Paul Buhle

MARXISM IN THE UNITED STATES

STATES

Remapping the History of the American Left

VERSO
The Imprint of New Left Books

British Library
Cataloguing in Publication Data

Buhle, Paul
   Marxism in the United States: remapping
   the history of the American left.—
   (Haymarket series).
   1.   Communism — United States — History
   I.   Title
   335.4′0973   HX83

   ISBN 0-86091-141-1
   ISBN 0-86091-848-3 Pbk

First published 1987
© Paul Buhle 1987

Verso
6 Meard Street London W1

Typeset in Times by
PRG Graphics
Redhill, Surrey

Printed by the Thetford Press Limited
Thetford, Norfolk

Contents

To the memory of my late interviewees and staff members from the Oral History of the American Left: Harry Brier, Pincus Caruso, Hugo Gellert, Sara Gudelman, Herb Gutman, Anton Kerzic, Bea Lemisch, Sam Liptzin, Luigi Nardella, Joe Norrick, I. E. Ronch, Warren Susman, Arne Thorne, Willard Uphaus, Fred Wright, Steve Zeluck.

PREFACE

As I sit down with the ninety-four-year-old editor of a Yiddish-language radical weekly in New York, I have the impression of whole eras passing before me. I'm his confidant—*mayne touere* ('my dear one' or 'dear son')—not really Yiddish-speaking, not even Jewish, but close enough to the old man's sympathies in a world that has outlived his time and his milieu. We talk about his problems of the day: raising huge sums from retired garment workers living on Social Security in order to keep the paper going; and his preparing himself, through reading and meditation, for the upcoming *Rosh Hashona* issue. He's preoccupied as always with questions of international peace, class struggle, and the unending contest for the Jewish soul (although he is too secular to put it that way). I ask him to analyze the accomplishments of the paper he has worked on since its founding in 1922. He says honestly that it has not been a success, despite its contributions to all those causes. He concludes that the paper discovered its own unique identity and mission within the Left too late. I see his point. I've read the old files and winced at the illusions, the hyperbole, the meanness toward competing radical entities and personalities—all seem so tragically mistaken.

But they are mistakes as historically inevitable, in one form or another, as the sectarian blunders Socialists made in 1871 or we New Leftists made in 1971. In the face of the errors (what my old friend would call, including his own mistaken actions, 'crimes against socialism'), there remains something of overriding importance: the life of radicalism itself, the survival of the movement through all its tragedies.

From a historian's viewpoint, his paper looks and feels like the last of an amazing tradition. The editor's own column is spiced with literary and biblical allusions straight out of the Russian nineteenth century where the critic, briefly but gloriously, became the great political voice of a generation. He takes his readers seriously—he knows enough of them personally from his endless lecture tours over the years—but he also cracks jokes of a typically ironic Jewish character. He demands attention and political response from eighty-year-olds barely mobile. He writes beautiful Yiddish in his weekly essay, the prose flowing and crackling over the issues at hand. The rest of the paper divides neatly into politics and culture, with a generous section devoted to death-and-remembrance notices. Like the papers of an older era it has few photographs, but it is animated by vivid prose portraits. Its other surviving writers—arthritic, deaf, straining visibly to complete daily tasks—have never stopped working at their craft.

Through him and through them, their collective memory of the Old World and their struggle as outsiders (even after seventy years!) to understand America, I seem to see a radical German-American editor at his desk in 1875 New York, or Chicago or St. Louis. Himself a capable literary critic, poet or *feuilleton* writer, this predecessor brings to the political tasks at hand his love of German literature and his understanding of Germanic working-class culture. Equally, I can imagine Italian, Slavic, Hungarian, Finnish or Japanese immigrant editors of whatever era in similar political and cultural situations, with analogous joys and sorrows. The newspapers I can actually read have a common flavor whether they are Anarchist, Socialist or Communist. This is far from the whole world of the American radical. But it has been a real world, larger in its collectivity and deeper in its intellectual character than all the Left political leaders and all the notable historians of the Left have thus far been willing to recognize. It has survived, and with different cultures and changing styles it continues to develop through the endless diaspora of immigrants from impoverished and war-torn societies into a chaotic and ethnocentric American order.

Another friend is my window on a different kind of radicalism. Former longshoreman and sailor who figures as the Trotskyist-syndicalist hero of Harvey Swados' novel, *Standing Fast*, he tells of a hundred incidents in his own life from the early 1940s to the present where the struggle for dignity assumed no overt political form, even found itself at odds with the existing 'progressive' (Communist or liberal) trade-union bureaucracies and public opinion. He helps me to understand those periodic uprisings and organizational innovations that seem to come from nowhere and disappear again. When I hear him talk, I can envision the unbroken Wobblies in their time, and before them the proud Knights of Labor. In this America, among a persistent rebel stratum of the working class, the wage-system remains unacceptable, economically or morally. Like my immigrant friends, he has seen other eras of accommodation and has learnt to tap the secrets of unobserved restiveness.

My other personal witnesses of the variety of American radicalism include: A retired coal miner from Elvira (he calls it 'Elvirey'), Indiana, a town that elected Socialist mayors in the pre-1920 days and kept a local of homegrown Marxists going through the Second World War. A Black activist since the thirties in Missouri, converted from the Bible to the *Communist Manifesto*, who recently joined a Sanctuary church and thereby reconciled the Revolution with the faith of his childhood. A retired garment worker, instinctive feminist with a sharp class edge who honors me with the love and serious criticism she gave her comrades in the shop. All three speak of universals in the history of the American Left.

None of my friends are famous people. They will not be found in the history books. But they and several hundred others have reached directly across the generations to me in interviews, across the lines dividing all sorts of radicals from one another. They helped bring me through the dark, suicidal moments of history when all the dreams of an age seem lost beyond redemption. They were there before, in 1920 and 1950; they have seen the betrayals and the disillusionment. And at their best moments, they know that endurance is not the only saving grace; every age speaks new truths and those who stop listening get old before their time. I like to think that they have made me wise enough to recognize that I belong to the same family as my radical antecedents, all of them.

In illuminating experiences of other generations of the Left, they have helped me understand my own generation. Like so many others in the New Left of the 1960s, I had sought in history what I couldn't find immediately around me: a Socialist tradition and hard analytical thought. These I had pursued for years, chiefly through mountains of old newspapers, while scarcely making conscious sense of the personal impulses and political tendencies that had brought me into radicalism at the close of the 1950s. In return for relating their lives, my interviewees wanted to know about mine, and they forced me to confront the significance of my own repressed family tradition from the Revolu-

4

tionary War, to Abolitionism, Spiritualism, Woman's Rights— and the Ku Klux Klan.

Today, when the excitement of the radical movement of my own youth has receded into the past, replaced (as far as those things can ever be replaced) with the usual variety of quasi-political activities from classrooms to picket lines to journalism, I find myself more like the old-timers than I ever imagined. This book, over the twenty years in which it has evolved, has become more than a reassessment of US Marxism from the wealth of new historical evidence available. It is by now, inevitably, an install-ment in collective autobiography, a family history of the left that has come to include my own generation.

*   *   *

There is little point in attempting precise predictions of the left's future from its past, or in gauging the value that a book like this may have for contemporary radical politics. Specific prog-nostication not only tempts fate but also repeats an error dis-cussed below: the collective egotism of one generation which seeks to impose its blueprint upon another.

Still, it is clear that the contradictions which shake the world and rumble like a distant thunderstorm back home in the United States will sooner or later return social protest to a wide arena. If American history serves as any example at all, a new unrest will surely break out with a suddenness and in forms that surprise no one more than the older generations of radicals. Some kind of internal coordination will again surely be assembled. Marxist ideas will return, as they have regularly, for use or abuse by people aiming at some kind of personal and political clarity.

As I hope this book will help illustrate, it is precisely the combination of the familiar and the unfamiliar, the repressed and the utterly original, which should catch our attention in any reflection on the radical legacy today. For example, the familiar immigrant link to world revolution remains a fundamental struc-ture of American history. The stormcenters of current world unrest—Latin America, South Africa, the Philippines—are either important sources of contemporary immigration or evoke profound sentimental ties in large sections of the US population. The parallels with the Irish and Fenianism in the nineteenth century, or with Eastern European immigrants and the Russian Revolution in the early twentieth century, are manifold and significant.

Likewise the utopian edge of American radicalism comes alive again in the simple notion of turning back the nuclear doomsday clock, and in protecting the earth from complete chemical devastation. Only dreamers can believe that these goals are any longer attainable—in a narrow, 'realistic' sense. We are not so far here, after all, from the old spiritual and Socialist vision of a Golden Age when all lived at peace in nature. Half-measures, the possible convergence of capitalism and state capitalism on one side of the globe or another, will no more satisfy future radicals than territorial compromises satisfied the Abolitionists.

Yet the next 'new left' will have to grapple with novel realities as well, including a worldwide, electronic mass culture, incorporating illiterate peasants as well as college intellectuals. This is the unavoidable terrain upon which any new movement will fashion its particular consciousness and identity. The Frankenstein monster of bourgeois sales techniques and totalitarian control mechanisms evidently has its own life, its own 'signs' and meanings. Readers will appreciate, I hope, how grudgingly American Marxists have moved toward interpreting the media world around them. That insularity has nearly passed. When revolutionary lyrics and bootleg versions of American films pass through the same subterranean channels of audio and video player-recorders, when computer access threatens the respective state monopolies on Russian publishing and American industrial-military secrets, Orwell's version of 1984 has become obsolete. But more than that: the interpretation of cultural symbols has become a potentially subversive and unifying global project. Only the division of theory from practice (not merely 'theoretical practice'), and the want of fresh political excitement, delay the interlinking and the drawing of the largest implications.

As this book goes to press, a political crisis in Reaganism threatens to expose the entire 'secret government' of Cold War hardliners to the light of media exposure and public reproach. At no earlier moment have the various contradictions, imperial and mass-cultural, so completely intertwined. Plentiful Marxist analyses will not be long in coming. The pertinent question is: will the left exploit the opportunity to mount a sophisticated attack upon the vulnerable monster? Or will its efforts fall between the two extremes of sectarian ranting and eager adaptation to an all-too-familiar 'damage-control' of the imperial presidency now planned by Democratic Party hopefuls?

All this seems to take us rather far from the traditional domain of Marxism, class and class struggle. Or does it? Cultural theory can no more eradicate class, and class organizations in some form, than traditionalist Marxisms can impose a rigid class determinism upon nationality and broad cultural developments. The sixteen-year-old hamburger slinger, the Black or Latin female computer keypuncher, need to understand the logic of commodity production (whether produced in the USA or abroad, and by whatever level of mechanization) and its famous 'mystery', as much as Marx's nineteenth-century factory hands. The psychic escape from work, now more prevalent than ever before, cannot evade the tyranny of the alarm clock and the paycheck. What will *not* remain the same, because it has never remained the same, is the form of self-defense and aggressive recuperation of surplus value. As the following pages show, the 'labor movement' has been not one but a thousand things, many quasi-political and quasi-cultural. Capitalism only guarantees the constancy of the essence of alienated labor amid its ever changing, ephemeral forms. The chief error of Marxism, beginning with Marx, has been the economistic limitation of a class model to the immediate means of production, a model based neither upon social membership of class within a wider, more inclusive social network, nor upon the subjective basis of individual perceptions. The recovery of women's history and Black history have taught us otherwise. 'Class' as a category will not become obsolete. The abstraction of class, in the old mechanical sense, has come to an end with the decline of the production-line worker. New definitions, more in tune with the reality of American social conditions and of the world labor-market, will undoubtedly follow.

This paradox—the vibrant prospects for change within a civilization on the edge of oblivion—has been the destiny of American Socialism from its utopian and class-conscious beginnings. Imperial crisis is the source of the civilization's origins and of its continual unrest. America, the attempted escape from the European past and simultaneously the apotheosis of Western values, refused lesser solutions on the model of European social democracies, the doctrinaire answers for the questions of class, nation, culture, individual and collective self-consciousness. Marxism in its original forms has been tested here, and the old universals proven insufficient. The history of American Socialism, and Marxism as a creative intellectual form, epitomize the fumbling search for new universals. The search accelerates as time runs out. Everything tell us our efforts can be fruitful.

From my initiation into the study of American Marxism more than twenty years ago, the task of understanding has remained a collective endeavour. Over the years my comrades at *Radical America*, *Cultural Correspondence*, the Oral History of the

American Left (Tamiment Library), and amongst the social and labor movements of Providence, Rhode Island have contributed immeasurably to the development of my thinking. Sustenance of a more material kind—in the form of grants and fellowships— has been provided by the Ford Foundation, the Rabinowitz Foundation, the New Jersey Historical Commission, the American Council of Learned Societies, the Immigration History Research Center, the National Endowment for the Humanities and the Rhode Island Committee for the Humanities.

I would like to pay tribute to some of the individuals who have helped me, and helped others, in trying to reconceptualize the history of American Socialism: Rudolph Vecoli, A. William Hoglund, David Montgomery, the late Herbert Gutman, James R. Green, Frank Brodhead, Linda Gordon, Harvey O'Connor, Itche Goldberg, Dan Georgakas, Jim Murray, Gil Green, Jon Bloom, Ruth Prago, Dorothy Swanson, Dave Wagner, Danny Czitrom, George Lipsitz, Franklin Rosemont, Thomas H. Fiehrer, Sue Benson, Scott Molloy. Special thanks are due to friends who read draft chapters of this work: Jim O'Brien, Alan Wald, Ron Grele, and, above all, to my comrade and companion, Mari Jo Buhle. My intellectual debt to C. L. R. James is evident in the book. My editorial debt, to Michael Sprinker and Mike Davis of Verso/Haymarket, *is* the book. Any errors, however, are mine alone.

INTRODUCTION

What has been the role of Marxism in American history? How has it been appropriated, construed (or misconstrued), even home-grown by previous generations of American radicals? What has happened to its latest major incarnation, the 1960s New Left, as political veterans entered middle age amid the Reagan Era? And what does the future hold? Can a theoretical system historically rooted in response to Victorian capitalism hope to come to grips with the challenges of the year 2000?

This book suggests broad answers to such questions while remaining self-conscious of their difficulty. The problem of American Marxism is irreducibly complex, and not only because the richness and diversity of the 'radical experience' defy simpli-fication. Variously native-born and immigrant, male and female, Black and white, rural and industrial, the disciples of Marxian doctrine deserve many volumes of description. Happily, that detailed work has become a long-range collective effort. My own contribution to that effort includes a more thorough documenta-tion of subjects discussed here, in forthcoming monographs on immigrant radicalism and reform literature, and in selected tran-scriptions from the Oral History of the American Left. *Marxism in the U.S.* seeks to synthesize preliminary findings of the com-bined research and to provide an advance look at interpretations to come.

The stock-taking of radical historiography coincides, not acci-dentally, with the New Left scholars' coming-of-age and with a generational crisis of sorts in left politics. Younger activists fre-quently express practical questions about the 1960s, especially 'how was it done?' and 'why did it fail?'. All the scholarly ruminations, all the warm personal reminiscences do not necessarily satisfy the questioner. The New Left's own meaning demands a systematic reconceptualization in the light of a deeper historical tradition. If I call this book a 'remapping', it is not because radical scholarship can not claim to plot a recent generation's exact historic location but because some sense of the coordinates has become both necessary and possible.

The starting-point is to discard the old saws found in the Marxist lumber-room and its anti-Marxist academic equivalent. According to 'orthodox', traditional Marxism, the history of American radicalism can be divided neatly into the world of honest ignorance before the classic Socialist writings became available, and deep scientific wisdom (or willful ignorance) afterward. The descriptive category of 'pre-Marxist' has required, since 1960, equally artificial categories of neo- and post-Marxism. Unfortunately for this schema, pre- and post- bear a striking resemblance to each other, from their emphasis upon Black rights to gender questions, peace and universal citizenship. The distinctions collapse. The arrival of Marxism on American shores turns out not to be such a singular event, but part of a larger and more complex flow.

Likewise, the mirror-opposite notion of an untainted radical radicalism (or innocent democratic impulse) enslaved by a foreign ideology will not stand serious scrutiny. No such creature can be discovered after the 1860s. Amid even the most idealist, indigenous non-class-oriented radicals. Marxist ideas spread widely to and through those who found them useful. 'Open your eyes and dethrone your rulers', the most famous Socialist editor of his age, 'One Hoss Philosopher' J. A. Wayland, wrote to the vast restless readership of the *Appeal to Reason*. Wayland, admittedly no sophisticate, challenged anyone to *disprove* the Labor Theory of Value and the inevitable crisis of capitalism which flowed therefrom. For him, as for so many others, Marxist ideas removed the scales from the eyes, supplied the why and how for the disestablishment of the wicked. To immigrants becoming Americans, Marxism offered more direct services: a strategic means to formulate demands for inclusion and a conceptual key to the vision of a truly democratic America.

Scholarship has taken care of the grotesque misconception (developed during the first Cold War) that Americans have shared a consensual view, in Richard Hofstadter's words, of 'the economic virtues of capitalist culture as necessary qualities of man.'[1] No such consensus has existed, not even in the most placid times, least of all in restless eras and turbulent districts. The role subsequently discovered of radical influences across the pattern of immigrant or Black life, of the labor movement and a variety of other social and cultural arenas, shows that the supposed marginality of dissenters is only wishful thinking, bourgeois *hubris*. The deeper problem which Hofstadter unconsciously addressed, the absence of sustained, popular *articulation* of Socialist ideas in the English language, remains the great question for scholars of the field to resolve.

Radical history has dealt a less lethal blow to Daniel Bell's familiar contention that Socialists and other dissidents 'lived in, but not of, the world,' *i.e.*, preferred a moral standard too high for mass acceptance. [2] The Puritan or perfectionist streak in the historical American left matches Bell's description, but it testifies more than anything to a solid grounding in national moral traditions. Even without sinking to the depths of the normal political corruptions, however, radicals have had a significant presence. Indeed, scholars are discovering them historically ensconced in a great variety of blue-collar, minority and middle class communities, considerably less aberrant to their actual neighbors and workmates than to outsiders.

I am simply astonished that most American historians and social scientists continue to consider the immigrant community fundamentally conservative. As scholarship on the Atlantic diaspora has begun to demonstrate so clearly, radicalism found a stronger base in the late nineteenth- and twentieth-century immigrant community than anywhere else in the United States, a fact well known before the Second World War but subsequently discarded. Conservatism existed also, of course. To an extent rarely appreciated by the surrounding society, the two lived side by side, sometimes but not always demarcated between the secular and religious functions. Not always, because class conflict and national sentiments frequently moved ostensibly conservative elements, including the clergy, to bloc with Socialists or Communists for such specific goals as unionization and homeland reconstruction. Readership levels of Socialist and Communist papers often reached fifteen to fifty percent of foreign-language groups, constituting a reading public we have only begun to understand. At important turning points like the mass strike wave of 1909–12, even such reputedly conservative communities as the Italian-Americans revealed a militancy and an affinity for radicalism that shocked native-born observers. [3]

Other myths likewise remain to be discarded. Histories of American Socialism which typically begin in 1900 and treat only English-language intellectuals as worthy of consideration are guilty of subtler sins of omission. Such book-centered and ethnocentric views, often the innocent productions of dissertations based on single-language and secondary sources, reinforce a traditional bias that mistakes the intellectual stratum at the tip of the radical iceberg for its ethnic bulk, submerged in a different cultural universe.

This is not to claim that Marxism in the United States became the ideology of large-scale, stable political parties in the European fashion. Or to claim that Marxist ideas became in any significant way hegemonic. But we need to explain why Marxists operating in the bastion of world capitalism could exert such widespread influence at times of national crisis and such sustained impact upon particular elements of society. We need to understand why ideas generally considered so marginal have recurrently had a powerful effect upon democracy itself.

A better grasp of the complex relation between Marxism and America should serve as antidote to the despair of those who bewail the 'backwardness' of the American left. European radicals have since the nineteenth century professed bafflement at the failure of the world's largest industrial working class to develop 'normal' modes of mobilization and representation via class parties. Yet as Eurosocialism and Eurocommunism have come to the watershed of late capitalism they encounter problems long familiar to the American Marxist: racial divisions, the impact of female labor and of feminism, the historic reality of blue-collar consumerism, and the steady erosion of industrial-extractive occupations. What European theorists excitedly celebrate as the 'new social movements' – including feminist critique and action, religious opposition to war, cultural movements to combat racism and so on—all have a reminiscent feel to American radicals.

One possible conclusion, and thesis for further development, would be that while European Marxism served as a force to eradicate pre-capitalist remnants, American radicalism has long faced the future that lay beyond. Perry Anderson's *In the Tracks of Historical Materialism* has indeed hinted at this possibility in his discussion of current intellectual trends.[4] I will not try to stake out such a broad claim here, or to elaborate its corollary: that in the contemporary Third World, Leninism as the final secular historical-materialist tendency is being steadily displaced by post-secular, post-Western chiliasms, heir to the same Radical Reform and Counter-Reformation, the same imperial intrusion into older societies and civilizations, that set the historic Marxist spiral into motion. Such argumentation must await another occasion.[5]

I seek to make some of the same points on a smaller canvas here. In its most organized, coherent dimension, Marxism in the United States has been a class manifestation of the National Question. Contrary to the apologists and to the hopes of many generations of immigrants, America has not been the Zion of world democracy. It has been the place where all worlds meet, but not on anything like equal terms. Marxist doctrine in its internationalist abstraction has run up against a vast tide of complex group loyalties and vernaculars; resolving at different tides to swim with the tide or against it, the radicals have sought to make the most of the possibilities.

Marxist movements have not necessarily coincided with the American working class trajectory as a whole. From the first days of the colonies, the American workforce has possessed, at its vital bottom-most layers, a pre-proletarian character. This has been the case from the Jack Tar anti-British rebels before the American Revolution to the slave and free-Black population of the Civil War and Reconstruction, to the European immigrants of peasant background, to more recent waves of Southern immigrants, white and Black, to most recently, the Latin and Asian populations accelerating their entry during the 1960s–80s. These tidal pulses of cultural and social recomposition have not generally flooded radical movements as such with new recruits. On the contrary, the most loyal followings have been drawn to an alternative Socialist autodidact culture which few bottom-most groups have possessed. Marxist political presence has therefore tended to concentrate in specific immigrant communities and native-born sectors with special needs and special cultural resources. But Marxist *leadership* of mass mobilizations, from time to time, has extended much further.

Marxists have strained against the limits of their constituencies to precipitate and to guide a comprehensive movement at once national and international. To fifty years of unremitting struggle with a successive series of nationalities, Leninism added the theoretical conceptualization of the National Question. However loaded down with dogmatic assumptions and with credulous attachment to Communist world politics, that conceptualization encouraged the formulation of self-understanding. As Germans and other nationalities organized themselves under Socialist auspices during the nineteenth century, a welter of successive groups—European, Afro-American, Latino and Asian—have struggled to grasp the nexus of national-class relation. Marxist ideas have fortified the sense of self-identity and dignity in an alien, exploitative America. Through a paradox more apparent than real, Marxism has simultaneously helped free individuals from constraints of their particular birth-right for a broader vision of Socialism in America and in the world.

Marxism has also been allied, in unorthodox ways, with typically American currents of democratic aspiration: radical, universalist, utopian. The same conditions which encouraged the bourgeois rapacity of the 'Robber Barons'—vast natural resources, swift technological development, a demographically sparse indigenous population, virtually limitless reserves of immigrant labor, and so on—also catalysed Arcadian counter-responses. Early nineteenth century communitarians, Abolitionists, supporters of Indian rights and labor reform, feminists and spiritualists had all seen the face of the devil long before he gained atomic technology; all had lived with exterminist Calvinism long before the world reckoned the full consequences.

In the mathematics of radical democracy the enlargement of citizenship rights to include the most oppressed groups signalled a challenge to the system's ideological claims as well as to its brutal practice. At the same time homegrown radicalism presented a practical challenge to orthodox Marxism, a sympathetic alternative which sought to avoid the modern class struggle by reaffirming and extending the ambit of republican 'citizenship'. Such ideologies often seemed crankish, outmoded, irrational, at times hostile to class forces or even xenophobic, but they could appeal beyond the limits of class and ethnicity-bound Marxism, beyond *homo economus*, to a recurrently troubled national conscience and democratic discourse that Marxist theoreticians failed to comprehend. Indeed on occasion radical democracy could also draw upon Marxist ideas to weave new and unexpected patterns: on the one hand, the continually revived chiliastic tradition; on the other, the critique of popular culture as embraced earliest and most relentlessly by the polyglot American masses.

Immigrant Marxism and utopian radicalism thus came to share a common ground neither could have anticipated. The pace of American development, the devastation of pre-modern ways of life and of understanding life, have left behind an often extreme sense of loss. Jews, with their ancient history of exile, have (at least until the founding of Israel, and arguably after as well) perhaps best articulated their feeling for America as diaspora where the worker is doubly exiled; but the sentiment is not unique. 'Homesick for the home I have never seen', wrote an anonymous poet in the grassroots Communist weekly *Truth*, of Duluth, Minnesota in 1920, '. . . I am here by some sad cosmic mistake'. That exilic sense has provided much food for melancholy. But it has also inspired a fresh will to redefine homeland as a multicultural Socialist paradise never been seen upon the earth.

American radicalism, via this National Question, has often been a force in world history. Immigrant Marxists have funded their homeland revolutions and assorted democratic struggles since the 1850s, often supplying both propaganda and a return-emigrant cadre. They have also sent back the advanced tactics and organizational forms pioneered in poly-ethnic American mines and mills. The Irish case is striking. Outside the famous General Post Office in Dublin—where former IWW organizer and SLP member James Connolly organized the 1916 Easter Rebellion—there is a statue of a major founder of American Communism (and onetime inmate of Sing Sing): James Larkin, father of the modern Irish labor movement. Likewise there has scarcely been a national liberation movement or struggle against racism that has not been profoundly influenced by the history of the Black liberation struggle in the United States. Marcus Garvey and W. E. B. DuBois helped galvanize a generation of nationalist militants across Africa and the Caribbean in the 1920s. The 1960s civil rights and Black Power movements had even broader international resonances: inspiring young activists and freedom-fighters from Derry to Soweto.

But the National Question in American history is two-sided. If on the one hand the dominant role of 'new immigrants' from Eastern and Southern Europe in the heavy industrial labor of the early twentieth century made Marxist internationalism a natural expression of discontent, then, on the other hand, no class movement, no set of Marxist ideas, could possibly attain significant *continuity* under such volatile conditions. American capitalism's unprecedented resources and its under-rated willingness to repress dangerous opponents, ensured that the cumulative force of radical tendencies could only be a sporadic threat to the home system. Between outbursts, they have been (which is to say, at least until recently, the prestige of Marxism has been) driven underground or absorbed. So much so, especially in the dominant discourse of the middle classes, that an argument for their non-existence, their unimportance, has been made continuously from earliest days to the present. Radicals have faced an endless 'end of ideology', with a secondary impact upon the undeveloped, recent character of Marxist scholarship in particular.

Yet Marxist and radical ideas remain alive, rooted in one milieu or another, a maddening discrepancy for bourgeois self-congratulation. At each objective juncture—the transformation of the workforce by composition or technology, the eclipse of some working-class culture, the bourgeois acceptance of structural economic reforms, the obsolescence of an ethnic press or specific types of cultural and self-help organizations—radicalism has been declared dead, sometimes by the older radicals themselves. At a later point it springs up again, with the new conditions assumed, the old ideologies tardily changed or discarded.

At the crisis moment—a strike wave, Black uprising, anti-war resistance—the apparently sudden influence of radicals seems to the same bourgeois observers quite beyond belief. The mechanisms for retrenchment, persecution, denial of fact and of interpretation, have already been set into motion; in the lull to come they are activated, and collective amnesia again ensues. The cycle is very old now, but by no means exhausted.

I have sought, more than anything else in this book, to cut through the web of forgetfulness. In doing so, Marxist critics in particular may complain, I have deserted the fundamentals of Marxism for some freakish conglomerates. That criticism depends upon a fixed view of Marxism rooted in Marx's later writings (excepting, perhaps, *Civil War in France*) and in the practice of the three Internationals. To my way of thinking, Marxism is as Marxism does, and the Latin American revolutionary who takes inspiration from Liberation Theology and economics from Marx and Lenin has as much claim to the mantle as Trotsky, Mao Zedong or Marx himself. Any other definition is the claim of an ideological holding-company.

If not, the title of the book may be a misnomer. But we American Marxists have lived with that contradiction a long time, and we shall presumably continue to do so. And we have a fine precedent. Wrestling with the contradictions of the American economy and its economists shortly before the Civil War, Marx wrote in his *Grundrisse* that they naturally belonged to a nation where: '. . . bourgeois society did not develop on the foundation of the feudal system, but developed rather from itself; where this society appears not as the surviving result of a centuries-old movement, but rather as the starting point of a new movement; where the state, in contrast to all earlier national formations, was from the beginning subordinate to bourgeois sovereignty, to its production, and never could make the pretence of being an end-in-itself; where, finally, bourgeois society itself, linking up the productive forces of an old world with the enormous natural terrain of a new one, has developed to hitherto unheard-of dimensions and with unheard-of freedom of movement, has far outstripped all previous work in the conquest of the forces of nature, and where, finally, even the antitheses of bourgeois society appear only as vanishing moments.'[6]

No one could have put the contradiction better. In looking backward to a time apparently disappearing from sight, Marx captured the nub of 'American Exceptionalism' that turns out to be not so exceptional at all. In the short run, Marx's own insight unwontedly laid out an objective and subjective reality which no amount of Marxist study, good will or political acumen could overcome. American capitalism's conquest of nature, its freedom from the restraints of the European past, have allowed recovery from every challenge. Radical movements expressed themselves as 'vanishing moments', one and all. In the long run, those moments predicted, perhaps, a universal process beyond the sight of the older Marx (and by now, the old Marxism) but not beyond the dreams of the philosophers and activists who have never ceased to feel Marxism's inspiration.

1

Immigrant Socialism, 1865–1900

Marxists, and those influenced by Marx, filled a yawning gap in immigrant life of late nineteenth and early twentieth-century America. They spoke forcefully to the emergence of industrial society, the hardening of class lines and the importance of a collective labor response. Other reformers and radicals prescribed social remedies more familiar to American traditions. Marxists had a unique dual contribution outside the body of those traditions. Meaningful transformation, they argued, and actually showed in certain limited but important ways, had to be based on the changing nature of production and the ways in which it prepared workers to seize their own destiny. Secondly, any strategy of transformation had to be rooted in the real lives of the workers, their cultural inheritance as well as their strategic industrial position.

Only the first of these two observations could be accurately described as part of Marx's, or the First International's, own programmatic insights. Immigrant socialists struggled to re-define the social relations of production in the American economy, their major contribution to nineteenth-century Socialist thought. However, the linking of social relations to culture, and specifically to national identity, constituted the most controversial, and in some ways the most important, problem for twentieth-century Marxism. The illusions of abstract, universal class consciousness and labor brotherhood to be achieved by imposing a dominant culture over subordinate cultures had to be overcome before this question could begin to be appreciated. The central significance of Blacks to American civilization, for generations recognized more clearly by native-born radicals than immigrants, had, paradoxically, to be integrated into an immigrant-based Marxism before it could be fully assimilated into revolutionary thought.

The immigrant Socialists did not succeed to the degree, or even along the same lines, that Marxism's European guides predicted. Nor did they impress the specifics of their Socialism very deeply upon assimilated America, prosperous or poor, white or Black, urban or rural. But they successfully promulgated the Socialist ideal and the methods of achieving effective organization among a scattering of indigenous labor activists and among large numbers of Germans, Czechs, Finns, Poles, Italians, Hungarians, Ukrainians, Slovenes, Lithuanians and other immigrant nationalities. They also impressed upon sympathetic observers from all quarters the certainty of industrial conflict and the zeal of idealistic activists pursuing the improvement of immediate conditions. Their successes did not come cheaply to themselves or to their theories.

North America, after all, played a strange and remarkable role in the fantasy lives of nineteenth-century Europeans, including those two very European intellectuals, Karl Marx and Frederick Engels. Many working people, especially those with relatives already in the United States, knew the 'Golden Land' to be tarnished by reality. But the promise of a better life upon emigration nevertheless played an analogous role to Socialistic visions of reform or revolution. (Famed German Socialist leader, Wilhelm Liebknecht, put it best when he promised German workers staying at home, 'Our America is in Germany'.) Each entailed social dislocation, uncertainty and risks; and each offered a fresh beginning at the end of a long road.

Marx and Engels, for all their erudition, battled phantoms in their efforts to understand the complex meanings of the relation. They saw in the widely disseminated image of pre-Civil War America, land of easy mobility and endless expanse, a potent ideological enemy. Socialists removed from Europe apparently abandoned the class struggle and ordinary working people seemed likely to do so as well. Emigration to the New World served as a safety-valve for releasing the pressures of working-class discontent and preserving capitalism in its European heartlands. From the end of the Civil War onward, the fathers of scientific Socialism sought to reverse the image. They drank in each tale of American poverty and economic-social unrest as proof of the opposite proposition: America would *precipitate* European Socialism, perhaps even arrive at the true Golden

Land first. Capitalistic expansion, from this perspective, had created the weakest link in the system. The absence of custom and tradition, which yesterday restrained class consciousness, today would plunge the society irresistibly toward the Socialist future.

The immigrants themselves, even those with a Socialist background in the Old World, inevitably saw the situation differently. They had entered, not an America which existed primarily as denial or fulfillment of European Socialist (or any other) ideas, but a vastly contradictory reality. It bore disillusioning similarities to the societies that they had left, and which Marxist descriptions fit with considerable accuracy; but the differences also loomed large, and did not grow smaller even when versions of the predicted social unrest raged around them.

Reality often had a bitter flavor. Immigrant Socialists, like immigrant Communists later on, tended naturally to grasp at European ties for a sense of security and self-definition. The weaker and more isolated their own movement in America, the more important those ties became, emotionally and intellectually. Attempts to groom English-language spokesmen not infrequently produced Frankenstein monsters, figures more doctrinaire and self-defeating than the immigrants themselves. Efforts to correct the misunderstandings of native-born reformers likewise seemed too often condescending and alienating. American disciples who took their own initiatives, on the other hand, strayed far from orthodox intent. Synthetic efforts to close the gap spoke imprecisely to the overriding issue. Marxists, even while adjusting in practice to their immigrant constituency's particular needs, conceptually tended to reduce social variables to class, while their native-born counterparts reduced class to an element of social variables.

The reasons for this difference went to the core of Marxist difficulties with American reality. Economistically telescoping the processes of industrial development and consciousness, Marxists anticipated in every class conflict the postponed arrival of class consciousness. The patterns of American radicalism would prove too complex for such conceptual reductionism.

Modern Socialism, it is important to remember, had arisen from a venerable utopian Socialism, and from a recent rise in class conflict on the European industrial scene. The conquest of Nature, the *Communist Manifesto* argued in 1848, had subjected the countryside to the city and the non-industrial world to the industrial world, effectively centralizing property, production and population. The unification of the bourgeoisie impelled the collateral unification, despite all internal divisions and backward steps, of the one revolutionary and universal class, the proletariat. By those criteria, American workers should one day soon compose the foremost battalion in the army of the international proletariat.

The adherents of the *Communist Manifesto* had distinguished themselves from previous Socialists, in particular the utopians, quite simply. Utopianism looked backward to a lost world of exploded property relations, or sought for the same idealistic reasons to impose a blueprint upon the emerging order. Communists perceived the new society already developing itself, objectively, within the old. The socialization of production contained the germ of that society. Workers' social relations, the understanding of collective labor required for their tasks, translated into political action. [1]

Karl Kautsky, Marx's and Engels' most prominent heir apparent, broadened this proposition into an economic-political determinism of means and ends. Socialists would work to eradicate the constraining remnants of the *ancien regime* holding back progress. The building of a class-democratic movement guaranteed the future. Kautsky's fatalism about America followed directly from this view. The rise of immense trusts, he wrote shortly after the turn of the century, had brought the American proletarians closer to power. [2]

European Socialism, as it developed out of the earlier struggles for democratic rights, did indeed register a certain political progress, if not at the level Socialists anticipated. Such successes had only an oblique relation to the prospects for Socialism in the United States. The American working class had arguably played a significant role in the completion of the bourgeois revolution, but in very different ways from their European brethren. Most obviously, and for the best of material and ideological reasons, American workers' early spokesmen and leaders historically demanded not only full male enfranchisement and comprehensive public schooling, but also free land in the West, *i.e.*, an economic citizenship in the bourgeois republic. The Jacksonian Democracy of the 1820s–30s encompassed and was largely exhausted by this issue. The Civil War was fought as much over free land as slavery. When the United States emerged from the military conflict that Marx considered a central event of the nineteenth century, labor's numerous middle ranks had not yet fully suffered the blow being prepared for them: a decisive class differentiation.

Artisanal republicanism overlapped the ideologies of other

'producing' classes, farmers and small businessmen, because of their shared real interests and historical experiences. The common democratic sensibility validated political and cultural challenges to the existing order and made possible the steady reformulation of citizenship. Against the interests of nascent monopoly and its palpable economic restraints upon individual initiative, a class coalition against class formulated early versions of Socialism. Europeans saw democracy in class and Socialist terms; Americans saw class and Socialism in democratic terms.

The legacy of American reform, even more than the unusual traits of the American working class, guaranteed this dichotomy a long life. The confrontation between nature and the forces of an unrestrained capitalism produced both monsters and utopians, Ahabs and Whitmans, Poes and Ishmaels, across the social spectrum. The conservative version of republican democracy, the joint-stock company theory of society derived from Locke and embodied in the Constitution, resisted thorough democratization with limited success. The political system excluded Native Americans, Blacks and women from participation, redoubled its defenses against potential 'mob rule' through the division of powers, geographical and judicial restraints upon the popular will. Yet the reform agenda advanced. A radical coalition of free Blacks, women, reformers and land-hungry farmers succeeded in rendering the Civil War a crusade. Labor reformers and women's rights reformers made smaller but not insignificant dents in the public consciousness. Roughly Socialist ideas, mostly but not entirely utopian in character, grew out of these efforts and out of resilient faith in America as salvation from a chaotic, brutal world.[3]

Marxism, as an alternative explanation of social ills and as a description of the future good life, offered only a proximate vision of US social realities to these radicals. Lacking the literal sort of class culture and class traditions which reproduced European-style (or better, German-style) social relations, American workers and middle-class reformers of various types interpreted industrial degradation and centralized financial power as rents in the social fabric, proof of the need for still further democratization. By contrast, immigrants who experienced the grinding poverty, exploitation and discrimination of the American order found Marxian Socialist ideas authentically helpful in explaining their lives and the world. The presence of age-old class traditions in their own culture, of militants armed with the skills for successful economic and social mobilization, held out to many of them a Socialist pole star as bright and meaningful as that northern light which guided the runaway slaves to freedom.

The problems looming before the Socialist faithful were, by any calculation, monumental. The power of expansive American capitalism, its apologists' head-start over any immigrants in defining class ideologies (except its own) as 'alien' and undesirable, made Socialist politics a difficult proposition. The system's ability to reinforce divisions among the underprivileged by marginally rewarding one group over another—organized craft workers against the unskilled and unorganized, or white over Black, men against women—often co-opted Socialists seeking advantages for their constituencies. Limited victory became the basis of long-run defeat. Impossible dilemmas produced pseudo-solutions, proud ideologues in splendid isolation, or adaptationists shorn of their ideals.

Faced by such overarching constraints, immigrant Socialists and indigenous American radicals could scarcely afford the luxury of sectarian isolation. Despite their differences, they struggled towards a mutual understanding. European-inspired Marxism and its native bed-partners, at the most conjugal moments, came together more splendidly and more peculiarly than any savant could have anticipated. Each side had something substantial to give; together, and alerted by intermittant social uprisings, they grasped at ideas still too advanced for the larger and more stable European movements. They effected very real changes in American society, not only in the labor movement but in many institutions touching the lives of the foreign born. They struggled mightily to break through the insularity of native-born Americans towards a class-conscious radicalism more feared than understood.

The American Socialist tragedy in the nineteenth century was that in seeking to cut through the webs of non-class reform and radicalism, the Socialists created impossible expectations for their own small movement. Unwittingly, they encouraged among their disciples an impatient class view of America still more reductive than their own. In so doing, they bore responsibility for the organizational debacle at the end of the nineteenth century. Their political descendants would have to begin again after 1900, in the construction of a Socialist movement and the recuperation of a legacy larger than themselves.

The Immigrant Origins of Socialism

We find our principal actors in the immigrant ghettoes which sprawled across the post-Civil War United States. Historians have only begun to appreciate how greatly these immigrants of all (but mostly lower) classes brought their customs and traditions to bear upon their new and unsettled situation. They faced a society nominally committed to absorbing their energies and talent, but more directly committed to turning them from human beings into factory 'hands'—and soon into consumers for over-priced, shoddy wares. Against this transformation into the 'trained apes' of capitalist machino-facture, the radicals among them threw the whole weight of their collective being.

The history of Black radicalism offers a comparable instance that will allow us to better grasp the specificity of the immigrant left in the USA. Cedric Robinson properly says in his *Black Marxism: The Making of a Black Radical Tradition*: 'Black radicalism cannot be seen as a variant of Western radicalism whose proponents happen to be black'.[4] Rather, he argues, it constitutes an autonomous response to exploitation by European societies, shaped by the interaction but bent essentially upon recuperating its own identity. The case is somewhat overstated. But the terms apply to European workers as well, to their families and their small business allies caught in the nexus of industrial transformation. Impelled by economic factors to relocate, they sought to regain a sense of self-identity in the new land amid a maddeningly chaotic cultural scene. No more than African culture could German, Bohemian or Italian cultures simply be transplanted to American shores. But 'survivals'—language, idiom, food, music and sometimes religion—helped to maintain resilience against economic and social adversity among those who lacked other resources. Abstractly, assimilation was available to every 'white' immigrant. Some upward mobility can be found in virtually every such population. But especially in the first generation, neither the opportunity nor the expectation was open to the overwhelming majority.

Marxist analysis admirably fitted the economic reality of these groups. Broadly speaking, the immiseration of the working class assumed real form here in two distinct, albeit related, ways. For groups from Northern Europe generally, the level of acquired skills allowed entry into the US labor market on relatively favorable terms—but only to a degree, and at a heavy cost for many workers. The pace of work, by all reports, proved more taxing than in Europe, the intensity becoming increasingly severe as progressive mechanization and primitive forms of scientific management blossomed. More important, the same mechanization pressed upon the skills themselves. To take one example,

German-American woodworkers, the most revolutionary segment, saw their way of life undermined and finally devastated.
The recurrent economic crises in the last third of the nineteenth
century plunged skilled alongside unskilled into the ranks of the
unemployed. In short, the expansion of the economy which drew
immigrant workers to American shores more than any appeal to
democratic participation, also periodically worsened the condition of those who had the highest expectation of gain.[5]

For the unskilled, especially those Eastern Europeans already
familiar with factory life prior to immigration, Socialism spoke
directly to a sense of class and national oppression. The immigration process severely damaged cultures already in shock from
recent change. Radicals promised to restore a community élan, a
self-confidence and creative adaptation, while bringing critical
aid to the struggles for change in the homeland. They offered an
alternative pole of attraction to the church or synagogue which
(with some notable exceptions) preached social passivity in
America and, for Christians, blind loyalty to the old country's
government. And they offered an alternative to the rule of ethnic
middlemen who enriched themselves by providing cheap labor
for American business, while declaring their patriotic attachment to the new land.

Radicals at times seized and at times failed to grasp the initiative on the particular 'national question', or on the immigrants'
immediate economic-social problems. But in many communities
they established important beachheads from almost the first day
of immigration, through sickness-and-death benefit societies,
unions, and anti-clerical, 'free thought' associations. From these
bases they developed and proclaimed their versions of Marxism.
No stronger, more popular and long-lasting constituency for
Socialism could be found anywhere in the United States.
Radicals thereby helped to construct a sense of pride in immigrant self-identity while supplying leadership for an otherwise
unorganized mass of workers. Their associations also provided a
safe haven for the soul-weary, tired of adaptation. They helped
to transform, but they also reinforced, immigrant Socialism's
limiting features.

This pattern had come into existence before the Civil War,
among the German refugees of the failed 1848 Revolution. Their
'free thought' opposition to conservative clerical influence, their
exercise societies, and their pursuit of an independent, progressive school system for German-American children made them a
rallying center within many immigrant German communities.
Predominantly artisans by origin, they found labor in the bur-

geoning industrial towns and cities at a time of shifting production when only their keen sense of organization—and at last, not
even that—could halt the downward slide of many crafts. They
instinctively opposed slavery and also the apportionment of the
war's burdens to the working classes. Led in many places by that
nineteenth-century rarity, the college-trained dissident intellectual, these circles espoused a generous, eclectic radicalism.

War sapped their ranks and the post-war industrial concentration fractured the artisanal faith. Veterans of twenty years or
more struggle in the USA and abroad had become suddenly older,
generationally exhausted, eager to accept the promises of the
emerging prosperity and to settle for well-earned laurels. They
had little interest in the emerging issue, American women's
political emancipation, conflating suffrage agitation with temperance campaigns which they viewed as nativist madness. They
were saved from nostalgic marginality by the onrush of new
German immigration following the War and again in the early
1880s: immigrants mostly from industrial districts who had seen
considerable changes since the departure of their predecessors,
young men and women with often sophisticated political understanding, they were not alien to the now *Alte Genossen* ('old
heads').

Here, more than in the formal traditions of proto-Marxist and
Marxist organizations in the USA, can be found the origins of an
immigrant Socialism. Printing and building trades, furniture
workers and scattered others already organized in the 1850s were
joined by a host of trades including cigarmakers, brewery and
metal-workers struggling to mobilize in the face of deteriorating
economic conditions. Building upon such foundations, linking
together unions and community organizations, the immigrants
combined the lessons from the old country with the demands
imposed by the new. Their ambiguous Socialist doctrine did not
make many of them self-conscious 'Marxists' until at least the
1870s. But it made them aware of Karl Marx, and even more
aware of the eclectic Socialist movement then sweeping across
sections of the German working class.[5]

Their experience varied greatly with location. New York and
Chicago can be seen then and for a half-century or more later as
polar opposites. New York, ideologically closer to European
trends and the natural intellectual center of any national movement, fostered a version of European Socialism. Its small industries, combined with the demography of dense and relatively
stable neighborhoods, reproduced as far as possible a simul-
acrum of the Old World conditions. Chicago, dominated by

large-scale industry spread outward across the urban area, encouraged a transformation of doctrine and of practice beyond the familiar European model. The small industrial towns stood curiously in between these extremes, both laboratories for preserving insular Germanic culture and alternatively places where Socialists had to blend in politically and to accept the leadership of Americans by sheer weight of numbers.[6]

Immigrant workers, their families and small property allies were held together politically through speakers and the press, often by the same individual leaders renowned for oratory and editorializing. What a remarkable crew these first Marxist intellectuals were! They had usually distinguished themselves on the other side of the ocean as editors, authors or lecturers, members of a cultural avant-garde. Leading lights of a political émigré wave whose farewell graced the pages of Germany's Socialist newspapers, and whose geographical abandonment of the Cause brought curses from Karl Marx, they left behind the relative certainties of European intellectual life for an existence politically and personally adventurous. Their genius lay in adaptating to immediate tasks, local crowds, sudden crises and long-term insularity. The largest group, around the editorial rooms of the New York and Chicago German Socialist newspapers, spoke for and to an organized constituency. Others, in smaller cities like Philadelphia, St. Louis, Cincinnati, Milwaukee and San Francisco, were forced to shift their tactics and models still more to meet local conditions. A handful toured regularly, because of the political or economic needs of their institutions but also from a prudent desire to see their constituents up close. Their tour diaries show a little universe with its planets pulled at once by the particular problems of the district and by loyalties to national and international movements.

Theoreticians with a background in free thought, the editors were often older men among a youngish constituency. Some represented the last of the radical-bourgeois traditions of 1848 updated to contemporary conditions, with a broader understanding of America than their constituent artisans and unskilled factory workers. Others represented an international Socialist intelligentsia which stopped over, usually for a limited time, in the United States. In either case, they linked the wide world of tradition and complex developments with the conditions at hand.

Adolf Douai was representative of the first type. A 'Forty-Eighter', he had written travel books for a German audience about American customs, edited an Abolitionist newspaper in Texas, penned a political novel, and earned his salary as a distinguished progressive pedagogue. He remained at the editorial post of a German-language Socialist daily until his death in 1888. Alexander Jonas, an example of the second type, returned from America to Europe in the 1870s to edit the German Social Democratic press, only to re-emigrate in 1879, remaining active in the German-American press well into the twentieth century. A German Jew (like a number of the '48er intellectuals), Jonas especially helped the first generation of East European Jewish radicals to get their bearings. These were steady hands. Other editors had more extreme and romantic reputations. Serge Schevitsch, journalist-agitator and a minor Russian noble, brought with him to America the countess (later a New York actress) over whom one-time German Socialist leader Ferdinand Lassalle had fought his fatal duel. A favorite during the 1880s, he was known to 'think American', to translate international ideas into the adopted vernacular so that friendly Irish and American-born workers could understand them. That Douai, Jonas and Schevitsch worked on the same *New Yorker Volkszeitung* suggests both the cosmopolitan nature of the effort, and the level of talent available.

Like other immigrant Socialist intellectuals, they admired Marx's theoretical contribution, which they sought to apply to the local situation confronting them. But the influence of Marx had distinct limits. They had other, sometimes competing loyalties and many non-theoretical obligations. Like their flocks, they felt the personal influence of Marx's *bete noire*, Lassalle (statuettes of whose countenance graced the Socialist locals and often served as raffle prizes). Until his romantic demise, Lassalle had overshadowed Marx in the German Socialist movement, and a curious death-cult around his memory had great staying power. The poetic spirits of Goethe, Heine and Freiligrath, along with contemporary German playwrights whose works were performed on the German-American stage, and were reviewed for their papers, greatly influenced the émigré intelligentsia. They had little time to go far beyond theoretical generalities in any case. Not one of them could be considered a scholar-ideologue such as the later American Socialist and Communist movements would produce in fair numbers, and European movements would create by the hundreds. They lacked the opportunity to write more than an occasional exegesis, and they lacked the conceptual distance to serve as sustained chroniclers of their own times. They trusted their power of generalization and the keenness of their penetration into the pressing problems of the day.[7]

Consider August Otto-Walster. Son of a leathersmith, early

editor and playwright in German Social Democratic circles, he traveled to America in the mid-1870s to take on the new weekly national paper, *Arbeiter Stimme*. Filling his columns with buoyant editorials on arts and life, serializing his own numerous historical romances, Otto-Walster moved from New York to St. Louis, and finally to Cincinnati, where Edward Aveling and Eleanor Marx Aveling found him in 1886, and recorded their vivid impressions: 'Poet, dramatist, an artist to his soul's core, he descends into the common ways of men so that he may help lead men from them. He makes the path out of the desert at once plainer and more smooth. He goes along it apparently carelessly, with a sort of devil-may-care swing; but he misses no flowers that may be noted by the way; nay, he plants many himself, and for the less favored souls gladdens all the journey with an external geniality and with flashes of an exquisite and pathetic humor.'[8]

This is not, of course, a particularly Marxist description. Neither could Otto-Walster's deepest thoughts be considered definitively so. His flashes of insight had other sources. He waxed especially eloquent on the subject of national identity. Cursed was the nationalism of the ruling classes, making differences into hatred for the sake of commercial wars; laughable if not so cruel was the American rulers' concept of a single, English-speaking nation with but one mind and one tongue. Democratic Americanism, Otto-Walster may have been the first Socialist theoretician to suggest, meant the freedom and strength of a voluntary diversity. This was an idea that it would take Marxists generations to absorb and refine.[9]

Another leading representative, now long forgotten, of this generation was George Stiebeling, perhaps the closest reader of *Capital* among the editors. He assayed in 1877 that the increasing concentration of American wealth had virtually eclipsed the unique features of the American republic, separating the democratic shell from the bourgeois kernel. Socialism might be seen in contemporary European terms, the struggle of a working class against arrogant capital. It was simultaneously, in American terms, the 'negation of the negation', *i.e.*, of a capitalism that had abandoned its origins. Here, too, as with Otto-Walster's observation, Socialists would require several generations to flesh out the implicit argument.[10]

These were the kind of perspectives and the necessary encouragement the ordinary immigrant Socialist craved. No wonder the editors could wield such influence over their flocks.

who regarded the intellectuals as a cross between great mentors and writ-large versions of themselves. The editors' patient insistence upon emancipation *of* the working class *by* the working class made sense, especially within the immigrant environment where few American reformers strayed. Socialist political movements (Communist Clubs, First International, Social Revolutionaries, Socialist Labor Party, then Socialist Party) made some sense, and between waves of political energy the presence of local branch activity kept alive the collective commitment and the inevitability of final vindication. Party intellectuals exhorted the ranks, reported results, and directed the patient task of education. Patience itself became after a time one of their chief virtues and simultaneously a serious fault; they had seen too many hopes smashed by precipitous and sectarian Socialist efforts to risk all their accomplishments in a single thrust.

They hardly needed to stress the importance of internationalism for their constituency. Understandably, Socialist progress in Germany loomed ever larger when disappointments in the USA recurred. Column inches of reports or editorials in the press, and no doubt discussions in the branches as well, devoted as much time and space to Europe as to America. German papers circulated freely, retailed by immigrant agents. Intellectuals had the special functions of coordinating Party fund-raising (important source for the German Social Democrats until the 1890s) and relief efforts for new—especially important political—arrivals. Notoriously, political exiles had to be pried loose from their Old World fixations and, where possible, given tasks outside their narrow milieux to help (or force) an acclimation.

The editors judged themselves by their steadfastness in a troubled pioneer era and by their more tangible accomplishments, such as aid to particular unions. All too typically, they neglected thereby one side of their contribution, especially the role of their own ideas in the monumental tasks of political adaptation. The interpretations of Marxism such activity produced were not considered, even perhaps by the intellectuals themselves, as particularly memorable. They were forgotten so quickly that not even the numerous celebrations of institutional birthdays, in their publications decades later, could produce recollections of strategic or theoretical innovations. And yet these now almost entirely forgotten immigrant intellectuals had forged an adaptation of Marxist theory that, in light of subsequent struggles and often tragic denouéments, can lay claim to a wisdom and prescience about the role of Marxism in the USA.

The disuse into which their legacy fell remains poignant evidence for the host of lost resources in American working-class struggles.[11]

Strategic Beginnings

Broadly speaking, we may divide nineteenth-century immigrant Socialist efforts into two periods. During the first, from the beginning of Radical Reconstruction to the Great Railroad Rebellion of 1877, a primitive Socialist movement struggled toward institutional existence. The second reaches from the aftermath of the same strike to the Socialist Labor Party in the 1890s, when the foreign-based activists, bolstered by immigrant Jews, attempted unsuccessfully to turn their greater resources into a mass revolutionary agency.

Deeply involved at its inception with the International Workingmen's Association (or First International) personally led by Marx, the movement gradually emerged under its own steam, mostly at the local level. By that time the pioneer generation of Socialist thinkers had grown up, suffered their share of disappointments, and learned to service their immigrant constituencies with ideas and deeds. Immigrant Marxism had made its definitive appearance.

The episode of the First International in America, the first of many catastrophic divisions between immigrant Socialists and their potential native allies, exemplified the fundamental problems of European Socialism in America. Marx's own role dramatized the impossibility of effective guidance from abroad; the more urgent the appeal for international guidance, the greater the miscalculation of American specifics. On the other hand, the success of the First International in small ways showed that Socialists had a place, or rather a number of related places, in American labor and reform, so long as they correctly understood their own limitations.

Native-born reformers emerged from the Civil War exhausted by their tireless efforts, still credulous at the Lincolnian hope for classless, egalitarian government, but also armed with new crusades and new constituencies located in wartime activity. Nowhere did their peculiarities, from a European worldview, stand out clearer than in the 'woman question', fulcrum upon which much antebellum reform rested. The increasing number of women in industrial or commercial occupations, and the terrible suffering of technologically obsolete seamstresses, dramatized the question of class while militant women and their allies brought forward suffrage as a decisive step to gender emancipation. The potential alliance of 'woman and the worker' raised expectations of a Radical Reconstruction South and North—and an opportune moment for the aroused German immigrants old and new to join the alliance.

In retrospect, such radicalism could not survive the coming defeat of Southern Reconstruction and its crushing blow to Blacks, both result and secondary cause of the consolidation of robust capital into a cohesive national, self-conscious body. The disintegration of wartime alliances between radical reformers and business, however, thrust the most militant sectors of reform into sympathy for Marxism (among other causes and ideologies), and produced an astonishing if shortlived experiment in radical politics.

Immigrant Socialists coalesced from post-war currents and sought to establish an authoritative international connection. Craft workers with a European Socialist background gathered themselves around the upswing of German-American labor organizations in Chicago and a number of other heavily German-immigrant cities, but above all New York. They sought to establish contact, on the one hand, with American labor organizations, and on the other, with the European movement's intellectual center, the trade-union based International Workingman's Association.[12]

It was a realistic aspiration. The National Labor Union, a loose federation of American unions under the leadership of William Sylvis, had sent representatives to the IWA's Congress, and showed signs of support for a potential labor political movement in the United States. The IWA, until the Paris Commune gave it an incendiary reputation and deprived it of its mostly British union supporters, appeared to be a modest and somewhat successful movement for coordination of solidarity across national lines.

The German-Americans immediately ran into their first formidable problem with the International itself. When various immigrant sections applied to establish a central committee among American comrades, Marx resisted, objecting to the foreign character of the operation. To the refusal of the International to grant full recognition, music teacher and emerging German-American leader, Frederich Sorge, responded sharply that American immigrants were not 'foreigners' in the usual European sense, but citizens speaking a non-English language—citizens, moreover, who dominated the progressive wing of the labor movement. In this exchange of views, European Marxists demanded an Americanization that the immigrant radicals felt they could not, and perhaps did not immediately need to, achieve as a basis for serious effort. One of the main bases for the misunderstanding of Marxism's American mission and American meaning had already been established.[13]

Another, apparently opposite source of misapprehension emerged immediately in the unease with which Sorge and his followers viewed their American-born comrades, a loose amalgam of workers and reformers. The Germans intuitively distrusted reformers for demoting the class issue to one among several, or even viewing it as a symptom of evil rather than containing a constructive solution to poverty and unrest. They thereby denied in their own minds the understandable sympathies of radical-inclined workers toward reformers and toward reformist electoral politics. Such an attitude, akin to Sorge's compulsive atheistic objection to spiritual ceremonies at the opening of each National Labor Union convention, bespoke an inability to understand the basic mentality of American radicals. The Americans, for their part, could not comprehend the complaints and ill feeling that the Germans seemed constantly to harbor against their predilections. Marx, the immigrants and the native-born radicals all held oversimplified views of strategic unity and, beyond that, of the process of transformation ahead. Neither immigrants nor native radicals could be other than what they were. No ideological alchemy would alter the material human equation.

The First International sections in the United States, numbering several hundred members in all, prospered for a few years precisely because of their heterogeneity. Various elements, as so often later in American Socialism, had tasks so different that their activities did not necessarily overlap. In this case, unfortunately, geographic proximity to New York City made a clash of styles and of power finally inevitable.

The American sections, a mixture of reformers, Irish and American-born workers, made splendid progress with the publication of *Woodhull & Claflin's*, a weekly with wide circulation in reform circles, especially among supporters of female suffrage. They led a dramatic and overwhelmingly successful march in memory of the Paris Commune in 1871, one of the great political events of the day in New York City. Their members also participated in a number of unions, particularly the painters, and they had some special influence among the radical Irish Nationalists. Taken as a whole, they believed in an advanced democracy, with liberty for the individual and government reorganization of monopolies. A national labor–reform party, they hoped, would supply a bridge to the ultimate goal. The Germans around Sorge contrasted vividly with this tendency. They exerted their energies directly in the unions, influencing the organization or reorganization of several important crafts, leading a near city-wide General Strike in New York and educating German-born workers with Socialist ideas.

The two sides might have achieved a *modus vivendi* if not for the international situation. As so often, the quarrels in European capitals found their echoes in American radical circles. We have the German-Americans' correspondence to Marx (with his replies) and the complaints of the Americans to help us under-stand the split which shattered the organization's efforts inside and out, and which left local Socialists to their own devices in the severe economic crisis to follow. Clearly, the division figured as a footnote to the IWA's internal troubles. Marx, pestered by Euro-pean anarchist challenges, had determined to rid the movement of interference regardless of the consequences. Sorge and his craft unionist friends saw their troubles mirrored in the larger scheme, despite the scarcity of anarchists in the United States and in the American First International.

The 'American Sections' (which phrase, for the next twenty years or so, would connote the American-born or assimilated branches) offered the real challenge, not anarchist at all but republican: that the International, and specifically the American wing, recognize not only working-class elements but also other citizens (in this case, women deprived of the opportunity of wage labor) as co-equals, including them as members by change of constitution (hitherto membership had been restricted to wage-earners). Sorge foresaw the organization of branch after branch built around middle-class reformers. He determined to make an end to the threat. With Marx's expressed approval, he resolved the difficulty through a bureaucratic purge, thereby accomplish-ing two ends. He cleared out the entirety of middle-class reformers, and he also proved the American Section so loyal (*i.e.*, insular) that it could tend the affairs of a dying home office of an International which Marx removed to New York for safe keeping. Correspondence and other forms of paper-shuffling filled the political lives of the survivors, no longer disturbed by women fanatics.[14]

The Sorge faction's manoeuver rested upon two theoretical and strategic propositions set out by Marx, both with special meaning for the American scene. 'The International', Marx reminded his US correspondent in 1871, 'was founded in order to replace the socialist or semisocialist sects with a real organization of the working class for struggle'. Internationalists regardless of location and immediate situation had foreclosed utopianism and had no need to compromise, least of all on the question of who represented the proletariat; that had been settled. Secondly, the Internationalists had no immediate requirement to undertake, to support, or even to tolerate any radical action outside trade-union work since (as Marx said in the same letter) 'every movement in which the working class as a *class* confronts the ruling classes and tries to vanquish them by pressure from without, is a political movement', destined to become overtly political with the passage of time and the progress of events.[15]

The logic of this decision needs to be examined more closely for clues to the fate of Marxism in the USA during the nineteenth century. However right or wrong Marx may have been about the pre-Marxist 'sectarian' groups in Europe (and anarchism continued to operate as a very lively ghost, especially in cultural matters), the case differed totally in America. Tradition, ethnicity, and the strength of American capital among many other factors precluded the hegemony of Marxists in radical circles for decades to come. Second, the presumption that trade unions represented the general interest of the working class, most especially in the United States, left an enormous hole in the entire logic. Craft unions had long held the door closed to working women. Sometimes these practices began or continued in trades with Socialist influence and notably without Socialist objection. The virtue of native-born Socialists in class terms, apart from the educational materials they offered self-motivated workers, was precisely their avid promotion of women's (and Black's) radical activity. Their effort was no mere pursuit of petty-bourgeois privilege. Marxist disdain for the women reformers who labored mightily in the slums to aid young women workers was condescending and badly mistaken. Their error postponed wider Socialist awareness by the reform activists and their following.

The same problem applied with equal force to Black workers South and North: failing trade-union organization, they had no place in the Marxist strategic scheme. The historical experience of Black activity in the Civil War and Radical Reconstruction left no trace in the Marxist sensibility. Other (*i.e.*, non-German) immigrant groups, prone less to organization than direct mass activity, likewise fell under this ban. Sorge and his friends suspected a mobilization of impoverished New York Irish, led by the most prominent working-class figure in the expelled International sections, because the unemployed and their representatives could not be disciplined like trade unionists. A hundred years later, Old Left labor leaders would cite the same reason for their distrust of the Black radicals whom they viewed as mere lumpen-proletarians. In the interim, similar doubts would be raised about the poorest European 'new immigrant' groups because of their purported incapacity to understand class issues.

Marx's injunctions unquestionably touched a major chord in the American experience, but not necessarily a Socialist one. Ironically, as French historian Herbert Perrier has noted, both Marxist historians of the American left and anti-Marxist labor historians have certified Sorge's *putsch* as necessary and proper: Marxists because Sorge cleaned out the bourgeois reformers, and anti-Marxists because Sorge set the pace for later conservative labor leaders' attacks upon 'impractical' Socialists. Both views ignore the depth of labor involvement with reform, and reformers' involvement with labor, in this period. Both also contain a grain of truth. In a society with few other unifying elements, the marketplace in general and, for workers, the workshop, seemed to many the single point of common ground. Some of the most important social movements in the next century would begin in the economic centers and move outward, at first heedless of or indifferent to electoral schemes. They could be revolutionary, conservative, or an ambiguous reform mixture. In a number of all three types, Socialist activists and Marxist ideas played an initial, crystalizing role.[16]

By Sorge's own later account, the German-Americans constituted an extraordinarily well educated and disciplined band, able to quote chapter and verse from *Capital* or to direct a trade-union struggle.[17] Critics regarded them as a quarrelsome bunch capable at labor affairs but given to hair-splitting on theoretical matters and organization-splitting on practical ones. Their surviving publications have a grey tone underwritten with defensiveness and a certain misogyny (after the expulsions, they nearly enacted an amendment to their program opposing woman suffrage as detrimental to workers' interests!). By contrast, *Woodhull & Claflin's*, full of every radical interest from free love to spiritualism, had the zest of discovering Marxism for a whole nation (here, *The Communist Manifesto* appeared for the first time in the USA in English), and the superficiality of placing every idea at the same level.

When the few thousand remaining socialists around the country reunified in 1876 (the year of German Social Democracy's unification) and reorganized the next year into the Socialist Labor Party, Sorge's intimates had hardened their position still further. Their Marxism could be summarized by cigar unionist Adolph Strasser in 1876: all failed utopias had in common an indifference to unions, in nucleus the true parties of labor and thus parents to the future social transformation. All else was folly. Their fellow union officials would soon conclude, in large numbers, that Socialism itself was the chief folly. Most of the Marxists' erstwhile reform opponents had also vanished from Socialist ranks, part of the downward wave of Radical Reconstruction. The first great ideological confrontation in American Marxism had imploded. Only the issues it had confronted, however indirectly, remained alive.[18]

Meanwhile, outside the pressures of New York, a more eclectic, less contentious Socialism emerged. The possibility of grand reform combinations had never been great elsewhere, and the immigrant Socialists felt no need for ideological claims. The Chicago *Vorbote*, by its length of service and political impact a stormy petral of immigrant radicalism, ran the gamut of immigrant Socialist enthusiasms, from electoral politics to anarchistic social revolutionism, with the same essential class-ethnic following. Never did its editors lose their admiration for Marx, nor confidence in their own ability to define a Marxism appropriate to the time and place.

Chicago had seen German-American workers' movements since the 1850s, but the post-Civil War immigration brought the first wide-scale movement and workers' press. The outbreak of Depression in 1873 drew German-language workers by the thousands into mass meetings to debate 'Labor's next step'. The Workers' Party of Illinois, as they constituted themselves, sponsored the *Vorbote* as their representative, responsible for protest, clarification of issues, agitation for their new movement and development of adequate strategies. The political party would not last. But the *Vorbote*'s strength resided deeper, in the German social clubs that dotted working-class neighborhoods, in the German craft unions, and in the sympathies of a wide-ranging radical constituency independent of any permanent Socialist affiliation. More than fifty per cent of the paper's columns would be devoted to serving this local constituency with information about the city, and above all about their own activities. The paper, like the audience, represented a distinctive Chicago German-American Socialism successful in its own terms.

Capitalism, *Vorbote* argued in its opening issue, caused the misery which readers themselves felt so keenly after the 1873 panic. Following Goethe's imperative, they called for more light on the darkness of social relations. The ancient struggle for justice, the cry for freedom on the lips of martyrs from Socrates to the Parisian Communards, sounded the tocsin again. The conditions that were necessary to spawn Socialism came, as Marx had predicted, through capitalism, an unwilling parent to the nearly-born child. Unions—the most discussed issue in *Vorbote*—offered a good opportunity for explaining simple social facts, while providing a first line of defense for wages and working conditions. Their faults notwithstanding, they were the available means of education and action.[19]

Here the future of the German-American Socialist movement lay, far more than in resolutions and national organizations. Its political efforts would wax and wane, but the local bases, supporting newspapers as symbols for Socialist presence and organizing tools for social struggle, survived. So solidly did Chicago Socialists build their larger apparatus that even when faced with mass unemployment in the trades, they held on through their own mutual benefit societies, their social clubs and their organized Sunday picnics in the country. Free to drink beer away from American blue laws and to engage in comradely conversation, they resisted for decades the loss of their radical identity. As a recent scholar of German Socialism observes, cultural practice became a political practice, and organization of various kinds was itself a culture.[20]

Eclectic Socialism faced its great test with the outbreak of class violence on a wide scale. Through most of the 1870s, the question of what Socialists might do in such a situation had been mostly of local concern. Very suddenly, in July 1877, strikes broke out along the railroad lines, turning into urban uprisings against grinding poverty and against the class privilege epitomized in the monopolistic railroad system. Accosted as 'Communists' in the press, foreign subverters who conspired to lead mobs, Socialists in most places remained distinctly on the sidelines of the mass action. Where well organized, as in Chicago, they supplied speakers and literature to the crowds. In an extreme situation, as in St. Louis where city government fell to the crowd, they became in effect the Executive Committee of a short-lived Commune. In general, Socialists could but point to the significance of the government's repressive response. The illusions of the republic had fallen, as Marx and the Socialists had long predicted; the day of reckoning now seemingly approached.

The strike and the organization of the SLP may properly be

considered the closing dramas of the first act. The encounter between Marxism and American life had been less spectacular than Socialists themselves often imagined, and certainly very different, but vital nevertheless. They had lost, arguably thrown away, their earliest contacts with an American-born population in search of the specific constituency they desired. They would have more opportunities but also more complex troubles in the future.

The Political and the Economic

At the time of the 1877 strike, the Socialists bitterly regretted their inability to intervene more decisively, with greater numbers and influence. Decades later, they recalled with amazement how much energy they had managed to mobilize. Organization raced ahead; Socialist literature experienced its first brief golden age as a dozen newspapers came into existence and pamphleteering flourished. A new group of American reformers, no longer dominated by the Civil War experience, came into the movement. Some, particularly women reformers, were middle-class. But even most of these had been drawn toward labor reform issues. Self-educated American workers, including a few prominent Blacks, also joined or supported Socialist candidates. For a moment the fires of optimism burned bright. A handful of party members gained elective office at the local and state level.

Meanwhile, a group of unionists around Sorge had effected an important coalition with native-born and Irish-American labor reformers. From the 'Little Lancashire' of Fall River, Massachusetts, they published a widely read Socialistic labor weekly and launched the International Labor Union to organize the unorganized, especially restive textile workers along the East Coast. An experienced, talented cadre, they made contacts quickly and encouraged hopes for massive unionization.

The political bubble predictably burst, and the support from the native-born dwindled almost before the German faithful could congratulate themselves upon their success. As would occur many times subsequently, the urban machines stole elections, recuperated their losses, and turned voters back toward the major parties or political apathy. Furthermore, American recruits often did not feel comfortable among the Germans, once the excitement had ebbed. The local meetings in the smoky tap-rooms of sympathetic barkeeps offended American women in particular, and the Socialists' apathy towards the suffrage question did the cause no good. The short-lived English-language press, divided between pure devotion to the labor movement and equally pure devotion to electoral politics, witnessed the unresolved contradictions in Socialist thought and organization in this period. The Germans showed too little concern for alternatives. They had understandably gained the reputation of believing they had an intellectual monopoly on Socialism, which they had equated with themselves. And they soon found themselves, much as before, with only their local sources of support.

The International Labor Union failed shortly after. Unskilled workers could not hold on against the power of the textile barons, who forbade even the distribution of ILU materials in the mill valleys. Labor reformers tended to go their own way, while the Germans drifted into the craft unionism they knew best.[21]

These latter could turn inward with good conscience because the work at hand among their own people became so promising through the modest, patient organization that Chicago Socialists had pioneered. New York became, in that sense, more like Chicago. The daily *New Yorker Volkszeitung* took the field in 1879, after a prodigious fund-raising campaign among union members and German neighborhood residents all the way to New Jersey. From its beginning, the paper became deeply involved in the type of labor struggles that showed the heart of Socialist efforts. The Brewery Workers Union, a truly international organization whose members brought their union cards with them from the old country, relied upon a combination of egalitarian industrial unionism, Socialist leadership, and mass-based boycotts against offending brewers. Within a decade it had won substantial improvements, and (along with coal miners) set an example for future industrial unionism. Around the same *Volkszeitung* sprang up labor lyceums in German neighborhoods, Socialistic German-language schools for children, and a multitude of cultural activities. In Philadelphia, Cincinnati, St. Louis and elsewhere similar stories could be told. If an insular existence was the fate of Marxism in America, these Germans had made the best of a difficult situation.

A newer German immigration simultaneously reinforced and challenged the level of self-identity achieved. Peaking at a half million in 1882, the new entrants were far more urban than their predecessors, more concentrated as skilled and unskilled labor in trades such as furniture, cigarmaking, tailoring, baking, meat-cutting, metalworking and construction. Thousands of them had already participated in the labor and Socialist movements in

Germany, a number (like the brewery workers) simply carried their credentials along, as did a handful of famous leaders. These new entrants found a place for themselves around comfortable institutions. They also saw more acutely than the veteran immigrants how inadequate such arrangements remained for influencing the larger scene.[22]

The unrest took its sharpest form in Chicago, where the whole swath of institutions underwent a subtle ideological shift. Embittered at the electoral duplicity that had cheated local Socialists of their political influence after 1878, and enraged at the brutal and chaotic conditions with fewer social amenities than ethnic New York, the Chicago movement drifted toward Social Revolutionism, a *tertium quid* between Marxism and the anarchism that Marx believed he and the International had killed off.

Chicago revolutionaries, editor August Spies argued in *Vorbote*, essentially adapted to changed conditions. Unlike the New York Socialists who kept their heads in Europe, Chicagoans had observed in experience with their fellow American workers both the necessity and the character of direct action. They reasoned that their own contribution was not to 'Americanize' by pretending to have cast off their origins, but rather to relate the understandings of their solid immigrant ranks to the tasks of the more practical-minded American labor radical.[23]

The historical evidence supports the accuracy of their assessment. Europeans of all classes would find the levels of industrial violence, especially in the West where miners and private armies faced each other with rifles over breastworks, simply incredible. American labor radicals of a new kind appeared at this moment in the Western states, publishing their own revolutionary Socialist papers, gathering real community support behind their labor agitation, and distributing quantities of imported British Marxist propaganda. These American revolutionaries did not have to learn German to understand their immigrant Chicago brethren. *Vorbote* did not have to stray as far as might be expected from the doctrines and ideals it had set out in the 1870s to meet them half way. The 'anarchist' propaganda of the day resounded, at one level, with natural rights doctrines of freedom, equality and fraternity. On another level, the Social Revolutionaries encompassed as much Marxian economics as European-style Socialists. 'We anarchists . . . remain socialists', proclaimed old Josef Dietzgen, 'philosopher of the proletariat' (in Marx's generous phrase) and fierce partisan of the Chicago movement.[24] They did not believe in *waiting* for change to take place.

When the opportunity for intensified labor agitation presented itself, the Chicago movement leapt to support the most practical of American labor aims: the eight-hour day for all workers. By May Day, 1886, Chicago had become the center of the struggle, not only for America, but for industrial workers across the world. That Marxists (or those influenced by Marx) could assume such leadership demonstrated their capacity to galvanize the deep needs of the working class for a real social citizenship. The famed ideological debates between Rosa Luxemburg and Kautsky or, later, between Trotsky and his critics over the meaning of mass strikes for socialism had already been argued out preliminarily, if not resolved, in Chicago of the 1880s. Mobilization, not the parliamentary vote or even the organization of stable unions and fraternal societies, brought the mass proletariat onto the field in its own name. *Vorbote* lacked the ideological finery to make this argument full-scale, but it set the problem of working-class revolution on the agenda for American Socialists.

Bohemian-Americans, the second most significant immigrant constituency of the 1870s–80s, recognized the importance of this perspective with special poignancy. Generally less skilled than the Germans, concentrated in trades such as cigarmaking and lumberyard work, they had their own traditions of free thought (dating back to Jan Hus and the resistance against the reimposition of Catholicism) and their own notable immigrant Socialist editors. Concentrated in Chicago, they followed the German lead in union organizing, electoral politics and revolutionary Socialism.

Socialists in other cities experienced diluted versions of the same sensations in the mid-1880s. As they wrote in their regular reports to the national papers, they worked hand-in-hand with unionists who established local labor federations, and made initial contacts with the Knights of Labor which grew to upwards of a half-million members by 1886. As they revealed in moments of candor, the Socialists did not quite know how to deal with Americans who could not grasp the inevitability of the class struggle or the need for tightly-organized unions, who inclined toward temperance and electoral schemes even as they went on strike. At their best, the Socialists approached their new allies sympathetically, willing to learn as well as teach. At their worst, unfamiliar with the language and style around them, they played a badly mistimed waiting game, confident that the future would bring the Americans to their positions. At the local level, labor made a surprising splash in the fall, 1886 elections, not electing many candidates but surprising the two major parties with their protest vote. Then the curtain really fell. In the face of repression and renewed nativism, reform allies drifted away. Except in the craft unions, Socialists were left alone and isolated again.[25]

In the *Neue Zeit*, the prestigious German Socialist theoretical journal, old Sorge railed, blaming the immigrant Socialists for being at once too American (*i.e.* insufficiently German in their tactics and understanding) and not American enough. Engels concluded bitterly that German-American Socialists could do American Socialism the greatest favor by disappearing altogether, so inadequate had they seemed before the task that had faced them.[26] Neither Sorge nor Engels acknowledged how the First International, and Marx himself, had prepared the dilemma by blessing German insularity from the reformers who could teach them something about American radical democracy. Social reality had again been reduced conceptually to class, and class to a caricature of the cultural mix in America.

Nor could Sorge or Engels fully appreciate the situation of the exposed 'foreign' revolutionary in the community when the tide turned against the Left. As so many radicals would discover in later periods of American history, local German-Americans found themselves after May Day, 1886, surrounded by a wave of nativist hysteria whipped up by the government and the press. Although not yet the foreign fifth column that Socialists would be branded as during World War I, or Communists during the Cold War era, they felt the sting of public hostility, and not only from the upper and middle classes. Activists also faced blacklisting in the workplace. No wonder they tended to stop talking politics openly and to withdraw to their bases.

By 1887 or so, the era of German hegemony over the Socialist movement had ended. Socialists fell upon each other in self-lacerating factional brawls. Some veteran intellectuals ended their careers tragically. Otto-Walster returned to Germany a broken man, forgotten in his homeland, lost in his cups, and soon an obscure fatality. Schewitsch returned home later to eventual suicide with his wife. Men and women in their mid-thirties viewed themselves as past their prime, more active in trade-union and, most especially, fraternal affairs than in politics hereafter. In many places, they still constituted a membership majority in Socialist organizations; and in almost every Germanic metropolitan area their language press remained both functional and cosmopolitan. They talked frequently afterward about the approaching moment when a genuinely Americanized Socialism would supplement and ultimately displace them from the center of Socialist practice. They were the first generation to age into an oldtimers' social club, with all the lost hopes and surviving stigma to Socialism of an insular culture that logically followed.[27]

In short, the German-Americans had never transcended their own success: the local movement based in specifically German cultural life and in heavily German trades. Marxism had aided them to understand the positive sources of their institution-building; it did very little to explain the limits of their project, or the political prospects ahead.

They had not, we should hasten to add, wholly failed to spread the light outside their own immigrant milieux. In slow, unsteady but definite and measurable ways, Socialist ideas had been transmitted to a growing number of Americans. These ideas were disseminated and gained a stable following with the formation of successful, local labor-Socialist newspapers. Historian David Montgomery has pointed to the underlying strategic struggle among native-born and English or Irish skilled workers which gave the Socialists a modicum of influence even under difficult conditions. American-born workers often felt the same pressure upon their position as immigrant artisans. Each decade in the later nineteenth century saw the further erosion of craft workers' treasured 'rules', the long-standing legislation between employer and employees governing procedures for the shop.

The de-skilling process had far to go, and indeed is not finished today; but the carpenters, machinists, wire-rollers, iron molders and others correctly recognized the early phases of a long road downward, even if they did not usually draw Socialist conclusions from their experience. As skilled workers organized successfully from the early 1880s, strikes to enforce work rules and sympathy strikes of one trade in support of another increased. Here, naturally, Socialists preached and practiced solidarity— that is, among craft workers. Newly-organized central labor federations offered Socialists a broad forum to state their case, and the local Socialist papers often found their financial backing here.

No one could call the Marxian analysis in the *Cleveland Citizen*, *St. Louis Labor*, or Providence, Rhode Island *Justice* either deep or consistent. Sometimes, as critics later charged, the unions were envisioned as the foremost agents of change and sometimes as mere defensive forces holding the line until a political Socialism could run large-scale industry as the government did the post office. Frequently, the unskilled and foreign-born were depicted as one pitiful, hopeless mass dumped upon

American shores for the purpose of lowering native wages. Yet, for all their faults, these papers carefully observed and reported the life of the crafts themselves—the first time Socialists had consistently done so in an English-language press—and spoke about the common interests of all labor. The papers succeeded on a modest scale, not enough to seriously threaten the AFL conservatism which they shared to a certain degree themselves but sufficient to make the Socialist movement respected. They were a viable although hardly (except to individual employers) a threatening presence. Tragically, for the crisis in American society and in Socialism of the 1890s, that would not be enough.[28]

Jewish Radicalism During the 1890s

The German demoralization and sense of spiritual exile propelled a newer group, the Jews, toward the center of American radicalism. Just when the German decline had become decisive at the close of the 1880s and early 1890s, Jewish Socialism offered new comrades for old. The massive immigration surge of the 1890s made them especially numerous in New York's Lower East Side, but also in many districts across the Eastern seaboard and the industrial Middle West. By the latter 1890s, the number and range of publications, of self-styled revolutionary activists if not necessarily union or party members, gave them an importance in the Socialist movement out of all proportion to their modest size in American society. It was a pattern other, smaller immigrant groups drawn to radicalism would repeat in following years.

No less millenarian-minded, no less gifted with autodidact workers hungry for Socialist ideas and arguments, they possessed many traits that distinguished them from the Germans. From their organized beginnings, Jewish Socialists had a radical self-awareness as spokesmen of an oppressed people and not merely, as the Germans, as spokesmen of an oppressed class. Jews' status as a nationality exiled into the *galut*, and the racist reception they received in America, made that response inevitable and, in many ways, potentially more volatile than the abstract internationalism of the Germans. Secondly, the material conditions of their arrival left the immigrants far more disoriented, in need of a unifying ideal. They had no prosperous Republican farmers, no Civil War laurels to rest upon, no easy assimilation into the American order awaiting them even in the second generation. The center of community gravity and especially intellectual and cultural energy leaned toward the left, almost from the first days of debarkation at Ellis Island.

Jewish radicalism had two distinct if related origins. In the sweatshops of the garment and cigarmaking industries, in suffering from seasonal labor and execrable housing, the need for organization was readily apparent. The intellectuals who responded to these conditions could trace their origins to the Russian literary revolt of the 1860s and to the political awakening many of them had personally experienced in Eastern Europe or London, surrounded by uprooted Jewish proletarians. Unlike the German 'forty-eighters who played such a large role in the German-American Socialist press, these intellectuals were still young themselves and capable of immense efforts with meager resources. Unlike the Germans, they had no political model to unlearn on American shores. They also had an existing Socialist presence with impressive labor institutions to teach them the nuts and bolts of organizing.

They also had to contend with, to oppose and to learn from, anarchism of a rather more doctrinaire character than the German Social Revolutionism—and not after a generation of experience but at the very beginning of their efforts. This was a Russian legacy reborn in the widespread Jewish sympathy for the Haymarket Martyrs and fueled by the sense of desperation at Jewish slum conditions. Anarchists had attempted with considerable success to join with Socialists in Jewish London during the 1880s, and they attempted to do likewise among the Jewish intellectual-political circles in New York. They boasted some of the most talented poets, most learned editors, and energetic organizers of the day. Unity soon failed, and fratricidal warfare briefly spread from the unions to propaganda societies. But this conflict took place so early, among a field of enthusiasts so young and so relatively small, that it practically burned out before the end of the century. Victorious Socialism absorbed an aspect of anarchism, as it did a hint of Zionism. Jewish Socialism, capturing more sides of community life, had more faces than its German equivalent.

Jewish Socialists learned from the Germans how to create newspapers, unions and fraternal educational-recreational-benefit societies, as they learned for themselves what ghetto Socialism meant. Organizationally, they hit the ground running. By 1886, a *Yiddisher Folkstseitung* appeared, an amateurish copy of the German-American original. By 1890, the Yiddish Socialist movement had its very first journal alongside a new and different kind of Socialist press, already staffed by some of the most capable journeymen intellectuals to have yet reached American shores.

Theoretical flagship, the monthly *Tsukunft*, might well be compared to the Sunday literary sections of the German-American dailies. It explored the wide vistas of modern life, science, and culture, aiming at the simplest levels of explanation. But by its very format, *Tsukunft* appealed not to a mass or working-class audience as such, but rather to a thin stratum of intellectuals, formally or self-educated. It also had a fresh literary tone, with its apotheosis of a William Morris, or even Shakespeare, rather than the Germans' classics and *Vormärz* heroes. (By the end of the century, Jewish Socialists even had a creative literary and critical journal, *Di Naie Geist*, 'the New Spirit', shortlived but likewise the first of its kind for any language in the American Socialist movement.)[29]

Tsukunft's editors included the most colorful intellectuals of the ghetto. Popular short-story writer Leon Kobrin remembered Philip Krantz, already a veteran of London Socialist journalism, as a hero from a Turgenev novel. His colleague, B. Feigenbaum (known as the 'Melamed', Hebrew-style pedagogue), specialized in anti-clericalism, both as a memory of the tyrannical power of the European village rabbi and as a response to American rabbinical hostility to the threat of Socialism. Abe Cahan, later editor of the *Jewish Daily Forward*, probably exceeded them all in energy and in his keen sense for adaption of Socialist ideas to Jewish consciousness.

The weekly *Arbeter Tseitung*, appearing from 1890, had a uniquely crafted message alongside and within the Socialist propaganda. Like the German papers, it argued forcefully for unions, and like the Yiddish anarchist *Freie Arbeter Shtimme* launched the same year, it carried poets' appeals in its first columns, a true Jewish emotional touch. But among its features, Cahan's own 'Proletarisher Magid', the Socialist preacher, leaps out from the page. Explaining Socialism with weekly quotations from the *Talmud*, Cahan made Socialist ideas accessible to those who had not broken and might never break with their own religious yearnings. It was an important point. Contemporary Jewish anarchists believed that once religion fell away, revolutionary identity would swiftly be realized. Cahan saw the transition better. Likewise, the *Arbeter Tseitung* quickly gathered a literary section surpassing the genial commentary-and-reprint format of the German papers. Young artists, playwrights, novelists, and poets considered it as their natural duty to work with the Socialist publications and their privilege to gain a sense of style and of audience for the Yiddish printed word through the Socialist columns.[30]

Taking nothing away from the German-American papers, they had not (except, perhaps, the weekly anarchist *Arme Teufel* from Detroit) become the site of an avowed search for identity; Socialism and their homeland traditions provided that easily, no doubt too easily. The editorials, the headlines, the formal understanding of the Jewish press do not seem so superficially different. But to the close observer, *Tsukunft* and even more the *Arbeter Tseitung* made that search the focus for Socialist politics.

This renaissance of Marxist revolutionary discussion, never fully realized in the heated days of German-American 1870s–80s, is a marvel to re-read. Not because the Marxist interpretations possessed any vast sophistication, but because the very effort, the paper trail and the lecture circuit, meant the creation of a Marxist intelligensia on a scale, even within the microcosm of Jewish life, hitherto unknown in the USA. Such a task could not be carried out overnight, or by Jewish immigrants alone. They knew they required an interchange with a constituency outside the ghetto, through the one cause to which they could give themselves fully, the multi-ethnic Socialist movement.

Socialism in Crisis: The 1890s

For all of their new-found energies and almost Faustian will, however, the younger generation of Socialists were in most cases disoriented and swept to the sidelines during the epochal social revolts of the 1890s. At the beginning of the decade the Socialist Labor Party retained a few thousand members, with a critical mass only in New York and Chicago, and scattered loyalists in smaller industrial cities and in the increasingly hard-hit AFL unions. The foreign-born parochialism of the movement was such, as one member of the National Executive Committee later recalled, that correspondence from native-born Socialists had to be translated for the benefit of non-English speaking Party officials. Virtually overnight this small Socialist nucleus was faced with a spectre of class war on a scale unknown since 1877: hunger marches on Washington by the unemployed, with local Socialists sometimes in the lead; bloody conflict in Homestead, Pennyslvania where ironworkers battled the Pinkertons and militia; the Pullman Strike with its national confrontation between the railroad unions and the Cleveland Administration; and, not least, the Populist threat to disrupt the two-party system.

This new class war also coincided with profound changes in the configuration of working-class culture. A revolution in printing methods made possible the publication of popular mainstream newspapers and magazines, with some element of sympathy for working-class suffering. Other mass entertainments, music, stage and sports, reached through and across class lines. The older ethnic political set-up, Socialist historian Morris Hillquit later charitably commented, could not withstand the changes. Weak as they were, Socialists felt themselves threatened with a kind of dissolution into the broader society. This posed problems the European Socialists still in Europe would not have to face for some time, or with the same paucity of resources.[31]

In response to these complex challenges the fundamentalism of American Socialism doomed it to marginality at the richest moment of political opportunity in the nineteenth century. German-American Socialists and their younger Yiddish brothers (with a handful of sisters) had so long and so thoroughly expected a European-style class awakening and an American Socialist upsurge that they created a *golem*, a clay figure, into which Marxist ideas breathed life. As he waxed strong, the *golem*, smiting Socialism's enemies, seemingly represented the incarnation of science and enlightenment. Only gradually did they begin to notice that he smashed everything in his way, including the little temples of understanding they had devoted their considerable energies to erect. Daniel DeLeon, the *golem*, might rightly be called the first American Marxist with renowned theoretical credentials if by no means the first of real theoretical skill and dexterity. He entered a Socialist Labor Party in 1890 ripe for a takeover.

The movement had seen educated men (and women), but none like DeLeon. Latin-American born, a former professor of international law at Columbia University, he had an apparent genius for adaptation to the native terrain, a universal mind, and a talent for the sweeping generalization. Self-taught workers idolized his breadth of knowledge and the intensity of his devotion, while oldtime German intellectuals put their reservations below their hopes for such fresh energies. Jewish Socialists above all were known to worship at his feet. Leon Kobrin recalls DeLeon as a fighting rabbi carried triumphantly through the streets by young Socialist Chassidim shouting his praises. Exuding sacred energy, he promised them and their faithful suffering a redemption in America.[32]

DeLeon became editor of the new weekly English-language *The People* in 1891, and swiftly put his stamp upon it. English-language Socialist papers had never, with the exception of *Woodhull & Claflin's*, been much more than labor reform sheets. *The People* had a different tone. Editorials by DeLeon created the sustained intellectual monologue that German-American editors had provided but no previous American felt competent to deliver. Without much need, or possibility, of the fraternal activities reports and homeland news that dominated the German and Jewish sheets, DeLeon subordinated reportage and incidentals to his ideological claims. This, he argued incessantly, was no paper for mere trade unionism or reform appeals; it offered the reader pure Scientific Socialism and a definitive political position from its principles.

DeLeon exploited many contemporary enthusiasms, synthesizing them into a single, apparently seamless doctrine. One ingredient was evolutionary theory, already bastardized by Spencer into the petty-bourgeois mania of Social Darwinism. DeLeon, in turn, adapted Darwinism to the vogue of American anthropologist, Lewis Henry Morgan, who had fascinated Engels with his hypotheses about universal laws of social development.

DeLeon also responded to the longstanding restlessness of rank-and-file Socialists, weary of Sisyphian attempts to convert the native craft aristocracy through patient education and organization. The depression of 1893 revived millenarian visions. No one could predict if the American Federation of Labor would be able to survive the slump and accompanying employers' offensive. Meanwhile its rightward-moving leadership under Gompers turned sharply against former Socialist allies as well as against the new immigration. Foreign-born, especially Jewish, Socialists railed against collaboration with double-dealing and often nativist craft leaders.

At the same time, DeLeon captivated many American-born Socialists, still small in number but increasing with the reform agitation of the early 1890s, who had never lost the old dream of independent political action. The formation of the Republican Party only two generations earlier had led to the freeing of Black slaves. Might not the reconstitution of a Socialist electoral machine lead to the freeing of wage slaves? The European example seemed to promise as much, while the contemporary depression, together with the widely lamented 'end of the frontier', suggested a radical turning point in American history.

'Science' to DeLeon thus signified clarity, which in turn demanded exaltation of the Socialist movement as the single, revolutionary beacon destined to survive the coming crisis and to transform American society. 'The question', he wrote in 1891, of 'whether society will emerge on the upward or the downward grade of evolution, depends upon the degree of clearness among the masses as to the road on which they are traveling. This clearness can only be effected by holding forth in all its [sic] purity the principles that guide onward and upward.'[33] Socialists heretofore had not quite imagined themselves capable of approaching power so rapidly without (as in the Social Revolutionaries' fantasies) a mass, spontaneous armed uprising. DeLeon and his coterie of mostly self-taught immigrant intellectuals believed Americans would vote by the thousands and then the millions for the one political party which knew its future. In a series of public addresses printed as mass-circulation pamphlets (and reprinted *ad infinitum* by the Socialist Labor Party as fundamental Marxist doctrine), DeLeon elaborated scientistic distinctions between reform and revolution, between revolutionary unions (those that preached Socialist politics) and mere economic efforts doomed to failure. Abstractly, as a complete system for the self-educated worker or neophyte convert from a disappointing reform movement, his conceptions had an admirable symmetry.

DeLeon's memorable *Two Pages From Roman History* (1903) later argued that the proletariat, unlike all previous rising classes, lacked the material power to establish its own infrastructure, and therefore needed political defenses built up against the lures of reform. This was a theory of working-class backwardness, disguised as an argument for pure revolutionary strategy. The argument had some historic basis in the capacity of the Democratic Party to absorb labor reform impulses, and in the eagerness of craft union organizations to make arrangements with politicians and industrialists at the expense of the unskilled, female, Black and more recently immigrant working class. But his solution went no further than attempting to regiment the same craft workers into a reliable Socialist formation.[34]

Even if the economic and political crisis of American society had been total, DeLeon failed to grasp the lineaments of a credible alternative. He treated the multiplicity of working-class internal divisions, the complexity of social unrest among wide classes of Americans, by levelling Marxist theory down to an impossibly narrow concept of class. He saw no class worth considering but the abstract working class. Its failure to heed his words seemed to him a certain indication that false prophets were keeping the flocks ignorant and confused. These charges increased his appeal, by providing simple arguments and effective leverage against internal critics. The more DeLeon showed himself intransigent and the more he was attacked by moderates within the labor and Socialist movements, the more his revolutionary integrity and scientific predictions seemed the issue rather than the prospects for proletarian uprising in the real world.

In short, DeLeon replicated and unwittingly caricatured the gravest errors German-American Socialists had made toward American social life. They had arrived at a cautious labor reformism by discarding the peculiar history and social arrangements of the nation they set out to revolutionize; DeLeon reversed the image and made that very reformism the result of insufficient determination. They had invested their strategic hopes in the unions, too little crediting their own cultural apparatus; DeLeon disregarded that apparatus as pointless and conservatizing, the unions a vessel for collecting Socialist ballots. The *alte Genossen* had failed for twenty years or more. He would succeed overnight.

DeLeon briefly sustained confidence with a grand plan to unite all revolutionary unionists, from the faltering Knights of Labor and the American Federation of Labor, into a single new union that would organize the unorganized and preach Socialist doctrine. The plan failed because Socialists possessed impossibly slender resources, and because of the political demands DeLeon placed upon even the most loyal union chiefs. As happened often during bad times for the Communist Party in this century, trade-union activity collapsed into building the Party, and Party activity collapsed into support of the press. Non-English language groups, pressured for the same reasons as they would be by Communist leaders thirty years later, either lost their supporters or departed with their institutions. In 1899, DeLeon eliminated all the planks in the Party platform calling for amelioration of conditions.

He could maintain leadership over the movement, amid this failure, only with a political bludgeon and the support of a loyal cadre. DeLeon moved, with the savagery attributed to later Leninist rule-or-ruin internal wrangling, to close down all other avenues of Socialist approach. On the one side, he would finish off the pesky American utopianism; on the other, he would cure immigrant Socialism of its institutional conservatism. With the same logic and almost the same wording as Marx and Sorge had used to expunge the critics from American First International ranks, DeLeon proposed to banish from the party once and for all the 'freelovers and such like riffraff' unfit for Socialist participation.[35] Laying down this law, he attracted the sort of fanaticism for political bloodbath familiar in subsequent sectarianism, including no few American-born radicals too young or too insular to understand the value of the native tradition. Reformers and cranks remained, of course, but only by quieting their criticism of DeLeon, who worked out a philosophy that would have done Sorge credit.

The petty-bourgeoisie, he increasingly argued, bore the blame. It monopolized radical ideas in America and confused the proletariat. Later, avowed Marxist critics of reform Socialism would repeat this charge, with the same grain of truth and the same incapacity to explain how and why that class succeeded. Internal life in American Marxist politics became a burlesque reign of terror, as petty-bourgeois opponents turned up and were dismissed from party ranks.

By the same standard, DeLeon increasingly decided, the older and established immigrant Socialists represented a petty-bourgeoisie in themselves. He treated as *de facto* proof of institutional conservatism their suspicions of his political demands upon unions and his imperious leadership style. DeLeon challenged the fundamental basis of ethnic Socialist localism, the publication of Socialist newspapers by private associations based in the ethnic community rather than by the Socialist movement as a whole. Much like the Communists thirty years later, he demanded Party control over their columns. Unlike the Communists, he had no mandate from a Socialist country to hold over their heads.

Inevitably, secessions began to take place on all sides. Local Socialist groups with their own newspapers had to depart or shut down their papers. Jewish anarchists joined trade-union conservatives in defending the AFL from devastation and in appealing for defections. The Germans, and a group of dedicated Marxist Jews, were the last to leave in 1899. A few years later, DeLeon would comment that he had to look in the office mirror to see if he himself had departed, so many loyalists had gone through the doors.

It is tempting to see the DeLeon episode merely as a false start (or false renewal) of American Socialism, a blind alley where Marxists unnecessarily hammered their heads against a wall. The episode reflected too many deep trends in the history of American Marxism for that comforting conclusion. Both the problem of the Marxist intelligentsia and the larger dilemma of Marxist politics found their reflections in DeLeon's sectarianism.

DeLeon had been converted to Socialism by reading in tandem Engels' *Anti-Dühring* and Lewis Henry Morgan's anthropology. Only later, and out of a distant sympathy, did the working class fit into his Marxism. He developed his hyper-proletarian strategy by choosing his enemies and identifying the obstacles to Socialism within the Socialist and labor movements themselves. The working class was the *deus ex machina* for his science of society. In this, DeLeon was far from exceptional. Remote as they usually were from the daily experiences of immigrants, Americans with education had scarce opportunities to live the lives of the German-American or Yiddish intellectuals, to mix with the basic human element of the Socialist movement and understand its compromises with reality. The immigrants could be fanatical themselves, especially when European events and the absence of meaningful American alternatives made them despair. They could also unconsciously negate their own best insights by blandly accepting the mainstream American view of reality, the marginalization of the foreign-born. But their concepts of Marxism had nevertheless an organic basis; the Americans who could make the same claim, a Socialist Eugene Debs or Industrial Workers of the World leader William D. Haywood, never aspired to similar intellectual status. They worked on instinct. Their practical prowess and intellectual limitations left the question unresolved: who would the American Marxist be, and how would he (or she) treat the fundamental problem of class?

The Left's isolation found its perversely logical conclusion here, in the *fin de siecle*. Trade unionism and reform politics had failed. The Social Revolutionaries of the 1880s, circling around against European parliamentary tactics displaced to America and craft unionist conservatism born in America (or England), asserted that Marxism was possible only with an insurrection around the corner. When that had failed, when the mass did not spontaneously rise and smite the enemy, a vanguard force in an un-class-conscious society seemed steadily more appealing. (Next time, that prospect would have a world revolution and a credulous ethnic movement in enthusiastic support.)

Socialists had paid an especially heavy price in the 1890s and so had the credibility of Marxist ideas. Contrary to what Socialists liked to tell themselves, then and later, DeLeon had not been an aberration. He spoke directly to the sense of disappointment the immigrants felt at their slow progress, to the despair at impotence in the face of mass suffering, and to the eagerness of American Socialists to field a political force beyond the ghettoes. *The People*, widely considered the first 'scientific' newspaper on the left, gave a badly distorted image of what Socialism meant to American practice. It made Socialists into know-it-all fanatics rather than community members one step ahead of their neighbors; and it made them agents of an organization that separated itself from their struggles in order to proclaim the absolute truth they would have to follow for their salvation.

*   *   *

Looking back from the next decade, Socialist intellectual luminary Robert Rivers LaMonte recalled he had known two totally different types of Socialist intellectuals in the 'nineties: the 'Americanizers', whose interest in Marx and in the class struggle had barely developed, and who were only a half-step away from naive utopias; and the 'textualists', who carried around *Capital* like a free thinkers' bible and who remained within the immigrant ghettoes, ignorant to the larger developments of American social life. Those were, he recalled, the ill days when 'the clearness of a comrade could be gauged invariably from the number of ear-marks on his [Communist] *'Manifesto'* and when 'the mental equipment of a Socialist of the rank and file consisted in a few ill (if at all) digested and parrot-like shibboleths and maxims borrowed on credit from some of the fathers and prominent leaders of the movement.'[36] Both contributed their share to the confused merger of evolutionism and class primitivism.

For those most heavily involved with DeLeon's party and union efforts, the generation of young Jews above all, the fallibility of prognostication along with the failure of politics left ineradicable scars. They, like the earlier Germans, became 'old', not by any means inactive but endemically suspicious of revolutionary slogans and revolutionary unions. Their Marxism became conservative, a waiting game. They, like craft union leaders disillusioned with DeLeonism, would for years afterward evoke the sectarian disasters of the 1890s as a defense against left-wing criticism of exclusionary, timid or plainly conservative unions.

What alternatives had been realistically offered? Numerous American Marxist writers later suggested that, had only Marx and Engels' advice been heeded, nineteenth-century Socialism need not have been so insular and the American working class so politically backward.[37] This kind of argument raised the shadow of Marxist omniscience over the reality of political practice, and scarcely aided the successors to the German-American Socialists in figuring out their own way. More importantly, it ignored the real course of events. Marx and Engels unceasingly, and correctly, stressed the importance of drawing Socialism into the class struggle. But they could scarcely appreciate the peculiar circumstances in which the immigrant radicals found themselves. America with its diverse labor force, its deep republican traditions, its overpowering bourgeoisie and its sporadically restive masses, would not readily yield to a literal class solution. Socialism's future rested in something more complex, and something deeper in the American grain.

2

American Socialism, American Culture

The migration of Marxism from its European homeland to the United States produced, as we have seen, results sometimes exciting but also deeply troubling to the Marxists. To succeed, any revolutionary movement needed to come to grips with the pervasive religious and cultural values, to understand and appreciate as well as to attempt to transform them. Homegrown radicals and class-conscious workers, for all their weaknesses, potentially provided Marxists access into the American mainstream. The process of discovery had to be mutual, a complex and protracted probing from both sides. The critical question was, what did each bring to the conversation? Marxism supplied a definite class view and a strategic instrument, the union, which could serve as means of transition to a new order. Indigenous radicalism stood for the most part outside these traditions. But its disciples held for that very reason a more sophisticated view of the multi-cultural, factory and non-factory, character of the American lower classes, Black and white, male and female. They also had a better subjective sense of the meaning, for Americans, of the old Republic's decline and debauch at the hands of monopolistic capitalism. At their best they understood the traumatic awakening into history which alone could bring a serious acceptance of Socialist ideas, and the moral or spiritual vacuum which only an expanded faith in democracy could fill.

The pre-industrial religion of a redemptive, benevolent deity watching over the republic fitted the needs of American radicals and reformers well into the late-nineteenth century. More than that, it placed the palpable deterioration of democracy in a great field of hope. America had failed the trust given its founders with the virgin continent. But that trust might yet be redeemed. The blasphemer, agent of Indian genocide, slaver, merchant-aristocrat, could not rule on. The shadow of his antithesis, the redeemer-woman, hovered in the background ready to bring salvation to a society that recognized its own heart of darkness and willingly marched toward the light.

No wonder Marxists found themselves strangers in a strange land. The sweeping bourgeois triumph Marx depicted did not, in America, consolidate an ideological victory over the past but rather ensured an endless revenge against the *hubris* of material progress. The Radical Reformation, where so much of the inner life of Protestantism first evolved (and devolved), had held as its foremost goal an *escape* from the history of kingdoms and slave classes to the pre-Mosaic paradise before the Fall. Jakob Böhme, mystic philosopher whose recuperation of the dialectic from the Ancients grew out of the challenge and out of the failure of that Reformation to create a heaven on earth, attributed the original Fall to the merchant who sold the fruit from the tree of life. Inspiration to William Blake and the German Romantics, Böhme envisioned a return, guided by Sophia the female deity, to an earthly paradise where androgyny replaced sexual polarization and where the new species lived in perfect peace with animals.

Crankish as this sounds, it combined the abandonment of a defeated armed struggle with the undiminished hope of overcoming mankind's sorrows. It promised a peaceful path to utopia, an alternative to Calvinism and the logic of the merchant. Utopianism and proto-bourgeois possessive individualism entered the New Word together. Despite its disproportionate influence, despite the particularistic and economic appeal summoned by post-Mosaic doctrine of the dark world touched by the light of the pre-destined alone, Calvinism could not uproot its ideological 'other'. Indeed, the rampant (and well-founded) sense of guilt in American religion has evoked persistent communitarian yearnings. Guilty Calvinism and innocent utopianism mixed strangely together in virtually every American radical reform movement from the seventeenth century. Perhaps they still do.

The terrors of colonists cut off from the collective European past prompted an apocalyptic doubt Harry Levin would describe as a special American 'blackness' at the soul's center. Hysterical forebodings must be accounted the proper precursors to radical criticism of the nineteenth century. The Rev. William Wigglesworth's *Day of Doom* remained for generations after its seventeenth-century appearance the best-selling colonial work, second only to the Bible in popular influence. Charles Brockden Brown's *Wieland*, the new nation's first major novel, provided a suitably gloomy national character study of fanaticism and madness at the edge of the frontier. That these took literary form more than political-philosophical analysis suggested that the official optimism could be penetrated only in the flight of fancy where reason no longer held sway.

Because secularism, fruit of the European bourgeois revolutions, here remained largely a genteel (and, despite the unchurched nature of large population sectors, generally marginal) phenomenon, political dialogue filtered through Biblical voices. John Locke's philosophy appealed to intellectuals, but Revelations possessed greater force to congregations who roused themselves against the British. Even Philip Freneau, premier radical pamphleteer of the 1790s, had written melancholy poetry bemoaning the despoliation of the New World. He ended his career writing under the pseudonym of a vanquished Amerindian chief watching the shadows fall upon the once-peaceful kingdom.[1]

Social alternatives had, from the beginning, posed themselves in utopian forms. 'West' signified the mystic locus of the new holy land on the compass of the Radical Reformation, final chance for heaven on earth lost in corrupted Europe. The 'Woman of the Wilderness', popular name for one prominent Böhmist colony, would there meet the outstretched arms of the pilgrim and bring everlasting joy. For many generations, the radical here seems both marginal and bizarre by contemporary European standards. What to make of the most productive press (and prestigious elementary school) of the early eighteenth-century colonies, the pietist hymnals and illuminated texts—all from the celibate Ephrata colony which brought Böhme's teachings to Pennsylvania? Or of the ministerial origins of American Revolutionary passions? Or of the Black and white churches which fed the radical reformism of the 1830s–50s, counterposing an anti-Calvinist Christianity of gentle feminine Jesus to the white man's rapacities? Or of the swift fanning out from Abolitionism into woman's rights, peace, dress reform and temperance? The horrific and utopian often stood side-by-side or combined in a single body like Edgar Allen Poe's, who was reputed to be at ease only when surrounded by his soul-mates, radical women intellectuals after whom he shaped his unattainable heroines.[2]

In practice, bourgeois goals and methods easily triumphed over the communal, frequently celibate settlements that spread across the frontiers. But the raging violence of the dominant order against the natural environment, against the subject peoples and seemingly against the very Edenic anticipation of the New World, made inevitable the patterns of a radical alternative. Not surprisingly then, race, gender and religion at once constrained and accelerated any American Socialism, making it both apparently archaic and simultaneously 'advanced' in ways that would take secular radicals long to appreciate.

Whereas to immigrant Socialists, Marxism offered a beginning point to assess their situation, indigenous reformers, intellectuals, and self-educated workers who started in a different conceptual place came to Marxism for confirmation and practical application of their ideas. Important immigrant groups with their own histories of quasi-religious radicalism also felt a certain kinship and instinctive understanding. In the broad sense, Marxist ideas have always and everywhere assimilated to indigenous cultures and politics. But among these old and new Americans, Marxism evolved towards something it had not previously been: an articulation of unanswered questions for class theory; and the germ of insight for a cosmology in which Socialism returned from its own insular development to the age-old traditions of millenialism.

The self-made Marxists, if they can be called that, naturally responded differently from European-style Marxists to the changes in American society. The grand transformation sweeping aside the pre-industrial society with its moral economy of relatively autonomous craft labor, subsistence (more properly labor exchange) farming and close family units, impelled them to broaden the terms of individual freedom while restraining the advance of monopoly controls. They sought to find in production something similar to the Marxists' notion of unionism but more clearly linked to a renewed civil society of virtuous producers. And they sought, in civil society, to reformulate the basis for order by adjusting existing institutions to self-evident moral laws.

From the factory and the farm, the decisive issue for redefinition was not, as the German-Americans and their Marxist successors believed, the purported 'backwardness' of the working class. The cohesion of the proletariat as a class did not figure as an assumed category in the first place. The remarkable (from an international standpoint, possibly unprecedented) steps taken during the 1877 strikes, Eight-Hour movement and Knights of Labor, demonstrated that sections of the working class could be extremely 'advanced'. The problem lay in the implications radicals would see in these struggles. On that question the long-postponed formation of a popular, English-language Socialist movement rested. The German-American Socialists could pass straight from the old country to Socialist organization in the new; native-born radicals, and the Jewish immigrants, had to pass through stages of awareness taking them closer to the society before them and closer to their own destiny.

Spiritualism, the American Socialism

Like their European Socialist cousins, American radicals found themselves compelled to complete the bourgeois revolution before moving onto grander goals. Like the Europeans they developed their ideas in the process. The peculiar radical ideology that grew out of the struggle for emancipation of Blacks, women and all Americans, offered a counterpart to Marxism's concentration upon the industrial worker. Spiritualism, the American Socialism, answered the need for a collective, egalitarian vision and nourished indigenous radicalism for decades.

The influence of women's agitation joined with abolitionist-minded Blacks can now be seen as decisive for the overthrow of slavery. That alone would have made unique the traditions upon which American Socialism grew. Abraham Lincoln himself said that without *Uncle Tom's Cabin*, no Civil War would have taken place. This may have been a hasty judgment upon the best-selling novel of the nineteenth century. But the ubiquitous dramatization of this novel recalls the function of the Greek theatre in presenting a social agenda. Like Julia Ward Howe of *The Battle Hymn of the Republic*, anthem of Northern soldiers, novelist Harriet Beecher Stowe was a product of the contemporary women's movement, of women's cultural strength and their relative autonomy from male values. The massive women's mobilization during the Civil War, supplying a popular base to Radical Republicanism, helped inspire Lincoln's decision for Black emancipation. The women were right: the war could be won on no other basis.

The Woman's Rights movement, launched the same year as young Marx and Engels published their *Communist Manifesto*, advanced a radicalism founded neither in class-economic complaints nor repressed nationalism but on a widely-felt utopian anticipation. As a prominent Abolitionist (and minister) wrote about woman's dress reform in 1857, 'The structure of our bodies, each limb, each member, is undoubtedly the best that He could devise. Is it not impious folly, then to corrupt, abuse, or prevent the development and right action of the body?' The same principle applied to every aspect of life. He signed his communication, 'Yours for the Improvement of Everything', not a spiritual hope merely but an expectation of certain fulfilment.[3]

Only such beliefs could have induced an ideological confrontation with slavery and, albeit to a lesser degree, with the racism deeply ingrained in the American experience. The foremost militants of Abolitionism and woman's rights quite properly connected these reforms with any fundamental change in the broader society. Elizabeth Cady Stanton, leading woman's rights advocate, insisted that 'government based on caste and class privilege cannot stand'. Her longtime collaborator, reformer Parker Pillsbury, believed with many others that a 'glorious, bloodless, millennial revolution' would follow a radical reconstruction of South and North.[4] How nearly these expectations conformed to the reality of Black Southern life before and after emancipation may be questioned, but not the sincerity or importance of the aim. When Karl Marx insisted that 'labor cannot emancipate itself in the white skin where in the black it is branded', he put the issue precisely from one important angle.[5] But he could not at such distance fully comprehend the problems posed by racism at all levels of the society, and the complexity of a solution most particularly for the labor movement.

Not that American labor lacked its own historic legacy of radical generosity. Proto-socialist Painite sympathies, utopian schemes and evangelical radicalism had all infused artisan and industrial reform circles through the turbulent 1820s–40s. Fourierism, the first Socialism to gain a major public following, kindled attention among Transcendentalist intellectuals and New York's powerful reform journalists but drew its main body from artisans of strong Protestant sentiment. Local ministers became the first milltown critics of exploitation, their women parishioners the shock troops for shorter hours and child labor reform. Artisan-linked movements and occasional third-party efforts stressed the dignity of labor and its social value; they also linked workers' rights to the salvation of the republic, a republic, that is, of producers.

Whether and how the dreamed-of republic might accommodate Blacks remained less clear. Racist sentiments outside the South were deeply embedded among the competitors for jobs and tolerable housing. White artisans sought to exclude Blacks for the same reasons, and sometimes in the same ways, that they sought to exclude women. Labor organizations did not accept the free labor ideology that with equal opportunity, Americans of every origin could rise up at will. Many workers knew such ideologies doubly false, because of prejudice against whole sections of workers (notably the Irish) and because schooling, family and other connections would continue to shape actual mobility. They chose, where organized, to remain largely with a Democratic Party mixing racial supremacist ideology and urban social services. Resisting Civil War conscription, New York Irish turned riot into anti-Black pogrom. It was a sombre note for the hoped-for bloodless revolution when the constituencies of the oppressed found themselves on opposite sides.[6]

And yet the very difficulty underlined the heroic character of the enterprise. The crusade against slavery raised idealism to new heights, and not only among the reformers. As in every crusade-like war, society had proven itself capable of great, sudden adaptations. The stirrings of labor activism during the war and after created potentialities for a breakthrough beyond 'free labor' to anti-monopolistic, pro-woman suffrage, even anti-racist labor. The deep doubts concerning progress on the bourgeois model, the horror at frontier brutality and civilized vice, the sense of time closing in upon the republic, stirred an imperative for change. The development of a wage-earning class, whatever its internal contradictions, provided a universal around which many other concepts could be organized.

We may begin to explore the nature of this combination by considering the most popular and most theoretical-minded, respectively, of the native-born American Socialist writers. George Lippard, the first best-selling Socialist writer of the nation ('America's Eugene Sue') and a pioneer labor activist, dramatized the dual vision of darkness and light within emergent industrialism. Philadelphia, industrial capital of the early nineteenth century, home of the 1835 city General Strike and of ugly internecine warfare between Protestant and Catholic workers suffering the handicraft decline, offered Lippard an arena to observe the betrayal of republican promise. He personally endured the most familiar American tragedy: he was driven from the family homestead (adjoining a vanished perfectionist colony) for the teeming city. Struggling up from penury, he watched with horror as a younger sister entered the swelling female workforce where prostitution served as recourse from underemployment, low wages and depressed living conditions.

The same tragedy unfolded in contemporary European capitals and found its way into European cult literature. But in a manner characteristically American, Lippard centered upon the cultural metaphor of virginal beauty raped by commercial evil. In his phenomenally popular melodrama, *Quaker City; or Monks of Monk Hall* (1845), Lippard foresaw a future Philadelphia with manacled workers paraded through the streets by the money kings. And he drew a contemporary Philadelphia moving almost inexorably toward that end, the wanton upper class debauching all that it touched. In a series of other novels, Lippard put into literary form the sacred destiny of democracy to triumph somehow over evil, through the mystic brotherhood of international labor whose redemption would be reached at last upon American shores. Lippard's greatest protagonists, handicraftsmen-socialists, prepared—with the inspiration and aid of gentle, visionary women—to lead the American masses toward that republic of honest workers and farmers.

Lippard's real life labor activity made the connection of prose and politics vivid. Lippard preached a variety of Fourierism: unity of workers across race and ethnic-religious lines, renewal of the brotherhood of toilers. Lippard's own secret labor organization (with its short-lived journal, *The White Banner*, full of spiritualism and broad class appeals) which emerged shortly before his death at age 32, was precursor in a half-dozen states to the Knights of Labor. From the 1820s onward other labor prophets wrote with greater clarity about the economy. Some, like labor-agrarian reformer George Henry Evans, had decades of sustained activity. But none captured more brilliantly than Lippard the unique spiritual-fantastic elements, the republicanism-cum-utopianism and the proto-feminist undertones of US labor radicalism. He considered Charles Brockden Brown his model, and Edgar Allen Poe his friend.[7]

The ultimate scholarly fulfillment of Lippard's Christian Socialist vision can be found in the massive two-volume *Ancient Lowly* by mechanic-reformer-intellectual C. Osborne Ward. First International leader (in the anti-Marx faction), Ward shared scholarly territory with his European contemporaries Kautsky, Eduard Bernstein, and E. Belfort Bax in exploring the religious-chiliastic revolution. But with an important difference: while the Europeans followed Engels' view of religious beliefs as mere metaphors of class unrest, Ward (more like Ernst Bloch and today's Liberation Theologians) accepted the millenarian beliefs at face value. Revolutionary religion was, to him, no mere symptom but the keynote of transformation.

Ward found hidden truths throughout history. Shrewd in his use of existing Biblical and archeological evidence, compulsive in his narration, he detailed the early Christians' absorption of a slave and handicraft culture many centuries in the making. He uncovered ancient labor protests ranging from uprisings against the Eleusian games, miners' riots, strikes and geographical escapes to the formation of primitive unions. As he saw it, the spread of the Roman Empire created the conditions for co-ordinated, widespread insurrection culminating in Spartacus's great action. Thereafter, energy was turned to the more modest trade associations which provided not only protective work rules but elaborated a fraternal-religious and ethical life wholly outside the imperial culture. Much of Ward's work documented these associations in sophisticated social-historical fashion, interpreting details of festivals, emblems, rituals and practices. Christianity met the declining conditions of trade, in this view, with a chiliasm recuperated from older religious forms—and with the promise of a better life on earth.

Betrayal lay ahead, a kind of historical Golgotha which only Socialism could redeem. Christianity in power inevitably repudiated its origins, repressed the traces of its radical and pagan origins, and ferociously persecuted undaunted believers in social doctrine. The ancient 'spirit of trade unionism' thus became the 'sickly feudalism which hovered over and ruled the dark ages of another thousand years'. And yet the example stood permanent witness, for Ward, to the thirst for justice and for inevitable *return* 'back to that sweet, loving, self-supporting Socialism . . . .'[8]

Ward's credo, if not his explicit Socialist faith, could be taken as the spiritual basis for resistance against the intrusion of large-scale capitalism into the life of native-born labor from the 1850s to the 1890s. And it could be taken as basis for a brotherhood of humanity beyond the color of the skin. As Herbert Gutman observed, Jesus the Brother Carpenter banishing the money-changers from the temple provided the apt analogy for anti-monopolistic efforts. And the goodheartedness of many among the local merchant class, 'producers' with their brother factory workers, underlined a common local resistance illuminated by numerous battles against nationally-owned railroad or monopoly mine kings. The Christian Socialist George McNeill, most prominent ally of the Marxists in the International Labor Union, put it clearly in 1890: 'Though the Mammon-worshippers may cry, "Crucify Him! Crucify Him!" . . . the new Pentecost will come, when every man shall have according to his needs.'[9]

Figures like Ward and Lippard were not (as they have usually been seen) mere interesting reformers with eccentric predilections but men in tune with a powerful minority view of the age. If they possessed a mentality nearly opaque to the twentieth-century mind, in their own time they were able to put their fingers upon real sentiments and made themselves heard widely. In all, the preparatory stages of American Socialism summed up a bold, distinct concept of spiritual progress without which the material development of the republic would be mere self-deceit. It remained to the political philosophers to explicate the contours of that peculiar pilgrim's progress.

Spiritualism fused this radical perspective with mid-century Protestantism. The third event of 1848 (or the fourth, including the European uprisings), the 'Spirit Rappings' of the Fox sisters in Hydesville, New York, set off a wave of excitement that would last a quarter-century. Prominent American intellectuals, especially on the radical side, enrolled themselves in Spiritualist ranks, predicting that the movement would sweep oldfashioned Christianity aside. Emanuel Swedenborg's doctrines (according to Blake, a retail version of Böhme), popularized at this time in America, helped give philosophical ballast to apparently fantastic claims. Soon, distinguished journals and Spiritualist church congregations had elaborated a growingly influential view of the cosmos as one great entity in which all life remained continuous and permanent.

Very soon, 'philosophical' Spiritualism distinguished itself from mere 'phenomenological' contact with the spirit world. Andrew Jackson Davis, the 'Poughkeepsie Seer', made himself the link between Swedenborg and the seance. Victoria Wood-hull's principal ghost-writer, Stephen Pearl Andrews, elaborated the philosophical implications of this fast-growing cosmology as the coming together of long-scattered human wisdom. Encompassing Pythagorean numbers theory, Spencer's philology of various sciences, Swedenborgian and Fourierist analogy and correspondence, his version embraced '*All that has ever been believed in, in the Past*; revised, clarified, systematized, by the Light of Knowledge'. Here was the heart of the matter. Spiritualism offered the framework for a super-organicism, an American version of left-Hegelianism with its theism intact. Until the early-twentieth century, homegrown Socialists by the thousands would cleave to some version of this belief. Lacking an experience or concrete reason for belief in the proletariat's power to supersede all pre-existing class structures and bring an end to pre-history, American radicals understandably pursued the inherent oneness of the spiritual world, all nature and human life present and past. It was their pantheistic, anti-racist and even ecological Socialism.[10]

The link between Spiritualism and the vision of a cooperative society had many popularizers. Best-selling novelist Elizabeth Stuart Phelps, who consoled the tens of thousands of Civil War survivors with *The Gates Ajar* (1869), became a prominent advocate of labor reform and author of the feminist-cooperationist classic, *The Silent Partner* (1871). Proto-feminist poets, such as Spiritualist Lizzie Doten, established 'contact' with Poe while blasting slavery and the monopolies. As late as 1879, the President of the American Spiritualist Association predicted that from 'Spiritualism will spring a merger of the two into the dominant thought of the age', and 'sole instrumentality that can save society'.[11]

Spiritualistic Socialism could be realized, it was obvious, only through women's emancipation and their unloosed influence. Political experience had told reformers (and not only women reformers) so. As Victoria Woodhull proclaimed in 1871, a new government had to be inaugurated to finish the political revolution of women's rights.[12]

A very peculiar Socialism. In practical agitation, this doctrine intended to bring together the temporal with the transcendental, and guarantee material realization through allying like-minded labor reformers, workers, women, Blacks, Native Americans (seen with unique sympathy by women radicals of the time) and the charters of celestial unity into one single indomitable combination. The notion was, so to speak, Leninist combination politics without the internally disciplined Party. But not without an International! Woodhull's vision of the First International may be closer to historic fact than the present-day image of the IWA. Full of European labor reformers and radicals of various stripes, some closely aligned with Spiritualist ideas, the International appeared altogether accomodating. From the viewpoint of Woodhull and company, Marx and Sorge, not the Spiritualists, were severely out of step.[13]

Woodhull's last hurrah, as she reeled from the disappointments of the early 1870s, was not surprisingly her effort to link the most excluded, women and Blacks, into an outright radical union. When all the prospects for a serious reform candidate for president had melted away in 1872 and she had lost most of her labor allies, she nominated herself for president and Frederick Douglass, still America's most prominent Black leader, for vice-president on the Equal Rights ticket. The convention-hall of radical women and their eccentric male allies ('long haired men and short-haired women', by the contemporary formula) may have been the only grouping of Americans to take such an effort seriously; Douglass apparently did not. The palpable failure, like the removal of woman suffrage leaders and Black leaders simultaneously from national reform into more parochial efforts, signalled the end of an era.

Subsequent obscurity should not, however, discredit Spiritualism's achievements. The non-Darwinian science preached by the Spiritualists required a more serious consideration than the late-nineteenth-century (*i.e.*, pre-Relativity Theory) world could easily give. The twentieth-century recuperation of the cosmic view, in theistic or non-theistic terms, suggests they deserve another hearing. According to savant and reformer Andrew Jackson Davis, Spiritualism also guaranteed the uncooptable tenacity of American radical thought in general. 'First, *the harmonization of the Individual*; secondly, *the harmonization of human Society*' in concert offered a program that the business class could not approach with its profane materialism. Those Socialists could count themselves the modern-day disciples in whose hearts the spirit dwelled, and who preserved the life-giving truth from forgotten or surpressed memories of the ancient days to premonitions of the 'good time coming' (as the popular Abolitionist song had it) in the joyous future ahead. And what if it could not be soon reached? The Spiritualists recognized, more clearly than did Marx, that the emerging science had no inherent bias toward the possibilities for emancipation. Indeed in their dark moments Spiritualists experimented with the opposite possibility, that what could not be discovered by the visionaries would likely be lost to the manipulations and debasements of the profit system.[14]

In American literature if not in reality, the circle was unbroken. Walt Whitman's literary heir, chief popularizer and first biographer, Horace Traubel—soon to be one of the most prominent Socialist editors and literary critics—gathered in 1893 with the Grey Poet's other intimates to publish *Cosmic Consciousness*, a memorial volume which set out many of the same principles. Whitman had, to this little circle, achieved in person what the Spiritualists held out as prospect for the race, a god-like contact with the infinite and a simultaneously thorough understanding of the physical world. Naturally, he became (most especially in Traubel's mind) more radical than the radicals, more democratic by half than the existing Socialists. Engels' contemporary *Dialectics of Nature*, intended as a Socialist exploration of science from the atoms to the stars, suggests how close a parallel sort of rumination cut to Marxism's core. But with an important difference: Engels saw the universe as spiritually inert, the Spiritual-Socialists interpreted it as cosmically alive with the super-organic lucidity which awaited Man's self-recognition.[15]

By the late 1880s to early 1890s, the essential patterns of utopian and reform thought had been reformulated around the aspiration for an indigenous Socialist movement. Utopianism, a recurrent impulse, renewed itself in a spiritual congruence with Marxism, sharing ideas and disciples aplenty. Out of geographical pursuit of utopia on the Western frontier, a vigorous political Socialism finally arrived, most prominently through the efforts of labor hero Eugene Debs. Meanwhile, a subtle but no less important tendency, a neo-transcendental mysticism blended with a Whitmanesque celebration of the ordinary, began to infuse new generations of radicals, both immigrant and native-born, with a sense of cultural purpose. The chief catalyst of the first group, class-conscious sentimentalism, stood closer to the furtive modernism of the second than scarcely anyone afterward would suspect.

The most important American radical writer of the nineteenth century, Edward Bellamy, had only a passing acquaintance with Marxism before the publication of his monumental *Looking Backward* (1888). But he must be regarded as a key precipitator of Marxism among the native-born, explicator of a particular Yankee reform version of Socialism, and himself the transitional figure from antebellum perfectionism to Debsian Socialism. His earlier writings are notable for their Sprirualist flavor, their determination to explore psychic transformation alongside social transformation, and their salvation of the lost man through the redeeming power of the all-knowing woman. In *Looking Backward*, an ordinary middle-class American from the late nineteenth century awakens in a utopian future where all the social problems have been resolved through a cooperative partnership. All the elements of potential happiness can be seen already in the time-traveler's own day; only a rational approach and a sense of Christian brotherhood are missing.

This kind of social transformation, couched in class reconciliation and the security-blanket of middle-class propriety, immediately struck a chord in an America shaken by the Haymarket events of 1886 and not likely to embrace a full-blown Marxism. Thousands of craft workers destined to join the Socialist Party had their introduction to Socialism through Bellamy's pages. Tens of thousands of others—the 'great Midwest of the American mind' in its idealistic variant—kept Bellamy on their bookshelves, voted Democratic or Republican, and pondered just a little that Capitalism might possibly *not* be the best of all systems.

William Morris and other European interpreters thoroughly misunderstood Bellamy's sentimentalism as puritanic, and his proposed system of organization, the 'Army of Labor', as authoritarian. Bellamy actually sought to fuse the lessons of the Civil War crusade with the mechanical futurism endemic among the Yankee population. Neither 1877 nor even 1886 had brought a new notion of civilization out of class turmoil. A leap of the imagination seemed more likely to succeed in winning hearts and minds.[16]

The extraordinary influence of Bellamy's novel upon women alone would establish its significance for prescribing styles of future American Marxisms. Virtually every prominent woman to reach the shores of political Socialism passed through Nationalist sympathies, from venerable Lucy Stone (a founder of the Woman's Rights movement at mid-century) to Frances Willard—the proclaimed 'Woman of the Century' and head of the largest women's organization in the world, the Woman's Christian Temperance Union—to pioneer twentieth-century feminist intellectual Charlotte Perkins Gilman (then Stetson). They and a legion of other activists recognized in Bellamy's novel, and in the short-lived movement it inspired, something immigrant Socialists had never grasped: the ethical imperative of Socialism restated in the native lexicon.

By the 1880s, Socialistic women had half a century of tradition behind them in the struggles of their sex and the cooperative solutions they had advocated and personally attempted. From the early years of labor reform during the 1830s–40s to the Abolitionism and Woman's Rights campaigns of the 1840s–60s and the Grange, Populism and the WCTU of the 1870s–90s, their leading activists had effectively articulated a native historical materialism that made empirical sense of the changes around them, especially of the impact of the industrial revolution on sex relations and roles. Above all in relation to working women, they had pioneered the Socialist movement's future accomplishments. Bellamy clarified their ideas and offered them a Socialist identity.

Class Conflict, American Style

Still broader classes of native-born Americans grasped at radical, Socialist ideas with a deceptive suddenness during the 1880s–90s.

They made the turn themselves, albeit with immigrant help, not only because the alternatives before them had dwindled, but also because they recuperated the power of their own radical traditions. So thoroughly had the industrial barons turned Civil War triumph into a charter for great fortunes, so little did the role of Blacks freeing themselves become known, so effectively did the emerging propaganda machine make class conflict out to be an immigrant conspiracy, that the vibrant earlier radicalism seemed a mere passing fancy. Bellamyism recalled radical democracy to the politically literate. Populism and the Knights of Labor reached deeper, demonstrating practically how another form of society might operate. The force of radicalism, whose genius lay in the melding together of immigrants, Blacks, women, skilled and unskilled workers, sent a shockwave through the system. Only their divisions permitted a wounded upper class to ride out the uneasy moment.

Populists felt the mixture of hope and terror, a mixture manifested in economic cooperativism and a chiliastic pessimism as dark as any offered by Wigglesworth or Poe. In its hard Southern core, Populism brought real success for small farmers in controlling the manipulations of parasitic middle-men. Such cooperators were heirs to generations of willful subsistence farmers whose 'household mode of production' lay outside Marx's analysis of commodity relations in the invading capitalist agricultural market. Mediated through a rough system of labor value, their forms of exchange had helped provide practical American utopians a model for their communities. Populists sought to restore this cooperative production in modified form as their only collective remedy.

As historians have tardily discovered, Populism's own equivalent of the German-American editors and agitators, the newspapermen and circuit lecturers of the Farmers Alliance, knew perfectly well what institutional system of exploitation they faced. The bankers (sometimes erroneously identified with an international or even Jewish threat to America) had, along with their allies the railroad barons, engineered the development of the agricultural marketplace into a system that combined the worst features of wage-slavery and debt peonage. Political action was required to take control of the menacing institutions and to regulate or replace them with democratic alternatives. A materialist if not a Marxist conception of history enabled the Populist press to interpret the eclipse of the republic, and to anticipate the dawning of another day brightened by the lessons cooperation had already taught them.

From the viewpoint of Blacks, Populism marked a decisive second phase of the freed slave's quest: the pursuit of allies against race competition among the poor and against the power of the merchant kings. Populism combined an articulate republicanism of the producer classes with a Christian ethic of mutual aid and milennial expectation. No wonder Populists swept Southern Black districts at the first signs of white farmers' willingness to attack a common enemy. Defeated in bloodshed, Black Populism nevertheless arrived at the common rendezvous of this generation. Tom Watson, Populism's foremost political figure (and, later, its greatest renegade), personally led white farmers to defend Blacks against repression. He had recognized the obvious: that the agricultural lower classes could not be free without mutual aid, and that American society could not be transformed without their cooperation. He had picked up the thread of Radical Reconstruction and its significance for the civilization.

The 'Empire of Gold' that Populists of all kinds attacked, moreover, correctly captured the imperial character of the real enemy. Troubled by past American expansionism and the moral price exacted, indigenous reformers better understood the threat posed to American democracy and to the world. Ignatius Donnelly, Populism's foremost novelist and one of its most astute politicians, provided the *Looking Backward* of the movement in *Caesar's Column*. In this novel, a Hitlerian monument is constructed with bones of victims cemented into a great tower which shadows over the destruction of civilization.

Elements of Populism would be trapped in their own pacts with the devil. The barbarity of racism fully restored in the South resembled the *Herrenvolk* consensus of aryan Nazi Germany, with defeated radical Tom Watson transmogrified into the champion of race hate. Populists in Congress who supported expansion of the American empire, willing to barter all principle for a share of wider foreign markets, made the same choice of blood compromise with mammon. Those left behind with their ideals, when not driven off by penury or brutalized into silence, turned in substantial numbers toward Socialism.[17]

A parallel process in the labor movement found less room for successful economic cooperation, but greater prospect for outright Socialist understanding. Like farmers, workers combined their vision of community with apocalyptic projections of violence or with a modest and pragmatic labor politics— sometimes with both. Contrary to most historical interpretations, these choices differed less than they seemed on the surface. They were, in any event, more distinct from European parliamentary Socialism than from each other. Sharing with Populists a real and pervasive class-consciousness however problematic its expression, and a relative detachment from the fate of a German-American Socialist politics that could neither aid nor understand them, radicalized workers advanced forms of class struggle without the European-style rhetoric.

From its inception, the American labor movement had repudiated the wage-system as an inevitable condition of working life. To many of the craftsmen who were brought together in the National Labor Union of the 1860s–70s or the Knights of Labor, this system appeared inherently degrading. For some, especially those schooled in British-style craft unionism, the patient strategy laid out by Samuel Gompers and his *soidisant* Socialist coterie seemed the only viable course. But the wage-system also rankled many by defying Christian virtue with its job-conscious exclusion of women, Blacks and new immigrants. Most of all, even when Gompersism raised wages and regulated conditions, it could only slow the erosion of skills and proud craft autonomy in the face of mechanization.

Alternatives depended upon the line of sight. Some, in contact with radical immigrants but by no means dominated by their ideas, considered violent seizure of power the inevitable outcome. Albert Parsons of Chicago, a former Confederate soldier, stood in direct descent from John Brown (and was embraced politically by John Brown, Jr.) in his relentless assault upon the industrial system. Joseph R. Buchanan, stormy petral of a powerful grassroots radical-labor movement in Colorado and a leading labor journalist, learned the ethic of violence in the mine wars between union men and company militias. The two men, foremost English-language propagandists for revolutionary Socialism, preached industrial doctrine steeped in Natural Rights and became, briefly, the principal distributors of English-language Marxian and anarchist texts (mostly imported from England).

Buchanan and Parsons rightly assailed the AFL abandonment of labor republicanism which had inherently embraced the various races and categories of workers into one potential citizenry of the 'producing classes'. They understood that such a shift signalled retreat from the cooperative viewpoint which had maintained since the 1820s that abolition of the wage system alone could prevent a fundamental degradation of labor. They also saw that contestation limited to the price of labor-power inevitably meant a turn in the direction of controlling (*i.e.*, limiting) the labor market at the expense of other strategies. Finally, they penetrated the veil of ostensibly non-partisan politics or no politics decreed by AFL officials to understand every form of unionism as political and to view in full light the implications of politics for the disinherited.[18]

But how to respond? For generations, following Gompers' and Sorge's lead, Marxist and academic labor historians alike described the republican reform vision as backward-looking and provincial. Whether personally sympathetic or unsympathetic to the Social Revolutionaries, they have distorted reformism's subtle relation to the revolutionary-insurrectionary alternative, and obscured a wider understanding.[19]

Women labor reformers, seasoned eight-hour day advocates, supporters of impoverished immigrant workers, and Blacks all knew that the AFL had no claim upon the 'typical' American worker. However briefly, the Knights of Labor *could* justifiably make that claim. By way of sympathies and of social services, the Populists or even the local units of the Woman's Christian Temperance Union could also assert equal contributions. More importantly, reformers and revolutionaries knew better than most AFL leaders that the question of labor had become a question of civilization: the issue of a declining republic had to be faced with a fresh republican formulation if democracy were to survive at all. They differed among themselves about how far the republic had already fallen and whether the justifiably enraged population could tear down and replace existing institutions overnight.

The Knights believed organization—as their friend, labor editor John Swinton put it—to be the 'key that unlocks the portals of that mysterious, majestic temple of the future, into which who so enters has felt the touch of the ultimate ghost'.[20] Organization could overcome the unnatural advantage monopolists had over the market, and lift to a higher level the achievements of democracy. Knights leaders, Terrence Powderly most notably, failed at the moment of crisis for the organization because they sincerely believed that organization of this kind could, like a magical Yankee invention, overcome entrenched privilege with combined virtue; and because they treasured the coming universal brotherhood so much that they scorned their fellow activists who had drawn different (and more correct) conclusions about the violence of the state. They shared with the revolutionaries the intuition that the time for great change had come. Their mutual failure, but also the historic phase that the Knights represented, could be seen as the rude beginning of a systematic and constructive class response to American social politics, prefigurative of major responses to follow.

One story illustrates our point. The Knights in Rhode Island, the original home and most concentrated single center of textile manufacture ('mother of industry'), encompassed nearly the entire reform-Socialist gamut. In the mill villages and the industrial cities, British, Irish and French Canadian textile workers popularly known as 'the Niggers of the North' had been a target of labor reformers since at least the 1840s. When the Marxist-led International Labor Union dispersed, its American-born activists turned to the small state's woeful operatives, voteless heirs to the unsuccessful insurrectionary 'Dorr War' of 1842 and victims of ten and twelve-hour working days. No movement had succeeded in stirring more than scattered groups of them from their collective sense of helplessness. Suddenly, in 1885–86, the Knights of Labor blossomed across the state. Knight meetings became town meetings, and locals took over day-to-day life in prominent textile plants.

This was a peaceful revolution manifestly unlike the railroad strike nine years earlier. Its watchwords, constructive change and cooperation among the classes rather than class strife, its apparently sudden emergence and thoroughgoing practical character gave the Knights an aura of the truly republican, dignified (and to listen to Powderly), vice-cleansed worker whose time had finally arrived. Close on the heels of organization, social networks proliferated, including clubhouses for the 'clean' entertainment of teenagers, reading rooms, and even 'socialistic' day-care centers in an occasional friendly church. Reformist ministers and defenders of working girls understandably rallied to the Knights. The organization had seemingly won its objectives with no bloodbath, few actual strikes, and much good will all round.

Exempt from this good spirit, of course, were manufacturers and their spokesmen in all the positions of power. When the concentrated power of the textile manufacturers was focused against Knights' locals, and when predictions of mass violence caused leaders to back down, the momentum disappeared and with it the Knights' membership. 'Socialism' as a word, Socialism as an idea, reached outside the small German-language community for the first time in Rhode Island in the form of conservative descriptions of a moral menace, drawn largely from fictionalized reports of revolutionary Socialist rhetoric elsewhere. Socialism as popular doctrine gained currency in the wake of the Knights' aborted revolution to install industrial democracy.[21]

The failure could not be attributed solely to cowardice or betrayal by the Knights' state leaders. Nor should the local AFL officials who stood by anguished at the tragic unfolding be made to bear the blame. Both (sometimes the same 'Lancashire Irish' men led craft unions *and* launched the Knights) failed to anticipate the swift recuperation of bourgeois power, and both led the transformation of the movement's remnant into a Socialist nucleus. The attempt to establish a new civil society had clearly lost. But not because of the inadequacy of the ideals. The state Knights' popular newspaper moved over easily into a labor-Socialist weekly, whose editor pronounced the defunct organization to have been foremost a 'school for ethics', model for a future organization destined to fuse craft unionists with the unskilled, the woman and the Black. He described the Haymarket Martyrs similarly, in a black-bordered issue mourning their death, as the successors to Prudence Crandall, the antebellum New England schoolteacher who had suffered popular hatred in her determination to educate Black children. The Knights, he admitted, had 'not fulfilled practically its highest ideal—no church ever yet has. The material from which they are made is too selfish. But it has made great strides . . . It must move on, ever developing, ever ascending, shining brighter and brighter until it becomes the Bethlehem Star of a new era, leading man to a social salvation.'[22]

This could be described as the Socialistic thought of an era. The defeat of the Knights threw back American labor as far as the destruction of the guild system had thrown back European handicraftsmen centuries earlier; and in an epochal sense, it seemed to many workers, only particularism and Socialism remained as alternatives. The first English-language Socialist branch in Providence, Rhode Island, meeting in the historical Baptist Church founded by religious dissenter Roger Williams two centuries previous, knew where it stood.

National Knights leaders did not take so advanced a position. But at the same moment they refused support for the Haymarket victims, Powderly drew WCTU president Frances Willard and her following toward the Knights and exerted special energies, albeit too late for great success, on behalf of organizing women workers. The Knights had sacrificed their finest forces rather than risk the loss of labor's republican heritage in class confrontation. Being who they were, they could not have done otherwise.

In a variety of other locations, the Knights were able to piece together coalitions of skilled and unskilled workers, erstwhile Democrats and Republicans (usually divided along ethnic lines),

Blacks and whites around a roughly common view of oppression and redress. Such coalitions had an inevitably fragile nature, and not only because of the manifest differences among the constituencies. What kind of society lay ahead? No one, except perhaps the German-American Socialists, had thought through the question with much precision. Many West Coast Knights, to take one small but extraordinary and painful example, did not envision permanent competition with Asian contract-laborers; Social Revolutionary leaders had joined in the hue and cry for deportation. Craft unionists in general, with early scattered exceptions, still upheld the dream of returning women from the labor market to the home once and for all. Women reformers drawn close to the Knights so abhorred class conflict that they hoped for a society free of violent Socialists as well as violent capitalists.

Beneath these differences lay the crisis in the conception of the republic. Lincolnian democracy had never intended the inclusion of Blacks or large numbers of new immigrants on equal terms, and even the most radical democrats found the vision of an egalitarian multi-racial, multi-cultural democracy difficult to comprehend. But they struggled with the implications more completely, stood on both sides of every question more openly, than the insular, industry-oriented European-American Socialists. Populism in decay, similar in this to the woman suffrage movement in a period of prolonged defeat, fed nativism and xenophobia. Radicalism had meanwhile absorbed the animating idealism and moved on.

Electoral politics, never the basic issue for the Knights, reaffirmed these divisions and confusions. At the local level, where the Knights' strength was concentrated, their activity tended to undermine the credibility of existing officials and promote new candidates more sympathetic to labor. In power, these relatively progressive officials attempted to improve public services. In line with these changes, a legion of erstwhile radicals entered factory inspection, state labor bureaus and the like. Florence Kelley, translator of Engels' *Condition of the Working Class in England* and a sometime SLP member, led the march into the state apparatus. Other women labor reformers, drawing the lessons of the time from the futility of cooperative production and the inevitability of state regulation, followed her. So did a scattering of local Socialist union leaders.

With all their positive value, such changes neither slowed the erosion of the craft worker's position nor altered in any fundamental way the exploitation of unskilled and non-English speaking minorities. Nor could reformism prevent the alarming spread of privation during the depression to follow. Involvement of craft labor in politics tended, moreover, to represent the advancement of a privileged section of labor, men against voteless women, whites against Blacks, craft workers and politically adaptable Irish-Americans against the unskilled and non-Irish. Radical democracy became unradical Democratic Party machine politics within a few years, an adjustment but not a fundamental change in the way political business had been conducted.

This form of political co-optation had recurrently been, and would remain, a permanent element in the life of American labor. But it had its historical benefits. While it corrupted its share of labor leaders, it also created a sense of political and educational possibilities heretofore unexploited by Socialists and reformers outside the foreign-speaking communities.[23]

In this limited sense, the Knights, the Populists and even the oldtime Socialists had to be swallowed up by history before the question could be reposed as capitalism and Socialism. With the Knights' smashing defeat (they persisted, mostly on a local basis, for more than a decade after), the republic of free industrial producers had failed at last. The dream of agricultural freemen stood only a few years from similar debacle. Ahead lay Socialism.

A Gathering of Folk Cultures

The road away from the Populists, the Knights and the craft unions through the dark valleys of the severe 1890s depression, illuminated the future possibilities for democratic transformation. Socialism became the dominant option, in a serious and popular sense for the first time, to the degree that it embodied the combined legacy of previous radicalisms and carried them forward. Railroad man, reformer and sentimentalist, Eugene Victor Debs epitomized these possibilities, and he effectively dramatized the necessity for Socialism through his own heroic failures to change the system from within.

Leader of locomotive firemen in the bustling railroad town of Terre Haute, Indiana, Debs represented a reformism still wedded to the hopes of class cooperation and economic expansion. He did not support the riotous 1877 strike, choosing instead the role of middle-of-the-road Democratic leader and state representative from blue-collar wards. He came to reform positions slowly as he began to discern the threat to the republic posed by the monopolies. He was shocked, as only an American revolutionary in the making can be shocked, by the repression of the 1880s and judicial murder of the Haymarket leaders. He moved steadily leftward as the pincers closed around railroad workers struggling to maintain their way of life.

The horror and mingled hope that emerged with the unfolding events during the 1890s brought Debs and others quickly along. Repression of peaceful, orderly strikes such as that of Brooklyn transit workers, or of the highly skilled, well organized iron workers of Homestead—both in 1892—raised fears of a cossack state. The widespread suffering and unemployment brought mass demonstrations and a gnawing sense of public desperation.

Debs' response to the steady destruction of railroad unionism exemplified the peculiarly American version of class-conscious behavior. The monopolies had violated the 'fundamental manhood' of the American worker, reducing him to a European serf. The 'Christ-like virtue of sympathy', as he called collective resistance against demoralization and degradation, promised to return that manhood and to redeem suffering in a fashion historically associated not with 'manhood' but with the androgynous Jesus that women churchgoers had substituted for the Calvinist deity. Recovery of self-respect, recovery of the republic, meant sacrificing individualism, if necessary, to the needs of fellow humans and of the future society as a whole.

The unprecedented use of federal troops to crush the Pullman strikers, and the unprecedented, mostly spontaneous response of Western railway workers to the call for a boycott of Pullman trains, forced Debs to a class-based view of social struggles. The public image of him as Christ-like martyr, suffering for the workers, made Debs the people's idol much as Martin Luther King, Jr., would become later. Pitting moral force against brute force, their vision promised the triumph of justice even against overwhelming firepower.[24]

An initial instinctive Socialism, linking class conflict with utopian strivings inside the mechanical heart of American civilization, supplied the answer or rather several answers for how the old republican dream of autonomy—and all the other threatened dignities of workers, the unemployed and the reformers—might be revived and universalized. 'The Debs of fable', wrote Horace Traubel ten years later, 'lighted a fire in the car yards of Chicago. The Debs of fact lighted an idea in the dangerous shadows of the republic. This Debs is not a threatener of the peace. He offers the only peace that is peace. He pushes aside all cheap and cheat truces. He insists upon the one practical and drastic measure of escape and affirmation.'[25]

While in prison, Debs read Marx, and a new day dawned for American Marxism. It had become nativized class-struggle and moral, social doctrine. A serious nominee for the 1896 Populist candidacy, Debs swiftly moved in the direction of the vision on the horizon.

The combined failures of Populism, of craft labor, of utopianism and even the failure of woman suffrage and temperance to sweep the country and bring their promised results all pointed to the conclusion Debs, still unconsciously, represented. But his sympathizers in many corners of American life correctly perceived that it had returned the onus of social guilt from the poor and the foreign born to the rich and had brought Socialism to the center of the reform message. Debs step by step, from his leadership of the Pullman Strike and the formation of the American Railway Union, his leadership of the last great effort at founding a utopian colony, and his acceptance of Socialist political leadership precipitated a radical combination as had not existed since the great divide of Black Reconstruction, Woman's Rights and labor reform.

In Debs' veritable image, the folk cultures of Socialism organized themselves toward an amalgamation. They did so under the sign of autonomy and self-realization. By way of contrast, Daniel DeLeon's fundamentalist revolt against craft union complacency had led directly to a levelling process, the reduction of 'the worker' to a static, abstract category destined to move in a certain way. Debs' new-found disciples did not articulate a much clearer message. But they expressed one through their very presence.

In the West, among Debs' rural and small town natural constituency, the grassroots Socialist press forged a mature propaganda apparatus. *The Coming Nation,* later *The Appeal to Reason*, for nearly twenty years one of America's best-selling political weeklies, epitomized the mixture of enraged individualism and idealism in the air. Erstwhile real estate speculator and utopian colonizer J. A. Wayland carried the message of the violated social contract to the Plains states' small independent or tenant farmers, the free-thinking petty merchants, the railroad machinists, schoolteachers and ministers' wives. Wayland raged against the shoddy aristocracy, the railroad kings and their Congressional supporters, who drained the countryside dry; he punctured the patriotic rhetoric that portrayed Socialism as unAmerican but bank manipulations and overseas expansion as impeccably American. He evangelized Socialism for his readership and, eventually, urged them to join the Socialist Party. How strange it must have been for European Socialists reading their exchange copies of Wayland's papers to interpret his eccentric blend of John Ruskin, Thomas Jefferson, Spiritualism, and Bellamy Nationalism — what Wayland called 'One-Hoss Philosophy'. How little a part of their world he was or wanted to be.

In the ultimate Protestant-Socialist *bildungsroman, Samuel the Seeker* (1910), Upton Sinclair described what Debs had in common with American grassroots folk beyond the resentment of class oppression and the loss of republican identity. The protagonist, born into a middle-income family ruined by stock investment, inherited from his father only three things: a working knowledge of the Bible, the memory of a dead mother, and a naturalist's love for the countryside as seen through the bucolic poetry of Eugene Debs' real-life intimate, James Whitcomb Riley. Struggling through poverty and unhappiness, learning about the artificiality and inner sickness of the existing order, he becomes an avid Socialist when he meets 'men and women of fervor' who turn away from organized religion to find their inner light. At the novel's close, his Socialist free speech meeting is broken up by thugs, and he lays in a pool of his own blood as the strains of 'The Red Flag' echo in the background: 'Yours is the power of clubs and jail, yours is the axe and fire/But ours is the hope of human hearts and the strength of the soul's desire.'[26] These masses had found a religion in Socialism.

Debs had another, surprising ally in the presumably most European of radicals: the immigrant Jews. Passing through the double alienation of cruel industrialism and the maddening response of the sectarian SLP, they turned to Debs as the fitting totem of their own unique Americanization, fusion of age-old messianic hope and egalitarian political-economic promise.

Their Socialism, too, involved a desperate struggle for folk culture. The Germans, dominant in the Socialist movement for decades and carrying over their culture fundamentally intact, had no need to demand the kind of autonomous cultural space that major immigrant groups would struggle for in the next period. Yiddish speakers and readers had their special pressing reasons to do so. Their effort had a hidden significance for the republican Socialism of the native-born and for Blacks at the heart of American civilization.

Among Jews, the language question had a unique internal history. Yiddish, a variant of Middle High German, had grown

up in Europe in the second millennium as the vernacular language of the Jews, increasingly displaced to East European
villages, the *shtetls*. Assimilationist, post-Enlightenment intellectuals had sought to banish the tongue, but without much
success. By the middle of the nineteenth century it had begun to
generate a literature of its own, a literature deeply touched by
Socialistic values. The pioneer Jewish-American Socialists
learned Yiddish, often writing in it for the first time in America,
in order to reach the mass population. Its development as a
language and as a culture bred pride in many who had seen it as
mere instrument. Thus Morris Winchevsky, famed poet and
editor of an eclectic Boston Yiddish newspaper sponsored by an
SLP local, declined to accept discipline from DeLeon, claiming
autonomy as a prerogative of any self-constituted part of the
movement. Challenged, Winchevsky and most of the other leading Jewish intellectuals seceded, giving a larger cultural meaning
to the Jewish unionists and political cadre who had broken or
would shortly break with the SLP for their own reasons.[27]

Between grassroots Protestant and immigrant Jew, related
messianic traditions were about to join symbolically. Jakob
Böhme, like a host of other Radical Reformation mystics, had
absorbed what secrets of Jewish Kabbalism he could gather
third-hand. These mysteries and heterodox readings of the Old
Testament hinted that the fall from grace had been an inevitable
and necessary step, something like the fall from peaceful
matriarchy to class society that Engels and Bebel elaborated.
The return to paradise, with the aid of some unspecified saviour,
had long been a staple of mystic promise.

From another, related perspective, the Jewish immigrant had
special reasons for reaching out to American Socialists. Other
New Immigrant groups would, in substantial proportions, regard
America as an economic convenience, a step up the ladder to
make a successful return home possible. Jews lacked the illusion
of a happier homeland waiting for their return. In a seeming
paradox, the descendents of the *galut*, greatly influenced by the
emotional and cultural elements of what would become Zionism,
nevertheless found in the American republic a personal and
collective solution. Some would escape the major social debits of
Jewishness by way of participation. Others would find in
America a place where a Jew could safely be a Socialist, and
where a democratic culture with a permanent Jewish presence
could be imagined. Socialism accommodated both scenarios, as it
accommodated the Protestant Socialist will to preserve and extend
democracy. This cultural pluralism, a concept vague but rooted

in the anti-racist and gender-conscious struggles of mid-century, would become twentieth century radicalism's strongest suit.

According to Winchevsky's testament, the Jews also found in Debs something else they had not found in orthodox Marxism. They admired Marx's genius and they had admired DeLeon's erudition. But without the poetic dimension, Socialism reduced itself to dry and unconvincingly rational theories. Debs was poetry come alive; he signified the birth of a movement that did not seek to reduce the symbols of Socialism but broadened them decisively. Here, too, lay the hidden future of radicalism.[28]

Perhaps, then, the two new key emerging constituencies, native-born radicals and the poor Jews, shared more than anyone imagined: in particular, a sense of exile from the Judeo-Christian promised land and an inner determination to regain their legacy. Their religious heritage made sense of their Socialism. Even the aging Germans, recalling their own romantic heritage and relieved now at last to discover an American disciple, fell in love with Debs. Defeat had washed the arrogance out of the political survivors. And now that they were old in a foreign land, they saw through Debs the meeting of folk cultures on equal ground finally taking place. From that event they took a rare satisfaction.

At the same time, the practical absence of Southerners Black and white, Irish Catholics and assorted others from the Socialist ranks did not bode well for the Socialist future. Such insularity was a historical legacy that could not be easily or summarily set aside. The crushing of Black Reconstruction, and of the Knights a decade later, drove these latter groups toward a particularism which could grasp at Socialism only in another form, primarily through the social doctrines of the Catholic and Protestant churches. Blinded by their backgrounds in white Protestantism and secular Judaism, Socialists could not encompass fully the lower-class realities of the American scene. In a paradoxical way the world war, with its exaggeration of nationalistic sentiments, would clarify the particularism inherent to this era of Socialism; the need for a Socialist self-identity, best seen by the Jews for linguistic and territorial reasons, would open strategic perspectives for Blacks migrating Northward. Generations later, the Socialist kernel within the churches would be understood better as well.

By the eve of the First World War, American Socialism would reach the height of its Debsian trajectory: a limited and even particularist movement *less* limited and less sectarian than in previous generations. Its very existence stood as a worthy legacy to all the striving and anguish of nineteenth-century reform When DeLeon complained that European Socialists seemed to have a straightforward task of embracing workers while Americans had to 'wipe clean the pothooks' of reform traditions, he had captured a part of the problem but responded with the wrong answer.[29] Socialists would perforce have to deal with the heritage of reformers or they could not situate themselves powerfully and effectively in American social reality. They had to break with the expectation of 'free labor', the doctrine of boundless opportunity. Most especially they had to repudiate the imperialism of expanded markets at all costs and to explain to Americans the moral alternatives of international peace and cooperation. In reality and in ideology, Americans stood at a turning point. To see past that point, they had to be drawn step-by-step from their spontaneous ideas of nationalism and unlimited commercial horizons to the doctrines of Socialism.

3

Marxism in the Debs Era

The political strength of the Debsian Socialist Party and the revolutionary *elan* of the Industrial Workers of the World have no equal in American radicalism. Together they reflect the capacity of the left to identify and equate with itself the key symbols from both historical sides of the great social transition: honest producers of the agrarian, republican past and cosmopolitan worker-intellectuals of the technological, multi-cultural future. In probing the secrets of full-blown capitalism based upon advanced heavy industry, state regulation and a vast consumer market, they interwove for a moment the immigrant and home-grown strains long incompatible. They also faced up to the emergence of the United States as the dominant military-industrial power in the world. Tragically, they ran out of time, out of strategy and out of forces before they could consolidate permanent social bases.

The first grand transformation of American society, sweeping aside the pre-industrial order with its moral economy of relatively autonomous craft labor, subsistence or labor exchange farming and close family units, had called the Socialists' home-grown predecessors into being. Utopians, labor reformers, even militant temperance advocates had sought to broaden the terms of individual freedom while resisting the social implications of total market domination. Socialists offered several constituencies their last chance to defend imperiled ways of life. The second transformation, coordinating Fordist mass production with a burgeoning 'culture industry', provoked the younger generation to attempt to make new cultural sense of the opportunities created by the objective force of the market. The linking

of these two large responses, drawing upon the past and project-
ing the future, made Victoria Woodhull or Frances Willard
parents not only to the Greenwich Village bohemian feminists,
but also to the IWW.

The expansion of the domestic labor market to a hitherto
unimaginable size and variety also brought radical responses
from forces wholly new to US society and the American left.
While struggling to save their cultures, the new immigrants also
sought to place themselves in the modern order where they
worked, lived and suffered. 'Socialism with its working clothes
on', William D. Haywood's definition of IWW unionism, offered
one possibility that could be linked somehow to radical politics.
Ethnic organizations more extensive and more intensive than the
nineteenth-century German and Jewish varieties produced tendencies toward re-internationalization of the labor movement
via links with volatile European events. Reaching simultaneously backward and forward, to age-old identity and to new
prospects, immigrant Socialists dramatized the situation for
radicals at large. By 1920 their response would be decisive for the
left.

Underlying all these new developments was the search for a
vision adequate to incorporate the central concerns of Marxism
into the emergent realities of the twentieth century. Which is to
say: comprehending the integration of the wage system into the
advanced consumer capitalism of the West, and the development
of industrial conflict within the global contradictions of capitalism. This vision, elusive as the invisible thread John Reed
claimed to have discerned connecting Cubism and the IWW, lay
somewhere beyond the available traditions of Marxism in the
USA.

Consider the gender-conscious Socialist woman (the term
'feminist' belongs to the post-1910 era) who was heir to generations of non-Marxist political practice. Her tradition spoke of
Socialism, an *American* socialism, and she could claim allies in
the largest, most impressive, women's movement on earth. Typically, such women joined the Socialist movement on their own
terms and sometimes formed separate societies of Socialist
women. The notion of subordinate status in relation to male
workers or agitators held no appeal. She had her own ideas of
what a Socialist movement should be, a notion closely linked to
the underlying ethos of the fading craft worker in the railroad
towns, the tenant farmer in Texas and Oklahoma, and all the
loyal children of Abolitionism. She knew that capitalism must be
restrained before it eradicated the last traces of a once pervasive

belief in the power and virtue of America's 'producing classes'. At the same time, she had to struggle with herself to understand a younger generation of women more interested in Freud and free love than in gender solidarity. Her world was disappearing, but not before she made a last statement on the finest dreams of older America. She captures best the backward glance from across the great historic divide.

In contrast to those who saw only corruption in the 'electric light towns' (the phrase belongs to Oklahoma, the homegrown Socialists' banner state in their banner era) stood the younger version of a very old man I knew briefly: Hugo Gellert, the last survivor of the group around the *Masses* magazine. Gellert recalled for me his growing up in New York, part of a working-class family attached to the Hungarian Socialist Federation and its popular daily *Elöre*. Winning an art prize, he traveled to Paris where the Academy and even the Louvre failed to inspire him. He was drawn instead to the streets and to a huge Michelin tire advertising banner. He returned to New York a devoted modernist *and* a loyal ethnic radical, not particularly burdened by either the supposed insularity of the immigrant ghetto or the presumed anti-modernism of Marxist conceptions. As an artist, Gellert recognized instinctively that consumer capitalism had seized upon the fluid motion of modernity and had placed its message in the public eye, a message that the old Socialist leaflets no longer could adequately express. As a Marxist, he reflected upon the contradictions that capitalism now presented to the left. *The Masses* embodied the result.[1]

Consider further the anonymous Wobbly, native-born or Italian, Slavic, even Mexican by origin, who considered himself a 'bird of flight', in ceaseless movement back and forth across oceans and borders. For this self-taught philosopher in work clothes with an ongoing mental dialogue in several languages and half a dozen cultures, the very notion of a single national conflict, or of a fixed hierarchy of skills and ethnic traits signifying leadership in Socialist or Communist movements, seemed absurd. He took Marx seriously, but Marxism—as then constituted—less so. Doctrine, organizational practice, had yet to be reformulated to suit his taste. He had figured out what the most brilliant of the parliamentary Socialists (including those who would become Communist leaders) did not know: that only by staying ahead of the Fordist strategy of connecting wages and consumption, by refusing the single identity of the 'home guard' worker in the conservative-minded union of the future, could he pose a revolutionary alternative. The Italian extra-parliamentary left of the

1960s–70s, reclaiming the 'revolt against work', would designate him as the crucial human link between the First International and the post-Leninist era.[2]

Or yet again, consider the young Black male or female who by virtue of family background and education knew not only about W. E. B. DuBois but had also heard, in the late 1910s, of Marcus Garvey and the Russian Revolution. Suddenly, in the age of emerging nationalisms, Black nationalism and internationalism seemed to have torn a hole in the web of repression. The world beckoned for Black culture and Black politics. The streets of Kansas City, or Chicago, or above all Harlem, became cosmo-politan centers for unprecedented possibilities. The youngster could grow into an aesthete poet, a nationalist militant, a Black Bolshevik, perhaps all in one lifetime. Social movements he or she observed would be judged, not even as the IWW had been favorably judged for its sincere egalitarian approach toward Blacks, but rather to the degree to which they recognized Black liberation in the fullest sense.

A loosely-organized, democratic movement could encompass these diverse elements; no movement could make them all the essence of its being. The English-language bloc of the Party, for all its good qualities, never quite transcended its origins as voice of protest for the petty bourgeoisie beaten down by industrializa-tion. Nor, despite all good intentions and some impressive ex-ceptions, did the IWW ever cease to be a predominantly white men's organization. Neither the republic of political virtue nor the republic of industrial virtue could become something they were not.

The Socialist Party's democratic claims, compromised on all sides by errors of omission and commission, epitomized the class ambiguity of the historic native-born American left. The Aboli-tionist movement, apart from its free Black component, could also be described as petty-bourgeois, and neo-conservative his-torians with a Marxist background would one day hurl those same charges at America's epic reformers. [So could the New Left, as *its* enemies trumpeted.] What else could a mass socialist movement be in a nation of an unstable, bitterly divided, and in its organized part, privileged and often conservative proletariat? No answer to this question could satisfy. The IWW stood in this sense directly descended from those older labor movements, narrowly economist like Sorge's 1860s–70s milieu or erratic with popular enthusiasms (like the anti-Chinese Social Revolu-tionaries of the 1880s), which saw the problem and the solution only in terms of production. The Wobblies fostered their own culture, rich and generous, but insufficient to the complexities of stable urban, working-class life. The Congress of Industrial Organizations, in its halcyon days, would not consciously advance much beyond this economist barrier, and the important factory network of Communists, Socialists and Trotskyists would not go beyond it at all except in adaptations to existing ethnic-racial cultures.

The Socialists sought to substitute themselves for a political working class that did not exist but might be successfully consti-tuted. The Socialist tragedy resided in their inability to grasp the dynamics which moved masses towards discontent but also towards longings and expressions that transcended the old re-publican imagination. The IWW attempted the same substitution with the same ultimate limits. In the meantime, the younger radicals who joined the radical ranks from the immigrant ghettoes or from Greenwich Village became tangled in the pace of events and the mirage of world revolution which favored neither Socialists nor Wobblies. In the face of unanticipated problems and opportunities, and despite their own defeats, they supplied some of the brightest intellectual moments of the cen-tury, the solid foundations of a Socialist culture that has persisted to our own day.

The Age of Propaganda

What could Marxism mean to such movements? It provided to millions more or less what it gave to Debs himself: an anchor, a philosophical center, for agitation and education. The Aboli-tionist and Woman's Rights movements, whose surviving acti-vists recognized their kin in the Socialist Party, had earlier succeeded in creating a mass constituency amongst the restless Yankee population by dint of ceaseless pamphleteering, lectur-ing and stump-speaking. But the task of forging an alternative public sphere in the United States was enormous. Unlike Europe with its far more centralized national labor movements, Socialism in America had to confront an extraordinary welter of local conditions and exceptionalisms. Despite the popularity of the *Appeal to Reason, Wilshire's Magazine* or even the more theoretical *International Socialist Review*, there was no American equivalent to the authoritative *Die Neue Zeit*, much less an *Iskra* to constitute the core of Party activism (although the *Weekly People* imitated this role in the sectarian microcosm of the SLP). Rather the public space for Socialism in America was invigorated by the extraordinary diversity of the local Socialist press, publishing in a score of languages. It was this local alternative press (not so different from that undertaken by the New Left three generations later) that attempted to answer Horace Traubel's question: 'Who will remind America that she has promised democracy to the head and broken it to the heart?'[3]

The Socialist press naturally reported national and international events, but its moral emphasis was on the eclipse of the republic and the promise of Socialism. An awakened citizenry had to educate itself to the history and destiny of civilization. Perhaps the emergence of an indigenous women's Socialist sector best expressed this fundamental aspect of Debsian Socialism. Women's Socialism first blossomed where nineteenth-century reform traditions had remained strong, in the small towns of the Midwest and West. Tinged by Spiritualism and its offspring (including Theosophy and quasi-Emersonian 'New Thought'), it resumed the Protestant mission for a purified world with woman's moral influence assured. For a time, in spite of a determined resistance by male Socialists, their movement flourished; their own press, with a circulation of 10,000, conveyed a unique Socialist message through the schoolteachers, ministers' wives and aging gender agitators. Marxism abstractly, and the Socialist Party concretely, had made possible the preparatory training women needed in order to take hold of their own collective destiny. Alliance with the working classes would bring a reconciliation between the sentimental values of the past and a Bellamyesque future. Socialist women had the right and the duty to demand their own share of the work and the glory, their own definitions of Socialism. In truth, the contemporary European avant-garde with its appeal to individual woman's emancipation did not aspire nearly so far or so radically as these stiff-backed, semi-rural women.[4]

The Socialist educational program, most popular in the Midwest and Plains states among native-born men and women in early middle age, demanded new kinds of books and new ways to read them. One may judge the movement's intellectual character by the most important educational text supplied to English-language Socialists, *The Struggle for Existence* (1904) by former Populist educator Walter Thomas Mills. Interpreting the history of the universe in one grand sweep, this widely circulated work simplified religion, culture, Spencer, Darwin and a little Marx into a graspable whole. Study questions following each chapter allowed little circles of disciples, meeting in public schools, union halls and taverns, to rehearse their own understandings and to raise their collective self-confidence. The local Socialist news-papers provided Marxism its first extensive popularization (or vulgarization), the most sweeping ever conducted in the English language, and pressed readers to go on to the books themselves.[5]

Chicago's Charles H. Kerr Company became the head-quarters for the effort to attain European sophistication without sacrificing popular accessibility. The SLP's New York Labor News Company, one of DeLeon's favored Party institutions, had published a dozen or so European classics, but lacked the distri-bution facilities and soon the scope to accommodate the growing potential readership. Kerr quickly took over the lead. Populari-zations of Darwin, Lewis Henry Morgan's *Ancient Society* (which owed its renewed interest to Socialists), Dietzgen's theories of cognition, Enrico Ferri's analysis of criminology and Edward Carpenter's lyric appeals for emancipated sexuality were all published and distributed as essential texts for Socialist reading. Ernest Untermann, dean of German-American intel-lectuals and in later years a translator of *Capital*, provided in his *Science and Revolution* (1906) nothing less than a cosmology for the proletariat 'conscious of its origin, its present and future place in the universe, its social, terrestrial and cosmic mission'.[6]

The *International Socialist Review*, published by Kerr, was the flagship of the entire venture, dedicated to bringing social thought in line with contemporary science. The *Review* indeed published virtually every famed European Socialist thinker in its early years, along with American hopefuls—more theory than all other US Socialist publications combined. Kerr had chosen A. M. Simons to edit the ISR. He was, after DeLeon, the most impor-tant and the most typical American Marxist intellectual of the age. Born on a Wisconsin farm, Simons studied with leading Progressive intellectuals and was active in settlement house work before he became the evangel of Socialist education for Americans. The coming writer who could 'bring a combination of clear English style and a thorough mastery of Socialism' to the problems of American life, he insisted, would 'earn the eternal gratitude of the workers of the world and have carved for himself a broad and lasting niche in the temple of fame'.[7] He especially looked to leading academic 'Progressives' who seemed to Simons more advanced than European Marxists because they had suc-cessfully broadened materialist analysis from economic prog-nostication to the entire span of the social sciences. Although he did not say so directly, Simons had effectively abandoned the Hegelian metaphysics that seemed to him a hangover from Marxism's European origins.

Simons took upon himself the unenviable task of persuading ordinary Socialists to become involved with complicated scientific ideas while convincing the educated non-Socialist that he or she had already come to Socialist conclusions. To do so, Simons had also to break the hold of indigenious metaphysics and messianic idealism upon the indigenous radical tradition. In his opinion American history constituted the crucial terrain for this confrontation, and Charles Beard's famous Constitutional revelations, so shocking to the Progressive Era, were the theoretical paradigm. Beard's stress upon economic *interests*, rather than *classes*, echoed the general Socialist emphasis on bourgeois venality in the American past, a resentment so deep in the wake of the 'Robber Barons' that the Civil War ceased in their minds to be a crusade at all. In this neo-Jeffersonian perspective, the practical yeoman farmer returned as the sole hero, and historian Frederick Jackson Turner, who invented the 'frontier theory' of American society, appeared as prophet. A. M. Simons' own works celebrated the farmer as 'the purest American type . . . the most unique of all the diversified social forms appearing on the continent'. The frontier experience with its 'communistic character' had conditioned American democracy, but had fallen prey to the cities and the exploiters.[8] The close of the frontier logically meant the dawning of Socialism, for nothing else could redeem American democracy.

One may well wonder, when looking back on Simons' pioneering works, at the absence in them of Blacks as anything more than victims, at the inattention toward radical ideologies in the Revolutionary and Civil War periods, and at the virtually total omission of American working-class history. Scientific Socialism appears a poor version of petty-bourgeois radicalism, stripped of its energizing ideals. But Simons, for all his weaknesses, represented a decisive stage in the theoretical development of the left: the first attempt to base Socialist criticism of American society upon contemporary scholarship. He also expressed popular disappointment at the betrayal of the Civil War's promises and understandable rage at the ceaseless historical self-congratulation in contemporary American lore. A more genuinely Marxist book, *Lincoln, Labor and Slavery* (1913), by old Hermann Schlüter, attracted virtually no attention. By contrast, Simons struck political gold. Over a thousand study classes were reportedly formed to discuss his books. Likewise Oscar Ameringer's more witty but interpretively similar *Life and Deeds of Uncle Sam,* (1909) reputed to be more entertaining to plain folk 'than a night at the movies', went through a dozen translations and half a million copies.[9]

But Simons' Second International style of scientific inquiry in the ISR, lacking this inherent historical interest, seemed dry erudition to most American Socialists. The limits of American taste for European theory became suddenly clear. The *Review* sales hit an early plateau of some 3,000 while the Socialist Party continued to grow by leaps and bounds. Kerr pressured Simons to publish more concise, accessible articles and Simons finally resigned. That phase of scientific socialism had been still-born. If much of European Socialist theory had adapted itself to the task of finishing the bourgeois revolution of the mind, Americans did not need or desire Socialist assistance. Socialist activists sought the certainty of evolutionary science but felt no need for extended theoretical discourse over the details. Very likely they also longed for a popular metaphysics which twentieth century intellectuals could not supply.

Only among the Jews, in the secluded Yiddish corner of the American left, did a serious theoretical project survive. *Di Tsukunft*, staggering through the years of defeat and disappointment, found a new leading spirit in Abraham Liessin, fixture in ghetto Marxist journalism for thirty years. Liessin, a melancholy poet of tragic Jewish destiny, had been a precocious Socialist leader in 1890s Vilna, one of the public champions of the Jewish Bund preaching working-class unity through Jewish workers' collective self-recognition. The *Tsukunft* he inherited, with a monthly circulation not exceeding 15,000, exerted a modest impact upon Jewish radicals at large. Its ample pages carried every Jewish Marxist writer of note on current politics, Jewish international and national problems, and especially Jewish literature. Strictly speaking it was the only typical Second International publication in the United States; but its existence was premised upon ethnic coloration. Here, as nowhere in the English-language Left, theoretical dialogue flourished continuously and at a relatively high level even if often marked by the contentiousness and the repetitiousness of the ghetto intellectual atmosphere. Reform Socialism and a European-style faith in science balanced ethnic self-identity with patience for the slow progress of American gentile society.[10]

Those *Tsukunft* writers who sought to purvey their theories in English were thoroughly disappointed by the lack of response. Close readers of classic Marxian texts and of *Die Neue Zeit* mounted categorical objections against the Socialist Party's vulgarization of doctrine only to be given polite but indifferent hearings. *The Jewish Daily Forward* lampooned Louis Boudin, the most capable American Marxist exegete writing in English, as being a man who 'talks pure Marxism even in his sleep', and who uttered wisdom that nobody could understand. Socialist sodbusters from Oklahoma could not have made a more devastating evaluation.[11]

Boudin's efforts bespoke a pathos self-avowed Marxist intellectuals would suffer until the coming of the New Left professordom with its clamoring for erudite discourse. His series of ISR essays, collected by Kerr in book form as *The Theoretical System of Karl Marx* (1907), gained considerable international attention as the first substantial American contribution to the classical European canon. He was, as Paul Sweezy noted later, the earliest American Marxist to interpret theories of economic crisis; and he supplied thoroughgoing refutation of Marx's leading international critics, chiefly Germans. His effort to explain the success of American monopolies showed his ingenuity (and his departure from Marxian orthodoxy) via an early version of overproduction/underconsumption theory. War and waste, as he could readily observe around himself, used up capital aplenty, postponing the gnawing crisis of inadequate consumption. In Germany especially, his work met with gratitude and enthusiasm. In the USA, Kerr had pleaded with Boudin to remove the word 'theoretical' from the title so as to encourage sales which, indeed, remained very low. As Big Bill Haywood once reputedly said, 'I've never read Marx's *Capital*, but I have the marks of capital all over me'.[12]

Yet the Party continually spoke of Scientific Socialism as integral to its political program. This was not hypocrisy, but use of theory at a wholly different level. The urban political leaders, Morris Hillquit of New York and Victor Berger of Milwaukee, typified the parliamentary twist. They identified Socialism with the inevitable growth of monopolies and the first countermeasures of government intervention. Somewhat more in the Bernstein than Kautsky camp of the great debate—but generally hesitant to say so—they believed firmly in stable unions (preferably of skilled workers), in propaganda societies and political machines to smooth the class struggle into electoral transformation. Socialism would in effect make the masses fit to rule.

'Utopianism', for them an extreme epithet, was the stigma they attached to visions of a stateless future with complete equality (Berger openly considered Blacks as biologically inferior, requiring watchful paternalism) and to the egalitarian, spontaneous industrial politics of the unskilled. Just as the patriarchal family was immutable, destined to be restored by the end of female labor and woman's return to the home, so the general standards of civilization taken over by the Socialist movement from the bourgeoisie had evidently been etched in stone. *Their* Marx, as reform Socialist popularist John Spargo wrote in his sentimental biography, had raised Marxism above such primitive notions. They wanted nothing more of anarchy or sudden change, but rather the steady movement toward a well-defined goal.[13]

The native-born Socialists had pinned their faith upon the renewal of a society half historical and half imaginary, a republican social order which in any case had no future in the complex, tentacular structures being erected by bureaucratic capitalism. The immigrant Social Democrats had staked theirs upon a European-style state reform which could be fulfilled only with Socialist content but which, as it grew closer to attainment, had no need for them and their ideology. Each group had understood the issue from one angle. They went down together in the firestorm of world war.

Unlike the majority of their European comrades, American Socialists did not grovel to the patriotism which swept sections of the working class as well as the middle classes. Vigorously, almost hysterically, they propagandized against American entry into the war. At their own peril, they campaigned—revolutionary and reformer alike, with few exceptions—for a peaceful, democratic settlement. Berger and Hillquit, for all their faults, carried the fight to the home districts of those who saw no stake of their own in the fighting. The native Socialists, repressed easier because of their rural isolation and vulnerability, struggled on as their newspaper mailing privileges disappeared. The Green Corn Rebellion, that extraordinary armed uprising by Oklahomans against the war, marked their eclipse just as the Russian Revolution's capture of young immigrant enthusiasts marked the demise of old-style ethnic Socialism.

The indigenous Socialists seemed to have sensed intuitively that time had almost run out, not only economically but also culturally, on their particular vision. Dissident rural and small town movements had another generation of protest ahead, but as strictly regional efforts no longer able to claim the republic as an image of themselves. The *Appeal to Reason* readers, as best as one can determine, were predominantly middle-aged Americans from the heartlands: craft workers, farmers and small businessmen who would be swiftly marginalized in coming decades of the twentieth century. Their credulity in the Lincolnian ideal would give way in the next generations to fascination with the speed, motion and culture of the cities. Young women, to take the obvious example, would no longer join the Women's Christian Temperance Union to affirm their potential influence. They ceased to live within a 'women's culture' defined in intimate terms by their female friends and increasingly were integrated into a volatile heterosexual order.

The same changes had a different but equally fatal impact upon immigrant and urban reformers. The refurbished middle classes defected from Socialism at the first prospect of serious reforms. Worse, the craft workers whom Socialists believed were their natural constituency remained, outside certain ethnic and industrial limits, loyal to the existing party system. Socialist leaders and intellectuals had fundamentally misconceived the nature of the potential Socialist constituency as they had (with the rest of the Socialist world, including V.I. Lenin) misconceived the steady European political march to socialism. They believed they had created an American Socialism. The truth was, they were not American enough. The most prestigious Socialist Party local political machines had, in effect, brought European parliamentarism to American shores by taking the hierarchies within the working class as inevitable and even desirable. As the older Socialism went into decline, a new radicalism—formed of the complex encounters between modernism, mass production and imperialism—began to advance its own agenda.

The new radicals assumed the irreversability of contemporary social transformations. The giant corporation and the multi-racial semi-skilled worker were taken as the starting points of political practice. 'Culture', for the first time, would be treated as necessary leisure and recreation rather than the uplift that elder radicalism had apotheosized. In many ways, then, the newer Socialists took the familiar tenets of American Marxism and turned them on their head. The road to revolution now opened via a society which had never existed, not even in the best days of American democracy, but which was *coming to exist* in the subtle and not-so-subtle shifts all around.

Industrial Workers of the World

The IWW, vehicle of industrial Socialism, rejected the patient educationalism of the socialist movement without abandoning the republican conception. Wobbly songs, agitational styles and their justly famous irreverance for bourgeois manners are the result of a dialogue with political socialism, the rejection of existing civil society in favor of a futurist equivalent which substituted one form of citizenship for another.

Industrial Socialism spoke to the utter hypocrisy of American politics from the viewpoint of the outcast. The historic Lockean-Jeffersonian assumption of property as the basis of the republic had never been abandoned in practice. Political power continued to be marshalled by the rich and the middle classes. Rhetorical claims of pluralistic participation as proof of egalitarianism (or proof of a 'natural', *i.e.*, racial hierarchy) defied common sense. Voters, especially impoverished voters, could be manipulated or their ballots counted out; they had no special influence between elections anyway. In all, the rule of government 'for the people' was government by specialists and special interests. The Wobblies projected, instead, the rule of direct economic democracy *sans* the political state.

It was true, of course, that Debsian Socialists had never forgotten the class basis of society or of the Socialist movement. But their conception of class remained more an ideal than a working reality. They sought an abstract working class to pull the irons of the republic out of the consuming monopolist fire. Thus Horace Traubel asked,

'The master workman—when will he come?
We crouch in the wilds of our black cities, we die of gluttony, we die of starvation,
Yet with one ear, listen.'[14]

Many socialists in the 1890s had believed that the labor movement could not survive the capitalist onslaught, and might at best only protect a few skilled workers while educating as many as possible to the Socialist message. Other Socialists, mostly craft union leaders, argued unconvincingly that the AFL would come over eventually to Socialism. With the economic revival, craft unionism solidified its status, its pockets of Socialist sympathizers important in many ways but never a serious threat to the Gompers-style corporatist outlook.

The insights behind the Wobblies flowed from different experiences. Socialists had played important roles in every previous effort to create industrial unions. With a few exceptions, like the brewery workers and coal miners, they had been badly beaten. But some of them had also discovered, among the poorest communities locked in strike situations, a readiness to sacrifice and a rare cooperative spirit. That lesson became more important with the rapidly-changing industrial scene, and with the initiative of Western miners to move away from AFL leadership of the American labor movement. Suddenly, dissidents of various kinds, ranging from ethnic anarchists to ordinary trade unionists outraged at the craft unions' lack of industrial solidarity, began to ponder the alternatives.

Discussion of a more radical, more democratic style of unionism precipitated new insights into labor and the Marxist tradition. Creative thinking about the uniqueness of American labor, abandoned to abstractions since the days of Chicago's Revolutionary Socialism, now recommenced. Thus California labor lawyer Austin Lewis, the most philosophically-oriented of English-language Marxists, wrote in his introduction to the first US version of Engels' *Anti-Dühring* that the elderly 'revolutionist of '48' had been essentially posturing against intellectual systems largely irrelevant to the modern working class. Marx's collaborator (and, Lewis seemed to imply, most of the Marxist theorists since) had written like 'a bourgeois politician possessed at intervals by a proletarian ghost', when the main task lay in examining changing industry with an eye to the future.

Mass production drummed the basics of Marxism into the industrial worker, who 'becomes a revolutionist by force of habit,' taught the transitoriness of phenomena by shifts in production and shown the necessity of class action by material compulsion.[15] This analysis also struck a chord with Daniel DeLeon, by this time reduced to a political leader with no resources for a new synthesis, supplied the stroke of genius by combining such industrial logic with the claims of social science.

DeLeon reasoned that the appeal for revolutionary parliamentarism was almost irrelevant in the United States. If European Social Democrats remained preoccupied with parliamentary tactics, it was only a sign of their relative backwardness: they hoped to capture the state and create the social and economic infrastructure for the emergence of a new society. In the USA, the class struggle had skipped stages to become a struggle over power in the direct production process. America, in short, was the one place on earth ripe for the proper 'execution of Marxian revolutionary tactics.'[16] DeLeon continued to argue the importance of educational activity as preparation, and believed the revolutionary union would create its own political organ to that end. But the actual agency of Socialism, preparing the society to come, was the industrial union itself. Its very structure, in DeLeon's conception, drafted the blueprint of a 'government of things' en route to replacing the government of politicians.

DeLeon's formulation of industrial unionism's revolutionary role marked a fascinating shift in American Marxist logic. Expounded by a handful of former SLP intellectuals and a multitude of common Wobblies, the notion also proved the most internationally recognized theoretical or strategic perspective developed in the USA. Its popularization coincided with the great international revolt of the unskilled proletariat, from Glasgow to Berlin, Turin and Petrograd, and gave those movements a logic outside Scoialist parliamentarism or fading anarchism. Thousands of craft workers, longtime sympathizers or new converts to a doctrine that met their own desire to resist the further degradation of their industrial autonomy, joined hands with the semi-skilled or held their own remarkable exercises in solidarity. The ideas and the drama of the Wobblies had helped make these developments coherent. Revolutionary industrial unionism was, then, also the first American doctrine to win *political* adherents in virtually every large-scale industrial center. In this case if none other, the more Marxist, the more American and the more American, the more Marxist.

DeLeon, long intrigued by the same anthropological and scientistic speculations that had preoccupied the elderly Engels. did not hesitate to interpret the IWW's vision of the state's replacement by workers' councils as the dawn of a new epoch in world history. Industrial unionism, in DeLeon's conception, inevitably recalled Lewis Henry Morgan's primitive *gens* and their primitive communism, now raised to an incomparably higher level by the already existing socialization of production. The proletariat—the US proletariat at any rate—had moved beyond the limits of nineteenth century Marxism and was reconnoitering the vast possibilities of corporate technology reappropriated by workers' control.[17]

The founding convention of the IWW in 1905—'the Continental Congress of the Working Class', western miners' leader Haywood called it—broadcast the conclusion that the wretched of the earth could create their own industrial theory and proto-political program. That message had been awaiting restatement since the Knights of Labor. But significantly, its articulation arrived with the conjunction of the indigenous and the international tendencies, European anarcho-syndicalism and American industrial unionism, in a fresh format.

The early IWW could not live up to its bold claims. The indifference of Jewish socialists, who had their bitter experience with DeLeon's radical unionism in the 1890s and wanted no encore, alone dictated that the Wobblies would never become a hegemonic force within radical labor. The rapid defection of political Socialists and the savage attacks upon the organization by the AFL made it a pariah. The organization utterly failed to organize the unorganized, and indeed lost the bulk of its affiliated membership with the departure of the Western Federation of Miners. By the 1906–07 recession, it nearly expired.

But the organization still had its driving purpose. Deprivated of other possibilities, the IWW became the industrial equivalent of what American Marxism has been so often: a vehicle of the outsiders. America's excluded—the foreign-born, unskilled, Black, Asian, the 'timber-beasts', 'bindle-stiffs'—found a welcome home in the IWW. So did ideological rebels, romantics of every ethnic stripe who distrusted parliamentarism but not the power of education and the efficacy of mass action. Even the Marx the Wobblies boldly claimed for themselves became naturally a 'hobo organizer,' in the words of one writer, a 'curious old codger' who 'did not seem to have any desire to be respectable' or to make the revolution genteel.[18]

The formation of a counter-culture, an alternative to flophouses and Salvation Army centers, i.e., a place where the workless and homeless would be treated with dignity and respect, should have called to mind the counter-culture briefly established by the Knights of Labor a quarter century earlier. But this time, rather than a republic of work with the restored dignity of early industrializatoin, the Wobblies promised a leap into the future. Their newspapers traveling with the mobile population through the fields, the hobo jungles and the flophouses, combined humorous attacks on bosses (and on reform socialists) with reports of direct action and a zeal for worker self-education exceeded by none.

This vision also stirred the enthusiasm of New Immigrants gathering their energies on the fringes of the radical movement. Italian-American radicals, uncomfortable with the reformism of the Socialist Party and organized in their own Italian Socialist Federation, offer a case in point. Italian-Americans had already taken part in violent, mass strikes during the 1890s and early years of the new century. Numbering only a few thousand, organized and led by mostly Northern Italians in a sea of largely illiterate Southern Italians, the radicals found organization difficult but agitation often fruitful. Their weekly, *Il Proletario*, edited by agitator-poet Arturo Giovannitti, emulated a European syndicalist publication in political outlook but with heavy nationalistic emphasis upon the humiliations 'dagoes' faced at the hands of native Americans. Their sympathy was naturally attracted by the IWW which was inclusive and generous unlike the racist, exclusionary AFL. Its romantic spirit also moved them. Along the industrial Eastern seaboard and in mining camps with

Italian immigrants, Karl Marx Circles preached the IWW and taught a brand of revolutionary Socialism kindred both to current European anarchism and the 'industrial Socialism' of the Wobblies.

A myriad of other nationality groups, Wobbly affiliates among Russians, Hungarians, Croatians and others with greater or less anarchist influences on their Socialism, also joined the crusade with high energy. Their Marx preached the evangel of socialized labor, and perhaps thereby they came the closest to 'pure' Marxism of any American movement. Through personal example and grand vision they summoned up the kind of enthusiasm among non-political Americans rarely seen again until the CIO and later the Civil Rights movement.[19]

The wave of mass strikes, beginning with the McKees Rocks (Pennsylvania) steelworkers' struggle of 1909, and extending through the great Paterson (New Jersey) garmentworkers' strike of 1912-13, seems to fulfil the industrial Socialists' vision. Not that the IWW organized all or most of the strikes, some of which were channeled into the older unions or found no institutional structure at all; rather, the IWW expressed the *spirit* of revolt. Wobbly editor Justus Ebert, who had been a member of the SLP from 1892 and understood best the larger meaning in DeLeon's industrial message, touched the essence of the revolt of the immigrant proletariat in his popular pamphlet, *Trial of a New Society*, written during the famous Lawrence (Massachusetts) textile strike. The downtrodden, foreign-born and discriminated-against workers who produced the wealth of the nation constituted in themselves the nucleus of the coming order. They had become, in other words, the true citizens of society.[20]

Said so simply, the concept disguises the sophistication with which Ebert reasoned. Austin Lewis put it differently, distilling concepts that he, DeLeon, and a myriad of Wobbly popularisers had advanced. In an important series of essays and a little book, *The Militant Proletariat* (1911), Lewis drew upon Thorstein Veblen's study of craftsmanship to argue that craft had been itself a form of property, analogous to the small holdings of the yeoman. The previous history of radical movements and Socialism in Europe as well as the USA reflected the stirrings of a fading petty-bourgeoisie which registered its resentments helplessly against present conditions. The hour had arrived for evolution's creature, the industrial worker, to take over both economic and political mechanisms, unions and the Socialist movement. Nowhere did the bell toll so urgently as in America. Had the IWW succeeded in its great strikes, the course of

American Socialism would have been altered. However the combined strength of the opposition—employers, police, craft unions and sometimes conservative Socialists as well—proved too great. Pushed out of the urban immigrant ghettoes, the IWW retreated to its Western enclaves. Immigrants would move on to unionization and to radicalism under other flags. The Wobblies had made the concept of the mass uprising in modern industrial society manifest and exciting. At the same time their promise highlighted (made possible really) the awakening of the radical intelligentsia to *its* twentieth-century mission.

The Newer Socialism

Life, meanwhile, provided other clues for turning the older transcendental rejection of American materialism towards a radical appreciation of the social *quotidian*. Where uplift ended, insight began, and with it the twentieth-century tradition of cultural criticism. Not the Socialist forebears, like the Whitmanesque Traubel, had lacked enthusiasm for the life of the masses. Rather, the Arnoldian division of blood and bowels from 'sweetness and light' made genuine appreciation, as opposed to mere sentimentalism, increasingly difficult.

In the notorious irreverence of Greenwich Village, a generational revolt promised freedom from Victorianism, search for inner meaning, above all the triumph of subjectivity as dominant principle. Ibsen and Freud, Bergson and Nietzche served alongside Marx, Engels and Kautsky. Somewhat down the social scale, the dance hall with its heterosexual encounters and jazz wriggling served at least as well. The sense of motion superceding history and tradition, the 'sexual revolution' which promised in mores what the ascendent suffrage movement had long promised in politics—all this blended into the discovery of big city excitements, the brilliant human landscape.

Floyd Dell wrote in his memorable *Intellectual Vagabondage: An Apology for the Intelligensia*, 'We were of the present. And, though we did not realize it, what we wanted was an interpretation of our own time.'[21] The new writers paused over past literature, *i.e.* high literature. But they set up the essential transition in thought by treating current literary culture as the test for spiritual revolt and by treating mass culture as 'fun', culture liberated from the usual criteria. The first had been accomplished already by the European anarchist avant-garde. In the second, they raced neck and neck with the Dadaists in claiming the stuff of modern anonymous culture for the revolution's own.

In America at large, the culture of abundance steadily moved through the social fabric. Recreation, public relations and celebrity increasingly displaced the ideals of hard work and self-denial. The materialist culture of the middle classes, as Warren Susman says, became a self-advertisement for the society. *The Masses* magazine, for all its socialistic political content and loving observation of the poor, exalted this culture. Where the previous Socialist culture publications found the artist's garret and the suffering of the slums their proper subject, *The Masses* placed the artist on the street where life became art. John Reed thus concluded a lyric tribute to a 'Broadway Night' with the pregnant phrase, 'This mad unconventionality, this magnificent lack of purpose is what I love about the city.'[22]

Dell was the reigning critical spirit. As precocious editor of Chicago's *Friday Literary Review*, the highest quality literary paper in the nation, he welcomed the birth of the midwestern cultural renaissance. he also developed the central logic of his commentaries. The most ambitious young man in American letters, Dell had sought to democratize the relations between writer and audience. Works that Dell 'discovered', notably the early fiction of Sherwood Anderson, invited this effort: they occupied no pedestal, offering up raw human material in characters and scenes that seemed to invite some unanticipated political conclusion. The old fiction of artificial manners, Dell hinted, could now be finished off, and with it the need for formal criticism. Rebellion itself was the law of 'true Art', destined not to make Art handmaiden to any given cause but rather, to return Art to life as only the rebellious spirit could do. 'I am not ashamed to say,' he wrote in 1918, 'that to me Art is more important than the destinies of nations, and the artist a more exalted figure than the prophet'. From the Socialist editor Dell, this was a political aesthetics. In demanding for cultural work the autonomy that its special tasks required, 'the evaluation of life' as he called the supreme end, he had blown apart the categories which placed Art in the possession of an elite until the maturing of a Socialist society.[23]

Thus, Dell found a 'refined burlesque' in the 'unswept streets of Hoboken,' with the top banana in apparent command: 'He has slapstick shoulders, slapstick eyebrows, ears, nose, legs, posterior; he acts with all of these, eloquently, and at each gesture some human dignity is overthrown, knocked over the head, tumbled on its nose. He sings, walks across the floor, makes love;

and these things, to the immense satisfaction of the audience, are revealed as essentially absurd . . . ' For Dell this was no true vulgarization, but rather a magnificent gesture of indifference to bourgeois civilization's genteel claims. The female star of the show, by contrast, was woman emancipatated: 'She defies the code of the dreamworld in which women burn with the ready fires of miscellaneous invitation; she is remote, unseizable, be-witchingly unsexed, cold as the fire-balls that dance in the Artic rigging. She mocks at desire as she mocks at the law of gravita-tion; she is beyond sex. Nor is she mere muscle and grace. She has, shining in contrast to this impersonal world of sex, a will of her own, an existence independent of the wishes of the audience.' These were passing glances, but ones educated by a profound understanding. Dell recognized the 'natural human impulse to create rthymical beauty'—long restrained by class society but now moving to become the guiding impulse of all arts—realizing and dissolving formalities, revealing to every person the universal flow of existence.[24] As *Masses* editorials patiently reiterated, the need for political education, voting, strikes and even insurrection remained. But a cultural awaken-ing gave the participant more than bread to fight for, more than determination to carry on the battle.

Immigrant intellectuals of the new type, romantics them-selves, felt at home with this crowd. No wonder Arturo Giovanitti, editor of *Il Proletario* and leader of the Lawrence strike, called *The Masses* a 'recording secretary of the Revolu-tion in the making, successor to the Bible, Marat and Garrison's tracts,' a 'battle call, a shout of defiance, a blazing torch running madly through the night to set afire the powder magazines of the world,' a possession of the 'realm of miracles as well as . . . the empire of portents.'[25]

The Masses was not alone in bringing cultural criticism into the twentieth century. Giovannitti, co-editor of his own Italian-language *Il Fuoco* (flame), counterpart to *The Masses*, had a unique poetic approach to the daily lives of his constituency. 'What Is Not Life,' each issue proclaimed on its masthead, 'Is Not Art', and 'What is Not Art, Is Not Life.' Likewise, *The Messenger*, subtitled the 'only radical Negro magazine in America' and edited by promising Black intellectuals Chandler Owen and A. Phillip Randolph, had a forceful cultural undertone to its ostensibly political-economic critique. The *Messenger* brought together a mixture of noted Black and white intellec-tuals, Socialists and liberal activists into a typically Debsian melange. It repudiated the War and ardently supported Black workers in the name of socialism. But racial dynamics deflected a laborist Socialism, and permanently frustrated Randolph's effort to create a Black Socialist milieu. The 'New Crowd' Randolph identified with the magazine in his words, 'educated, radical and fearless', had the flash and sophistication of a self-styled avant-garde. It would find itself drawn to the Harlem Renaissance, and later to the only political force, the Popular Front, which could carry back the message to the white community.[26]

In a peculiar (and from the radical standpoint rather perverse) sense, *The Jewish Daily Forward* recognized most brilliantly the modern popular culture of the metropolitan immigrant—and built an empire upon it. The Yiddishist revolt against DeLeon had, after some complicating developments, placed Abe Cahan into the driver's seat of the *Forward*, symbol of Jewish Socialism and the most popular Yiddish newspaper in the world. Cahan reorganized Socialist journalism around the sensationalist style of the yellow tabloid. Cahan's reporters also combed the Jewish streets for the daily life of the real masses who suffered, hoped for social change but also looked to individual advancement.

Cahan, himself a living archetype, represented the *Allrightnik* (from the Americanizing phrase) personally prospering but restrained from embrace of the system by the continuing realities of the ghetto and by a tug of Socialist conscience. That conscience, or perhaps the anxiety of the immigrant who seeks to impress the natives, also kept Cahan from embracing the details of the urban environment with the type of zeal the bohemians displayed. Even as a sensationalist, Cahan still sought to uplift his readers from the vulgarity of bad table manners and all-too-Jewish body language. This Socialism would finally exhaust itself as the adjustments in American society permitted middle class Jews entry on something like equal terms. Rebels from assimilation and the cult of upward mobility would turn elsewhere.

The fatalism of Cahan, no less than the wide-eyed optimism of *The Masses*, reflected changes already apparent in the political terrain by 1915. Precisely those *outside* the familiar constituencies, *i.e.*, the unskilled, foreign born and Black, along with a sympathetic minority of the new middle class, would speak to the future of radicalism. The old faith, the old constituencies had foundered.

And Debsian socialists were not the only ones to lose out. The revolutionary ideals of the IWW also took a back seat when newly-chartered AFL or independent unions—led, especially at the local level, by many of the old Wobbly organizers—seized the advantage of tightening labor markets to install bread-and-butter industrial unionism. No wonder the Russian Revolution, just around the corner, came as a godsend.

Socialism at the Edge

As intensifying war 'preparedness' put an end to the carefree days of bohemia, the prospects for Socialism became central to the fate of the intellectual. The corporate transformation of American society increased both the numbers and social prestige of mental workers, raising the fledgling social sciences in particular to a crucial position in the reform of industrial institutions. At the same time, the strikes and unrest, the warlike character of capitalism and the pitifulness of its victims cried out to the waiting conscience. The problems of the left—disparate communities, disparate goals and perceptions—no less than the problems of the corporate society seemed to demand the skills intellectuals could supply. But which path would they choose?

The *New Review*, published from 1913, was the first journal to emphasize the role of intellectuals *as intellectuals* within the Socialist movement. It sought, more than anything else, to convert the contemporary sense of discovery into theoretical terms. Its difficulties speak to the problem of *The Masses*' cultural insights, the elusive quality stemming from their impressionistic nature and the corresponding absence of any clear political implications. Its editorial and executive boards included a few activists, but were mostly composed of radicals identified as thinkers, including W.E.B DuBois, William English Walling, Floyd Dell, Walter Lippman, anthropologist Robert Lowie, scientist Charles P. Steinmetz, Horace Traubel and a young intellectual, Louis C. Fraina, destined to take the editorial helm. The *New Review* carried the earliest serious discussion of Feminism within the socialist movement, the first significant contribution on the 'Negro Question,' and early discussions of such artistic matters as the Armory Show then in progress. (By comparison, the literary pages of the daily *New York Call*, the other major refuge of New York socialist intellectuals, remained stuffy and traditional, the weekend section of a nineteenth century immigrant paper rendered into English.)

The *New Review* thus crystalized what became known as the socialist "New Intellectuals," those openly discontented with the older socialist expectations and practices. William English Walling—popular muckraking journalist, a founder of the Niagara movement which led to the NAACP., and a vitriolic polemicist against reform socialism—epitomized the journal. On the one hand, he was the first notable Socialist intellectual to become an unabashed pragmatist. On the other hand, he memorialized, in his literary study *Whitman and Traubel* (1916), the faith that had been passed down from one mystic American Socialist philosopher to another. The two sides contradicted each other less than might be imagined, and showed themselves alike in Walling's widely heralded works: three major books on the evolution of the State between capitalism and socialism.

Science applied to sociology and philosophy had, for him, banished archaic materialism and idealism alike. What remained of traditional Socialist philosophy was only 'that truth must come from social activity . . . that all culture and civilization of the future must come from the active struggles of that social movement which represents the future against the present'. The archaic expectations of the Socialists had blinded them to the unanticipated strengths of capitalism, its powers of self-regulation and its complex internal dynamics. Craft workers had been incorporated into the system, allied with the petty bourgeoisie. Socialism was no longer the immanent result of the class struggle at all, but simply 'a struggle by those who have less, against those who have more' in 'matters of income, hours, leisure, place of living, associations and opportunity'.[27]

This was neither a superficial nor conservative view. It made American sense of European Social Democracy's real tactics by abandoning determinist claims for the high ground of Whitmanian observation and moral purpose. It gave meaning, if not necessarily a viable future, to the municipal reformism which brought most American Socialists into local public office. It also provided the outline for a *Kathedersozialismus* or academic Socialism of younger college intellectuals. In so doing, it superseded A. M. Simons' efforts in the old *International Socialist Review* to merge Second Internationalism with American Socialism; in Walling's version, class orthodoxy had entirely given way to the cool if beneficent gaze of social science.

Walling's expectation of stage-by-stage development—first state capitalism then a state socialism in behalf of the skilled workers and middle class, and only at last a real Socialism—disregarded the wild streak in American society. His enthusiasm for the IWW and his scorn for old-fashioned socialism notwithstanding, Walling could not explain the explosive significance of the contemporary mass strikes by the unskilled workers, or the contrary implications of official violence. Walling's middle class, key to the prospect of peaceful, long-term change, might share Whitman's *desire* to be truly free, but its members lacked the industrial muscle and probably the political will to carry through social transformation against a powerful, determined ruling elite.[27]

The *New Review*, along with the revived and more direct-action oriented *International Socialist Review*, sought to sketch out alternatives. They published the latest prophecies of European ultra-radicals on the international wave of mass strikes, as well as a stream of close analysis on the American industrial scene. (The *ISR* in particular sought to interpret the changes in the labor process and its implications for future action.) And they struggled with the inevitable question of the intelligentsia's potential contribution. Here was intellectual revival of a new kind.

Yiddish writers simultaneously pressed ahead with their own theoretical leaps. To young, radical Jews who had emigrated after the *pogroms* of 1905, Cahan's style and the growing complacence of the older 1890s generation had to be replaced with a new forcefulness and a radical self-identification. From the Amalgamated Clothing Workers, a mainstream but radical industrial union, to the rebellious ranks of the International Ladies Garment Workers Union restive at bureaucratic socialist leadership, to the young cultural *tuers* (activists) in the fraternal *Arbeter Ring* (Workmen's Circle)—a new day had dawned. The Russian Revolution would give them, for better and for worse, a singular sense of direction. But before the Revolution they already took part in a cultural renaissance that was unanticipated and indeed unwanted by the reigning giants of ghetto Socialism.

Around 1910, the Yiddish literary world had come alive with the fresh spirit of *di Yunge*, the young writers and critics who were America's most spectacular example of blue-collar modernism. Painters, pants-pressers, shoemakers and common-day laborers, they strove for the perfection of the Yiddish word through recuperation of the 'classic' literature (mostly I. L. Peretz and Sholom Aleichem) of twenty years earlier that Socialists had disregarded in favor of more directly political and class themes. Not that *di Yunge* disregarded the *reality* of blue-collar life, their own lives, but rather, they saw reality itself in a more imaginative fashion. The wonder of the city occupied the center of their literary attention. The skyscrapers and streets of the urban neighborhoods became for them, in the Jewish mystic tradition, a mundane key to the secrets of the heavens. Aesthetes moving in all milieux of left politics, the *Yunge* had fallen in love with popular culture more than Cahan, who only respected its importance.

A larger sophistication, expressing itself in *Yiddishkayt*, Yiddishness, took hold in the ghetto. Major European intellectuals, generational predecessors of the emigre Frankfurt School, began to propound their doctrines among growing Jewish audiences. Chaim Zhitlovsky, one of the great popularizers of new ideas into Yiddish vernacular, typified the quintessential radical cultural approach. Revolutionary Socialism, he insisted, had to have a spiritual (if not necessarily religious) side which Marxism as such palpably lacked. Yiddish culture, for Jews at any rate, supplied that element from its own classics and from its hungry absorption of dreamers and thinkers, even those (such as Nietzsche) touched with anti-Semitism. Yiddish language and culture, Jews as a people, *could* survive with a sufficient commitment to their own identity and to world Socialism—that was the message Zhitlovsky pressed upon his eager listeners.

The anarcho-Zionist critic B. Rivkin, less popular than Zhitlovsky but more profound, clarified the essence of Yiddish as the province of a people with no geographical basis of their own, and of Yiddish literature as the barely secularized response to homelessness and suffering. Its messianism had a deep purpose, the particular Socialist message of the Jews. The straightforward assimilation of Jews into American culture, and into American Socialist politics as such, would induce a sense of uncertainty, a lack of self-fulfillment. Socialist transformation, Rivkin hinted and a handful of intellectuals began to argue, had to mean a society of equals, including cultural and even linguistic equals. Socialism without a pluralistic culture of folk and modern idioms combined was no Socialism at all.[28]

This was a serious and ambitious cultural goal. But it could be carried lightly. For many young Yiddishists, the act of reading (or writing for) the anarchist weekly *Freie Arbeter Shtimme*, or one of the *Yunge*'s own small publications, did not exclude the practices of their Americanized contemporaries, movies and necking sessions. Cultural bohemianism flowed into sex as into politics. Moshe Nadir, later to become the leading Yiddish Communist litterateur, grew famous as the Bad Boy of the ghetto, penning a minor erotic classic and (if urban folklore serves) making every attempt to live his fantasies.

The Italian immigrant youngster, Louis Fraina, captured his generation's spirit at its least individualistic. Fraina, who joined the staff at *Modern Dance* magazine for a few months in 1917, found his universal in jazz dancing. Here, he wrote, the artificial civilization which represses instinct and creativity fell away; humanity's original 'mass action', religious ritual, came alive again in the dance halls of ordinary working women and men who expressed themselves freely. They represented a spontaneous popular aspiration, corresponding to the national music, the slang of life. Without culture, no revolution; cultural revolution among the immigrant masses promised that both could be realized.[29]

The Marxist gadfly among the bohemians and the premier theoretician of American Leninism, Fraina was a child of the Italian-American slums and the precocious protegé of DeLeon. *The Daily People* sent him as its reporter to the Lawrence strike where he imbibed the apparently spontaneous creativity of immigrant labor. A few years after breaking with DeLeon, he became a leading figure at the *New Review*, where he too commented on the rise of state capitalism. Unlike his colleague William English Walling (whose favoured Pragmatism he dismissed as 'the totem-god of efficiency'), Fraina saw ominous possibilities in the growing role of the state. State capitalism, to the extent that it entailed the iron heel of administrative centralization and militarization, was 'compelling reactionary', and rendered parliamentary politics in the old Socialist style almost impossible. Yet at the same time the state was the central problem of class struggle that the militant, mass production working class needed to understand. Socialism had to provide this new proletariat with the program and theory that would allow it to turn its industrial revolts into a political revolution. For without the mass workers' rise to power, capitalist crisis and imperialist war would ensure 'the collapse of all civilization'.[30]

Culturally and politically Fraina had virtually cut the nexus with the older Marxist intellectualism. Rand School functionary William J. Ghent had years before answered a mild public suggestion that after the revolution intellectuals might disappear as a category into shared work and thought throughout the population, replying that such a notion filled him with 'repulsion and disgust' as it would, he assumed, anyone 'to whom civilization has any meaning'.[31] Precisely. In raising the spectre of mass subjectivity and popular culture, Fraina had provided new terms for a reconciliation of Marxism and American experience outside the old civilized standards. He had done so at the moment when a breakup of the old Marxism had not yet been followed by the crystallization of new dogma, and when the changes in social life still seemed most promising and filled with liberatory possibility. His own thoroughgoing contributions, *Revolutionary Socialism* (1917) and the pathbreaking anthology, *The Proletarian Revolution in Russia* (1918), simultaneously summed up and buried his own creative thrust. Fraina captured the sense of mass industrial activity rooted in modern industry, the conditions of the unskilled workers and their exclusion from state capitalism's privileged classes. He saw the Russian Revolution as a breakthrough for that global class of workers who understood and *lived* the revolutionary cultural promise. But he lost the image of the everyday in the rush of world events. And he fatally misperceived the consciousness and capabilities of the foot-soldiers for American Communism: the immigrant Socialists enthralled by Russian events.

Socialism and the New Immigrants

The first ripples of industrial unrest among new immigrant workers outside the Jewish ideological orbit should have instructed reform and revolutionary Socialists. Isaac Hourwich, Russian-Jewish theoretician much admired by Lenin, showed statistically how immigration had not lowered wages nor diluted proletarian combativeness but, on the contrary, had pushed the immigrants' immediate predecessors upward and introduced a new level of community-wide struggle. Fraina, one of the immigrant workers' first public champions, recognized the industrial implications but not the underlying cultural institutions of the immigrant community itself. Making the obverse error from the reform Socialists who drew ethnocentric conclusions from the Slavic and Italian indifference to voting for Socialism, Fraina viewed their industrial uprisings as premonitions of an imminent revolution. He had no common knowledge, no articulated interpretation of such momentous events to draw upon. No one, including assimilated immigrants or even the long-standing Socialist groups in the communities, could grasp the implications fully, or anticipate the change in radical ideas that the new constituencies required.

An inflexible Marxism reinforced the complacency of the Socialist Party, to the movement's future peril. Party leaders, certain that Marxism mandated the unity of all proletarians under the banner of the dominant culture and language, looked upon the national groups as mere auxiliaries. Only in 1912 did the Party grant them official status as semi-autonomous units, and then with unease. By 1916, when the groups had reached near-parity with the native-born and assimilated, Party leaders had hardly begun to suspect that Debsian Socialism had encompassed such totally different creatures from themselves under its ample wings.

Finns and South Slavs offer two particularly well-documented cases of this development. Both had suffered severe cultural as well as economic-political repression in the Old World, and had built up resentments against collaborationist-authoritarian clerics. Both possessed budding intelligentsias with desires for cultural and political expression, and both groups had a limited but crucial urban-industrial experience prior to immigration. When they relocated to the mining camps, steel towns and fishing villages of America, a sizeable proportion became supporters of inclusive unionism and some variety of Marxism. Socialism, including Marxist ideas, permitted a national-cum-ethnic sense of identity to blossom, a sustaining relationship with the language, culture and politics of the old country to grow amid fearful European crisis. Socialism further enabled a significant element of the community—workers, family members, small shopkeepers and political functionaries—to undertake self-growth and personal expression in forms that would otherwise have been inconceivable.

In the Finnish case, the rare college-trained intellectual, not infrequently an erstwhile Lutheran minister, became the natural editor of the early workers' newspapers, the teacher of schools the Finns themselves created for adult education, and of course the theoretician. The most outstanding of these thinker-activists had been prominent Socialists in the old country, sometimes Diet members who would return to prominence. The prospect of an international militant carrying on life in a small town of the Mesabi Iron Range might have struck the American urban intellectual as daunting, but no more perhaps than the fate of the Oklahoma City editor (Oscar Ameringer) or other sophisticates scattered in rural Socialist pockets. What made the Finnish immigrant intellectual unique was the literalness of his (and, emphatically, also her) Marxism when adapted to the specifics of nationality. Class lines hardened for most new immigrant groups as they never had for German-Americans, and never would for significant numbers of Jews. Much of Finnish-American Socialism leaned heavily upon religious metaphor, and played constantly upon the themes of cultural deprivation that Swedes and Russians brought to Finland and that American capitalism's agents reinforced. Otherwise, class perspectives had a straightforward character little diluted by republican traditions and property aspirations — even for those thousands destined to leave the mining camps for the 'stump farms' of hard work and meager rewards. European-style Marxism, with minor variations, seemed to apply directly to the USA.[32]

The geographic concentration of the Finns contributed to this compact sensibility, but various groups of close-knit industrial proletarians in the urban neighborhoods and one-industry towns attained something similar. Intellectual leaders could be said to have helped create communities from mere ethnic aggregations. In the old country, clerics had succeeded in repelling every secular challenge to their prerogatives outside the cities, in accordance with the wishes of imperial authorities. National and class resentments developing among urban workers gave a secular intellectual class a mission and a constituency. In America poets, theoreticians, and indeed intellectuals of all kinds tended to be, among these national groups, either clerics or Socialists, each with an evolved command of popular attention and a program for salvation of the community. Fraternal associations embraced very wide sectors of the working class, providing various services and a decisive link with the Socialist intelligentsia. Theoretical and strategic debate focused on strikes, industrial exploitation and the national question, jettisoning almost entirely the small property dialogue of the English-language Socialists.[33]

Editors such as Slovene novelist-theorist Ivan Molek won wide community respect with their interpretations of issues immediately facing their readerships. Although hardly exceptional by Second International standards, they gained mastery as interpreters of doctrine and adaptors of patient education in the volatile conditions of immigrant life. By American Socialist standards, on the other hand, the nationality papers displayed a surprising sophistication. According to a well-known immigrant proposition, the more difficult the adoption of the English language the more resilient the group identity. Among those groups, including Hungarians and Lithuanians, who took unusual pride in their language and literature, not only politics and economics but also culture occupied front pages of their press. At the same time they were often vigorously attuned to the native culture and political scene around them.

Tragically, native-born and even older Jewish Socialist leaders remained indifferent at best, hostile at worst, to the emerging culture and sensibility which seemed to them more threat than promise. Contrary to that leadership misunderstanding, faithfully repeated by generations of one-language historians, it was the insularity of the Americans, and not of the immigrants, which had the most destructive effects prior to the Bolshevik Revolution. Given the kind of intellectual and political opportunity that the Socialist Party should have afforded, an Ivan Molek might have been able to understand a Jewish *Yunge* intellectual, a Finnish editor, and a Jack Reed. The task was daunting and the time short. But the insight American Socialists required to amalgamate industrial militancy and American culture could be achieved no other way. Despite an electoral revival stirred by anti-war sentiment, the Socialist Party had begun to collapse in upon its own internal incoherence.

The Mass Strike and the Breakup of American Socialism

The foreign-language federation members and other self-styled revolutionaries within the Socialist Party would certainly have been drawn to the Russian Revolution, and to the new Third International, whatever American Marxism had been or done. The world revolution suddenly looked too large, and the difficulties of American radicals too pressing, for any other result. The otherwise convincing anti-war positions and political regeneration of the Socialists, re-establishing institutions amid repression and electing new candidates to office in 1918–20, pulled little weight among the Russian enthusiasts. But it was the mass strike wave of 1919 which made the very essence of the old movements evidently archaic and the prospect of something new, the Russian Soviets, convincing—especially for the young. The Wobblies had been knocked out of action by the sweeping repression. Meanwhile, the confusion and timidity of Socialist leaders on everything but the war issue deprived their Party of any alternative or even a constructive contribution to the emerging proto-communism.

At the end of great wars, class and cultural forces turn sharply one way and another, sorting out possibilities, as the authorities seek to reestablish the old order and insurgents to establish a new one. The Seattle General Strike, a massive display of the labor movement's capacity to organize public order and welfare (and the only strike in American history waged expressly with that demonstration in mind), offered the most convincing American argument for great changes to come. Workers' councils, some joined by sympathetic returning soldiers, arose in Butte, Astoria, Portland and Buffalo. Purely economic strikes reached a new climax with the national steel strike (directed by William Z. Foster), and a new dimension with the interracial packinghouse workers' struggle in Chicago. As a veteran Socialist editor observed a workers' parade, he remarked, 'The workers awakening from their long age of slumber are astonished at themselves and are seeking out their fellow workers to relate the new and wonderful change in their being. They imagine that they have taken possession of a new idea. They will soon learn that the idea is very, very old and that it has taken possession as other ideas have done when arrived at fruition . . . For two centuries [the] bourgeois class has patronized a professional class and their association has so related them that their psychology is one and the same. The worker has been taught to look upon his labor energy as a thing for sale, that it might bring a little savings to get educated in order to get into the bourgeois class. Now the workers are changing. Now the workers are saying and doing radical things . . . It is grand. It is inspiring. Life takes on so many new meanings when Labor is found to be thinking.'[34]

If the Russian Revolution roused the Slavic and Jewish workers in particular, it at least momentarily stirred broader sections with the dual vision of workers' councils and Socialist emancipation. (In Seattle AFL dockers refused to load arms for US-supported White Guard armies in Siberia.) At the same time, however, that the left was responding to this new internationalism it was losing sight of the international significance of *American* culture-in-transition, and to American radicals' potentially unique role within it. As faction-fighting tore the Socialist Party asunder in 1917–19, culture vanished from the foreground of Marxists' concerns. In the especially important case of Fraina, sensitivity to avant garde and popular culture was eclipsed almost entirely by insistence on the proto-insurrectionary 'crisis'. Surviving activists from that era recall him as a wonderful young hero; but he was also the dangling man as well, suspended from all he had known and intellectually recognized, across a crater of uncertain political change. He spoke for the immigrant federations, the most clearly 'cultural' of the working-class Socialist organizations, but purely in a Bolshevik political voice.

The failure to maintain a critical interest in the experience and sensibility of the real masses proved equally disastrous for embryonic American sovietism. The 'national question' in the United States—that is, the extreme national, race and ethnic consciousness of the variegated working class—could not be apprehended via immediatist slogans or telegraphic injunctions from Petrograd. Likewise even the brilliant distillations of Bolshevik practice which Fraina edited from the Russian for eager American readers added nothing to insights about what the real revolutionary reshaping of consciousness in America might entail, nor how the search of the worker for a fuller life in the interstices of leisure entertainment might overlap with their struggles for control in the work process. Nor, it goes almost without saying, did the adaption of Bolshevism to Wilsonian America grapple with the issues raised by the triumphant woman suffrage movement or the confused, but fervent aspirations for a freer sexuality. Radical thought retreated to a higher version of economism, giving up the special insights so arduously gained, and sacrificing in the process the moral-utopian qualities which gave radicalism much of its currency in American tradition. The problem was not so much the uncritical embrace of Russian Revolution as the uncritical relinquishment of American Marxism's most advanced positions and insights into the national reality.

'We are in revolt', precocious *Seven Arts* intellectual Waldo Frank wrote in 1919, 'against . . . Industrialism which would deny to America any life—hence any unity at all—beyond the ties of traffic and the arteries of trade'.[35] But to revolt *against* meant also to revolt *for*, and the new intellectuals, hardly active in the radical movements, had no forces to effect the changes they sought. Their isolation was part of the tragedy of the moment for even a prestigious writer like Frank, who felt his Jewish identity deeply but who lacked the contacts and the language to touch the vibrant labor movement and organic intellectual community merely a subway ride away. Greenwich Village, *The Masses,* Jack Reed and the Ashcan School had all brought hope because they seemed effectively to bridge the gap between intellectual and industrial life. The contact had been brief and unsustained. A terrible price would be paid for the loss, which by this time epitomized the dilemma of American radicalism.

The language groups for their part, contrary to what most historians would later write about them, struggled for a bridge between their Old World and New World expectations. By 1917, many of them already had lengthy and complex histories of their own in the United States. Most groups leaned (as they had always leaned) toward homeland or America as the moment led them. Their future remained to this moment undetermined.

The Communist movements everywhere, as Eric Hobsbawm has pointed out, had two origins: national experience and the Russian events. American Communism had a third, the international experience of the immigrant members. The strategic effect of the Russian Revolution on the immigrant groups may be measured best in the changing political weight of the federations themselves.[36]

The most politically important of the federation papers in the wake of the February Revolution was understandably the Russian-language *Novy Mir*, remembered principally for its editors, veteran Russian revolutionary Lev Deutsch and later Trotsky and Bukharin. Celebrity leaders tucked away strangely in the immigrant world, compulsive writers and lecturers on questions Russian, they were by all accounts little concerned with the scene before their eyes. *Novy Mir*, its attention fixed upon Russia, paid scant attention even to the Union of Russian Workers, 10,000 to 50,000 strong and one of the most important IWW-affiliated immigrant proletarian groupings—it was too anarchistic for Menshevik or Bolshevik tastes.

The intellectuals' alienation from Russian immigrants in the USA was an old story by 1917. *Novy Mir* long had the reputation of wanting to make a revolution, but not with the largely illiterate, often religious constituents of the Russian immigrant community. Struggles and intrigues, like the unseating of Menshevik leaders who had guided the paper through most of its life, took the form of palace coups. Probably in no other group did the leaders hold themselves so seldom accountable. Certainly no other group grew so much overnight—from the mere six hundred in 1917 to the mass of 12,000 only two years later—and with so little sense of building and guiding stable cultural and political institutions.

The paper, and Trotsky in particular, stood or fell with the Marxist rationale for an extreme anti-war position. His widely-attended lectures centered on the European war, the decline of European civilization and the redemptive promise of international Socialism. From that policy, and fidelity to the Bolsheviks, *Novy Mir* and the Russian Federation unquestionably benefitted in the short run. Not only did the Federation draw Russian immigrants who had never previously taken it seriously: its sudden power and prestige gave it a weight in factional struggles vastly out of proportion to its day-to-day political influence and still more out of proportion to the political maturity of its functionaries. The Russian Federation leaders orchestrated, or blundered into, the breakup of the Socialist Party. A few years later, the revolution not made, almost everything fell away. The Federation became a perfect arena for government infiltration and the activities of agents provocateurs. The membership largely disappeared, the cadre were forced underground, and the press ceased operation. The Russian-

American left, never recovering more than a fraction of its
momentary strength, remained among the Communist foreign-
language groups one of the weakest and most dependent upon
news from abroad.[37]

Groups with greater maturity and internal strength acted more
cautiously and saved themselves from such a fate. They all suffered the hangover after the celebration: the collapse of
immediate revolutionary hopes and the loss of contact with
native radicals. Although sectarianism and despair also followed
in the wave of the radical fractures of the 1890s, this time there
was also systematic government repression to deal with. Immigrant radicals, inflamed by Russian events and hammered by
official persecution, tended to forget they lived in the United
States and conflated repression with the imminence of revolutionary crisis. In the process Marxist thought drifted to doctrinaire and (to the outside world) almost unintelligible
formulae, unanchored in any national specifity.

A few years later, in the 'normalcy' of the Harding administration, it would seem difficult to believe that in 1918, Socialism
had commanded the attention of so many ordinary Americans.
'Not so many years ago,' the *Appeal to Reason* mourned in 1921,
'hardly a week passed in any community without some Socialist
speaker bringing to it the Socialist gospel. Whether it was on a
soapbox or whether it was in a public hall, the principles of
Socialism and our interpretation of current events were delivered amid great enthusiasm . . . The number of speakers
now on the road you could count with the fingers of one hand.
Soapboxers are practically extinct'.[38]

What had it come to, then, the experiment, a half-century old
by 1919, of homegrown radicalism meeting Marxism on something like equal terms? One irony of the great divide of 1919 and
the eclipse of American Socialism is that, native- and foreign-
born, Marxists or non-Marxists, the open-minded radicals had
come so far in formulating problems and possibilities later to
become core values of radicalism, and not in the USA alone. The
optimistic utopianism of the nineteenth century had died before
Bolshevism came on the scene, although a rigid doctrinaire
interpretation would bury history unnecessarily; the feminism,
the embrace of popular culture, the fluid futurism which left
much to spontaneous choice would all takes decades further and
the discrediting of yet another generational politics to resurrect.
Only radical nationalism lived, and that in a mostly self-
restricting form.

In the larger sense, the entire transition from supposedly

utopian to supposedly scientific socialism had been made too easily, too carelessly. Lack of self-consciousness in this enterprise betrayed an eagerness to avoid the reality of the self, to escape into comforting abstractions. Marxist claims, Marxist texts, neither guaranteed political understanding nor political continuity. They validated class concepts and class expectations for specific sectors, and permitted an interpretation of the recurrent economic crises. They failed worst in the precise area where they seemed to succeed best, inducing self-confidence in the activists to know omnisciently the next developments ahead. Without that kind of humility, the creative contribution of Marxism would remain forever suspect.

4

Leninism in America

In 1919, the Kansas City Communists' *Workers World*, organ of future Trotskyist leader James Cannon and future Communist leader Earl Browder, had proclaimed 'For centuries the eyes of the oppressed masses of Europe were turned to the West . . .

'But with the development of industry an industrial autocracy has arisen in the Western Hemisphere more crushing as it is more efficient than the ruling class of Europe and now—And now our eyes turn East—to Russia and the rising Industrial Democracy of Europe for inspiration that we do not grow faint and weary in this struggle for freedom.

'In the West the night cloaks the land. In the East is the Red Dawn of the rising sun coming with the new dawn.'[1]

American Communists awoke from their revolutionary dreams to the reality of the 1920s. Pilgrims in the dark-shadowed land, they set out to conquer the capitalist beast in its home lair and to rescue a working class seemingly unaware of captivity. The rampant racism, xenophobia and anti-labor attitudes of native-born America confirmed their worst fears. They *needed* the light from the East, because they seemed to have none other.

The basic assumptions of American Marxist thought had by now shifted decisively. Nineteenth century immigrant Socialists and anarchists never got much beyond the concept of a workers' republic. Wobblies and Debsian Socialists, in their different ways, had sought to reconceptualize that republic as society (civil or industrial) redeemed from bourgeois deformation. Only the more bohemian Wobblies or Wobbly-oriented bohemians seemed to draw together the futurist implications of the mass society around them. Faith in the national citizen-workers' republic and in a mass culture breakthrough were simultaneously destroyed in the world war and its reactionary aftermath. Communist thinkers rushed to articulate a substitution. In place of American civil society and the prospective workers' republic they offered the Russian example, *i.e.,* supreme faith in the revolutionary leadership of a new state in the making. In place of the putative worker-bohemian alliance for a new world culture, they married Communism as class value of the producers to Communism as representative of the world's suffering nationalities and races.

The National Question now openly defined American Marxism, despite all official Communist efforts to render nationality into class. Previously, as we have seen, more time was spent denying the role of race and ethnicity than in assessing their importance. Immigrants themselves had built formidable institutions, but they had only begun to interpret the complexities of their situation in America when 1917 arrived. Russian leadership, helpful in some areas, ultimately compounded the American left's difficulties. But mass participation of immigrants, Blacks and a new middle class in the Communist movement also renewed the creative efforts begun by activists and theorists in the teens and abandoned during the insurrectionary excitement. The National Question became a metaphor embracing capitalist society in transition.

Less confidently, American Leninists confronted other problems unknown in Lenin's pre-revolutionary Russia, and groped for satisfactory solutions. The notorious twists and turns of Communist policies, from ultra-revolutionary to semi-reformist to revolutionary to virtually evolutionary, confirmed in critics' eyes the workings of international conspiracy. Indeed, American Communist policies continually coincided with Moscow's directives. But the same critics were hard-pressed to account for the changing reception of Communists by sometime sympathizers and a broader American public. Communist theoreticians, and the anti-Communist accusers, shared similar delusions in the power of a few to shape history.

The consumer economy more than any Marxist doctrine ultimately defined viable left strategy as the demand for a share of national abundance. The rising tide of anti-fascism set the framework for other demands, democracy in the European mother countries and pluralism in America. Behind the constantly-shifting constituencies of the American left, the Communists had consolidated their influence among those who identified simultaneously with Communism and with the social changes they themselves had helped to bring about. If not (in Earl Browder's claim) 'Twentieth Century Americanism', Communism provided a true Americanizing experience. Unions, Social Security, and an anti-fascist liberalism struck a true chord among people who had been made to feel like aliens, outcasts and enemies. They had—they thought at their optimistic moments—at last come home.

The particular experiences of different Communist constituencies underlined the movement's contributions and its inevitable dilemmas. An intimate understanding of the unskilled worker's centrality to industrial strategies solidified the older radical insights, and helped make possible a more sophisticated understanding of race and ethnicity for the prospects of American socialism. Identification of the surviving folk cultures, and of radical potential within the evolving popular culture, permitted intensive activity if not much greater theoretical understanding. It also permitted Communism to become remarkably middle-class. All in all, Communists cast off a large measure of their primitivism in almost every respect but their credulence in the Soviet Union and in the vanguard party model of hierarchical political relations.

The limits of American Communism, as a generational and multi-ethnic movement, could be found in the same experiences. The National Question, the status of an oppressed group within a state or empire, tended by its very nature to raise questions about the entire Marxist class analysis. The commonalities of European-born workers who filled the Party's early ranks did not carry over even to their children, many of them the white-collar generation of Communists. Afro-Americans and other racial minorities stood on very different ground yet. Generalization of population categories to one submerged mass, or to a pattern of groups uplifted through Communist efforts inside the New Deal, did not make Marxist sense of things. The sheer unfamiliarity of the immediate terrain lent itself to pseudo-solutions, a wild gyration around a resistant reality. It was a symptomatic error.

Class categories also fell apart in another way. Labor's own objectives, imperfectly articulated but evident in a variety of quotidian actions and demands, included desires that followed Wobbly traditions but that took the Communist left by surprise. Many workers sought not only improved wages and shorter hours but also a measure of control over factory life, a half experienced and half fantasized hope more extensive (or utopian) than union representation could provide. Communists had not counted upon *this* kind of transition, new demands rising with the scale and sophistication of advanced production. Their meat-and-politics approach had already lost touch with younger workers by the golden years of 1930s labor mobilization. Their fascination with state capitalism's gross redivisions of wealth disguised from them the nature of the discontent—even before their Second World War policies of labor discipline placed them firmly on the side of labor bureaucracy. Conditioned by Soviet-style economic planning, but also by their own past, they lost out to a working-class shift in aspirations.

As a Communist return to isolation in the later 1940s would show, the misalliance could easily become absolute. Contrary to Marxist theory and despite the expansion of global misery, the United States moved in the direction of a consumer *nation*. The rising popular culture's raw materials and (in the case of Blacks and Jews) many of the key personalities, the music, film, and radio that articulated the values of mechanized leisure, all had deep roots in working class life. The development of the service economy that socialists had predicted in the teens marched through the prosperous 1920s, then revived in the boom 1940s and 1950s like an engine for the expression of the masses—albeit in a very different way than the bohemians had anticipated. The rituals of material production would less and less dominate the mundane consciousness of the US working class, as culture and its ideologies replaced the primacy of work in a fully consumer society.

Production's hold upon *consciousness* had never been entirely secure. The less satisfying production came to be, the less wage labor would be defined as means of subsistence and more as means of bankrolling a lifestyle. Marxism's intellectual heirs apparent, middle class young people so plentiful in the Popular Front but also in other radical movements, felt these desires with special intensity. But Leninism of all varieties responded clumsily to this other world of consciousness. Individual radicals as artists, critics and organizers went far to give the emerging culture a democratic shape and meaningful artifacts. Yet the left remained intellectually alien, especially in formal Marxian theory, from a sphere beyond production and its immediate woes. Similarly, and for the same reasons, the average worker-Marxist faced generational upward mobility in their own ethnic circles with a combination of individual optimism for his or her own children and theoretical-strategic confusion for the class implications. The new issues did not seem to be 'Marxist' issues.

Not coincidentally, the category of empire emerged suddenly with the consolidation of Leninism in the middle 1920s. It had played a negligible role previously, even among that handful of socialists who pressed for some recognition of what came to be called the 'Negro Question'. Not since the 1890s had American military imperialism had much popularity as a radical issue, not even during the Mexican incursion which Socialists boldly denounced. In general, anti-imperialism had never escaped the abstract denunciations of capitalistic greed. The First World War burst apart the Central European formulae on the national question, and set the Socialists furiously against American militarism, while the racial and ethnic groups themselves ruminated over the implications for their self-identity and their particular futures. Still, empire proper as a concept, empire in particular as the domination of the white western world over the non-white 'backward' societies, remained outside the dominant theoretical accounts of American capitalism's expansion.

When early and later revolutionary fantasies dissolved, empire tended increasingly to become the all-inclusive explanation for the indifference of America to Communist dreams. Despite the material reasons for believing so, the idea was at its base a moral, even a Christian guilt at America's feasting while the world starved. It was also a half-conscious pronouncement of bankruptcy for the West, and of futility for a popular western radicalism.

Up From the Underground

In the reflected light of the Russian Revolution and amidst titanic labor struggles on the homefront, left-wingers had hastily reorganized themselves. For a moment, they consolidated their strength in the foreign-language federations and sent out an appeal to the wider movement, capturing whole state districts of Socialists who wanted an up-to-date, uncompromised revolutionary party. Indeed, even most rightwing Socialists still in the Party cheered Russian events and recognized as inevitable some kind of left reorientation.

Events, and government agencies eager to destroy the left, conspired against the revolutionaries. Lenin's call for parties affiliated with a new, disciplined Third International made any phased capture of the Socialist Party impossible. The bureaucratic maneuvers of the National Executive Committee on the one side, and of hyper-revolutionary American Bolsheviks on the other, caught most native-born revolutionaries in the middle. The overwhelming numbers and prestige of the foreign language

groups joined in the chiliastic immediatism of the Communist
Party, a precipitous breakaway from the Socialist Party. A sizeable number closer to the traditions of the IWW stayed on within
Socialist ranks to fight for their positions, until the tumultuous
1919 convention made that impossible, and then set up shop as
the Communist Labor Party.

The promise of the moment exploded. Even as unrest continued to rock working class life, the Socialist Party virtually
collapsed and the two Communist entities spent their energy in
internecine polemics. A field day for government infiltrators and
wild-eyed sectarians, 1919–21 passed in a rush of charges and
counter-charges, arrests, deportations and disillusionment. Old-
timers recall that ordinary workers determinedly loyal to the new
Communist movement largely sat out the disputes, waiting for
the smoke to clear. When it did, and the Third International had
imposed a unity of sorts upon the factionalists, most of the ninety
thousand or so leftwingers had drifted away. The residue of five
or ten thousand radicals with a following several times that size
cold undertake important practical interventions. But only in
their own fervid imaginations did they constitute a serious revolutionary threat to Calvin Coolege and J.P. Morgan.

Of course in their more sober moments, no one understood
this better than the Communists themselves. As a leading participant later reflected: 'A few slogans have served like hallelujahs
at a revivalist meeting. Hell has gaped before us in all its fearful-
ness, even more terrifying than the portrayals of Billy Sunday,
the hell of being the minutest fraction under one hundred percent Bolshevik. To escape this fearful peril most of us have been
more than one-hundred-percent Bolshevik—somewhere to the
Left of the Left Communists in the other countries . . . What has
dominated the Communist movement in the United States up to
this time may be described as the big bluff of Bolshevism . . . A
ready-made Bolshevism was superimposed in this country upon
a left-wing movement of many years standing. The adventure
element—with the revolution in the process in Russia, in
Germany, in Hungary—was so alluring that none stopped for
questioning or analysis . . . The Communists, lo and behold,
were the bearers of a new revelation! And ever since the summer
of 1919 we had an official Communism in the United States
which proceeds by incantations, counting of beads, salaams to
the East, Jubilees of phrases and slogans, pieties unending to
Bolshevism—to a Bolshevism consisting of a mysterious com-
pound of words and ritual which cold only be known to the high
priests!'²

How to escape from this never-never world without falling back into the Socialism they had rejected proved as puzzling to Communists as the changes in America around them. Nothing typified the break with the past as much as the indifference, hostility, and worse, simple ignorance about the history of women's rights. The republicanism of the earlier movement repelled Communist theoreticians, and the trans-class character of the movement gave them an easy target. Their belated discovery of women activists (at the insistence of Comintern authorities!) revealed more about themselves than they knew. A 'vast and fertile . . . mature yet one might say, virgin field for our work', an American correspondent to *Imprecorr* in 1927 styled the potential female constituency for Communists.[3] The unconscious humor suggested a clumsiness inevitable in the reductive, formulaic approach taken.

Dismissal of feminism as bourgeois did not even correspond to the experience of the new immigrants, some of whose group memberships (notably Finns) had ardently supported woman suffrage and maintained their own forceful women's organizations. Least of all did it conform to the personal experience of the mostly Jewish intellectuals who set the theoretical pace. But it suited the generational rejection of everything the Socialists had seemed to represent, from coalition with bourgeois reformers to faith in elections. Communist theory reduced women's own political traditions and their role in revolutionary change to the lowest level reached in the late nineteenth century. Women came to be viewed as a mere auxiliary force with a few widely heralded but mainly symbolic leaders. Communist *practice*, with its dynamic women Party members, trade-union and neighborhood activists, taught very different lessons, eventually forcing minor theoretical modifications. Overall, the paradox remained of an organization denying the personal sources of strength upon which so many activists drew, and which on pain of exclusion sought to ignore the obvious and ever-present implications of everyday political practice. That kind of self-destructive behavior symptomized the negative side of enthusiasm for the Russian experiment.

In the Communist underground, J. B. S. Hardman had asserted, 'no real activity was carried on or expected', and a leadership emerged 'whose real capacities existed only when their leadership was not required and whose faculties, except for local ones, were completely atrophied'.[4] But this was the view from the top, one that would soon be translated, in the Popular Front period, into a dismissal of Communism's early years. Some of the reasons can be readily comprehended: the emphasis upon European events; the repression which closed down much of the radical press and made formal communication within the left both difficult and unwise; and the dramatic loss of constituency. Another, equally compelling reason has, however, been generally overlooked. Decentralization of political initiative, with the inevitable persistence of old habits, encouraged a wide experimentation at the local level that remained largely invisible to Party leaders—and has so remained for most historians.

In the unions, where the ordinary (especially foreign-born) Communist focused most of his or her energies, the frantic pace of industrial unionism sometimes continued from the war through 1921 and 1922, merging with a backstairs struggle against the employers' counter-offensive. Despite legal limitations, Communists and future Communists had already done yeoman duty in the Chicago packinghouse and national steel strikes, among dozens of proto-industrial unions, and in a multitude of immigrant and Black communities.

In scattered localities, often but not always immigrant-dominated, the Party reappeared as a cleansed Socialist movement, working with trade unions to coordinate the fight-back, setting up educational classes on the old Socialist model now improved by readings about Russia, revering the old heroes and creating new ones. (*Workers World* apotheosized as its American martyrs two recent fallen comrades, science popularizer Arthur Lewis and Whitmanesque Horace Traubel.) Here, and not only among the working class, the expectations of a world-revolutionary breakthrough immediately touching America had not entirely faded.

How exactly their influence could be most effectively manifested remained unclear. Communist national leaders squabbled among themselves on plans for reorganization. Local activists followed their own instincts. Local Communist papers, like the Duluth, Minnesota *Truth*, edited by former Christian socialist leader F. O. Bentall, or the Chicago *Voice of Labor*, edited by Irish-American Jack Carney, even began to argue for a Communist pluralism of techniques and strategies.

Most ethnic federations, unlike the English-language branches, never ceased functioning—even during the worst years of repression—along the lines they knew best. Their public activities quieted somewhat, but they maintained the fraternal and cultural associations, correctly anticipating that another day would bring them manifold opportunities. In some of the largest and most important groups, the political hotheads who had first urged the split with the Socialist Party faded into the background. Leftish functionaries initially skeptical about Bolshevism recognized that their future lay in the Communist Party. So far as their press continued, they also viewed the world situation in general and the American situation in particular with an increasingly realistic eye. Many had seen worse repression in their homelands. They anticipated revolution in the old world, perhaps imminently, but not necessarily a sweeping change in America tomorrow. After a moment of fantasy, they began to make the necessary adjustments for the long haul. The very maturation of the New Immigrant groups as communities and political constituences made the elaboration of the fraternal network a struggle that could be won.

The Party encouraged the uncertain relationship between revolutionary politics and ethnic culture, providing the immigrants with essential services: labor defense, propaganda, English-language spokesmen and organizational contacts. The groups in return gave the bulk of funds for the Party's operation, produced enthusiastic crowds, and formed an authentic radical proletariat. And by the thousands these immigrants proved doggedly loyal, unlike the American recruits who had few social settings in which to participate collectively.

This simple demographic distinction shaped the inner character of American Communism as much as the continual late-breaking news from the Soviet Union. The flourishing of daily papers in Lithuanian, Hungarian, Finnish, Yiddish and other languages demonstrated both the riveting interest in the fate of the homeland, and the ability of ethnic activists to make use of conditions and sentiments at hand. In the most extreme case, a Central Committee effort to commandeer the ethnic press through its most powerful member, the Yiddish *Morgen Freiheit*, collapsed when the *Freiheit* Association—acting altogether like the nineteenth-century ethnic papers—responded to imposition of an unfriendly, unliterary editor with their own *Umparteiishe* (non-party, independent) conference where they threatened a split. The leadership backed off, as it did in a number of these early encounters, biting its tongue and biding its time. The power of expulsion it assuredly had, but not necessarily the respect of immigrants whose reverence for Russia did not extend to the American party leadership.[5]

Lithuanian-Americans offer a more extended case in point. Formed as a party within the Socialist Party until they were forced to reorganize as a loyal section, the overwhelmingly working-class Lithuanian immigrants sought, along with

Socialism or improvement of labor conditions, the freedom of Lithuania, *i.e.*, the defeat of the Czarist Empire. Led by self-educated workers acutely aware of labor struggles, they spread their propaganda and recruited nearly five thousand members by 1919, developing an influence that would survive repression. They made the move to Communism easily, through an array of ethnic sports groups, choruses and fraternal societies whose members overwhelmingly considered themselves supportive sympathizers rather than cadre. For most of the Lithuanian radicals—ordinary workers more spontaneous than studied in their beliefs—their movement remained a state within a larger, somewhat alien state which they had no need or wish to challenge.[6]

Still smaller nationality groups within the United States, significant at the local level, struck up similar political relations. Armenians, prominent across New England, recognized that the fate of their homeland rested largely with the Red Army's stalemating of the Turks. Like Bulgarians, they owed more to Russian nationalism than to Communism. But their sympathies naturally inclined them towards a fraternal style of activity at the fringes of the Party. At high times of mobilization, when the homeland was in particular need, those fringes grew sometimes as visible and influential as the Party proper. Even in less exciting times, an Armenian-language film in a local theatre might draw a bigger crowd than any other local left event.

Marxism re-Americanized itself ambiguously and in some ways reluctantly as the New Immigrant communities settled into America. They had struck upon Socialism in One Country independently of Stalin's prognostications, and for altogether practical reasons: even imperfect Socialism had a better influence upon their homelands than no Socialism at all; and then, too, they needed their dreams as they lived out their lives in an unrevolutionary land. They built new halls, reorganized benefit associations and cultural movements after the split. They devised a Communist approach to history and to society equally dependent upon the survival of the Soviet Union and transition, fast or slow, to the kind of institutional influence which would make Socialist transformation in the United States possible. They moved, often painstakingly, from general pronouncements in their press and propaganda to a practical and even theoretical approach suiting their particular constituency. (Secularization, *i.e.*, the break from the Church's reactionary influence, thus could be sold to younger ethnic women as a part of Americanization, a radical Americanization which did not threaten the good aspects of their dual identity.) The exegeses and lead editorials often continued to be translated from the English-language leadership's words, but the content of their adaptation they devised increasingly on their own.

Party trade-union policy had a way of making sympathizers (if not necessarily converts) by virtue of the energy and sincerity of its adherents. For groups in trades where Communists had extraordinary influence—like the Greeks, Hungarians, and Lithuanians in the fur trades directed by the Communists' own genuine labor hero, Ben Gold—the Party's union influence would be decisive. By the early 1920s ordinary Communists had learned to put ideological questions aside in trade-union matters. They could, with favorable conditions and shrewd leadership, mobilize significant numbers behind their positions. Their first institutional entry into the trade-union arena, the Trade Union Educational League, benefited from the accumulated experience of grassroots union reformism. With the decline of the Wobblies, the Communists were able to assume the mantle of leadership in the struggle for industrial unionism and the organization of the unorganized.[7]

The dynamic of *this* Marxism quickly moved beyond Party circles proper into a vague zone of left-labor influence. Hardman, undisciplined trade union ideologue and Party free-lancer, thus published for a few years the remarkable *American Labor Monthly*. It provided an open, intelligent forum for the problems of radicals within the labor movement. Placing demands on the labor leadership in such a way as to garner maximum rank-and-file support, it epitomized a style that won over more than a few mildly socialist functionaries. (For instance, a large section of the Italian-American labor leadership belonged to the Party.) Marxism seemed to present a loose tolerance of tactical differences alongside a strong fidelity to the Soviet Union. Until this entire effort fell afoul of the AFL rightward drift and the broader collapse of militant unionism, the Party momentarily resembled what it would become fifteen years or so later: a place for aspiring labor leaders to cut their organizational teeth, and for old radicals to join with the young.

The blush of enthusiasm for early Russia (even the ferociously anti-Communist *Jewish Daily Forward* remained positive about Russian reconstruction until the end of the decade), and the constructive Communist policies won the Party another chance at recruiting or influencing native-born radicals. Former Wobblies and longtime progressive AFL unionists, along with veteran Socialists and activists in the dissident rural and farmer-labor movements from the Dakotas to Minnesota, tended to view Communists as ideologically high-strung but also hard-working allies. Groups of coal miners, Black industrial workers, even farmers came over on the basis of specific campaigns or because of older radical loyalties. An influx of mostly second-generation immigrant youth eager to become cadre brightened the prospects for an early consolidation of ranks.

It is tempting to speculate what the Communist movement and what Marxist ideas might have become if, for even a few years more, Communist practicality had endured and homespun radicalism had not faded. Oldtimers still meditate on the 'farmer-labor' alliance which briefly caught fire and made anti-war crusader Robert LaFollette the most powerful third party candidate since Eugene Debs. That movement could hardly survive, as a national force, the AFL's steady retreat and LaFollete's own death. But even a more modest persistence, like the regional farmer-labor movement which held strong in Minnesota, would have prepared radicalism for the 1930s and prepared the Communists as natural leaders of a coalition.

Alas, mixed signals from faction-torn Moscow and a series of drastic tactical errors by American Communist leaders sheared off most of the potential support. Seeking to outbid moderates in the farmer-labor movement, Communists once more thoroughly isolated themselves. Moving too swiftly across the retreating progressive currents within the AFL, they lost J.B.S. Hardman and a host of other left-leaning functionaries. Outside the immigrant communities and a few trade union outposts, American Communism had bungled its first attempt at sustained influence. Communists had, arguably, also lost the opportunity to put together a 'Popular Front' on far more favorable terrain for Marxist ideas than the New Deal-dominated era to follow.

Another aspect of American Communism remained maddeningly unresolved. Contrary to frequent predictions, the 'science of revolutionary leadership' had proved far from infallible. True, the collapse of parliamentary-style Socialism, with its patient expectation of educating workers into radicalism, seemingly demanded another model. So did the moribund Wobbly slogans, further away from realization than ever before. The character of 1920s labor and political mobilizations certainly demonstrated the value of strategic direction, but what precisely did Leninism mean in America? None of the contending factions of American Communism, themselves busily competing for Comintern blessing, had any clear ideas beyond the necessity of leadership and the requirement of discipline. 'Democratic Centralism' had become an all-purpose rationalization for the practical absence of internal democracy and the chaos of power-centralization. Assessing their loyal ranks as proletarians who happened to be Jewish or Finnish or Hungarian, Party leaders deceived themselves. Only the loyalty of the immigrants to their own newspapers and their own leaders as well as to the Soviet Union saved the Party from internal collapse. Attempts to alter the equation would lead more likely to calamity than to perfecting the vaunted Vanguard.

Communism in Stasis

Communist leaders had obvious reasons for wanting to uproot the autonomy of the language groups and to end the undeclared polycentrism within the Party. Well before the Bolshevik revolution, Ohio functionary and future Communist leader Charles Ruthenberg expressed dissatisfaction with the inadequacy of Socialist Party discipline over the language groups. Moderate Socialists had ordered the 1912 expulsions of left Socialists, an act which proto-communists bitterly denounced, partly over the same essential issue. By the mid-1920s the shoe was on the other foot. 'Resistance to centralized leadership,' as a party document characterized the activities of old Ludwig Lore, whose *Volkszeitung* remained the most historic and certainly the most literate of the Communist papers, took a thousand forms then and later. Despite their considerable contribution, the language groups constituted a living infraction to discipline. National and international pressures persuaded Communist leaders to take the immense risk of cracking down. From that particular maneuver, it would take the Party a decade to recover.[8]

The remaining cadre suffered from the welter of mixed signals. Whatever headway they could make by leading strikes of workers in 'sick' industries like textiles and coal, Communists lost through the sickness of their own internal party life. It is difficult now, for the ordinary participants in those melees, to understand what the argument was all about. They recall finding themselves lined up with one side rather than another based on friendships and regional loyalties more than clearly-defined political differences. The harassed rank-and-filers – except, of course, the considerable number expelled on charges of 'right' or 'left' deviations—were mostly glad to see trouble end through Russian-commanded bureaucratic fiat. The male and female 'Jimmy Higginses' of the movement made their own low-profile adaptations to the stubborn phantasmagorias of the Party leadership on one side and the stubborn realities of American working class life on the other.

Thus ordinary Party members and low-level functionaries developed a pervasive cynicism toward a leadership evidently out of touch with reality. The leaders, presiding over a largely immigrant Party with its extended union and fraternal network, felt themselves trapped between exciting international developments and overwhelming day-to-day bureaucratic tasks, between ideology and American life. As they struggled to balance obligations, they took little added trouble to consult their flocks. Such dissatisfaction on both sides did not begin or end with the Communists. But they confirmed its presence in practice while stoutly denying its existence in principle.[9]

That denial, reproduced at all levels by the incessant cant of 'Democratic Centralism', attested to the most melancholy fact of American Leninism. Unchallenged authoritarianism and the wild factionalism of the 1920s CP (to be replayed later among the Trotskyists) were two sides of the same coin. The command theory of Lenin, present from the beginning, moved from a guide to practice into a form of, and even a substitute for, practice. What might have receded into the background of a youthful movement's errors became a deformity in premature middle age. None of the nineteenth century leaders had outlasted their time, even Debs remained more figurehead than actual leader in a complex and shifting Socialist movement. By contrast, leadership for all Leninist movements was like an American judgeship—rule for life. The disgrace of one leader present at the founding day usually promoted another; their successors, 'youth' of the 1920s–30s, took control too late and with too heavy odds against them. No wonder aging leaders valued international contacts as highly as elusive success in the United States; they remembered the glories of 1919 and lived off those memories all the days of their lives.

The Party achieved a remarkably disciplined internal integration with the limited forces it possessed, at the cost of debasing its loyal constituency. In part, blundering organizational measures simply reflected Russian international policies. Twice the Yiddish membership faded away, in 1929 and 1939, circulation of the popular *Freiheit* fell drastically, and Jewish Communists feared for their safety as street speakers. The prestigious intellectuals the Party lost on each occasion were never recovered. Later, it would lose virtually all standing in Slavic communities when Yalta enforced the end of anti-Fascist alliance and the imposition of Soviet-style regimes in Eastern Europe.

Amei can Communist leaders could, and did, commit their own blunders. Their power over the federations, unchecked except by the inevitable defections and loss of revenue, guaranteed errors. Half the Finnish membership disappeared, their suspicions against New York functionaries amply borne out by the Party demand for the Finnish treasury which cooperators had built up over many years. Other, smaller groups fared even worse. Hardly a fraction of the syndicalist-minded Italian group survived. Districts rich in mass industry but poor in English-language Communists practically ceased to function, some never to return to their strength of the mid-1920s. In a few cases (notably the aging German group), there was mass exodus from the Party with former quasi-Party institutions intact. In general, individuals left one-by-one, tired of the trouble and disillusioned with the internal life of the left. Had the uprising against reformist Socialist leaders meant only this after all?

In another, deeper sense, Lenin's theses on national self-determination notwithstanding, Communists had made minimal advances upon the nub of the National Question. The Russian promise of 'autonomy', cultural or otherwise, began to wear just as the disillusion of the foreign-born with the US Communist leadership first became apparent. On the theoretical level, Communist functionaries reverted to the assumption of the Socialist leaders that ethnicity and language were transitional features, tolerated for the comfort of the older generation. The actual burgeoning of cultural activities, most readily apparent in popular Yiddish culture but obvious across the spectrum, left them deeply suspicious. Their recognition of these developments was opportunistic.

Some in the Party leadership put the best face on this uneven policy of coerced assimilation and tolerated plurality. Foreign-language cultural activities did, unarguably, often become mere 'banquet socialism', an insulation against an uncertain world. Pressure upon the local ethnic cadres to establish shop-oriented newspapers that were strong on local complaints opened a new front for industrial union agitation. In optimal circumstances, such initiatives could exist alongside ethnic-fraternal activities.[10]

The same leaders also sincerely sought to give Americanization a positive educational side. The Party established its own educational apparatus and arranged (or, more properly, permitted) contacts with the surviving and renascent reform tendencies in labor, such as Brookwood Labor College. International Publishers had begun to offer new editions of Lenin,

Marx and Engels, as well as fresh theoretical works from Bukharin, Trotsky and Kautsky. The Workers School (which used non-Communist instructors, like Louis Boudin) took as its slogan, 'Discover America', and organized English classes for new immigrants just as the Rand School had done earlier in the Socialist Party milieu. The leading intellectual spirit for this new turn was Bertram D. Wolfe, whose star briefly shone brightest amongst the Young Communists. He directed the theoretical energy of the movement away from the abstract 'timelessness and spacelessness', toward the necessity to understand the real problems at hand in *this* civilization.[11]

Wolfe and his collaborators argued that the rise of US imperialism had augmented the power of trusts over the largely immigrant workforce, corrupting indigeneous working-class consciousness as early as the 1880s–90s. Unionism had become no more than the economism Lenin denounced, as one relatively privileged sector of the proletariat falsely generalized its immediate perceptions. In short, revolutionaries were necessarily outsiders in relation to a corrupt and evil order. They had hitherto lacked the vanguard to carry them to success, but ultimately, capitalism would be stricken by crisis. Led by a vanguard embracing the super-oppressed minorities, social revolution would conquer.[12]

The argument had a distinct novelty to it. It worked too simply, ignoring all the signs of solidarity among specific skilled sectors, and it actually retreated from the sophistication of Austin Lewis' more precise industrial interpretation. But it had the virtue of being an initial approach. The vision of the Party as all-sufficient unquestionably lent moral strength to those who remained within it. They looked to themselves, correctly perceiving that the revolutionary impetus could be found nowhere else. Such ideas rang true, at least, during the late 1920s. Unfortunately, the analysis seemed to many a counsel of despair.

From the viewpoint of the dizzy stockmarket spiral of bourgeois optimism, Wolfe (and his patron, Party factional leader, Jay Lovestone) opted essentially to strengthen their own ranks and wait out the lull. In practice, they proposed that the Party continue its propaganda patiently, making peace with those parts of the labor movement prepared for alliance.[13] Ten years later, long after Wolfe and Lovestone had been branded as rightists and class traitors, the Party would revive this line of thought in the Democratic Front.

The alternative was Draconian. Under any other strategy, the Party had to enter upon a forced march of accumulating human resources. It had to overcome objective difficulties by a matter of will—the will to mobilize every energy and to believe the crisis of capitalism lay just around the corner. Characteristic of his break with an adaptationist past selling war bonds and organizing within the AFL, William Z. Foster voiced the belief that Communists found themselves in a society sick almost beyond redemption with the poison of its own avarice. 'Opportunism', where it did not mean unwillingness to follow orders, signalled an infection spread to the Communist ranks and to the working class at large by the outside society. 'American labor', Foster wrote in 1927, 'is still asleep, drugged into insensibility by bourgeois propaganda . . . And the worst of it is that it is making no effort toward . . . awakening . . . American labor takes capitalist economics and morals for granted . . . It is our calamity and discredit that [one] had to come to America to find the spectacle of a great labor movement which has not yet freed itself intellectually from the bonds of capitalism'.[14] This was a very strange kind of Americanization, indeed.

One delegate to an early Comintern Congress told his more prestigious colleagues, 'Comrades, for us in America the Soviet Union plays an extraordinary role,' compensating for the absence of favorable domestic forces. For a few years, Communists pictured the American masses as suffering under the same yoke as other world peoples, common (if extraordinarily deluded) victims of imperialism. By the later 1920s, they swung back toward the IWW version of the AFL as agent of oppression, its well-fed workers those social layers Lenin had labelled the pawns of the bourgeoisie. 'Americanization' became a common term of opprobrium. Reform insurgencies like the briefly powerful LaFollette movement now became a 'drunken debauch' of sentimentalism. America the nation, maybe even Americans—if that mean white, middle class and comfortable working class Americans—had become the enemy of humankind.[15]

Communists emerging from the disappointments of a false start and alienated from America thrice over, by class, ethnicity and even more by fidelity to Soviet Russia, saw things with special eyes. Lenin's authority, and the stunning significance of revolution in a 'backward' society with promise of more such ahead, dramatized a larger and even unintended point to Communists everywhere, nowhere more (at least outside the Third World itself) than to American Communists. Imperialism *had* to be the final stage because the weight of Empire hung so heavily upon the life of the nation and the tragedy of an unhappy world.

The Christian dissident tradition dovetailed with Leninist

critique more than either side could easily acknowledge. Most of the early popularisers of the Russian Revolution in America had been religionists. *Christianism and Communism* by 'Bad Bishop' William Montgomery Brown, venerable Episcopalian leader drawn step-by-step from the race question to the entirety of capitalist evil, easily outsold official Communist works of the 1920s. A handful of intellectuals from Christian backgrounds, often old missionary families, formed a cohort of journalists preaching the regeneration of peasant life under Communism. They rightly saw themselves as heirs to a tradition which included nineteenth-century Abolitionists and supporters of Native Americans. They also included contemporary constituencies as unlikely as women explorers who had returned to civilization praising the virtue of the natives they had known. These people shared, at the extreme, the meta-critique of anthropologist Robert Briffault, who argued that the post-revolutionary populations of the West would need to be cleansed, perhaps for a century or more, from the corruptions they had acquired. The Third World, in this turnabout of chauvinistic Socialist interpretations, was on the contrary more prepared for Socialism because closer to the sources of age-old human life. A diluted version simply but eloquently hailed every anti-imperial revolt, from Sandino to Gandhi, and worked hard to educate Americans to their share of collective sin.[16]

Only a relatively few Communists, none in positions of internal power, consciously imbibed this non-Marxian logic of national guilt, moral redemption of the outcasts, and overthrow of the West. But a handful of popularizers created an influential milieu, not only in the American religious community but among the Protestant middle class at large, indeed among all those who could feel wistful at the pages of *Soviet Russia Today*. The personal sympathies of Party members as well as their agonized isolation made the moral outlook of the Protestants a sub-text of the movement. Here, in what might be seen as a decisive permutation of American Marxism, lie some of the tangled roots of Third World support, post-New Left terrorism, and even Liberation Theology fifty years or more later.

Anti-imperialism led Communists to a fresh emphasis on the question of racial oppression. Communist hopes rose dramatically when the most prominent Black left Nationalist organization, the African Blood Brotherhood, together with its *Crusader* newspaper and the Crusader News Service (mimeographed bulletins sent out to Black papers of all kinds) merged into the Party. Cyril Briggs, the leading spirit of this enterprise, was indeed an extraordinary figure. West Indian-born theorist and cultural critic, Briggs argued a precocious version of Popular Front perspectives based around Afro-American perceptions and social needs. *The Crusader*, distributed in a few thousand copies mostly among urban Black neighborhoods, touched the sophisticated minority who understood the limits of Marcus Garvey's programs. Garvey's counter-attack upon them under- lined their ideological importance, while the Black Socialists around A. Philip Randolph practically abandoned their attempts to create a radical milieu. The opportunity did not bear many immediate results. Only among the cultural avant-garde and a few working-class recruits did the Communists have any immediate success, and the *Crusader* group (which folded its newspaper and press service in 1922) seemed simply swallowed by the Party apparatus. The Nationalist fervor died away almost as quickly as it had come into existence, leaving behind it poli- tical uncertainty on all sides.[17]

Still, the Communists proceeded to establish enormously im- portant principles for the entire left. The Sixth Comintern Con- gress in 1928 introduced a new responsibility for Americans to support Black nationalism. Black *race* consciousness was identi- fied as revolutionary in and of itself. White Party members were pressed theoretically, practically and personally to wrestle with the Black question, to encourage Blacks and to treat them with perfect equality or risk censure and expulsion. Within Harlem, metropolis of the Pan-African world, Communists began by the end of the decade to press beyond the familiar denunciations of Garveyism, conservative politics and religion to a concrete analysis of eroded living conditions. Especially prominent in this new turn was the denunciation of an exploiter, the landlord, whom Socialists had criticized only haltingly. With their street rallies and free speech fights, Communists—mostly white, even in Harlem—signalled that they believed in a distinctive Black contribution to class struggle. In point of fact, their appreciation for the fine points of racism and racist oppression left much to be desired. But in advancing Black liberation to the foreground of revolutionary politics they had opened a new strategic and (potentially) cultural dimension.[18]

It is often forgotten how significant was the Party's ability to mobilize reservoirs of empathy amongst the immigrant pro- letariat. For Jewish radicals (indeed, most Jewish liberals in these decades of well-intended paternalism) the pariah status of Blacks was poignantly redolent of the horrors of anti-semitism. In an age where the virulently anti-Catholic, anti-immigrant Ku

Klux Klan drew upon a nativist mass base North of the Mason-Dixon Line, the other harassed ethnic groups—the Finns, Slavs, Hungarians, Italians, and others—could often manifest some solidarity with Blacks. When *The Hammer*, Yiddish-language Communist monthly, published expressionist 1920s covers of African primitivist motifs, and inside offered hard-hitting material on conditions of Blacks together with bitter diatribes in essay and cartoon form against the racist exclusionism of the AFL, the combined effort to educate readers had no forced or doctrinaire quality. Its more sophistcated readers, workers and the lower middle class, knew their way around Harlem. Some of the other ethnic groups, less enlightened, had to be monitored by leadership, especially where conflicts over work or housing had already broken out in the neighborhoods. At this point in history, the problems were no greater, probably less, than struggling against anti-Semitism within Party ranks. Left-wing workers and many others could grasp from their own practical experience that only unity could overcome employers' divisive stratagems, and that only the liberation of every individual group could bring the liberation of all.

From such understanding to the bold anti-racist conclusion that Black resistance against all white racism at every level constituted radical action, Communists advanced with greater difficulty. To begin with, the theoretical legacy for analysing racial oppression as a 'national' problem was fragmentary and ambiguous. The formulations by Marx on the Irish Question and on the American Civil War, or even by Lenin on the importance of achieving proletarian unity by supporting the rights of national independence, provided only vague pointers on the US situation. The putatively 'scientific' formulations attempted by Stalin in his 1913 article ('Marxism and the National Question') were scarcely any better. (Indeed, even after the 'solution' of the 'Negro Question', the Communist Party would continue to twist in the wind over other cognate dilemmas. For instance, they failed to define Mexican-Americans as a nation-within-a-nation, despite precedence in the Southwest and previous citizenship in Mexico. And while recognising the national rights of Hawaii, the Philippines and Puerto Rico, they contributed little to understanding the cultural adaptations of their immigrant populations on mainland USA.)

The ultimate perspective on the national dimension of Black revolutionary prospects was achieved only through the intervention of the Comintern. At Stalin's own initiative, a temporary formulation described Black activity for liberation as a first step toward Socialism. In provisions added by the ultra-revolutionary emphasis of the time, American Blacks in the South had become an oppressed proto-nation on the verge of revolutionary uprising.

This was, contrary to later Popular Front revisions and to Black complaints, a *ne plus ultra* of American Leninism. The National Question—which since Sorge and the First International had so uneasily coexisted with classical economist Marxism—finally forced a major recasting of theory and practice. No longer was the hope for Socialism simply coeval with the maturation of the industrial proletariat and the working out of its specific ethnic traits. Now the Black community, conceived of as a 'Black Nation', would be admitted as a parallel, overlapping revolutionary agency. Communist leaders who, organizationally, did not even staff a full-time Black organizer and who fretted continually over the dangers of Black nationalist tendencies among minority Party members, yet moved toward furthering the new strategic goal.

A mixture of sheer audacity and foolhardy bravado marked the Communist entry into urban Black politics. This was already traditional Marxism only in a remote sense, because it no longer based itself (as among the ethnic groups) primarily on the industrial proletariat but also on the Black *community*, unskilled and underemployed. The Party went about things in a clumsy, and often unpleasant, manner, holding show-trials against internal dissenters and excoriating the Black petty-bourgeoisie. Only slowly, and not without continual misjudgments, would it make its adaptations. With all that, the approach to race was still the noblest, and the most unique, of Communist contributions to the American left and to American society.

It was also—and here Black critics of the Party like Harold Cruse are hard to fault—inevitably condescending. Neither Leninist theory nor Christian spirit restrained Communists from treating Blacks as victims waiting helplessly for direction. Even the original Party Black cadre, many of West Indian origin, manifested their own subtle paternalism toward Black Belt immigrants. Through its dedication and hard work, the Party recruited and would continue to recruit outstanding Black thinkers and organizers. It repeatedly alienated those recruits, however, from a community which, like the rest of America in this respect, could not help judging Communists as fanatics who did some good things. For all its idealistic zeal, the Party con-

veyed the impression that it understood better than Blacks themselves the nature of and the solution for the race problem in
America.[19]

The other single, most unique element of American Leninism
came directly from the human resources of the ethnic radicals.
Encouraged and coerced to begin factory agitation, little groups
produced the first 'underground newspapers' of the labor left,
hand-out tabloids and mimeographed sheets with complaints
about local woes. Some of the finest of the factory activists were
lost to factionalism, notably in the expulsion of suspected Trotskyists. But for most working-class Communists who survived
coerced Americanization, the tasks remained very clear and
obvious—life had taught them so, and a revision of the old labor
newspaper style gave them the form.

Inasmuch as Communists consciously represented the unskilled worker as potentially triumphant, their immanent new
society within the old had presumably to reflect upon itself,
develop itself intellectually, understand itself. The consequent
experiment in workers' own writing, 'Workers' Correspondence'
initiated in the mid-1920s across the spectrum of Party papers,
aimed to elicit reports, commentaries, intelligence from the
bottom-most levels. Socialist and Wobbly editors had often tried
the same thing, but without much success, and without the
high-flown formulation. Their Communist counterparts found
themselves in fact writing the contributions for the most part, on
verbal reports mostly factual rather than interpretive. The experiment had too little chance amid factional warfare, shifting
membership and hard political times.

This failure pointed to a lasting contradiction between theory
and practice, hidden by the economic crisis just ahead but never
entirely overcome. The basis of the old Socialist movement, and
the ideal of the Communist movement, was the autodidact proletarian, thirsting for knowledge that only Marxism could give
him. US workers, especially skilled workers, often had public
education backgrounds by the 1920s. But quite apart from a
general lack of political sympathy for Communist literature they
considered daft, they had already bypassed reading as a major
form of entertainment and enlightenment. The desire for a truly
proletarian literature symbolized the urgency of a missing
dimension in American Communism's first decade. How could
the Communists dream of taking power when they lacked the
rudimentary indications of a class-conscious working class? The
devotion to Blacks, the limited successes in heavily ethnic unions
like the fur workers or in the struggle for union reforms among

the mineworkers and garment workers, could not compensate for that absence.

The Zenith

History, not internal politics, transformed the Communist situation. The Wall Street Crash seemed almost like a biblical confirmation of the Party line. With hoopla turned into despair, the Communists could confidently prepare themselves (like DeLeon in the Depression of the 1890s) to become the Army of Conquest. But they found no large number outside their own modestly swollen ranks ready for the final conflict. Disappointment and disgust with capitalism as a social system certainly spread through the population, but the main battlements of the system proved amazingly stable. The left-leaning intelligentsia, sickened by the execution of Sacco and Vanzetti and now convinced of capitalism's decrepitude, voiced a desire for radical change. But traditional intellectuals hardly marshalled the forces required for an authentic revolutionary mass base.

Communists could count on wider influence only amongst the traditional left constituencies. Ethnic working-class communities, mortally wounded by industrial lay-offs, responded to the long-standing predictions of the Party with grudging but sometimes warm acknowledgment. These Marxists *did* know something after all. But the Party's new-found popularity did not usually translate into mass recruitment. The ultra-sectarian attacks on Socialist Party members, the bloody charges on police lines or city hall, and the continual internal heresy-hunting, frightened many off or caused them to drop their active membership within a few months. The Party captured and held, one might say, only those who had consciously or unconsciously sought a single cause for their lives.

But thousands did enter the radius of the Party's mass activities: rent strikes, hunger marches, defense campaigns, union organizational drives, strikes, and so on. In the early days of the Depression, mass organization remained at a protean level. An elderly former leader of the National Textile Workers Union told me that the organization had no treasury, no fixed membership, and barely enough funds to pay for an office. It responded to strikers' requests for help by canvassing funds at neighboring plant gates and in the community. It supplied speakers, duplicated flyers, and provided a sense of solidarity and interconnection with a larger movement. Like many of the Communist-led 'dual unions' it failed to organize in the usual sense, or even perhaps to impart the kind of *élan* that had once characterized Wobbly struggles; but in a field of timid and generally immobile AFL unions, it bridged the gap to the formation of the CIO a few years later (supplying a veteran kernel of organizers and militants).[20]

The Party also moved, step by step, to reorganize the fraternal side of the movement. The decisive break with Socialist fraternalists left behind thousands of sincere activists with no meaningful differences on the crucial questions the fraternal organizations dealt with—camp facilities, language schools, hall maintanence and the like. But the new International Workers Order did bring the assorted groups under a single umbrella, for the first time. Fraternal leaders could meet with each other (albeit under the watchful eye of Party regulars), discuss differences and work out strategy. At first the IWO's top leadership, veterans of the sectarian days, held back the eager identification of the ethnic activists with their communities. By the later 1930s, younger and more flexible replacements gave the activists freedom to coordinate the increasingly impressive network. From urban neighborhoods to industrial villages, the Bronx to coaltown Pennsylvania, the IWO flourished in a hundred different ways. It proved, far more than the Party proper, that Communists could be unfanatical, ordinary working people uplifted by their special commitments.

The insurrectionary fever largely passed by 1933–34. Although the evidence appeared tardily in the official publications, Party activists had learned many difficult lessons. The futility of ultra-revolutionary language had been driven home, and the go-it-alone spirit vanquished. Wiser heads already observed that Party activity made more sense in concert with other forces of various kinds. Party functionaries might work out high level relations with a Father Divine in Harlem, or later on, that once-notorious red-baiter, United Mine Workers leader John L. Lewis. Local Party members made less formal but no less important arrangements with non-Communist fraternal societies equally enthusiastic for industrial unionism or Social Security. So neatly did the shift in Party policy coincide with the international changes in Communism that contemporary observers, and later on historians, believed there had been a mechanical transfer of ideas from Moscow to New York, Chicago or Detroit. In truth, the reorientation of the Party's mass work was undertaken for hard-headed practical reasons and against the resistance of such old guard sectarian leaders as William Z. Foster. The moving forces for change within the Party, mostly younger activists, had maneuvered Party practice at local or regional levels before the official shift of position. They had already, almost imperceptively, begun the march to the Popular Front.

Young Party leaders, and the anonymous factory or community activists who supported them, carried the energy of Communists into American life. But their secondary mission, to transform the Party into a mechanism appropriate for an American Socialism, could not succeed. They shared with the most credulous neophyte the myths of Russian democracy and well-being, and of Stalin's heroic world-revolutionary leadership—indeed, had they not believed, they could not have remained in positions of power. Second, they unwittingly absorbed the habits of their predecessors in dealing with the Party faithful and the public. Again, they had little choice: most of the leadership slots had already been taken by the mid-1930s, so that official policy would not bear their imprimatur in any case. But they were compelled to battle blindly against the old sectarian preoccupations. Their consequent enthusiasm for influence outside the Party prepared them to accept almost uncritically the promise of alliances with the New Deal. They had no alternative.

Only for a moment, during the first appearance of disillusionment with the New Deal and the phenomenal appearance of one mass strike after another in 1934, did they hesitate. Perhaps one could yet imagine Soviets in Toledo, or Minneapolis, or San Francisco? That fantasy ended with the 'Second New Deal' and the consolidation of the Democratic Party around Roosevelt in the approaching 1936 elections. By now, Comintern directives coincided with the sentiments of immigrants stirred to vote for a first time.

Over the next half-dozen years, as with Communist parties elsewhere, American Communists were transformed from a persecuted pariah into a semi-legitimate left-of-center force within national politics. The Popular Front attracted considerable sympathy on the left flank of the Democratic Party, which needed a ginger group committed to rally constituents and bring out working class and ethnic voters. Meanwhile, the Communist cadre supplied the CIO with an indispensable shock-force of organizers and functionaries, willing to risk death for their cause but also-ready to discipline the ranks in the name of larger social objectives. With big labor victories in maritime and electrical manufacturing, in particular, Communists and their close friends thus became the leaders of some of the most powerful new unions.

With allies in upper echelons of state Democratic Parties and even the White House staff, they had *entre* to the powerful on a variety of issues. They simultaneously became a major force in the Black community, especially Harlem, and a significant if less central element among Mexican-Americans, Asian-Americans and other racial minorities. Among a multitude of European immigrant communities their influence swelled to new heights. By the brink of the disastrous Stalin-Hitler Pact of 1939, the Party seemed poised to resume the victory march of American Socialism from the point left off by Debs in 1912.

But at the very peak of Communist influence, the riddle of Marxism and American life seemed more baffling than ever before. How were the proletariat and its allies to transmute modern production and social relations into a successful movement for socialism? How would support for the CIO and the New Deal open the road to revolution? To what extent was the new-found influence of the Party in direct proportion to its low-keying of anti-capitalist demands? A veteran of the Popular Front recalls that in the Party's adaptations to the complexities of the New Deal political climate, the sense of definite transition disappeared. In turn, this loss 'intensified the powerful and ever-present pressures for total immersion in the issues of the moment with the Socialist vision relegated to the back of the mind or the tail of an omnibus resolution.'[23] The vision of the Soviet Union as prototype for Socialism was partly to blame. But obsession with this identification also disguised a deeper and more indigenous problem.

Not even the Communists' most forceful radical opponents, uncompromised by blind faith in Moscow, could provide a strong alternative vision to the emergent mass production-mass consumption synthesis heralded by Fordism and democratized in the promise of the New Deal. No basis for a Socialist constituency seemed to exist outside the Popular Front, and no cultural prefiguration of the new society within the old seemed to be possible except the *idea*—no longer as revolutionary as twenty years previous—of a radical modernism. Some of the Communists' opposite numbers renewed, for one last time, the old Socialist faith in patient education of workers and defense of the unions against all political manipulations. Others, primarily Trotskyists, identified with the revolt of rank-and-file workers against the union bureaucracy and raised the problematic of self-organization. At their most lucid, they began to apprehend that Popular Front Marxism reflected the very triumph of the new middle class that Fraina and Walling had warned against. That perception had, inevitably, more intellectual than political significance.

Socialists thus floundered while 'left' and 'right' opposition, Trotskyists and Lovestoneites—together no more than a thousand in number—increasingly exchanged the Marxist view of civil society for versions of syndicalism. The world outside the factory lost its importance save for the cadre, while the world inside the factory, beyond the day of successful unionization, hinged upon authentic democracy and/or 'good leadership.' No doubt the centrality of the labor movement and the limits of their respective forces scarcely permitted any wider perspective. But they narrowed their own strategic terms as well. (An acerbic internal critic of Trotskyists wrote that they would be more interested in 'the Ukrainian Question' in the Ukraine than in Detroit.)[24] Syndicalist terms so dominated any debate within the left that still different views, other and more eclectic efforts, tended to be swallowed and digested.

The attempt to argue from educational socialism to trade union democracy and back again fell to the Socialist Party and to Norman Thomas as the final champion of a lost politics. Thomas, more influential among YMCA staff workers than industrial workers, essentially convicted capitalism on a morals charge. He doubted the intentions of the New Deal, even while he sought a creative use of the state not so qualitatively removed from Rooseveltian programs of the 'Second New Deal.' Running a strong 1932 presidential campaign, Thomas evoked a great moral response, especially on the more elite campuses, and a last burst of Socialist fervor from the ethnic constituencies who for a variety of reasons had disdained the Communist Party.

Thomas himself cut a most impressive figure. But in one of the American left's true misfortunes, the crusading orator could carve out no version of socialism between liberalism and Leninism. Another age might have made him a lesser version of Eugene Debs or Martin Luther King, Jr., rather than Middle America's pesky conscience.

Generational conflicts precipitated the determinant crisis in Thomas' effort to restore Socialist influence. The grizzled Germans, Jews, Slavs, Finns and scattered Yankees who maintained, to this point, a sizeable press and neighborhood presence (including several vital electoral operations at the local level), had next to nothing in common with the restless, semi-bohemian Socialist youth.

Fresh-faced intellectuals and union activists made numerous contributions, among them the mobilization of students and the

unemployed, the support of southern tenant farmers, the formation of a Christian Socialist bloc and the brief revival of a revolutionary press (the weekly *Socialist Call*). But they had no source
of cohesion like the Communists' faith in Russia or the Party,
and no firmer ideology than did Thomas. The more they pressed
for a renewal of Socialist dynamism, the more their uncertain
initiatives rattled the old faithful. By 1936, a parting of ways had
become inevitable. Unlike the Popular Front Communists, who
maintained their ambivalence even in their enthusiasm, Socialist
ethnics went over to Roosevelt with both feet. Youngsters
scrambled for alternatives.

The Socialist Party still had a historic role, but now as a source
for other movements. A bloc of militant Socialist youth became
Trotskyist converts, many of them soon rebels from Trotsky's
own orthodoxy. Old time Socialists briefly joined Communists
and independent radicals in New York's American Labor Party.
But the struggle of the Socialists for a non-Leninist Marxism had
disappeared. Increasingly, especially for the Socialist following
in the garment trades, anti-Communism became the overriding,
obsessive issue. The *Jewish Daily Forward* and *The New Leader*
would be the first liberal publications to call for the Cold War.
Disillusionment with the Soviet Union and defense of existing
union styles of leadership fit an acceptance of what William
English Walling (himself a convert to conservative unionism in
the 1920s) had called State Capitalism. In less overtly ideological
terms, it signified the acceptance of Socialist ideas as immigrant
ideology, the assimilation of subsequent generations into democratic capitalism. A surprising number of onetime rebels from
the 1930s Socialist movement later found themselves reconciled
to this logic and even to Ronald Reagan.

The logic of these positions dovetailed with 'right-
communism.' The Lovestone group, reduced after their expulsion from the Communist Party to a corporals' guard of
intellectuals and labor functionaries, devoted almost a decade to
working out versions of critical Leninism. Still expecting the
Communist party to reform itself, and anticipating no revolutionary alternative to it, their foremost figures entered the
bosom of the union leadership (most especially ILGWU, Local 22,
for a time the largest union local in the nation). Unlike the old
Socialists, they emphasized not education (the Lovestoneites'
own small-circulation newspaper, *Workers Age*, perhaps the
most literate of the left's weeklies, was aimed at intellectuals and
a cadre) but industrial union management. Their driving purpose
became the resistance of Communism. Defenders of such unions

against Communist insurgency. Lovestone's leadership, spread through cadre to other unions, increasingly embodied an enclave mentality. Himself announcing a series of ideological shifts over the later 1930s, Lovestone explained (much as the cigarmakers' Adolph Strasser had sixty years earlier) that all social change had to come through unions, and that this would be possible only through stability. In this perspective, Will Herberg (one of Lovestone's chief ideological lieutenants and later a conservative theologian) concluded all other American radicalism had been exotic, unhealthy and unreal. Sorge could not have put it better. A few more steps and Lovestone would become architect of the American labor movement's international anti-Communist policy, extending the defense of what was presumed to be true American unionism onto the world scale. Through Lovestone's lieutenant, Irving Brown, this Rogue Leninist intervention lasted into the 1980s.

In lieu of these defaults and right turns, the left version of labor radicalism landed squarely in the Trotskyist camp. This destiny stemmed not only from Trotskyism's particular roots within the 1920s Communist milieu (where James Cannon and Scandinavian-American left leader Arne Swabeck had operated in the midwestern, trade unionist faction) but also according to the space remaining open in Marxist movements. The new Workers Party, founded in 1934 (with less than a thousand members) by the joining of Trotskyists and the Brookwood Labor School-connected labor reformers around minister-educator A.J. Muste, proclaimed in almost DeLeonist fashion that the revolutionary movement would develop internally in the working class, albeit with the help of educated cadre. It was a sensible approach, given American conditions and the consciousness of workers engaged in a series of dramatic industrial strikes prefiguring the CIO. The goal of revolution would be not the 'dictatorship of the proletariat' but workers' councils, self-educated (according to A.J. Muste, in a proposal that echoed Wobbly logic) through understanding of machine production. This stratum of activists and ideologues lacked the resources to rival the Communist Party or even the fading Socialist Party. Besides, Trotskyist leaders had other plans: invasion of the Socialists.

Trotskyists and their version of Leninism successfully swallowed up the labor reformers and vigorous Socialist youngsters. But years of maneuvers only netted them different personnel, not increased numbers even in a period of wide radicalization. They appeared, as Trotsky himself complained at his influential Minneapolis truckdrivers' cadre, themselves quintessential syndicalists of the 1930s: battling Communists in numerous unions to restrain the bureaucratic devolution of the CIO organizations, playing important roles in various localities, but keeping a generally low political profile among workers. They gained a reputation, as an Akron, Ohio, supporter said, of 'thinking that everything was going to be solved by economic organization.'[27] At best, they could propagandize against the Communists' failure to break with the New Deal after Roosevelt's rightward turn in 1938. Their fresh opportunity for intervention (amid their own repeated, almost debilitating factional warfare) arrived with the Second World War and the Communist support of the No Strike Pledge. Trotskyism did have a final major theoretical contribution to make, in the tradition of syndicalism which passed through Leninism while retaining its own peculiar identity. That contribution can be understood best by returning to the Communists' emerging dilemmas.

Shadows on the Wall

One straw in the wind, years before the Comintern's Popular Front declaration, was the self-criticism of the party and even of the bureaucracy which followed in the wake of expulsions and the midst of the futile insurrectionism. one of the most perceptive and independent-minded of Communist functionaries reflected in 1931 that in the Party, as in American life at large, 'workers are looked upon as "hands," cogs in the machine— mere machine tenders—the system that gives great power to the executives and stifles the masses.'[29] Against this healthy impulse stood the myth of what some called the 'perfect inner apparatus,' the bureaucracy's faith in its own special ability to create a comprehensive Marxist logic through an intellectual forced march, the massive reading of Stalin's *Foundations of Leninism* in ultra-didactic methods so suggestive of Mao's Little Red Book some thirty years later. One tendency recognized the limits of a pre-determined logic, the other gloried in apparent limitlessness.

It is fascinating to observe how these notions worked out in practice for the industrial workers on the periphery of the Party's ideological influence. From the first days when the mostly foreign-born industrial workers began publishing their own 'shop papers' during the later 1920s, a new logic had been introduced into Marxist politics. William Z. Foster's own marginal Syndicalist League of North America had, more than ten years earlier, urged a non-ideological approach to labor agitation, but within the existing unions. Even in their third period 'dual unions', Communists implemented a practical policy of commenting on day-to-day complaints without drawing revolutionary conclusions. In the short run, this gave the local Communist visibility as an activist and not a mere left-wing crank. In the long run, it raised the troubling question of just what role Marxist ideas and Marxist organization could ultimately play in the labor movement.[29]

Until the Popular Front took hold, the prospect for industrial insurrection held these opposite impulses in tandem, more and less prominent according to the particular union situation. Where Communists fought bitter wars, in the garment trades, the appeal (especially to Jewish workers) had always been tinged with theory, with support for the Soviet Union and with the influence of the left's Yiddish institutions. In short, Marxist politics came as a package. In steel, auto, electric, rubber and other major sections of industry, Communist efforts at independent left unions operated sometimes like Wobbly minorities had, issuing leaflets and calling strikes without local consensus. Communists gradually came to support the issues, wages-and-hours or 'control' matters such as work rules which most stirred workers, and to tailor their general policy of work within or outside the AFL according to the best option for viable organization. Here the ideological perspective fell away almost entirely, save for the never-ending effort to recruit a minority into the life and duties of the Party. The more successful the union organization, the ever-smaller the proportion of *Daily Worker*, to say nothing of *The Communist* or *The Foundations of Leninism*, readers amongst the radicalized workers.[30]

Communists of course might have claimed with justice that events had come upon them so quickly as to make any organic understanding almost impossible. Much of the working class, especially foreign-born and racial minorities, seemed to rush from apathy to New Dealish sympathies with a left-wing tinge, bypassing revolutionary expectations of the old electoral Socialist or syndicalist-Wobbly variety almost entirely. Working-class militancy in the heroic age of the early CIO (1935–1938) might challenge private property in action, but hardly ever in politics. Something more was required to wed Marxist theory with the most important blue-collar reality of the period.

On one level, by the middle to late thirties, the Party had prospered. Over six-hundred shop nuclei published some three hundred newspapers, and nearly a quarter of the 30,000 party membership (as well as many others, several hundred thousand at the least, who felt close to the Party) were concentrated in heavy industry. In those 'pulsative, formative years' of the industrial union movement, a Communist functionary later recalled, 'we had the illusion that an iron bond united party and class'.[31] Workers' bitterness over the failure of the Roosevelt administration to *defend* their right to organize encouraged visions of a labor-political movement that could sweep past the New Deal.

But the 'iron bond' was an illusion. The *Party Organizer*, internal organ for the cadre, was pervaded by the self-criticism that any discussion of Marxism, the Soviet Union, or the nature of the Party, continually retreated to distant priorities. 'Discussion of the Party line' was postponed for weeks while more pressing local activities intervened. The CIO shop papers made the CP's own papers seeming redundant or divisive. The CP fraction around (or against) the union local's leadership replaced the old shop nuclei with a very different movement. Earl Browder later commented realistically that the workers themselves viewed the nuclei in this situation, as 'rival and competition' to their elected leadership. No doubt the Party activists had so many meetings to attend already that they welcomed the relief.[32]

Many older Communists who had maintained their long-standing presence with alternative expectations, and many younger Communists as well, naturally wondered about the deeper meaning of this development. Browder attempted to rationalize the significance of the cadre as concentrated 'technique', the 'process of history' personified. If sympathizers, even of years' standing, now had no particular reason to join and add to their own obligations, it meant that they failed to grasp that no reform effort could be complete without Party building and Party recruitment.[33]

It was a weak answer, as weak as the internal effort to raise quotas on literature distribution, establish a Marxist book club, or convert the unreadable monthly *Communist* into a more lively publication. In New York, the one place where intellectual interests could always be found, even among sections of the proletariat, the Workers School blossomed to some nine thousand members by 1939. A Chicago Workers School was, however, more typical. After a week of attempted theoretical training in 1936, pupils concluded unanimously with their teachers that lessons hereafter should be 'based on a study of immediate problems and issues served to equip the party with a more conscious core of people for active work' rather than upon theoretical generalities. *The Communist* itself reflected these weaknesses on a deep theoretical level. It was read, one critic estimated, by perhaps ten percent of the Party, a figure not surprising given the preponderance of foreign-born until the very late 1930s, and given the sheer dullness of the publication. It improved, but it never ceased to be written for the hardened insider who could wade through old-fashioned slashing polemics, endless didactic exegeses of Lenin and Marx 'updated' to some current question, coupled with sycophantic tributes to current Party leaders.[34]

The early Red Scare of 1939, when Franklin Roosevelt opened the door to government investigations of the then isolationist-minded CP, brought a hint of what would come. Congressional liberals and conservatives joined in passing the Smith and Voorhis acts, providing a rich climate for the House Un-American Activities Committee and its state equivalents. The Party's removal from the ballot in many states for the 1940 election signaled, again, that it stood in some sense outside civil society despite all its efforts to enter the mainstream. Defeats at the highest levels of several CIO unions, and severe government repression of defense plant strikes in which the Party figured, revealed a precariousness even in its strongest centers.

The confusion of theory reflected that of practice, and tended to become an unconscious grappling with the ghosts of radicalism past. The *Communist*, at its peak prestige in the late 1930s, featured Alexander Bittelman's essays on current topics and William Z. Foster's categorical ruminations. These were the deepest political thinkers American Communism could claim.

Bittelman, a Party veteran of the earliest days who came into his own during the Popular Front, became the key spokesman of strategic adaptation. He deftly turned Marxism into a realistic pressure-group perspective tied to the immediate position of the Soviet Union, but also to the changes the New Deal precipitated in the American political system. He interpreted working class movements as such with somewhat more unease except when they could be comfortably treated as the raw muscle behind a power-bloc. Bittelman, that is to say, repelled every form of syndicalism. By dint of faith in the forces of transformation, he sustained a sense of a potential transition beyond Roosevelt, unspecifiable but nonetheless real. This was, in fact, the Communist version of social democratic theory. In sophistication if not consistency, it marked an improvement upon the earlier thinking of reform Socialists. But it was woefully inadequate for the prospects of American radicalism and the problems soon to engulf the left.

Foster, the fundamentalist, sought to keep the Party's shift within Bolshevik bounds. Rather than opposing the Popular Front squarely, as he could not do, he directed his sharpest blows against the memory of syndicalism and against its palpable continuation in all forms. He had the grey image of Party discipline for an alternative, but this made little sense after 1935. He thus returned ritualistically to old categories, fumbling for some new insight. That insight could not be found within the history of the Communist parties, either in the Soviet Union or the United States. He had hit a dead end.[35]

Here stood the tortured saga of American Communism. The very success of the Party since the mid-1930s affirmed Leninism in a way Communist leaders had never anticipated, not as the theory of proletarian insurrection but as a decisive clue to the polycentrist quality of American democracy. Communists had no chance to make the most of the revelation. The simultaneous surge of industrial unionism and the decline of New Deal reformism at home, the approach of world war and the degeneration of the Russian Revolution abroad all diverted attention. In any event, the lack of Party democracy prevented the real lessons learned at the base from transforming the upper echelons.

Leninist formulae for a social democratic practice merely postponed the Communist Party's day of reckoning. Neither Social Democracy nor Leninism spoke to the deeper radical impulses that a young Brooklyn Communist touched while leafletting Ebbets Field for the integration of the Dodgers. Neither encompassed the protean rebellion of workers restless at their new CIO taskmasters. Neither could chart the transition through and beyond the New Deal to a different America. Communists lacked the self-confidence, independence from Russian imperatives, and the background to think through, let alone carry through, that kind of program. Perhaps Socialism had little prospect within capitalism about to recover through the expansion of the behemoth state. But the left would pay a terrible price for the American Communists' failure to face the issues of Socialism and democracy. No one paid more heavily than Communists who realized how much precious time they had lost.

5

Rise of the Culture Critique, 1925–1940

'The most characteristic sign of our times,' a prominent socialist wrote in 1924, 'is the lack of confidence in all our pre-War ideals, and especially in our pre-War conception of how we are going to realize our ideals.'[1] This sense of doubt constituted the greatest crisis in the *idea* of socialism that American Marxism had yet experienced. Marxists could no longer console themselves, as they had previously, that American conditions were not yet ripe for the doctrine. The revived strength of capital, increasingly focused upon mass production and industrialized leisure, suggested instead that the moment of socialism had come and gone. Communists had a fierce faith in the young Soviet Union and in their own ultimate destiny. But even the radical intelligentsia could not quell its doubts about the vanished Socialist project. The Depression temporarily blasted confidence in capitalism, but no convincing alternative emerged. Intellectuals would nevertheless contribute much to Marxism in a variety of areas. They could hardly appreciate themselves how great were the odds against their success.

The Marxist thinkers of the 1920s–30s possessed an educational level, and a familiarity with culture in the broadest sense, that their predecessors would have envied. Individuals succeeded in attaining high levels of formal theoretical sophistication. They lacked something more important: the rootedness of previous intellectual generations. Neither the organic ties of their German and Jewish antecedents to segments of the working class nor the grassroots audience of earlier socialistic reform intellectuals could be theirs. Likewise, they remained as a group strikingly out of touch with the rich intellectual legacies. The sentimental, spiritualist native vernacular and the variegated immigrant Marxist approaches to American conditions had been practically lost to collective memory. The literary-political 1910s came down to them fragmented, falsely dichotomized into culture on the one side and class conflict on the other.

The defeat of the American left had suspended the intellectuals in an all-too-familiar political vacuum where popular radicalism seemed the lucky fate of people in another time or place. The task of reconceptualizing socialist prospects under the changed conditions of mass production and mass society found them tragically ill-prepared. Marxist texts and formal training therefore helped them very little in understanding their own milieu and the particular prospects of the white collar worker. Marxist parties offered them a variety of practical experiences, but at a heavier price than most would finally be willing to pay.

Their common source of wisdom was 'Progressive' social science and its methods, the liberal side of contemporary higher education. But the militantly empiricist character, if taken seriously, deepened the all too familiar division between the real and the ideal. This promoted vulgar Marxism in the short run and a corresponding vulgar idealism when radical hopes had been dashed. 'Progressive History', the most radical element of mainstream scholarship, had for instance a valuable muck-raking slant, but by focusing attention upon the misdeeds of the upper classes, it tended to reinforce an economism and a fatal blindness to race. The Progressive currents in philosophy and economics, from Pragmatism to Institutionalism, inclined young radicals toward analogous over-simplifications. With abundant energy and clarity, the radicalized intellectuals thus excoriated the inequities, exploitation, and self-made mythologies of their time. Rarely did their probes satisfy their own intuitive sense of more complex relations between ideas and reality. Nowhere, neither among professed orthodox or heterodox Marxists, did the dialectic find a secure home in America.

Attempts to make literature part of the working class and the working class part of literature symbolized the problematic of the intellectual's place. This bold effort to fill an evident cultural gap on the left and in working-class life had little chance of success and much likelihood of demagogic abuse, because the task itself rested upon archaic assumptions. The projection of intellectual perspectives upon a working class moving away from old-fashioned autodidact styles and away from mainly literary entertainments put the would-be pedagogues in the impossible position of teachers without students. Moreover, the very effort both postponed and ultimately distorted the concern for the cultural sensibility and desires of the intellectuals' own middle class. The links of their own culture (especially under Depression conditions) to the real American working-class experience, a fusion of class, ethnic and mass cultural strains, offered potentially useful ideas. So difficult was it to keep this connection untangled from the political barbed wire that little headway and less mental clarification were registered until the end of the era.

Popular creative artists and writers, folk collectors, musicologists and folklorists had a better time of it. Few guidelines already existed on the left or elsewhere for popular art. That very absence provided breathing space for the cultural innovator. Just as important, the cresting of the left coincided with a swelling interest in anti-fascist, New Deal-inspired national self-recognition. The lack of coherence also took its toll. No one could say what the significance might be, for instance, between Marxism and Black field hollers or Marxism and *Watch On the Rhine*. Practical accomplishments begged the question, as Marxist political breakthroughs among the ethnic and racial groups had begged the question. The folk music revival, which bridged the gap between the activist 1930s and 1960s, outshone all 'proletarian literature' altogether. Hollywood made Humphrey Bogart a more likely candidate than Earl Browder for radical apotheosis. All popular culture accomplishments, moreover, would be recuperable by a liberal anti-Communism no less capable of intoning 'This Land is Your Land' and cheering the US military victory over fascism.

Such a prospect, evident to the Communist Party's critics in the later 1930s, did not render the cultural innovations invalid. But it drew attention to the inadequacy of Marxism as currently understood. The further Marxists succeeded according to the terms available in America, the less did their success seem to depend upon anything resembling the familiar tenets. The same was just as true for the alternative and more cerebral Marxist scenario, the creation of a literary culture. Where this culture assumed life of its own, as in the *Partisan Review*, it seceded from its radical origins. What, then, did the so-called Marxist worldview mean for culture!?

Only rarely did Marxists broach the implications inherent in the originality of the terrain, or the problems raised by the New Deal national-populist discourse. Instead, efforts at culture critique fell into loyal exegesis (doubly constrained by the unavailability of the 'Young Marx' until the 1950s) of the few classic Marxist writings on art and literature, or hasty justifications of an often artificially constructed 'People's Culture', or savage attacks upon the entire Communist cultural position. Real energy and insight went into each of these tasks, but in relation to each other they remained obsessively ideological and self-pleading. They collectively lacked depth and precision.

Timing above all worked against the necessary rethinking of the intellectuals' labors. Irving Howe's lament that the New York Intellectuals arrived 'late' applies to the overwhelming majority of radical thinkers who came of age in the mid-1930s or early 1940s, scarcely setting out their personal agendas before the imagined streamliner of history had turned into a freight car on a spur line leading nowhere. A season or two of youthful Marxist creativity and sometimes intense political involvement would be followed by years of isolation, factional acrimony, and at last the erosion of commitment. This generational experience helped to explain the meanness of subsequent Cold War debates among middle-aged men (and a few women) whose youth seemed to have been devoted to a lost cause. Brilliant essays and well-sculpted novels notwithstanding, only a new social movement could reignite the sense of radical purpose. That new movement would not arrive in time, and when it did, it would not be theirs either.

And yet good piecemeal work had been done. The rough hand of Communist Party influence generally reinforced the intellectuals' original limitations. But contrary to subsequent myths energetically cultivated by neo-conservative intellectuals, the effects were neither predictable nor uniform. The despair and the cynicism which touched upper levels of the American Leninist movements necessarily had an effect upon the radical intelligensia's *elan*, even before Stalinization. Yet America was a big country even for fifty thousand Communists, and the opportunities for radical activists during the 1930s offered a multitude of possible roles. Intellectuals did more than write essays and join committees. In often spontaneous collaborations, they wrote leaflets and edited newspapers for unemployed organizations, union, anti-fascist and Negro rights groups; under-employed and exploited themselves, they also marched and picketed with multitudes of ordinary non-intellectuals.

The radical intellectual had thereby ceased to be an *avis rara* outside the ethnic ghettos. He (more rarely, she) took a front seat in cultural and occasionally political events, wrote brilliantly in magazines ranging from the Communist *New Masses* to the Trotskyist *Partisan Review* to the liberal *Nation* and the *New Republic*, and turned out a large handful of useful books. By indirect statement, by description and by deed, that intellectual had for a time made socialist ideas and ideals part of the American lexicon. Such effort paved the way for those successors who would refuse to tie their criticism to either Cold War camp, and who themselves refused to disappear when radical criticism became highly unpopular. Considering the small and not particularly socialistic class the intellegentsia had been as late as 1920, and what confusion America had passed through, these piecemeal efforts added up.

The full importance of such efforts for the 1940s and 1950s would become clear only in retrospect. At the height of the Cold War, and despite their own political fratricide, radical intellectuals had established their efforts to look at civilization as an organic entirety. Marxist ideas, with a backspin, had made that view possible. Capitalism, it could be now be more clearly understood, did not satisfy *as a way of life*, and the cost it exacted upon the world had proved too dear. The postwar advance of consumerism so readily embraced by the masses contained fresh and, in a philosophical sense, final contradictions. Beneath the surface placidity, millions already knew this, expressed it in their daily behavior far more than in their political action. In such ordinary people's insights and yearnings lay hidden the basis for the new society within the old that Marxists had predicted and searched for. The spectre of atomic annihilation and the traditions of disdain for popular entertainment badly constrained recognition of this subjective development. Yet the trajectory continued. Here in the critique of culture, coupled with the related interpretation of the empire and its manifestations, the future of Marxism would be found.

The Birth of 'Culturalism'

All radical critiques of culture were prefigured in the work of one extraordinary but symptomatic figure, V.F. Calverton, whose worldview his collaborator Samuel Schmalhausen called 'revolutionary culturalism.' Born at the turn of the century, Calverton came of age in time to imbibe the revolutionary hopes of 1917–19, but not to live them as political practice. He could be called the first, and the most prescient, of a generation of latecomers. He is also the prototype of the intellectual as organizer of intellectuals, the jack-of-all-trades generalist, and the social scientist as utopian. In his faults as well as his strengths, he summed up the Marxist intellectual of his generation.

Left intellectuals had, with difficulty and considerable attrition, survived earlier dry periods. But not with the unique prospects for recovery that the 1920s held out. Calverton could rely upon no English-speaking working class constituency of any size, and for that matter, most immigrant Marxists remained distant from his intellectual world. Instead, he spoke to a new white-collar following. Well educated and intensely curious about itself, this group stood on the verge of a cultural radicalism. It now included sprinklings of Blacks politicized by their condition, and a large number of women restive at the limited gains of suffrage. It also included frustrated politicals aplenty, seeking the personal identity of a journal not so different from the identity immigrant workers received from their formidable press. Intellectuals, to put it another way, had become an ethnic group. Calverton encouraged them to meditate on their own nature.[2]

His *Modern Quarterly*, founded in 1923, promised essentially a metaphysics of synthesis for all the new and exciting social sciences: history, anthropology, sociology, psychology and literary criticism. The last had become already during the final years of the old *Masses* a touchstone for a growing dissident intelligentsia. Through the leadership of Calverton and the avant-garde expatriates, criticism became a consolation for world lost, and a laboratory for experimentation with fresh ideas. Never before had such as ostensibly romantic pursuit become self-consciously scientific. Nor had manifestations of intellectual feminism previously played so great a part in the formulation.

In practice, the Marxist analysis of social science had most often diverged sharply from the study of literature, not only because of the different personnel involved but because neither history, economics nor philosophy were expected to 'become proletarian,' *i.e.*, to be written by as well as for the proletariat in anything like the short run. For Calverton and his magazine, aimed at the intelligentsia, the distinction between a proletarian culture and the bourgeois sciences never quite emerged.

Calverton himself reasoned in a common sense fashion that literature would become, had to become, the expression of the masses. Unlike the literary communists at the end of the twenties, he did not purport to create with his scant resources a proletarian literature himself, but to understand the background and current conditions for its future development. Unlike the formal left literary critics, Communists or otherwise, Calverton never intended his literary analysis as an end in itself, but sought rather to make it a symptomatic study of wider society. He unfortunately grasped the Marxist component as a strict materialist perspective. In the words of his friend and confidant, Arthur S. Calhoun, 'literature correlates with social life in as precise a fashion as does government and law . . . art is but a reflex of the economic basis of society.'[3] From that all-too-narrow standpoint, only elaboration remained. Constrained by a mechanical Marxism, Calverton nevertheless acted upon the implications with great vigor. He was hardly (as F. Scott Fitzgerald called him) a 'modern Lecky.' But more than any other Marxist writer, he *tried* to place everything within Marxism's purview.

Calverton's major volumes, *The Newer Spirit* (1926), *Sex in Modern Literature* (1926) and *The Liberation of American Literature* (1932), elaborated a sweeping overview. Literature evolved in three great stages of human culture: the pre-industrial culture dominated by the nobility; the bourgeois culture of the eighteenth and nineteenth centuries; and the proletarian culture from the last quarter of the nineteenth century forward. 'Liberation' signified the step-by-step shedding of past constraints that had prevented the full development of a realistic social literature. American writers needed to lose their 'colonial complex', which relied on English literary models and on a Puritan moralism devastating to subsequent American intellectual methods. Equally they had to shed the repressive sentimentalism of the nineteenth century and to jettison, finally, the petty-bourgeois individualist response to a bourgeois consciousness which had itself only appeared on the stage. Soon, the working class would create its own cultural products, joined by the special folkish elements alive in Black culture and by the freed sexual-social expression of women. This massive 'psychological' preparation for a working-class seizure of power would then be understood in its true significance. The Left (even if Calverton did not bluntly say so) would be revolutionized along the road to a definitive social transformation.

What Calverton called 'sex and the social struggle', the replacement of hypocrisy with frank and easy relations, became the most immediate means at hand to reconcile the smashed promises of the 1910s with the real changes that had taken place in young people's lives. Freudianism, it had already become clear, led as much toward personal adjustment as social change, and toward a rigidity of gender definitions that rivalled Victorianism. Sex had to be studied in relation to social struggle and in direct perception of woman's advance. Calverton and his collaborators on this question, from Havelock Ellis to Waldo Frank, had no ready solutions beyond sex education and open discussion. But they knew freedom could advance no other way.[4]

Altogether, Calverton's ideas constituted an extraordinary advance toward producing a systematized perspective on American life. His project was so ambitious that Marxist cultural critics would not attempt anything on the same scale for decades. It fairly outlined the general objective of the generation just coming to age: to interpret through literature the larger trends in the national culture. Had Calverton not become enmired in factional jousting, he might have reasoned his way considerably further, with the help of the critical commentary he so badly needed from the ranks of the younger intellectuals. Or, even if he had written himself out on the subject, the *Modern Quarterly* might have continued the project on other fronts. The hurried efforts which cost him a lasting reputation speak to the loneliness of the task at the time when he began, and to his manic drive to make sense of tradition before the arrival of the revolutionary crisis.

Later critics would make Calverton a scapegoat for the thirties literary outlook that seemed (in Alfred Kazin's phrase) just another 'totalitarianism in an age of totalitarianisms', a Leninist 'search for fulfillment by the word'. He had become, symbolically, the mixture of political commitment and scholarly indelicacy that soured radicals rejected in their own past. They duly noted the haste and frequent superficiality of his judgements. They had little appreciation for the historic role he played in the creation of radical intellectuals, or for that matter his strident, uncompromising feminism. Such critics judged his work unfairly, as product and not process. Only from hindsight was *The Liberation of American Literature* 'ill-fated' (Kazin's phrase again). It might have been, as it was widely considered at the time, the bold beginning to move *beyond* sloganeering to an authentic cultural understanding.[5]

Besides, Calverton's *Modern Quarterly* (for a few overly ambitious years, the *Modern Monthly*) spoke for him in all its contents, wiser and more eloquently than he could speak himself. Nearly every non-communist radical intellectual of importance appeared in his pages as a welcome friend, a participant in collective effort, a radical intellectual unashamed of being just that. Black intellectuals, for instance, achieved an expansion of their role unimaginable in the communist or Trotskyist press. Anthropologists, sociologists, historians and others from the academic world made themselves heard without either guilt or academic cant. Here, the dream of the *New Review* almost gained fulfillment.

Calverton's project could be sustained, with difficulty, as the Depression changed the issues facing intellectuals. It retreated before the white collar allure of the Popular front. Yet, despite the meanness of Communist attack, only toward the magazine's end did the *Modern Quarterly* become a repository for sectarian response—and never, as in the case of the *Partisan Review*, for the defense of bourgeois ideas or institutions. In that respect alone, Calverton had triumphed.

Calverton sought to leap over his own limits. Why didn't the real-life proletariat coincide with the recent fictional version, or for that matter why did American literature's manifold curious and dark sides not coincide with Calverton's neat schema? He fell back upon a notion he called 'cultural compulsives', the *deus ex machina* Marxists would later rename 'false consciousness' and which in explaining away everything unpleasant resolved nothing at all. Calverton's theories shaded into an uncomfortable but typical contemporary intellectuals' belief that 'psychological conditions' (in the popular social science version, 'cultural lag') were now the main obstacle to Socialism. Other than the often-predicted mass disillusionment with capitalism, he had no particular idea of how the psychological conditions might change. If Leninism for the activists became a theory of will to power, for Calverton and his crowd Marxism tended to be reduced to a tool for studying 'group behavior' whose objective conditions were to be accounted for only by unspecified mediations. Compared to vulgar Marxism, this was still a heuristic notion, and in the pages of his magazine there was encouragement to the kind of independent thinking that could take place nowhere else. But without more concrete analysis into the sources of group thinking and its relation to the steadily emerging mass culture, Calverton's insights lay fallow.[6]

In the narrow sense, Communist abuse destroyed Calverton, their annihilating attacks upon his independence leaving him only a fringe audience of anti-Stalinist intellectuals who mostly enrolled in the Trotskyist movement or moved steadily away from politics altogether. In a larger sense, the specific project that the *Modern Quarterly* had launched in the early 1920s had failed with the Crash, and would revive in more sophisticated forms only after the Second World War. The metaphysical super-science he sought became less tenable as the novelty of the mores explored by modern psychology and anthropology was displaced by the dismal realities described by economics: the destroyed subjectivity, the ruined middle and lower class lives of the Depression. Feminism, a conceptual key to the entire theoretical edifice, faded entirely, leaving in its wake a forgotten vision and a Freudianism no less mechanical than the Stalinist 'boy and girl meet tractor' which later intellectuals so ridiculed. When Calverton died an early death in 1940, he had written the first installment of a projected trilogy on a subject carrying him back to the other side of the old reform-Marxist duality: American Utopianism.[7]

Future Socialist intellectuals would have no choice but to repeat Calverton's journey through the social science of culture back to the wellsprings of revolutionary faith. But few realized how thoroughly he had trekked the course. Calverton's project failed not because of its inherent unworthiness, but because the lessons of previous radical generations had been lost almost entirely. No proper Marxist basis for understanding the complex problems of modern society had ever been laid. The contrast between rising expectations from existing Marxist texts and indifference toward the now forgotten Feminism expressed as vividly as any other phenomenon in society the depth of the problem. Calverton, too, unable to confront the sources of the difficulty, had written on the wind.

The major Calvertonian intellectual developments, if they may be called that, took place not in the ideological sparring arena of literature at all, but where social science methods and radical objectives met on less contested ground. By and large, what passed for Marxist thinking could be more accurately placed somewhere between the margins of Progressive thought—Charles Beard, V. L. Parrington and John Dewey—and a rough understanding of Marxian economics. The main proponents were, almost without exception, men (virtually no women) on the outside of Left party politics, younger members of a growing specialized academic world seeking political verification. Their methodological ambition and their political marginality marked them from beginning to end.

In each field, ambitious syntheses foundered on the difficulty of reconciling Marxist theories with contemporary reality as well as academic orthodoxy. The authors never quite sparked the critical discussion on the Left that they expected. After political conditions changed, they returned chastened, almost without exception, to the familiarity and warmth of mainstream American thought: on one side to the pragmatism and empiricism of the social sciences; on the other, to the aestheticism of high culture. The handful of hard-line political intellectuals differed little methodologically from these others when they tackled their monographic subjects, relying upon their own intuitions and formal training. They, too, failed to close the gap that had steadily expanded since the early years of Socialist educational and theoretical projects, between popular knowledge and specialized information.

All but forgotten, the ill-fated cultural-political *wunderkind* Louis Fraina resurfaced after Comintern misadventures in the 1920s as economist Lewis Corey, ripe for another tragic intellectual encounter with the left. The one leading political survivor of the heady theoretical adventures in early Communism—albeit no longer a Communist—he struggled to come to terms with the great economic questions posed by the Depression. The result read like an unconscious synthesis of Louis Boudin and A. M. Simons.[8]

The Decline of American Capitalism (1934) presented six hundred rambling pages of statistics and analyses intended to uncover the roots of crisis. Corey treated overproduction as the contemporary manifestation of Marx's Labor Theory of Value. Leaning heavily upon Charles Beard's non-class interpretation of American history, he detected the intrusion of monopoly into the post-frontier economy, its effects combatted by purgative crises until the turn of the century. Afterwards, prosperity appeared increasingly artificial. By the mid-1920s, with long-run exceptional factors exhausted and demand rising more slowly than productivity, prosperity relied upon speculation. The Crash issued in a period when state intervention aggravated the crisis. The American Dream had come to an end, confirming Marxian hypotheses.[9]

Corey's attempted comeback provoked unforseen Communist polemics. His partial reconciliation with marginal economics and even more his heretical suggestion that American problems might be resolved within the national context rather than in the greater contradiction between socialism and capitalism, *i.e.*, between the Soviet Union and the USA, provoked a Party pamphlet, distributed along with the *Decline* at Left bookstores as an antidote—an intellectual first in Communist history. What might have been hailed as Americanized theory twenty years earlier, became, in effect, an instance of nationalist revisionism. Moreover, a few years later, after the change in Party line, *Decline* was seen as *too* radical for its charges of proto-fascism in the New Deal.

Crisis of the Middle Class (1936), almost a Popular Front book (Corey was invited to edit a special *New Masses* issue on the middle class, but withdrew when it became clear that he would not exercise full editorial control), revealed him en route from Marxian ideas to uncertain alternatives. Later a militantly anti-communist Socialist and professor at Antioch College, Corey repeatedly sought, without much public recognition and with less influence on the Left, to refashion a democratic approach to economics and politics. He died awaiting deportation and attempting to write a biography of America's first feminist utopian, Francis Wright. Like Calverton, he devoted his final energies to searching for the road back.[10]

Contemporary philosophy offered another example of a theoretical minefield, in this case because Communists made so many claims and, with few exceptions, knew so little. Lenin's *Materialism and Empirio-Criticism*, first published in English in 1927, had set out to destroy interpretations based on spiritual faith and to prove human perception an unmediated 'copy' of the real world rather than a fiction of consciousness. Stalin's *Dialectical Materialism* presented a yet more mechanical scheme used by the Americans to attack idealism. Non-Diamat Marxism, as particularly represented by Korsch and Lukács, had been roundly condemned in Russia and remained untranslated into English. But it had influenced at least one young American philosopher: Sidney Hook.

Hook, a Dewey student who had helped translate Lenin's work, argued among academic philosophers that Lenin had simply borrowed Engels' 'copy theory', thereby sacrificing the balance Marx had achieved between sensationalist empiricism and absolute idealism, and thus falling into the trap of claiming that ideas merely reflect objective laws of nature and history. Such a scheme left no room for conscious intervention into history. In *Towards An Understanding of Karl Marx* (1933) and *From Hegel to Marx* (1935), Hook broadened the criticism by rooting his alternative in the hitherto almost unknown (in the USA at any rate) Young Marx. Marx's concept of alienation allowed him a view of praxis that authorized a recovery of self as an agent in history.[11]

This was more than a keen reading of Marxist philosophical origins. It was, potentially, a thrust against dialectical materialism as a fatalistic and presumptuous theory of omniscience, and an argument for Marxism as an open system. Hook unhappily failed to reach that conclusion when he returned to his own Pragmatist origins, holding that Marxist doctrines had no objective content. Marxism became, then, a corrective to Deweyism, an alternative means of structuring social engineering to create the new society.

Hook's subsequent move to the Right evolved out of the inner consistency of this Pragmatism. Understandably, he began looking upon Marxism in power as non-rationalist, a feature which he connected to the emerging Third World and its messy messianics: Russia became the center of a neo-barbarism embracing all the remaining barbarians (*i.e.*, those seeking to escape the grip of neo-colonialism). Hook's defense of the Enlightenment entailed the command form of society, limitation of civil liberties where abused by subversives, and the championing of business as the logical opponent to Communism in the world. Hook, who denounced the return of religion, embraced the religion of capital, the indigenous myth of the West.

The hypocritical Communist attack upon the earlier Hook, however, did focus the issue of methodology as the Party saw it: a true Marxist would join the Party, therefore political renegade Hook (a non-party Trotskyist) had demonstrated his methodological renegacy. Trotsky himself proposed the same line of reasoning at the end of the decade, defending Marxism against his own disillusioned American disciples by assaulting them as personally petty-bouregois. The uniform and uncritical celebration of Engels' *Dialectics of Nature*, published in English for the first time in 1939, showed the ideological conformity amongst the Left regarding the fine print of the founding fathers. There was no room for equivocation on Marxian science here, even for the well-intentioned. Rejection of the slightest detail tended to produce, in actuality, the self-fulfilling party prophecy of the heretic's flight from Marxism entirely.[12]

In history proper, the great field of Socialist exposition if not of theoretical sophistication, the Progressive historical legacy continued to dominate except where Marxists made original contributions (notably, in Black history). By the end of the 1930s, Earl Browder was warning young Communists against sneering at Charles Beard. Popular Front Communism had itself come around to Beard rather than Beard to it; Browderism had nothing better to substitute for the democratic struggle of contending interests. This was quite an evolution, but one common to virtually all Marxists.

There were good positive reasons for the historical shift away from orthodox Marxism. V. L. Parrington's *Main Currents of American Thought* (1927–30), by no means Marxist, schooled nearly every young radical in the richness of intellectual culture and the ferocity of debate even within the bourgeois framework of American history. Parrington failed in many particulars, as the aesthete ex-Marxists-gone-New-Critics would tirelessly observe during the next two or three decades, but his intentions could not be doubted. Neither, for that matter, could those of Charles Beard, a truly public figure in American life as no historian had been before or since. His basic histories of the nation, written with Mary Beard, had a crude economic sensibility and no concept of working class, Blacks, or for that matter any other non-genteel presence beyond the yeomanry. But the Beards' polemics against the elder and modern Alexander Hamiltons possessed an authority no contemporary Marxist could match. Thus Bertram Wolfe, probably the leading Communist intellectual in the 1920s, argued that the Beards' and Parrington's writings marked the civilization's 'growing self-awareness . . . the beginning of inner activity, of introspection, of consciousness of self'. Communists felt so themselves.[13]

But they were desperately unable to examine critically and to build upon that Progressive legacy. The proof lay in the all-important 'Negro Question', for here the unique Communist perspective on American history could take its full measure. Communist scholarship, notably that of young Herbert Aptheker, discovered slave revolts where there had been believed to be none. The larger meaning of this discovery remained clouded in political mystery. Had slaves essentially lacked (as was argued in the first important Communist history text, Lithuanian-American leader Anthony Bimba's *History of the American Working Class* (1928) a *vanguard* to bring them to success? Why had Northern workers, and for that matter Southern workers, failed to support them energetically? Why had they failed to win equal admission into the 'nation'? In the old reductive Marxism, the last and critical question could not be asked because only classes were recognized as poltical agents; in the emerging Popular Front Marxism, by contrast, the positive embrace of Jeffersonian-Lincolnian traditions made any harsh answer impossibly painful.

Marx himself, in his writings on the American Revolution and Civil War, already combined national and class categories to a certain ambiguous degree. But American Marxists had seen the connection of class and nation in an historical way only when they took the road away from orthodoxy. The pressures of nationality questions during the late 1930s became overwhelming—save for the smaller movements, such as Trotskyism, which simply chose to deny them in favor of old-fashioned, abstract internationalism. The official Communist position moved toward bourgeois history. Foremost theorist Alexander Bittelman confessed that when he discovered Frederick Jackson Turner's Frontier Thesis in 1939 he began to 'see the light of day' concerning the duality of capitalist and democratic traditions. A great space opened to the left of the Popular Front, a space where someone would inevitably come to identify the Turnerian thesis of inevitable expansion, the 'American Assumption' of individual economic advancement, as the curse of the world's oppressed.[14]

The groundwork had therefore been laid for the most important methodological dialogue about Marxism in the thirties, neither literary nor economic nor philosophical but historical: the left's stake in the American heritage. W. E. B. DuBois, who had educated the Black American about modern ideas and race pride, and had denounced Communist tactics as recently as the Scottsboro Case, had also subtly, steadily, embraced Marxism in unprecedented ways. Communist orthodoxy, mirror of loyal Marxism since the 1870s, found the DuBoisian view almost impossible to assimilate.

Here, the limits of every Marxism, emphatically including Leninism as it had been understood, stretched and began to give way. At the base of the magnificent edifice of DuBois' monumental study, *Black Reconstruction* (1936), was the explosive assertion that the failure of US *labor* to throw itself behind the Black struggle had been an international calamity, for 'the world wept and is still weeping and blind with tears of blood' from the consequences. Unlike the Beardian (and most of the older Socialist) history that treated Blacks as passive agents of a voracious bourgeoisie, and unlike the Communist efforts to add in Blacks as a revolutionary afterthought, DuBois looked to Blacks as the central figures in the American historic melodrama, the key to the unique nature of the society.

DuBois had been gesturing in the direction of this conclusion, in a very general sense, since his earlier study of the slave trade and its consequences upon both the South and North. But the effect of the First World War in revealing Europe's bankruptcy, together with the impact of the Russian Revolution in throwing up new forces on the side of the colonial peoples, forced DuBois to re-examine Radical Reconstruction as a turning point in Western history. With pardonable exaggeration, he called it 'the finest effort to achieve democracy for the working millions which this world had ever seen . . . a tragedy that beggared the Greek . . . an upheaval of humanity like the Reformation and the French Revolution . . . .'

DuBois showed a certain clumsiness of categories, interpreting the massive slave abandonment of the plantations during the conflict as a 'general strike', the strongest term he could discover for a concerted and decisive mass action. The notion of Reconstruction state governments as dictatorships of the proletariat likewise rings strangely, recalling the kind of jargon the Communists at their worst moments misapplied. But these miscoruptions were hardly the issue that vexed DuBois' detractors.[15]

The theoretical implications that could be seen so clearly by DuBois at the time, and which reflected so badly on white radicals of whatever affiliation, touched at the core of orthodox Marxism's limitations in the United States. DuBois had written in 1921 that the Russian Revolution might indeed be the key event in modern history—and yet still not be demonstrably the answer to the Color Question. Neither its Vanguard Party or its millenarian proletarianism were self-evidently applicable. The history of Blacks in the USA and in the colonial world did not have to fit into the Marxist context; Marxism had to fit into theirs or lose its relevance, most especially in the United States. Like Richard Wright, whose *Native Son* provoked contrary reviews in the Communist press and made party functionaries exceedingly nervous, DuBois thus insisted upon a test of group subjectivity which Marxists of almost every variety found impossible to understand, let alone accept. Decades later, Ralph Ellison would analyze the problem as an unwillingness, perhaps an inability, to see Blacks as more than symbols or symptoms, rather than an extremely complex part of a complex society moving along their own trajectory.[16]

Sadly, Progressive history, despite its bourgeois origins and indifference to class, served the existing worldview of Marxists better. The nineteenth century the Progressives had interpreted thus purportedly showed social movements with a primitive, unfinished character—naturally, because these movements lacked Marxian science. The successful rule of past elites made perverse sense to a self-styled vanguard, rulers of the future. C.L.R. James's writings on the West Indies already published in Britain (but not the United States) had pointed to slave activity and its modern equivalent, the Garvey Movement, as manifestations of Black self-consciousness. The Marxist left, from

Trotskyists to Lovestoneites, remained virtually unmoved.

This intellectual climate produced *Reconstruction—The Battle for Democracy*, by James S. Allen, the Communists' leading (white) expert on black history. Written in part to 'correct' DuBois, the book referred only obliquely to northern labor's limitations, and put forward a rather modest version of southern Blacks' contributions to American democracy. This was no outright polemic, and Allen had in fact done everything himself from street agitational work in Harlem to serious research on nineteenth century Black life. Sincerity was not the question, but rather how far any of the official versions of Marxism could yield ground to Black nationalism.

Black Communists of that era, looking back from the wisdom of old age, recall that the prestige enjoyed by Black history in Communist circles significantly influenced them and circulated through the educated Black community. But something limited their consolidation of this advance. Communist solidarity with Blacks was grounded less in theoretical or political analysis than in a moral critique which Marxism could not absorb without transforming doctrine at large. No one, save perhaps a few stubborn Black nationalists forever facing expulsion from the Party, believed that transformation possible.[17]

Literary Communism

Ironically, the major concentration of the intellectuals fell far worse victim to the same basic ills, albeit expressed in very different ways. Literature, not in the Calvertonian sense of culture critique but rather literature as symbol and substance of American ideas, reigned supreme for two generations without supplying any satisfactory solution to the problems radicals pursued. Not that good work failed to be produced. But the politicization of the context clouded the discussion at every point. Neither modernism nor its presumed opposite, literature by and for the working class, was the monopoly of any political faction, claims notwithstanding. Stalinist, Trotskyist, Socialist and aesthete intellectuals shared the same methodological dilemmas and the same world that first encouraged, then shattered radical dreams. The intellectuals' own marginal status reinforced the air of unreality that surrounded sectarian bickering in the eyes of an America which neither knew nor cared about such fine points.

Calverton's personal style, the sheer intellectual labor of anticipating the class-radical merger of interests and sympathies ahead, grew increasingly less satisfying after the politically passive mid- and later 1920s. *The Liberator*, which succeeded the suppressed *Masses* and attained a monthly circulation of 60,000 at one point, briefly achieved a balance of avant-garde spirit with popular journalism about Soviet Russia. By the early 1920s, both had lost much of their popular allure. When William Z. Foster wrote privately that a revolutionary movement could never be built on the basis of such a publication, he was regrettably correct. The fading I.W.W.'s *Industrial Pioneer*, or the *Liberator*'s Yiddish Communist equivalent, *The Hammer*, or even the N.A.A.C.P.'s well-circulated *Crisis* in DuBois' hands, had working class links and a continuing sense of purpose beyond the *Liberator*'s capacity.[18]

The *New Masses*, formed in 1926 with an openly Communist leadership but with a policy of a 'literary NEP' that enrolled such independent intellectuals as Waldo Frank, Van Wyck Brooks and Lewis Mumford on its editoral board, showed the uncertainty of direction. Sympathies notwithstanding (and the higher Communist bureaucrats had precious little sympathy for such independent intellectuals beyond their immediate usefulness), the sources of the *Masses* and *Liberator*'s vitality had widely diverged. Mumford was no John Reed, nor even a Floyd Dell; and the Communist Party was no Socialist Party or IWW, loose and vaguely confident of success.

In its first several years the *New Masses* tried to occupy both camps of Communist literary practice and artistic experimentalism, even publishing an attack on Soviet Russia by Ezra Pound because he was a leading younger literary figure. The general feeling of paralysis among younger American writers, rather than the vitality of the avant-garde itself, broadened the desire for some publication of this stripe. The Sacco-Vanzetti execution proved the injustice of the capitalist system and (despite political infighting with the anarchists) the ability of the Communists to bring together concerned intellectuals in a defense campaign.

This impetus was not sufficient, however, to sustain a monthly magazine. The *New Masses* lacked its predecessor's larger constituency and financial backing. Flailing around, it nearly expired. Then, encouraged by the ultra-left turn of the Sixth Comintern Congress and by the development of a 'proletarian literature' in the Soviet Union, the magazine began to press a less eclectic view. Party Communists, as opposed to sympathetic intellectuals, proclaimed their determination to resolve the contradiction between mass and avant-garde.

The hard-line politico on the staff, Mike Gold, won effective control through personal determination and by driving from the magazine those who could not abide either political sectarianism or proletarian posturing. Not that Gold lacked sincerity, but he believed too literally in a specifically literary proletarian culture. In this he epitomized the Communist weakness for triumph of the will. If proletarian literature did not as yet exist in the USA, if real working-class writing (*e.g.*, the Yiddish novel, short story or poem) dwelled upon bourgeoisification or working-class despair rather than on the triumphant spirit of a rising proletariat, Gold and the magazine would themselves create, *ex nihilo*, an American proletarian literature.[19]

Who was this mythic writer-to-be? In his call for the undiscovered autodidact, Gold described the vision of proletarian virility the *New Masses* sought: 'Send us a giant who can shame our writers back to their task of civilizing America. Send a soldier who has studied history. Send a strong poet who loves the masses and their future . . . Send us a joker in overalls. Send no saint. Send an artist. Send a scientist. Send a Bolshevik. Send a Man.'[20]

This had a lyric appeal. In contrast to the lack of self-confidence and the sheer despondency of many intellectuals before the Crash of 1929 had made the bankruptcy of the system evident, it carried the verve of a radical battle-cry. But in combining affirmative nineteenth-century literary ideals with the lived reality of the overworked factory operative, it created a false expectation. Small numbers of authentic working-class intellectuals did appear, but none fit the heroic mold of Gold's prototype nor met the expectations of a veritable cultural revolution. In the event, the Party's turn toward proletarian culture had the perverse effect of concentrating mental labor where it had always been: in the hands of educated sympathizers and self-trained workers who had moved beyond their class origins by becoming writers.

In the contemporary Yiddish press, critic Sh. Niger raked hardline Communist litterateurs over the coals for imagining that Yiddish writing had even been — or would ever be — a proletarian' rather than a 'people's' art. The crucial difference would be clarified after the declaration of the Popular Front. Yiddishists had in effect debated the same points for decades. A people's art conveyed broad, collective values, especially intense when persecution or international crisis placed an entire culture at risk. Proletarian art assumed, on the contrary, the possibility of an autonomous, self-contained and in some measure universal working-class culture before the day of Revolution. In the

America of diverse ethnic groups and trans-class popular culture, this was precisely the wrong optic through which to view cultural production.[21]

On the other hand, to insist upon the impossible gave writers of ungenteel origins a club with which to thump the privileges of well-connected intellectuals, from snobs like Wallace Stevens to sympathizers like Mumford or Frank. It also gave writers' own revolutionary commitment a palpable shape. But it opened the floodgates to much pointless personal abuse, especially by Gold himself, asserting the purported manliness of proletarian literature against the effete (and, it was often hinted, homosexual) artificiality of the reigning literature.

Moreover, proletarian literature itself failed to live up to the standard demanded of it. Honest literature about the working or sub-working classes had few happy endings. Yiddish literature continued to frustrate Marxist critics with its emphasis not upon the heroic proletariat but upon the corruption of Jewish upward mobility. Much of the effective English-language writing was actually regional literature, semi-agrarian in focus, and its authors tended (like the circle around Missouri writer and editor Jack Conroy) to be openly iconoclastic toward the Communist cultural functionaries' claims. Writers who treated the real irony of the working-class writer (Albert Harper, for example, in his laconic *Union Square*) felt the blows of Communist propriety. Those who could posture most effectively and create an artificial politicization out of real misery and a sense of helplessness won the bulk of the left literary prizes. The experiment tended to destroy its own accomplishments by overselling the product in advance and by degrading those allies who could not or would not meet ideological demands.[22]

The zealotry of the proletarian novel, however, did not entirely displace a more serious literary criticism on the Left. A parallel discourse continued in the *New Masses* which, even at the height of the proletarian fervor, was more concerned to establish radical lineages than discontinuities in the history of American writing. Joseph Freeman, Newton Arvin, Bernard Smith, Gold himself and a host of lesser lights produced solid work on this front. They shunned the crude equation of material conditions with the writer's consciousness that had been a staple of Calverton's equations. Instead, they began to deal directly with both social context and individual psychology, treating form and technique in the first instance independently of content, returning to content only for a final evaluation—a creeping Modernism. In this perspective, as in Calverton's, the literary era of Sandburg, Dreiser, Norris and Crane was now finished. But the *New Masses* critics lavished praise upon Sinclair Lewis, Sherwood Anderson, Eugene O'Neill and others who had opened new imaginative territory in their exploration of machine age America.

This critique reached its apex in *The Great Tradition* (1933) by Granville Hicks. Like *The Liberation of American Literature*, Hicks' book attempted to assess the American literary generations in the light of their historical milieux. Unlike Calverton, Hicks was careful to stop at the literature itself, and in that sense he set the agenda for subsequent Marxist literary studies. He sought evidence in the personal mediation of aesthetic form as it was made manifest in the actual literature. Beginning with the heritage of the Concord circle among the post-Civil War generation, he singled out Whitman's adaptation of Enlightenment ideals to the material possibilities of American life and the particularities of the American people. The realism of regional literature after the war helped to develop a more concrete cultural basis for this perspective. Tragically, that promise went unrealized, foreclosed by the eclipse of the frontier and the dynamic upswing of urbanization. The central task of writers became analysis of the emerging social forces, but even those like William Dean Howells who were sympathetic toward the masses, could not break through their own gentility and middle-class individualism to see beyond surface conditions. A generation of writers became 'fugitive', trapped like Henry James in artificialities. Only a wave of reform struggles could bring a new literature into being.

The uncertainties of the transitional generation—Hamlin Garland, Frank Norris, even the self-educated proletarian Jack London—doomed them methodologically. Only when literature fell from the hands of the old middle class to a fresh group of rebels—Dreiser, Wharton and Anderson principal among them—was a 'rebirth of American literature' possible. Frustrated by its own class basis, stopped short by the war, this latter group nevertheless perceived the literary imperative as truly as the Lost Generation had perceived the absence of alternatives. Proletarian literature held the future, the Communist political movement a guide and mentor to acceptance and simultaneous transcendence of the 'Great Tradition' of critical literature.[23]

F. O. Matthiessen and others rightly blamed Hicks for a sin not far removed from that of the more careless Calverton, what Claude Levi-Strauss would later call the reduction of Being to Meaning, an undervaluation of the text and the psychology of the writer in favor of 'social significance'. Kazin was not wrong to attribute Hicks' difficulties to a 'monumental naivete'. But it was the naivete of those who believed—among the last who believed—that literature had an active social significance beyond the education of the *literati*. Besides, the charge failed to take into account the problems inherent in Hicks' chosen task: to describe the broad terrain of the major traditions in American literature. Hicks' project left little space for detailed textual analysis. But Kazin did identify the flaw common to Hicks, Calverton and Floyd Dell, the conservative Humanists, and indeed every school of American literary scholarship going back at least to nineteenth-century historian Moses Coit Tyler. There was nothing unusually Marxist (or for that matter, nothing peculiarly 'Stalinist', as others would later charge) about Hicks' project, nothing more Marxist at any rate than Parrington and the general infusion of materialist criteria into liberal-radical scholarship. Hicks had tied his *political* loyalty to a view of militant populist-cum-socialist-cum-modernist literature.[24]

Hicks' work, with its grand sweep and its inherent limitations, was as characteristic of 1930s Marxist theory as DuBois's was uncharacteristic. Within the Party, Hicks had written a largely non-Leninist work whereas DuBois, the critic of the Party, had come into line with Lenin's major positive contribution to twentieth-century revolutionary ideas. This paradox framed the strangeness of the emerging literary/cultural debate on the Left, for the problematic stood not on methodological Marxist grounds at all but on political loyalties and unarticulated, politically unpredictable aesthetics.

So long as the *New Masses* and the broadening Party cultural apparatus did not make loyalty the overwhelming issue, Communist literary initiatives could flourish. The John Reed Clubs, a Party-sponsored experiment of young writers in the early 1930s, mixed Marxist discussion with the encouragement of such young writers as Erskine Caldwell, Jack Conroy, Nelson Algren and Richard Wright, to name only a few. In the vital period of 1934–36, they seemed open even to correction of their errors. Film activist John Howard Lawson complained in the *New Masses* about Gold's 'sentimental and mock-heroic attitude toward revolutionary themes' which gave the 'impression of self-satisfaction and glibness and condescension'.[25] A Communism that could indulge in public self-criticism had bright prospects for intellectual and ideological growth. Everyone knew that the Party's own intellectuals often admired Eliot and even Faulkner—privately. Public taste was still a matter of obligation, but many expected it would not remain so.

The high point of Communist literary clarity and technical sophistication was surely the first American Writers' Congress in 1935, and the early years of the *Partisan Review*. Literary criticism, as Phillips and Rahv said, could put literature to 'its own uses, which means that it is not necessarily conveyed in terms of correct politics'.[26] The Writer's Congress, by intention if not achievement the IWW's 'Continental Congress of the Working Class' thirty years later and with another class, expressed the extreme optimism that bourgeois styles would give way with the widening of the literary audience, creating a relationship of intellectuals and workers equal to the experience and skills each brought to the relationship.

The weak side of Communist literary criticism showed up whenever political loyalty became a central issue. Early blasts at Calverton for emphasizing 'our century' and 'our generation' were self-revealing, because the spirit of the *Masses*, the *Liberator* and even the early *New Masses* rested precisely upon such sensibilities: the revolt against the stupid archaism of bourgeois culture. Generational denials of this sort signaled that loyal intellectuals stood ready to abase themselves whenever politically obligatory. It is difficult to distinguish between the Party leadership's cues—based most upon the perceived utility of a literary movement that otherwise did not greatly interest them—and the megalomaniac sectarianism of literary czar Gold. The two coincided in short-sightedness and self-destructive energy, driving the more inventive and hetertodox contributors (*i.e.*, the more true to life) from the Party ranks or into subject matter and treatment where they could not succeed. Nor did the Party give the experimenters encouragement to launch their own small publications, perceived as threatening competition. Until the Popular Front, pseudo-realism rode high in the saddle with Gold, punishing the alternatives and cloaking with a pall radical rage at the literary mainstream.[27]

Happily, events overwhelmed literary sectarianism. In American aesthetics, a radical version of the documentary form had already begun to seep through popular culture, not because of any particular support from Communist officialdom but due to the participation of many hundreds of talented radical individuals. The CIO's singing picket lines, together with the rising Black struggle, added a political-artistic verve. From the *New Yorker* to Hollywood films to modern dance to the Yiddish folk chorus, the imprint of the left and the wide acceptance of the need for drastic social change could be felt. The contribution of

Communists to the preservation and popularization of folk culture alone constituted a major, if by no means unambiguous, achievement. The Party cultural apparatus could not accommodate real political diversity. But it was large enough for the time being to encompass Woody Guthrie and Leadbelly, Dorothy Parker, S.J. Perelman, Kenneth Fearing and many, many others.

Only to a minor extent would most readers or editors remember the Popular Front *New Masses* for its proletarian ideological exercises. Indeed, the class shift of the magazine from a fantacized constituency to a real one marked its new importance. The *New Masses* carried some of the best strike reportage in the world of journalism, but about rather than for the emerging working class. As a factory leader in East New York once said to me: the workers didn't read it. Rather, *The New Masses* turned to the most likely intellectual constituency, and broadened its literary self-definition to include a wide range of culture. Real writing talent appeared in its pages, with keen style and a humor not seen on the English-language left in twenty years. The magazine now correctly saw itself as the expression of a large-scale turn in popular middle-class opinion. From its eclectic cartoons to its ambient columns by Ruth McKinney (of *My Sister Eileen* fame) to public ruminations by major writers like Heminway and Wright, it *implied* without ever adequately stating that Marxist ideas had a place in American life.

Outside the *New Masses*, in the liberal magazines, similar Popular Front work was carried on without even the reminder of the ideological mailed fist. Malcolm Cowley's essays in the *New Republic* present a signal instance. Cowley described a world of literature, written by those he admired, for the delectation of non-Marxist 'progressives,' those critical of capitalism and even of the New Deal but hopeful for some peaceful social resolution at home and the victory of democracy with the aid and friendship of the Soviet Union abroad. He did not insist or bludgeon, nor draw the line too narrowly on literary method. He would have been more comfortable in the old Socialist movement, probably, than he could be in the Communist milieu. He carried the imprint of Marx and Marxism, but very lightly.

A still more subtle impact of the Popular Front was achieved in specific approaches to popular culture. The *Daily Worker* never lost its hamfistedness in general, but its sports column by Lester Rodney attained a high standard of journalism while carrying on the righteous battles for recognition of the social struggles on the playing field. The *New Masses* carried hundreds of film reviews, often of rarely-seen political films but also of movies with Cagney, Garbo, even Frankenstein's monster and Jeanette MacDonald. A Kenneth Fearing, himself a screenwriter for standard Hollywood adventure films, could argue for a Socialist society on grounds of a practical aesthetics: the desire which actors and actresses, writers and directors felt for the full potential of film to be realized. Such arguments had never been made so clearly before in relation to popular culture production. New levels of sophisticatoin were apparent in analyses of 'anonymous' culture, the pulp magazines and the teenage musical culture beneath the contempt of serious art critics. In short, the Communist cultural press could, with difficulty, cover challenging new novels and serious theatre. It was better at baseball games and the young Communist League's Madison Square Garden 'Socialism in Swing' concert.

This casual commentary, and also the more serious book essays that were not distorted by the grind of political axes, gave Marxian ideas (and Marxists themselves) a reputation for ease and rootedness in the culture of the time. 'If you like America . . . if you like its Rocky Mountains, its Storm King highway, its low-priced automobiles, the hot and cold running water in your well-tiled bathroom', a *New Masses* advertisement pointed out, *i.e.*, if you enjoyed the pleasures of middle-class life in America, you had better join with the Marxists to struggle for them. An unembarrassed, radical middle class: here was an idea with a future.[28]

The *New Masses*, the like-minded columns of Malcolm Cowley in the *New Republic* and the readable pages of the *Daily Worker* came to stand for, and to dialogue with, that very middle class, the largest Communist constituency outside the ethnic groups. The effectiveness of the alliance can be attested in one rather spectacular case: the Hollywood Communists. These latter played a major role in helping to form the Hollywood unions in the days when studios were dominated by far-right moguls. Such extraordinary left intellectuals as Albert Maltz, Lillian Hellman, Clifford Odets, John Howard Lawson and Donald Ogden Stewart (and on the outskirts of the Popular Front, a galaxy of stars—Humphrey Bogart, John Garfield, and Bela Lugosi among many others) could be counted among Popular Front sympathizers. They injected into film a socially-conscious perspective on international politics and domestic racism. They did not succeed, or even seriously attempt, to develop anything like a public presentation of Marxist ideas. (Few could say exactly what Marxism in the raw, proletarian version might mean in Hollywood's image world anyway.)

For a moment, *New Masses* writers and readers rode the crest of Popular Front optimism, a mixture of good causes and sad illusions. All this did not change the fundamental problem of the radicalized intelligentsia. The question for Marxist intellectuals and artists, to make sense of these developments and their potential in terms larger than the usual intellectual concerns, remained to be faced squarely. The political divisions imposed by international events placed a tragic burden upon creative response. From the early 1930s, the prestigious League of Professional Groups for Foster and Ford, with such luminaries as Lewis Corey, Waldo Frank, Lewis Mumford and Edmund Wilson, found itself sabotaged and ultimately destroyed by a Communist fraction uneasy with any tendency toward intellectuals' political autonomy, the Party functionaries had driven its public doubters into the arms of Trotskyism. Despite sincere efforts by Communists to unite intellectuals around anti-fascist sentiments a few years later, the public compulsion to defend the Moscow Trials understandably drove loyalists toward a hard-nosed sectarianism, and many more to an early and bitter political silence. Stalinist machinations—resented and regretted, but not openly rejected by thousands around the Communist Party—in a certain sense propelled the return to the scholar's study, to vicarious attachment with the Modernist classics, to *Weltschmerz* and kneejerk anti-Communism. Warren Susman points out that the culture of the 1930s, especially middle class culture, expressed a desperate need for security—not ordinarily considered a revolutionary temperament. The international and the personal insecurity of the moment manifested as Marxism for the unsatisfied need to believe in something—and as return to the emotional safety of individualism free from political obligations.[29]

For middle class Communist sympathizers in general, the more plainly Marxist ideas (in their available versions) were delineated, the less appealing and more aggressively destructive to real discussion they became. The less these ideas were explicitly employed, the more they seemed to imply. Did this suggest, as demi-Trotskyist critics such as Irving Howe later charged, that Stalinism had not only corrupted the left but also conspired with the establishment to invent that diaphanous mass culture of the post-World War II years which destroyed any popular basis for classical learning? The charge contained a grain of truth. Communist writers had intelligently observed that sports, the tabloid press, radio, the detective novel, science fiction (or for women readers, romance and medicine), and popular film quite understandably preoccupied blue-collar leisure. Literature and culture had been socialized rather like the means of production. The Popular Front practitioners of mass culture creation drew their own conclusions, both politically and for the sake of their individual careers. They worked more comfortably than most other radicals with elements of popular culture (although here and there, especially in science fiction and detective pulps, individual Socialists also functioned). As individuals imbued with humane ideals, they made considerable contributions to contemporary culture. Among other accomplishments, they took the lead in calling for the integration of major league baseball.

The problem lay not so much in the concept of the 'People's Culture', as in its application. Broad enough to cover anything, it relied too greatly on current international positions and on the overkill so common to Party propaganda. For instance, ordinary Americans felt revulsion both at Fascism and at war; the Left and its cultural extensions played both keys inconsistently. It dredged up all sorts of pseudo-patriotism to cover its tracks, much as hard-line Communists had expunged every concept of nationalism in its earlier phases. Perhaps worst of all, it never escaped a didacticism, a narrow affirmative or preachy quality which ill-suited the very entertainment value of popular culture. As Lester Rodney, the brilliant Communist sports writer, told me in an interview: the *Daily Worker* several times nearly became a good daily newspaper, but a mediocrity style based on political criteria (and enforced by the presence of political commissars) always pulled it back. Communists as Communists never could quite imagine themselves outside their little world in America; it gave them too great a sense of security in a very large and complex order.

If the Popular Front can stand as the litmus test of Communism's adaptation to American life in the late 1930s and 1940s, the Party itself constrained and stifled its activists' best instincts. Marxism of any variety had scant contribution to make to the *form* of creative contributions, the mediation between contemporary styles and the individual talent. As had been the case with the National Question, the very success of the Popular Front-style film or the appearance of Detroit Tigers manager 'Red' Rolfe in the *Daily Worker* during the World Series raised the question of Marxism's ultimate utility. The point of 'progressive' culture came down to providing the masses *better* entertainment, better in moral content or characterization than the standard mush. That kind of approach 'worked'. But no existing theory had evidently been necessary to accomplish the task.[30]

Herein lay the larger contradiction inherent from the time of Calverton's earliest efforts at the *Modern Quarterly* to create a science of culture. Marxism, as it was then understood, had little to contribute directly to the project of culture. Yet the shift in radical constituency demanded that a non-reductionist theory of culture be developed. Efforts to bridge the gap tended towards worse schematism than ever the class reductionists of the nineteenth and earlier twentieth century had produced. Not that Marxists of political and intellectual repute, Mike Gold included, failed in observation of particulars, especially in literature. But the theoretical context, the mediation between crude economics and cultural life, could not be simply willed into existence.

The radical intellectuals of the 1920s–1930s had, in this respect, not realized the promise of the John Reeds and Floyd Dells any more than they had the promises of the Austin Lewises or Louis Frainas. One very good reason became clear only during the latter 1960s: the feminist awakening which gave shape to Greenwich Village optimism had been dampened in American life in general, and nowhere more obviously than on the Left. With the collapse in feminism, broader hopes for culture became schematic and affirmative—uplifting some future society entire. Or they became mundane: more and better economic opportunity for culture under socialist reorganization. Either way, the notion of *liberation* had been lost.

Another good reason became increasingly obvious as the spread of working-class literacy did not bring a greater readership to Plato or a greater listenership to Beethoven. What if the fulfillment of great bourgeois (and pre-bourgeois) culture in the triumph of the proletariat, should prove a false goal? And if the Popular Front creators of a progressive-tinged popular culture had blundered into a whole new world of aesthetic politics? The entirety of the left cultural discussion, to the limited extent that it transcended the world of books and fine art, may be taken as a subscript upon these imponderables.

1939–41, disaster years for Marxism among American intellectuals generally and literary intellectuals in particular, made the question of a viable cultural theory and practice unavoidable. Cowley, Hicks, Newton Arvin and many less-remembered critics close to the Party renounced the left and its intellectual presumptions. Along with the death of V. F. Calverton, the open manifesto on the death of Marxism by Lewis Corey, published in the *Nation*, beat the sound of retreat. Mike Gold put the matter squarely in 1945: The thirties had been the best. But the thirties were over.

At the last moment of that era, Edmund Wilson in his own odd way drove home the futility of clinging to the older credo. *To the Finland Station* (1939) argued that history had provided the weapon which Lenin grasped, because philosophically and actually, history 'worked'. Wilson's banishment of the Hegelian element left the instrumental, heroic (or pseudo-heroic) view uncontestedly in charge of Marxism, even among intellectuals who alone could challenge accepted doctrine.[31]

The moment for a different kind of Marxism, rooted in the lessons of the CIO on the one hand and the Popular Front cultural achievements on the other, had definitively passed. The drama of the War and the horror and the disappointment that followed only underlined Marxism as Leninism, and Leninism as a quasi-military mental preparation against the West's failure of nerve. Or, in the opposite view, preparation *for* the West's collapse, with barbaric state capitalism ready to pick up the pieces.

Literary interpretation, then shifting towards its postwar captivity as an academic discipline, reflected this loss of vision and nerve. In only a few years a burgeoning Henry James cult would announce the new emphasis on literary form rather than literary politics, and, both cause and effect, would promote the golden bowl of Lionel Trillingism, its many facets gleaming with sharp insights and an uncritical attachment to bourgeois culture.[32] Between the leftist 1930s and the conformist 1950s something had taken place below the level of political argument.

6

Somewhere Beyond Leninism, 1940–1960

By 1940, massive changes had already begun to sweep over American Marxism. Confronted with the hard truths of Russian cynicism (or *Realpolitik*) and American Communists' blind loyalty, the intellectuals as a group visibly wavered. Even Trotskyists, before Trotsky's assasination, had in large part come to consider his political leadership a disaster. Rich idealism and rife discontent had not abated, indeed would reach new intensities. The unfamiliarity of emerging forms, however, defied the familiar logic not only of international Marxism but of the whole working class and ethnic tradition. Younger activists and radical thinkers, many of them already self-conscious post-Marxists, floated at the surface of events, hopeful—naively, as it turned out—of anchoring themselves within the swiftly moving tide. Their fresh interpretive efforts, their experiments in form and content, experienced rare moments of creative intensity.

It was not at all a gloomy time until the Cold War and the changes in social patterns had pushed the left to the margins of American political life. World war and its immediate aftermath gave myriad activists real sources of excitement. Ethnic Communists and socialists, flushed with optimism by community support and even government patronage for their war-support efforts, involved themselves with guerilla wars in their homeland and in plans for the post-war European order. War production needs inspired federal support for considerable unionization left incomplete during the 1930s. The tight labor market prompted resistance against the official no-strike pledge. Black activists took advantage of democratic war sentiment and of the need for Black labor, despite residual and virulent racial intolerance.

Organized women's activities, likewise influenced by the labor shortage and a government campaign stressing their worth as creative contributors to society, reached a high point on the left unknown since suffrage days. Each constituency discerned reasons for optimism.

Superficially, the 1930s left reached a crest: the reform-minded Communist Party claimed 80,000 members, while the relative handful of revolutionary Trotskyists exerted unprecedented shop-floor influence through their syndicalistic militancy. This conflict seemed to many old-time observers a reprise of the reform Socialist/IWW conflict under different slogans, but joined at a higher stage of working class organization. Observers on both sides assayed the developments with a gleam in their eyes. Perhaps Communism had won a long-denied place in the midst of American life; or perhaps the working class would break through all barriers, against capitalism and state capitalism alike.

What happened, of course, was more complex and less susceptible to anyone's teleology. Popular (now United) Front Communists had consolidated and extended their earlier successes through a subtle, polycentrist drift away from Party central authority; their activities increasingly converged with democratic tendencies by no means Marxist. The rest of the surviving Left had begun to move beyond Marxism entirely, en route to a variety of post-Leninist, anarchist and neo-conservative destinations. Those who openly rebelled were, especially at first, not so much disillusioned with Socialist ideals as with the inability of the Left to change with the times. This generation had mostly come of age since the leadership of Marxist movements had hardened; they struggled for a breathing space that leadership could not (and did not wish to) give them. Ironically, the Cold War, while a catastrophe for the Left, had the short-term effect of reining in this internal opposition and of disguising the secessionist mood at large.

As militants told themselves in a thousand different situations, all the activity surely would add up later. Indeed it did, but not to the sum they imagined. Atomic warfare and the revelations about the death camps dispelled the heroic-optimistic confidence in science, kin to scientific Socialism. Just as surely, the postwar rush to commodity culture—all the items denied to workers during the 1930s and now available to ordinary people for the first time—signalled the end of the historic Left. In a war-ravaged and desperate world, America had for large classes of people banished poverty as a central, political issue. A generation of young radicals of every ethnic stamp and racial hue emerged from their war experience eager for something different, something that they could not articulate and that the Left did not know how to supply.

Thousands, perhaps tens of thousands of GIs and younger people from middle and working-class backgrounds felt the sense of dislocation that Norman Mailer dramatized in *Barbary Coast*. The reality of the postwar world disputed radical predictions and promoted disillusionment. The proletarian revolution would not likely take place, at least not for a long time; and younger rebels began to think of themselves, for want of another category, as intellectuals. Prodding, pulling conceptually at reality before them, they worked to arrive at such cultural, personal solutions as the absence of any revived radicalism would allow. At best, they hinted at civilization—the West, the way of life arrived at in place of a proletarian revolution—as a reality to be seen whole, a reality previously and abstractly designated as capitalism. At worst, they gave themselves over body and soul, through a series of ideological rationalizations, to the same system.

A decade later, with the disintegration of the organized Left virtually complete and the faithful ethnic milieu in ripe middle age, intellectuals of various descriptions had become *the* constituency for radicalism. They would have seemed at any other time in Left history an unlikely crew: veterans of the Left emancipated from their organizational past and most of their dogmas; children of ethnic and Popular Front radicals; and a stratum of anarchists and pacifists previously treated as marginal. Together, these bent but unbroken dissidents defined the new territory. Joined by an array of emphatically non-Marxist intellectuals—descendents of the isolationist Middle Border— they effected a pre-New Left conception of the world, and of American society, that was almost precisely the reverse of the wartime Left's. Philosophically hostile to the state, suspicious of union leadership and even of definitive class categories, they carried the virtues and faults of rebellion against received radical truth. Faced with the power of nuclear imperialism at the noonday of the 'American Century', they made their own statement. That simple act was an achievement.

Tragically, they lacked the other elements which had made an American radicalism occasionally strong and original. The Cold War and Stalinism had dispelled utopianism while the evolution of popular life seemed like a grim deception. They distanced themselves from Imperial America's corruptions as much by distancing themselves from ordinary Americans as from the power elite. They had, inadvertently, frozen 'the intellectual' into a rigid category, or perhaps they had merely accepted categories that had been passed down since the 1920s and were reinforced by disappointing events. They had ideas that would live, but could take flight only in the political practice of another, still younger generation.

Puzzled Communists

The reorganization of the Communist Party during the 1940s, one of the more flexible oldtime leaders once remarked to me, had taken place with the proviso that middle-class recruits were now just as useful as, perhaps more useful than, blue-collar workers. It was a momentous sea-change, scarcely recorded in the formal documents where Party statistics of industrial membership continued to be exaggerated at the expense of housewives and lower professionals. From one angle, it signified the completion of American Leninism's historical mission, not the Leninism of the pre-revolutionary Russian Bolshevik Party by any means, nor the Leninism that Trotskyists imagined might exist if only the Communist Party did not, but Leninism as it had reached its organizational pinnacle on the American scene. Acceptance of the ethnic groups as blocs rather than merely proletarians in ethnic form, and acceptance of the 'Negro people' as a revolutionary agency, cleared the way. By the late 1930s, the Party achieved its aim in a certain measure by the multiplication of influential sectors and the creation of a social movement. To do so, it had ceased to be a working-class party in the strict sense of the term.[1]

Already in the later 1920s, Bertram Wolfe and Jack Stachel made such an aim entirely clear: 'To comrades who are afraid that . . . multiple activity in all the strata of the population will destroy the proletarian character of our movement and of our work, Leninism replies . . . with more clarity of principle, a higher theoretical level, a more ruthless struggle gainst all deviations, a more active "interference" of the Party in all the work of its members, the organization of the entire party into fractions in all the organizations in which we work and the control of these fractions by the central authority of the party.

'Indeed, from a certain standpoint, Leninism can be characterized as a theory of allies of the proletarian revolution, that is to say, the strategy of gaining allies, accumulating reserves, taking from capitalism and imperialism such reserves as it may have, and neutralizing such sections of the population as cannot be wholly won as allies'.[2]

Wolfe's true heirs, not the grizzled veterans of 1919 but the rising stars of the Popular Front, had carried this plan into action. In doing so, they had unwittingly recapitulated the ambiguous class nature of American radicalism, mystifying the process with Leninist terminology. Unlike the old Socialist Party which they now emulated in so many ways, they could not, however, make the best of the situation by openly accepting diverse regionalisms or racial and ethnic interests as legitimate and simultaneously conflictual. Nor could they seriously claim to present an American Socialism distinct from foreign models. Familiar dynamics shaped them, but they had difficulty with the mediations.

Whether any organization could have created a mass working class party under the conditions is unclear. Outside the ethnic groups, rates of turnover among working-class membership had constantly reminded organizers of the difficulties at hand. Workers, and not only workers, generally found Party meetings routine and boring. A society where they expressed their class politics mostly within the factory, made any extra forum an overload. No amount of literature sales (purchases of the 'classics' fell off sharply after 1938), or sporadic study sessions or attempted popularizations of the *Communist*'s format could change a fundamental attitude. Communism in America, unlike France, Italy, or pre-Hitler Germany, was a culture essentially for the intellectuals, the foreign born, and the exceptional autodidact.

Communists in large numbers, inside and outside the leadership, had recognized the problem early. They contented themselves with a three-fold solution, each aspect of which bore heavily upon American Leninism. Among the rank-and-file of unions whose leadership they monopolized or shared, they accepted the inevitability of an ambivalent relationship in which class consciousness and union loyalty translated into personal trust rather than prospective conversion to Marxist ideas. (For Communists who had risen to leadership out of the ranks, discovering the Party with their own rising aspirations, this was a natural attitude anyway.) Among ethnic and racial nationality groups they tended to yield, as far as possible within the Party, autonomy from day-to-day direction. With the middle class, they became more assertive, recognizing that their constituency had broadened both quantitatively and qualitatively.[3]

Inevitably, these policy adjustments accelerated the process of

Communism becoming the 'petty-bourgeois' movement that left Socialists had vehemently denounced the Socialist Party mainstream for being. Thirty years had so thoroughly altered the structure of American society, however, that this progressive petty bourgeoisie had relatively fewer small merchants and scarcely any significant rural element. (Rural Communism, never numerically large although important in some ethnic districts of the Midwest, virtually disappeared with geographical relocations during the war.) It found its new locus among the ranks of white collar workers euphemistically described as professionals but accorded neither good pay nor dignity. *This* middle class enthusiastically attached itself to an advanced New Deal and a version of state socialism, seeking freedom of ethnic-racial access to all occupations and an international world order framed by peace and justice. Marxism of the old variety maintained formal prestige, in the absence of another language to describe the economic contradictions of capitalism. Meanwhile, thousands of activists from the lower middle class who went into the factories for personal and political reasons either during the war or afterward received a fresh dose of class struggle basics. But they no longer had the prestige or the opportunities of their political predecessors. The centers of action, especially after the postwar strikes, had shifted toward the upper circles of union maneuvering.

As the Party became more of an American radical and substantially middle class organization, its historic strictures against women's gender-conscious participation naturally eased. During the war, precisely at the moment when membership reached its peak, draft-age men had gone off to fight—leaving women with an unprecedented opportunity for leadership, albeit at the middle and lower levels of the organization. Over half the local organizations had women at their head. Working women drawn back to the factories together with middle-class women active in housing, cultural and United Nations-style work exerted pressure for theoretical adjustment.

Mary Inman, a West Coast Party journalist, offered the first notable challenge to orthodox ideas on the 'Woman Question' in a quarter of a century. Inman presented the subjugation of the housewife as the unpaid labor behind wage labor. Party thought, heavily economist, ran against this position, and it had so little support from career-minded progressive women then or later that it would not be put forth again until the 1970s. Yet the very expression of Inman's views suggested the process of feminist rethinking alive in some sections of the Party.[4]

More visibly, Communism had become the intellectual fashion, and even more the cultural fashion, in Harlem. The Party's shift toward the middle class generally allowed a focus upon an integration demand more achievable and far more popular among Black professionals than earlier demands for separate statehood. Moreover, the Communists seem to have learned, as Mark Naison says, to leave Black culture to Black radicals. Social affairs for left integrationist groups attracted a galaxy of Black luminaries, and close supporters of Party positions worked at the highest levels of official Black organizations. Their credibility suffered, perhaps fatally in the long run, from the repeated change of line during the late 1930s. But they re-emerged in wartime seemingly stronger than ever.[5]

In the white ethnic sector, meanwhile, the transformation of the left proceeded at a rapid clip. Greek-American Communists, for example, built upon the ardent traditions of republicanism and their own long-standing two-stage approach to Greek Socialism by way of political democracy. The right sought to unite Greeks around the monarchy, the left around the working class. Both sought to escape the humiliating racism directed toward Greek-Americans prior to the heroic exploits of anti-fascist Greeks during the war. Marxism supplied the proletarian argument for a successful United Front at the moment of successful Greek entry into mainstream American life. Enthusiastically pro-Roosevelt and pro-Russian, the left consolidated its support in unions through the powerful Greek-American Labor Congress. At a time when the important seamen's section of the Greek resistance worked out of New York, Communists justifiably saw themselves as the center of the action.

Where they did not directly lead, ethnic activists worked effectively in coalitions that would have been impossible a few years before. The powerful American Slav Congress enrolled the left fraternal groups at its core. But it ranged outward to Socialist and liberal support, especially among Tito's solid backing in the large South Slav fraternal groups that had remained within the Socialist movement. Never before, not even at the peak of thirties anti-fascism, had the Slav Communists achieved such unity with their communities or such confidence in their own worldview. The clerical forces, discredited by their links with homeland fascist collaborators, could only hold onto their hard-core supporters and outwait the Left.

Hungarians (whose countryman, horror film star Bela Lugosi, served as president of the Hungarian American Council for Democracy), Bulgarians and other Eastern European Leftists enjoyed liberal backing and real working-class enthusiasm, especially among the older generation in their own communities. The editors of their papers basked in the glow, now unambiguously unified with a wider American view of social peace and their own children's upward mobility. With an aging constituency, this would be the papers' final moment of glory. Marxist ideas did not so much disappear as change subtly and, in the case of some venerable slogans, simply recede toward the margins. Contrary to subsequent anti-Communist claims, the ethnic activists' enthusiasm bespoke no cynical underlying attitude. They believed, or convinced themselves for a time, that in America Communism became democracy and that democracy would become Socialism in some peaceful postwar world order.[6]

If postwar amity did not prevail, if the Party no longer represented United Front strengths, if it blundered in seeking to coerce loyalty from those who no longer needed its protection, then its elements would go their separate ways. Scarcely observed, traditional constituencies were already shifting beyond Party control. Much as the secession movements began among the Socialists after 1910, they emerged among the Communists after 1940, and largely for the same reason: the founding program of the forefathers, even severely adapted, no longer served.

The shift came earliest, and most articulately, in the Jewish sector. In 1943, the leading pedagogue of the Jewish People's Fraternal Order, largest segment of the IWO, had practically declared ideological independence from the Communists' long-standing assimilationism, insisting that 'the melting pot has a scorched bottom'.[7] Heavy-handed ideology no longer had a place in Yiddish children's curricula, as Yiddishists placed the preservation of their language and culture above other political demands. Although they continued to deny Soviet misdeeds (even through the 1952 murder of Russian Yiddish writers), a long process of detachment had nevertheless begun at the cultural core. Yiddishists wanted a different kind of movement, even if they could not get it. They also wanted, and began to fashion for themselves in subtle ways, a different Marxism. Albeit only in Yiddish, this they could create for themselves.

In the little circles around former Popular Front Yiddish publications, the meaning of the secession became most evident. Middle-aged activists, protean proletarian stalwarts of the Left since the days of the Russian Revolution, no longer held back from their own potentially heretical intellectual elaborations. The Yiddish-American poets, essayists and cultural heroes received careful scholarly attention and close interpretation in book editions of a few thousand. In numbers of writers or readers, this was of course a small and steadily diminishing milieu. But by the standards of the Marxist intellectual following in the USA it was a substantial milieu with a symbolic importance of its own.

The Yiddishists were perhaps best suited to assess the cultural distance traversed from the late nineteenth to the middle of the twentieth century. Despite all that had passed, these diehards retained a vivid impression of Sholem Aleichem and I. L. Peretz as reflections of the centuries-old *shtetl* facing fragmentation, the collective yearnings that led to *Weltschmerz* and to widespread Socialist beliefs. They still swam in a current where Marxism and messianism had come together as long-lost relatives. Now, despairing the unforseen results of Socialism but not in the original ideals that made the radical movements possible, they grasped acutely the crisis in the messianic imagination.

The Yiddishe Kultur Farband, founded during the Popular Front enthusiasm and fueled by stubborn cultural resilience, thus published anarcho-Zionist B. Rivkin's *Grunt Tendentsin fun Yiddish Literatur* (Basic Tendencies in Yiddish Literature), explicating at full length the Yiddish messianic criticism in its social-economic context. Socialism, Rivkin argued, supplied the form, but Jewishness itself—the *galut* and the miseries of the immigrant generations in particular—the content for the revolutionary worldview. Thereby, Rivkin could contemplate the change in literary generations as the coming to consciousness of the spiritual element within Socialism. A writer like David Ignatov, author of the trilogy *Euf Veite Vegen (From a Far Horizon)*, exemplified the worker-intellectual drawn to the labor movement and to Socialism but repelled by the emptiness of mechanical secularization. The pilgrim's journey led not toward the degraded path of Cahan's David Levinsky grown materially wealthy and spiritually hollow among the New World's temptations, but rather through impoverishment and alienation to find at last in America the keys to the secrets of an elder wisdom. Rivkin had, in his earlier polemic against positivism and crushing rationalism, helped provide *di Yunge* a meaning for their instinctive messianism. The elder Rivkin summed up the results for the Yiddishists who remained. So much had passed and the survivors had to make themselves clear. The smaller tragedy to the larger one of the Holocaust was that only at the last moment could Marxists consciously break with the economist simplifications of the early twentieth century and begin to speak in their own theoretical tongue.

The ferment around the creation of Israel understandably tapped similar sources and an overlapping constituency with *Yiddishkayt*. Indeed, as the Soviet Union alone among the major world powers defended the right of a Jewish state, American Jewish Communists joined hands with the quasi-Socialistic, quasi-chauvinistic Zionist movement against the more assimilationist-minded reform Socialists. The election of a single Progressive Party Congressional candidate, Leo Isaacs, to Congress in 1948 from the Bronx dramatized the overlap. The fact of Israel, however, ensured a competing loyalty among the ardent defenders of Jews, a competition that would grow dramatically with time. The Party's English-language expression of Jewish consciousness, *Jewish Life*, struggled to find a middle ground. Ultimately, it found itself, along with the old *Morgen Freiheit*, the sole representatives of organized Euro-Communism in the United States.[8]

'Progressivism', the leftward edge of the New Deal now threatened by Truman's accession to power, competed more broadly for the loyalty of the Party's new middle classes, Jewish and gentile. The emotional power of the crusade against Fascism evolved into a vision of a new world order in which America would no longer play successor to European colonialism but would be the advocate of popular national revolutions—most immediately, the Chinese—and co-guarantor with the Soviet Union of a lasting world peace. Devotion to Roosevelt's legacy required considerable credulity in many areas, among them the continuing imperial role in Latin America, the wholesale abandonment of republican Spain and of endangered European Jewry. But the quixotic project of renewing this legacy captured the sentimental imagination of a number of New Deal veterans, from Henry Wallace to Rexford Tugwell. So long as the seeming return to Depression conditions at home and the seeming impossibility of bourgeois recovery in Europe remained fixed points of reference, international peace and some form of state socialism remained viable goals.

Earl Browder sought to make the best of the situation in a dramatic series of gestures during the final years of the war. Envisioning a postwar world of peace and reconstruction, he declared for collaboration between class and nation, with Communists subordinating their own considerable resources toward that end. 'Perhaps we could say', he added in 1944, 'that our

Party is standing on its own feet for the first time' in proposing such a direction. Given the strength of American capitalism, as well as the dangers of a postwar anti-Soviet reaction, Browder perhaps opted for the only strategy that seemed to promise continuing legitimacy and membership growth. That he made such an appeal for extended class peace, for the abandonment of Socialist prospects into the indefinite future *in the name of Marxism*, seems remarkable in retrospect. But what, in fact, it revealed was that the Party apparatus stood above even the vision of Socialism which had called it into being.[9]

Browder's bold opening disguised a paradox. *Without* the vision of Socialism, the Party's activists no longer had any particular need for the organization. The Soviet Union looked very large, flush with its epochal victories over Hitlerism at Stalingrad and beyond, but, Browder notwithstanding, the leadership of the American Communist Party looked very small. Its grip upon its own members rested upon loyalties no longer firm, while its alliance with the larger New Deal coalition would soon be exposed as superficial. The state and the trade-union bureaucracies began to dispense with their erstwhile Left allies. Hard-pressed to move back into now badly eroded bases, the Communists stood vulnerable in a way they were not during the more reactionary, but also more insular 1920s.

The fatal consequences did not show themselves evenly, or all at once. The *Daily Worker*, to take one obvious example, reached its second apex (after the late 1930s) during the immediate postwar years. With a modicum of editorial autonomy from the party, it took up a variety of cultural subjects and improved its investigatory journalism until hard times and political backpeddling forced a reduction in staff and column space. Meanwhile, in blue-collar districts where party activists did not find themselves compromised by pacts with labor leadership against industrial restlessness, the Communists effected new coalitions while holding their ranks firm.[10]

The beginnings of political self-destruction both dramatized and delayed the Communist awareness of impending crisis. The Party could neither carry out Browder's last political stroke (reorganization out of the Leninist mold into the 'Communist Political Association' in 1944), nor could it formulate a viable alternative. The overthrow of Browder in 1945 on French-Russian inspiration, amid his pleas for independent American Marxist thought, offered up a scapegoat for the internal troubles and confusion, but also opened a can of worms. Where had the Party gone wrong? What could be done? Expulsions 'right' and 'left', of talented Popular Front operatives and old former Wobblies alike, showed the machine to be out of control.

Foster, who as usual survived his opponents, returned ceaselessly to old categories, fumbling for an appropriate restatement. The older vision of Leninism as champion of working-class revolt, commander of mass action, had long since faded, and Foster, the tactical unionist, had genuinely never been its proponent anyway. Bold phrases aside, no one had a credible, thoroughgoing program.

Quite suddenly, calamities befell the Party one after another. The appeal to ethnic nationality collapsed under the weight of Yalta and the realities of Russian hegemony in most of Eastern Europe. The Right began to exert itself strenuously on this front, joined by a wave of former fascist collaborators and democratic anti-Communist dissidents who provided the final wave of European language-speakers. Catholic activists in labor, having grudgingly cooperated with the Left in the formation of unions, rallied their considerable energy to drive the Communists out. Liberals and mainstream labor leaders hastened to distance themselves from the Left. Previously restrained, they gave vent to full Cold War rhetoric. Meanwhile, the government witchhunt had begun.[11]

No doubt the resurrection of the Party after the Second World War would have been extremely difficult in any case. Returning Communist soldiers, like other GIs, had lived through a profoundly nationalizing experience; in the next few years, many would follow the mass trajectory via the GI bill to college and the professions. Suburbanization and automobilization, taking the younger people especially from the ethnic ghettoes, fragmented old solidarities and rechanneled aspirations. To take a single example: the neighborhood social club, central to blue-collar life and accessible to left-wing variants, suffered immensely from the automobile. Or again: the street-corner speech, whose decline as a popular art had helped eradicate an older Socialism twenty years earlier, was now completely eclipsed as an electoral vehicle for a Left politician like Congressman Vito Marcantonio when television took hold.

But these consequences became fully apparent, and final, only at the end of the 1940s. Postwar strikes showed a labor movement that was still vigorous, if increasingly hamstrung by its own bureaucratic apparatus. Veterans returned home to bolster picket lines. Middle class activists, seeking to maintain and extend the New Deal, exerted wide influence through their organizations. Nowhere did labor or liberal organizations exclude

Communists until 1948 or so; indeed, their leaders usually combatted divisive efforts as a threat to Roosevelt's legacy.

Communist leaders responded to these changing circumstances with a maximum effort to control their own ranks
regardless of the cost. Intellectuals, prominent Black leaders and
others who showed signs of independence were struck down.
Trade-union officials felt the pressure of demands that finally
forced them to choose between politics and economics. Efforts
to interpret the contradictions, meanwhile, produced a strange
vacillation from class struggle to class collaborationist rhetoric,
from the language of the 1920s to the language of the 1940s, in
the same issue of *Political Affairs* (adroitly renamed from *The
Communist*), sometimes even in the same article.

What passed for theory exhibited an increasingly strained
quality. Attempts in the writings of a few bold (soon to be
castigated) theoreticians to weave together democratic and
Marxist ideas culminated ingloriously with Foster's pathetic
Twilight of World Capitalism (1949). In these pages, if nowhere
in reality, capitalism faltered while the Socialist countries
marched forward. Bourgeois influence over the body of the
masses, through social-democratic union leadership, showed its
bankruptcy, while bourgeois control over the mind, through
religion, was refuted scientifically and stood on the veritable
edge of disintegration. The creation in the Soviet Union of an
authentically Socialist humanity of well-rounded citizens demonstrated the validity of Marxian precepts once and for all. How far
such 'scientific Socialism' stood from Stalinist concentration
camps on the one side and the robust energy of postwar capitalism on the other can be calculated more easily in psychological
than in political terms.[12]

The popular effort to stave off Russian-American conflict
moved ahead despite such narrow-mindedness. Resistance
against the Cold War had a heroic quality tainted but not ruined
(at least until 1948) by Party leadership maneuvers. The populist, mystic former vice-president Henry Wallace, meanwhile,
articulated a real desire for Americans to cut loose from right-
wing dictators, take domestic racism in tow, and seek some
cooperative form of mixed economy. The same complaints
against US foreign policy would be echoed, often by the same
individuals, when Vietnam protests began in the 1960s. The
Wallace campaign indeed pioneered the campus as a political
arena. But the more the Party tended to fill in, to substitute for
the mass support that the Progressive Party fell short of accumulating, the more it fostered the Progressives' schism from the

mainstream of American radicalism or liberalism.

From another angle, the peace sentiment uniting behind Henry Wallace's candidacy crystallized a progressive milieu which no longer accepted Party guidance as the price for political help. The *National Guardian* weekly, launched in the wake of the Wallace campaign, displaced the *Daily Worker* in many homes, especially when it assumed a leading role in the Rosenberg Defense. Run by professional newspapermen, dedicated to battling Cold War propaganda, it became a kind of *New Masses* descendent, unembarrassed about its mostly middle-class readership and increasingly determined to establish its own independent presence.

Many other such activists sought to strike out on their own, free of Party interference but with their constituencies intact. Former Congressman Vito Marcantonio, against official Party advice, threw himself into one last Congressional campaign before dying of a heart attack. Left unions which refused to buckle under to the anti-communist provisions and join the mainstream, as the Party advised, also went their own quiet way. Younger Party leaders, champions of the Popular Front, privately shared these sympathies. But they found themselves unavailable, driven into hiding, just as the rumors of Stalin's crimes drove home the necessity of democracy in the Party and in society at large in order for a Communist Party to thrive.

'Underground', resisting repression through an internal exile monitored by thousands of FBI operatives, these activists remained hapless to the larger degeneration of party life. Reprimands for 'male chauvinism' in a Party not previously known for honoring women's rights, expulsions of aging immigrants on 'white chauvinism' charges for the crime of wintering in Florida, proved that sectarianism had its own logic. The Party's very lack of democracy encouraged police agents and provocateurs. It staggered through the fifties somnambulently, a ghost rattling phrases from the past, while its best talent increasingly found themselves a place in non-ideological movements pointing to the future, or simply resigned to living their private lives. A score of talented functionaries remained, along with thousands of mostly middle-aged rank-and-filers, determined to survive the government harrassment and the bad leadership of the organization. They did indeed survive McCarthyism, and even (albeit in numbers and talent far diminished) the 1956 Hungarian Revolt and the Khruschev revelations. But their movement had once and for all lost hegemony within the left.[13]

Not surprisingly, it did not leave many intellectual monuments behind. The most promising new Party journal of literature and criticism, *Mainstream*, had been shut down after three issues in 1945–46 as a distraction from political priorities. The new *Masses & Mainstream* (1950–60) had little resemblance to either of its namesakes. Despite some interesting Black cultural material and a television commentary then rare on the Left, it mostly became the cultural version of *Political Affairs*, hard to read and hardly worth the effort.

The further the distance from the Party proper, the more capable of life and new ideas—this was the climate on the left during the fifties. Thus *Freedom*, published by Paul Robeson and his supporters in Harlem, did not make much headway in the Black community but kept together an array of veteran and younger talent. Radical forefathers like Langston Hughes (whose Finley Peter Dunne-like 'Semple' columns, wittily analyzing contemporary conditions in street-talk, circulated in Black local papers) joined newcomers like Lorraine Hansberry, author of *Raisin in the Sun*. Such popular and talented entertainers as Ossie Davis, Ruby Dee and Harry Belafonte could be found at the fringes of the Popular Front remnants. *Freedom*'s successor, the monthly magazine *Freedomways* (1960 on), took even more independent distance, forging a permanent Left presence in Black intellectual life that was acceptable to many who were wary of the Party and of Marxist ideas. The same principle reigned in an array of other ex-Party cultural and intellectual institutions, driven into a premature Eurocommunist-style exile.

Theoretical creativity began at the point where the break with the Party became permanent. The future editors of *Monthly Review*, formulators of 'world system' theory and the key source for the examination of the US empire had, like many intellectuals, always been more attached to the Popular Front than to the Party proper. Paul Sweezy, prominent Marxist economist, had briefly bruited the idea of launching an intellectuals' organization *against* CPUSA isolationism in 1939–40. He and his co-editor, popularist Leo Huberman, believed roughly in extension of the New Deal into state socialism, with heightened democratic participation and international détente. The Wallace campaign's momentum on the campuses gave hopes for a new intellectual revival, while the disintegration of CPUSA influence threw them back onto their own resources. They urgently wanted to make Socialist ideas in the USA comprehensible, to render them less dependent upon emotional loyalties to Russia and the special pleading of Marxism-Leninism and more reliant upon historical and political analysis. *Monthly Review* reached mostly committed radicals, but those of a notably intellectual bent. In their efforts to revive domestic Socialism, they had little immediate fortune. Their increasingly systematic view of monopoly power within the US state and economy did not yet have an audience. But in one area, they exceeded all their own expectations. MR did not rightly know how to refurbish a worldview beyond disillusionment, save, in part, for a displaced identification from Russia to China. But it understood the punishment American military and economic power rained down upon the dependent nations, and the fateful connections between imperialism and the permanent war economy. MR looked beyond the familiar hopes for working-class revival and/or improved liberalism to something like an intelligentsia put in touch with the reality of world suffering.[14]

Paul Baran's *Political Economy of Growth* (1957) was a milestone in the careful research and analysis of imperialism. Baran saw that the historical advance of monopoly tied to the expansion of the world market meant a programmed 'backwardness' for Third World nations, a backwardness by no means inherent in their economies but, once developed, inescapable short of revolution. Baran's signal contribution, to interpret the internal effects of neocolonialism, foreshadowed the criticisms of US Vietnam policy and the entire 'world systems' discussion of the 1970s–80s. Disruption of internal markets, 'industrial infanticide' of potentially competitive industries, the creation of a comprador class tied to the imperial powers—these were universal structures of underdevelopment. Sweezy himself, both in his own essays and in collaborative editorial statements, sought to refine Marxist theories of imperialism from a rather more theoretical quarter, and to draw out the implications of emergent neo-colonialism for the internal US economy. One might say that in Sweezy's writings, Lenin's *Imperialism* subsumed the rest of the canon and, considering the historical period, not entirely without reason. Indeed, if the Popular Front had expressed one principle of Leninism in action, the abandonment of domestic proletarian expectations in favor of a world-wide view of imperialism summed up another. Each tendency had been immanent from the beginning of American Communism. Only the pressure of events had decided the survivor.[15]

Trotskyism and the Search for Alternatives

American Trotskyism, despite its limited human resources, filled a political and intellectual gap during the 1940s, and exerted an intellectual force from the Second World War until the dawn of the 1960s out of all proportion to its numerical strength. It developed a point-for-point attack upon Popular Front positions, missing a great deal along the way (especially in appreciation of unassimilated ethnic life), but aiming much of its fire in the right directions. It often hesitated at its goal, sometimes providing a stalking horse for Neo-conservatism, but it stuck to its principles with formidable tenacity. The repeated crises of the CPUSA fulfilled Trotskyist predictions without usually leading to significant recruitment by the latter. A hard reality, shorn of the hubristic moments enjoyed by the Popular Front, forced the Trotskyists toward a more creative approach in the direction of an uncharted post-Leninist future.

Other radical groups had virtually disappeared from sight. Jay Lovestone's followers, growing fewer and more conspiratorial in their labor involvements, dissolved with a last statement of their hopes for a democratic Socialist presence somewhere in the labor movement and in American life. The Socialist Party, where some of the faithful Lovestoneites found a home, itself shrunk to a support group for Norman Thomas and for the conscientious objectors imprisoned during the war. A few Socialists were still elected to local office, as in Milwaukee or Reading, where ethnic ties and gaps in the two-party system permitted holdouts against the kind of pressures that had lured Minnesota's Farmer Labor Party into the Democrats and broke up Wisconsin's Progressive Party. Men like Frank Zeidler, Milwaukee's mayor for many years, kept the municipal Socialist spirit alive—but just barely.

Only among the Trotskyists, then, could a collective vitality still be found, and even here that vitality was as strange as the Communist adaptation to liberalism. The Workers Party, formed in 1940 by a few hundred predominantly middle-class Jewish youth who opposed both war camps and Trotsky himself, conducted a lively labor agitation. Its newspaper, *Labor Action*, circulated in the tens of thousands in war factories; its militantly anti-bureaucratic supporters figured in hundreds of illegal strikes and thousands of less-remembered internal mobilizations. It carried on with an economism that would have done the old Communist rank-and-filer credit, putting aside all questions but shop complaints. The support it gathered as a group was, as veterans recall, 'a mile wide but an inch thick'.[16]

These younger, sometimes quite militant, workers showed far less eagerness to join an isolated and rather fanatical organization than had their fathers and mothers who joined the CPUSA a generation earlier. The ethnic tradition of self-education had ended before the Trotskyists really emerged, and Trotskyism had no foreign lode star to inspire admiration. One of the other 'industrialized' Trotskyist factions, the strongly unionist followers of Bert Cochrane and Harry Braverman, soon made its peace with the stumbling Communist apparatus in the auto industry and took over the editing of the left UAW press. It was an emblematic decision, either capitulation or realism depending upon the perspective. Other Trotskyists, including most of the ever-smaller Workers Party cadre, chose to throw in with the anti-Communists supporting Walter Reuther and the Cold War. Either path led to Socialist oblivion.[17]

Seeds of hope were nevertheless planted for another season. Nourishing small shoots of practice and thought through the old system and beyond it, heterodox Trotskyism impelled individuals and groups almost entirely away from the familiar fix of the American Left (Leninist and pre-Leninist) and into fresh engagements with American reality. Trotskyists of several varieties, all well-educated and usually unprotected by any ethnic or sectarian cushion, set forth original conclusions.

By the early 1940s, the *New International* became the most intellectually vigorous journal on the Left—when not obsessed with discrediting the American Communist Party or contesting the mantle of Leon Trotsky. So long as Trotsky himself ruled, the journal had served mainly to amplify his opinions, and often his own essays seemed to crowd the rest of the contents to the margins of journalism and intra-Left sniping. Following the split, the magazine found a life of its own. During the war it sought to redefine the terms of world socialism. Later, Trotsky's over-optimistic predictions of postwar world revolution led the *New International* to considerable stocktaking, a mixture of understandable despondency and the brave search for new grounds.

C. L. R. James became the journal's most outstanding and original author. He was, to many inside the Trotskyist movement, a living enigma, at once a theorist of Black nationalism and of strictest class struggle, of Leninist formulae and post-Leninist interpretations. Like DuBois, he had grown into Marxism by recognizing in it a confirmation of his evolving political views. But as a Trinidadian-born intellectual nurtured in the Caribbean popular culture of calypso, carnival and cricket (he was for a while a prominent cricket journalist in England), James had a distinctly different background from the genteel DuBois. James was steeped in lower-class life. By the 1940s, he came to see that the dialectics of popular culture, related both to Black consciousness and the volatile industrial scene, were largely unrecognized by the reigning paradigms and organizations of the Left. He saw the masses themselves struggling out of the disasters of contemporary history toward goals of their own making, past concepts of the vanguard party leadership to a more dynamic mixture of politics and culture.

James emigrated to the USA in 1938, already renowned for his incomparable history of Toussaint L'Ouverture's Haitian revolution, *The Black Jacobins* and, among the British, for his cricket reporting and his leadership of Pan-African agitation. But for the next fifteen years he lived in semi-obscurity, familiar only among Trotskyists and to occasional public lecture audiences. But in his own small circle he was an influential and prophetic figure. In the Workers Party of perhaps a thousand, concentrated mostly in wartime production, James gathered a little group including Raya Dunayevskaya, Grace Lee (later Boggs), and Martin Glaberman. They shared an almost messianic faith in the revolutionary capacity of the mass production worker, who, they insisted, could not be considered 'backward' in the usual European Marxist sense. He or she did not join Marxist parties, or rigorously follow radical leadership in the unions, but nevertheless sought fundamental changes in the way production was organized, and in that sense understood more than the Marxist intellectuals could explain.

To advance this claim in the name of an updated Leninism was iconoclastic, even extraordinary, but not without native precedent. Daniel DeLeon, it will be remembered, had seen the IWW as a new phase of civilization, heir to an industrial and historical evolution become quasi-anthropological in its effects on the entire culture of human development. James and his collaborators put forward similar claims about the CIO unions and the mass-production working class in general. In the USA, the group's document *State Capitalism and World Revolution* argued, the combination of Henry Ford's system of sweated labor and a complicit local state authority had already anticipated the essence of modern totalitarian social relations: rationalization of production with the coordination of the state. Such a development marked the culmination of a long history, from the reduction of the medieval European artisan to wage laborer, to the ravage of the Third World peasantry and the undercutting of the Western craft laborer. At every step resistance had flared, from the Low Country weavers' temporary seizure of production to the Levellers and Diggers to the Black revolutionaries of Haiti. The modern class conflict brought this

process to a conclusion. Concentrated in enormous work collec-
tivities, the new mass workers strove, consciously or unconsciously, for the abolition of all hierarchies inside the factory and
outside--an end to the division between mental and manual
labor.

The most formidable obstacle became the labor bureaucracy
itself—an analysis that made experienced readers think of
Wobblyism rendered philosophical. State Capitalism had indeed
grown within the framework of the system, as had been long
predicted, but the functionaries in the early years of the C.I.O.,
often Communists, demonstrated by their constraining presence
the reality of a *new social formation*. From this perspective,
symmetry to the bureaucratic denouement of the Russian Revolution was increasingly evident. Stalin intuitively relied upon the
party bureaucracy, or even the foreign bourgeoisie, rather than
the Russian proletariat itself, while the Comintern, an extension
of the new power base within the state bureaucracy, acquired an
affinity for bureaucratic power within unions around the world.
Unlike the reformers of the Second International, these were not
racists nor representatives of some skilled working class segment, but products of the mass industrial phase, thinking in
terms of industrial rationalization and international consumer
marketing analogously to their corporate opposite numbers.
State Capitalist functionaries-in-progress, they had repudiated
private capitalism without believing that the classic proletariat of
Karl Marx's vision could in the foreseeable future rule without
rulers.[18]

James cut through the moralistic criticism Trotskyists and
liberals unthinkingly made of Stalinism. How Communist parties
manipulated their unquestionably idealistic ranks seemed to
these critics an unresolvable problem which they covered over
with verbiage about 'totalitarianism'—a rhetoric borrowed from
anti-Naziism and soon turned against Marxists of all kinds.
James had a better, because more historical, answer. 'Stalinism
is a concrete truth . . . a necessary, an inevitable form of development of the labor movement', no distortion of history in the
final sense, but the working out of a logic inherent in the uneven
pace of world revolution. The one-party state he viewed as a
similarly inevitable 'attempt to respond to the contemporary
necessity for the fusion and transcendence of nation, class, party,
state'.[19]

From the rampant pessimism engendered by Stalinism's coop-
tation of all organized resistance to capitalism, James drew hope.
When the society as a whole perceived the forces of production

(the working class) to be essentially *social* and not merely economic, the working class stood subjectively closer than ever before to cutting the Gordian Knot. The old categories that had held fast since the beginnings of capitalism, the mysterious origin of the commodity in workers' labor-power on the one hand and the supposed autonomy of party and state on the other, lost their essential definitions. As Engels had predicted in *Anti-Dühring*, the last major text of the founding fathers, 'concealed within' the very contradictions of this more highly organized capital were 'the technical conditions that form the elements of the solution.'[20]

There was much to be said for this sweeping critique. James and his collaborators neatly identified the logical error of Trotsky, but also of Communists and Socialists since at least the Second International, as the identification of socialism with the *form* of state ownership and not the social relations that prevail within that form. Socialism—although James did not quite spell it out this way—had become a means for overcoming the precapitalist obstacles to modern production and social relations in Europe and the emerging Third World. Socialists, and now Communists, carried out the abstract ideal of the bourgeois program of 'progress'. No wonder political socialism had so little effect in America, born bourgeois and relatively free of state encumberances. And no wonder Black aspirations, especially those of the Black proletariat, had such a threatening aspect. In this sector of the national working class, the global reality of capitalist exploitation impinged upon the American delusions of bourgeois utopia.[21]

Contemporary Trotskyists outside James' little group regarded this as virtual madness, but the New Left and Black nationalists who recovered James from American obscurity some twenty years later recognized something of his accomplishments: his prescient use of Marx's 1844 *Economic Philosophical Manuscripts* as a means to identify fundamental social alienation, on the one hand, and his belief in autonomous Black revolutionary potential on the other. They were too late, or perhaps too early, to accept the corollary: James' discovery of autonomous work-cultures whose members had instinctively developed their own patterns of resistance and mobilization, not in the interest of any socialist revolution but with their own immediate needs in mind. However limited this tendency might prove, it offered the hope of industrial democracy from the bottom up, out of the lives of ordinary people rather than the plans of experts.

James' critics easily identified a kind of neo-Hegelianism that came from his reading the *Logic* side by side with *Capital*. Certainly James and his followers idealized workers, not in the one-dimensional fashion of other left-wing parties, but in their own way. Anarchists or Wobblies though they seemed to many observers, James' group followed Lenin's teachings as if the Soviets were virtually in formation, and the potential resistance of the Party, any Leninist party, was about to become the chief obstacle to overcome. In the carnival atmosphere of the postwar strikes, where masses of people took to the streets in defiance of employers and labor leadership, it might have seemed a possible perspective. They took too little notice of the deep racial and gender attitudes which penetrated working-class social life, and the consequent psychological appeal that anti-Communism made to the self-image of the white, male worker in particular. They could not grasp, in theory, the individualistic impulses that home ownership and suburbanization, commodities and wage hikes, gratified in return for industrial pacification. And they had no appreciation of the real plight of the unrecalcitrant radical, the anti-racist, anti-war Communist or Trotskyist or independent, factory operative or minor leader, who simply did not find in fellow workers the traits that James described. It was a perspective for immediate transformation which, like so many others of its type, did not account for the human and institutional sources of defeat.

Yet for all this, James and his collaborators had essayed conclusions no one else had dared in the collapse of a political era. The economic fatalism and faith in the construction of political elites, the ancient working-class hopes, state ownership of production—had all become archaic or, worse, a part of the logic of continued capitalist development. The potential forces for change had to be re-examined. That sort of initiative required too much courage and energy from movements reeling from the natural loss of rank-and-file membership to the economic boom and the extraordinary loss of cadre from rampant harassment, threatened deportation and other repression. James' crew embraced Black mass struggles against bureaucracies of all kinds, detecting before anyone else the racial element and political significance of the wildcat strikes in predominantly Black auto factories. They also boldly experimented with journalistic forms, lineal descendents of the 1920s 'Workers' Correspondence' efforts, to let workers speak for themselves on politics, factory life, racial or sexual struggles and popular culture. They brought a New Left perspective to the working class, with an impact less political and more cultural than they imagined.[22]

Culture as Tragedy

The alternative march away from the Old Left, wholly ruling out what James (after the young Marx) had called the 'self-activity' of the working class, turned political vanguardism into a melancholy critique of mass delusion. Trotskyists and ex-Trotskyists who argued in this fashion had the best of authority. 'Trotsky declared that the proletariat does not grow under capitalism and declines in culture', James and his collaborators had noted.[23] If so, a protracted capitalist recovery meant catastrophe for culture generally, and a cruel dilemma for Marxist intellectuals. Clement Greenberg first signalled the mood with his frequently reprinted essay, 'Avant-Garde and Kitsch', in which every grain of popular culture expressed a fundamental flaw in creation, and everything in modern society encouraged a grotesque parody of civilized values.[24]

From this optic the failure of revolutionary politics and, worse than failure, the betrayal of human values, had been a *symptom* of pitiless drift from the promise of the nineteenth century (or the Enlightenment, or even classical antiquity), to the self-annihilation of the human spirit. The intellectual obviously had only narrow choices: to join the celebration of the coming barbarism as patriots seemed too eager to do in Russia and America; or to refuse to participate. The 'great refusal', as Herbert Marcuse later called it, would at least leave a record of personal integrity and perhaps some worthwhile ideas for those who followed.

These choices, over the long run, implied others. To withdraw from the Marxist-historicist faith of an intellectual generation might mean resignation to the reigning temporal powers—acquiescence in the Cold War, pursuit of a career and upward mobility—so as to preserve the narrowed space for the life of the mind. It also might mean just the reverse: a collective intellectual crusade *outside Marxism*, outside all existing orthodoxies, to find new ground for opposition. The two solutions intermixed, as events foreclosed the possibility of any immediate social transformation.

Irving Howe, who speaks for the faded but authentic survival of radicalism in his generation, has sketched the cultural background that prepared the emerging intellectual for personal solutions. The larger public culture of New York during the 1920s–30s reputedly made the great literature and the humanistic values of the West widely accessible to the lower classes, most especially to the determined young idealist. This was a world already fast disappearing to a popular audience, but still accessible to those seeking its rich fruits.[25]

In retrospect, the naive intellectuals in the making had begun their quest by exiling from their own minds much of what their predecessor Jewish intellectuals had striven to create. The conscious turning away from a ghetto-tainted Yiddish and *Yiddishkayt*, a denial reinforced by the compulsory assimilation of public schools and of professional occupations, signified an unconscious acceptance of their middle-class American status even before they took on their radical political identities. They successfully escaped the lower-class ghettoes, mixed freely with native-born Americans of all types, and in time graduated to distinguished status with all the accompanying perquisites. On the other hand, they did not and could not accept the trans-class middle American culture of unvanquished religiosity, sports enthusiasm and generalized indifference to European high culture. They were repelled by the mass culture presence in their own neighborhoods and in the working class they sought for a time to revolutionize. In a strange way, their background left them both more and less adapted than the Yiddish revolutionaries who envisioned a peacefully chaotic multi-cultural society without any necessarily universal standard.[26]

Squarely on the middle ground that Adorno called the home turf of the critic, half in and half outside the phenomenon to be studied, they spoke for the results of the bourgeois nineteenth century and its modernist negators and continuators among whom they numbered themselves. And they spoke (as long as they retained their radicalism) for a future society which would one day hold these values high. At best, this perspective gave them a tenacious sense of self in the tradition of the idealtypic European intellectual. They were the first Marxist-related group outside a political party to have that kind of collective stamina. No palpable lack of real political influence, no momentary obscurity from the main radical paths or mainstream academic paths, could deter them from their continual self-clarification. At worst, their disaffection with popular culture (save perhaps for film) tended toward snobbery, a philistinism in its own right that blended all too well with the sophisticated cynicism of the postwar intellectual establishment. In both senses, they were the mirror opposite of the untenacious, influential but ephemeral Popular Front intellectuals.

Their self-developed worldview encompassed the unconscious assumption that mass society meant mass manipulation, confirming their suspicion of the ever-deteriorating condition of public intelligence. The influence of the Communists before the war and the triumph of commercialism afterwards seemed to vindicate this pessimism. The cultural loneliness of the New York intellectuals, their total sense of opposition on all fronts, confirmed Trotskyism as a shaping worldview even where it had become rogue Marxism and State Department Socialism.

Originally, in the *Partisan Review*, they had tried to reach beyond the mental reductionism of the Left, attempting (although key editors William Phillips and Philip Rahv would not put it this way yet) to be more revolutionary along those lines than the revolutionaries themselves. They identified the problem with the absence of a meaningful American past, and the solution with Europe. They sought to contextualize revolutionary culture, but mainly in the artistic upper reaches. Art 'worked' when it captured reality with the full sense of that tradition intact. Literary criticism for them, as for the Communists, offered the arena of shared sentiment and insight unlikely outside 'good' books, plays, music and painting. Modernism, if it failed to capture the entire imagination of the masses, yet retained all the promise of the avant-garde and could with a little imagination be seen as precursor of a critical, perhaps even popular, American radical culture.

Such a position had real importance for writers seeking to escape Party literary formulae; but the ultimate implications, the shape of the envisioned art or criticism of the future, remained inchoate. The Communists' own move toward the Popular Front and the rallying of liberal culture against Fascism placed a revived and independent *Partisan Review* in the ambiguous position of speaking for revolutionary (and against reform) culture through the high literary canon and the avant-garde. Hardly any one still believed in the writer's burying self in the proletariat. But who was the writer and where *did* he or she hang the hat of identity?

The Moscow Trials fixed Phillips's and Rahv's politics, and willy-nilly made the *PR* a mechanism for intellectual resistance, *i.e.,* Trotskyism. But their politics bore little resemblance to classical Leninism, and was only tenaciously allied to the main partisans of Trotskyism. The defense of Trotsky became their *cause celebre*, and rightly so. They also took individual potshots at Stalinism wherever possible, in the pages of the *Nation* and elsewhere. With some notable exceptions, most of the milieu around them felt little inclined to join a Trotskyist organization or even to pass out a leaflet. The public attacks they suffered at the hands of the *New Masses* writers nevertheless reinforced their own sense of importance. They would speak for the American intelligentsia, slice off the intellectual head of the Stalinist gorgon, and set out new critical standards.

The further the Popular Front moved away from revolutionary aspirations, the more readily *Partisan Review* could attack from the left. For a moment, in 1938–40, they spoke in the name of a modernist-radical vision which still resonated, albeit in a much diminished fashion, with echoes of the old bohemian self-liberation. They lacked only the connections with a real movement that the *Masses* once enjoyed, its circulation, and its vanished *joie de vivre*.

The war and the sense of impending doom that hung over socialist prospects imposed upon the *PR* group the obligation of preserving values threatened with extinction by the prevailing barbarisms. Hardening anti-Communism and, by the 1950s, creeping conformism or complacency, played curious roles in this development. As the ideological compromises of many Communists during the 1930s and 1940s did not necessarily deflect them from their practical and creative tasks (or did so in ambiguous ways), so the open call for alliance with the postwar bourgeoisie, the hysterical attack on the peace camp and on anti-McCarthyism, even the overlap in personnel and finances with the CIA-funded Congress for Cultural Freedom during the 1950s did not close the *Partisan Review* to heterodoxy of non-political sorts, or (more important) to contributions by younger avant-garde types who had no other outlet.

It might be said, with some justice, that such power tended to constrain these latter writers much as Communist publications had earlier young people, by setting out the rules (this time, kneejerk anti-Communism and obeisance to existing literary authorities, in place of uncritical support for the Soviet Union and obeisance to Mike Gold) for making personal connections and for publishing. *PR* personalities used their cultural power ruthlessly, much as Communists would presumably have done in their place. But in both eras, serious interest in cultural criticism, with a vague avant-garde or demi-Marxist flavoring, was otherwise confined to small literary circles. Where else besides *PR*, until the 1960s, did the door open to current French philosophy? Certainly not in the academic journals, nor in the surviving Marxist or Socialist publications.

PR's limitations, from a cultural point of view, grew more obvious as the decades passed. Because it had nothing positive to substitute for the mass cultural politics it attacked, the *Partisan*

Review could not supercede the Popular Front cultural approach but could only help to drive it underground. Red scares, black-listing and the intellectuals' own disillusionment, not the protests of avant-gardes, cut the Communists from the mainstream and shut down their cultural presses. The specific thirties presentational modes identified with Communists and the Popular Front nevertheless returned ceaselessly to popular films and television, not because of continuing Communist influence (although many younger militant liberal writers and directors would owe personal debts to blacklisted figures), but because no other form of social issues drama (by the 1970s, a Popular Front descendent comedy-drama) could be successfully devised. A few of film's and many of television's proudest moments originated in this milieu. The *Partisan Review* crowd, despite its prestige in the intellectual world, had little useful criticism or any contribution to make to such developments. It is staggering to think that during the Golden Age of popular culture, with glorious phenomena from Bebop to Hank Williams, Sr., to *Mad Comics* to Sid Caesar, New York intellectual conversation remained centered on Flaubert and Henry James. What tunnel vision for all that critical energy!

This extreme myopia posed once more the ultimate contradiction in American intellectual life. Without a means to establish contact with, or even acquire a serious perspective on, the culture of ordinary Americans, the European foundation which the *PR* insisted upon tended to become precious, the mental hoard of the few who were increasingly devoted to defending their turf and their historic reputations. As American Communism disappeared and the *Partisan Review* further narrowed its agenda, its personalities grew larger than life. They were talented, hard-working, and increasingly absorbed in their own minor celebrity. By the later 1960s, Rahv fled. In his brief effort at a new journal before his death, he sought to set up shop again as an avant-garde critic and true radical. The most brilliant of the crew, he had seen through the self-delusion. The ignominy heaped upon him by former co-workers said more about the moral disintegration of the old crowd than about his purported masquerade as the savant of radical chic. He at least had tried to recover the original, core purposes of criticism.[27]

But the *PR* had one other great negative virtue. Its intellectual commitment and rightward-turning politics tended to spin off the loose energies of intellectuals still determinedly radical. One such byproduct was *Politics* (1944–49) magazine, Dwight Mac-Donald's brainchild and without doubt the clearest collective voice of the radical non-Communist intelligentsia since the *Modern Quarterly*. MacDonald, coming from a genteel WASP background utterly unlike the humble Jewish origins of the other New York intellectuals, had enlisted formally in the Trotskyist movement on the eve of the Second World War only to abandon his membership two years later for the status of permanent renegade. Similarly, for kindred reasons, he abandoned the *Partisan Review* when its own party line (actually a version of the uncritical support the Communists lent to the war effort and its ominous domestic accoutrements) blessed the leviathan state.

Politics—the name had been suggested by C. Wright Mills— ultimately became the definitive intellectual link between the Old Left of 1930s–40s and the New Left of the 1950s–60s. In its pages can be found a willful withdrawal from the historical agendas of the Marxist movements, a withdrawal interpreted and explained with the aid of the Marxist intellectual tradition. It recognized the barbarism of Stalin's slave-labor camps and the equally barbarous American atomic war against Japanese cities as twin phenomena of an inhuman age. And it sought, mostly on uncertain ground, to take a moral position *against*, like the old Dadaists who assayed the bankruptcy of Europe after the First World War. Like the Dadaists, the attempt by this newer intellectual fringe to reconstruct the pieces proved less successful than its useful deconstructive efforts.

Intellectually, *Politics* introduced Mills, Paul Goodman, Irving Howe, Lewis Coser and, to a US audience, Albert Camus and Victor Serge, along with such future conservative savants as Daniel Bell, Oscar Handlin, Nathan Glazer, and Irving Kristol. More important than the contents, more important even than MacDonald himself, was the journal's readership. They spoke through the editor and the contributors, as far as they ever would, about the vast disappointments and the fresh insights the age had forced upon them as a group. As MacDonald later commented, the overwhelming majority of his 5,000 readers were male college graduates under thirty-five. Although not a large audience, it included most of the rebellious intellectuals coming out of the war experience. *Politics* helped explain to this generation why wartime progressive hopes were inflated, adding to trenchant analysis an existential element—*felt* not reasoned— that became a solace for the new isolation of the radical intelligentsia.[28]

A descendent of both *Partisan Review* and *Politics*, more subdued but also more solid in its analytical style than either, was the last distinguished journal of the Old Left, *Dissent*. Now liberals of a Cold War, democratic-socialist sort, editors Lewis Coser and Irving Howe retained a number of the *Politics* contributors along with that journal's passion for the precise statement of political morals. They sought to bind together the university intellectuals, Socialist trade unionists (mostly local officials), and free-ranging intellectuals around a common program of support for democratic institutions East and West, and a less well-defined concern for the common culture.

The particular way in which *Dissent* reached out spoke to generational politics. According to Howe's own testimony, editors and contributors sought to pick up the pieces of decomposed Socialism, to re-examine them, to survey related current developments and to wage polemics against their former comrades who had moved more swiftly and further rightward. Even in looking toward the future, they carried the particular burdens of the past, much as the politically surviving *Masses* editors had carried their generational passions into the 1920s and 1930s. 'In the fifties, for better or worse,' Howe said, 'almost everything began that would dominate our life in the following decades'.[29] The operative word here, 'began', might be better written, 'crystallized'.

Although *Dissent* touched a handful of younger intellectuals, it tended like any other quasi-Old Left institution to cast them in its own image exclusively. It sought not diversity but agreement, perhaps because *Dissent* saw Stalinism in nearly every quarter where dismal conservative trends did not dominate. Obsessively it applied the litmus test and found the radical specimen turning suspiciously toward the red end of the scale. By way of contrast, the more pictorial and short-lived *American Socialist*, cousin from another version of abandoned Trotskyism, sought to separate friendly intellectuals from their Communists pasts. *Dissent* had no taste for such Christian charity or the wider confraternity it might have encouraged. It remembered every wound, as Howe and Coser drove home with their vindictive history of the American Communist Party, written at the very moment the Party was disintegrating.

Dissent represented a peculiarly chastened Left eager for Democratic Party openings toward a wider welfare state and for genuine material advances among the poor, but utterly hostile to the changing intellectual tastes it perceived as mere fads and fashions. The great questions had, as far as *Dissent* was concerned, already been settled. Further efforts at revision, particularly those moving toward the non-Democratic Party left or toward some intellectual compromise with popular culture, were excoriated with all the editors' polemical energies. *Dissent* expressed a more polite (or perhaps dry-witted) dismay at the slide of its own surrounding milieu toward neo-conservatism. It stood fast, decade after decade, proclaiming its values into the 1980s. It seemed little changed by time and the addition of new editorial talent. Still echoing the original *Partisan Review*'s rejection of a hostile and corrupting reality, *Dissent* continually hinted at the anticipation of further betrayals, something almost inevitable in a lifetime of disappointments.

The polemical bluster disguised great quantities of anguish, nowhere more apparent than in Irving Howe himself, who became a kind of pessimistic Floyd Dell with the hopes of the 1910s now stood upon their head. Howe sought repeatedly in his own criticism to recover from the nineteenth and early twentieth the then–new sensibilities and new cultural politics, and to describe their dismal outcome in real life (including, he usually hinted, his own). In his moments of candor, he spoke for the New York Intellectuals. He was their otherwise vanished social conscience and their final, melancholy scribe.[30]

Toward the New Left

The 1950s motor-cycle driving radical-professor-as-existentialist, C. Wright Mills, was part of the same *Politics/Dissent* milieu; but he was already escaping to the borders of what would become the New Left. He was also the embodiment of a category that had to be reinvented: not a New York Jewish but a Western talent, fascinated at the congealed circles of avant-garde intellectuals but contemptuous of their compromises and, even more, their *mood* of political futility. Mills knew America would listen to radical ideas if they were explained differently. He and A. M. Simons (or John Reed) would have had a lively conversation.

David Riesman's *The Lonely Crowd*, a favorite book of liberal instructors during the early 1960s (speaking as it did to *their* generational disappointments), pinpointed the importance of a cultural change which seemingly made leisure more important than work, consumption more decisive than production, and as a corollary, the middle class itself both chief subject and object of concern. Not surprisingly, in a prosperous age just emerging from the shadow of Hitler and Stalin, 'conformity' had displaced material want at the apex of social concerns. The pervasive sense of rootlessness and alienation escaped the charges of disloyalty that hounded other criticisms of the US order and simplified for

Americans the Frankfurt School view of an advancing totality crushing the individual mind and the collective conscience. Mills added a significant Germanic sophistication (by way of a Frankfurt School lesser-known, Hans Gerth) and a vital prose style. The fusion of native idiom and cosmopolitan resources energized Mills' critiques of labor bureaucracy (*The New Men of Power*, 1948), the middle class (*White Collar*, 1951), and the upper class (*The Power Elite*, 1956). *The Sociological Imagination* (1959), a virtual demand that intellectuals return to the barricades of social commitment, evinced all the weakness of the general critique. But having abandoned the class perspective of Marxism for something closer to Max Weber or Robert Michels, Mills could locate no other possible dynamic. One found in him more personal example than intellectual mentor. *He had not given in*. His popularity would wane, his attachment to the sociological standards would not survive his generation—at least among radicals—but his example would shine. Abandoned to its own devices, the intelligentsia had no choice but to act, with and upon the conditions at hand. Mills issued a cry into the wilderness that fell upon waiting ears.[31]

Mills was not alone in his protest. C. L. R. James published a formidable (but at the time, very obscure) book-length treatment of Melville and *Moby-Dick*, locating the heart of darkness within the totalitarian Ahab, the antidote in the spontaneity of the promethean working-class crew, and the vital middle term in Ishmael, the intellectual who must choose. F. O. Matthiessen, a Christian Socialist and homosexual as unlike the *Partisan Review* crowd as the Texan Mills or the West Indian James, had earlier traced in his monumental *American Renaissance* (the most read major literary study of the USA, certainly the most important radical one until Fredric Jameson's writings) the tragedy the West imposed upon itself, not by Philistinism or weakness toward Communism but by its own triumphant individualism. Matthiessen took personal cognizance of the tragic element in American life as immigrants and the children of immigrants could hardly do. The nation's sins were deeper than the most avaricious and manipulative ruling class could by itself create, and deeper than a victorious proletariat could eradicate in a day. Like the radical democrats of the nineteenth century, Matthiessen understood America's 'ruthless individualism', its opposition of intellect to practical life, as a fundamental flaw. Unlike his contemporaries, the aesthetes, he saw no reason to celebrate the literary results. Matthiessen seized upon the promise of American life in the nineteenth century's most brilliant group of thinkers and artists, viewed through the individual artist and his work, as keys to the whole. The organic view, the healthy American attempt to learn directly from nature and from practical life, he struggled to reconcile with Transcendentalist dreaminess on the one side, and narrow Calvinist property obsessions on the other. Matthiessen was himself a martyr to that dichotomy. 'Socialist without a party' (he was branded a fellow-traveling Communist), peace advocate without a movement after 1948, he committed suicide at the height of the Cold War, leaving a crucial legacy of his own funds to the young, struggling and independent-minded *Monthly Review*.[32]

Equally tragic, for American radicals afterward, would be the sudden departure of James and Mills from the intellectual and political scene. James faced deportation shortly after his Melville book appeared. Mills, the radical individualist, died in 1959, leaving his premature testament, 'Letter to the New Left'. Such intellectuals had no *minyan*, no collective openings to a dissident American intellectual life which existed hardly anywhere in the 1950s.

One exceptional location did stand out already in the mid-1950s, and in bringing together dissidents of a new type, it forecasted better than any of the New York publications the intellectual phase just ahead. Shortly after the New York Intellectuals evolved definitively toward accommodation with *Pax Americana*, a less prestigious but—from the retrospective viewpoint of the New Left—more important group moved in the reverse direction for precisely opposite reasons. The University of Wisconsin had been a center of anti-monopolist, anti-imperialist thought since the days of Robert LaFollette. It was shortly to regain its historic role, in New Left guise.

Many intellectuals in the old Middle Border had bowed uneasily to the inevitability of war mobilization, suspecting—with a handful of Trotskyists, unrecalcitrant pacifists, and Charles Beard—that militarization of American life would become permanent. They had their own reasons for thinking so, which were as deeply rooted in regional tradition and the historic resistance to World War One as in the growing dangers of the Cold War. The postwar US rush to world domination alarmed civil libertarians, recalcitrant Jeffersonians, and quirky Midwest radicals who might be found at the height of the McCarthy Era seeking public signatures on a disguised Declaration of Independence. A new generation of scholars, mostly refugees from Old Left families and from the Henry Wallace campaign, joined these odd ducks on the Madison campus and relearned radical history with

native coloring. The same youngsters were also, and not coincidentally, the first generation of immigrants' children who could
fit comfortably into a field now comprised not of gentlemen
scholars but of middling professionals. They took their models
and their immediate constituency, respectively, not from the
William Z. Fosters or the flagging trade-union movement, but
from the quasi-isolationist, anti-military tradition of Progressive
historians and from the new mass student culture.

Ironically, the signal weaknesses of homegrown Progressivism
which Marxists had excoriated in the past had become almost
positive features by the 1950s. The rightward march of Cold War
liberalism toward justification of American business leadership
made the older surviving Progressivism seem, by contrast,
further to the left of the mainstream than it had been since its
heyday at the turn of the century. Moreover, the defense of civil
liberties, including academic freedom, had become almost subversive. Scholarly criticism of something so apparently removed
as nineteenth-century Indian policy signalled suspicion of current racism; commentary upon Woodrow Wilson's maneuvering
of the nation into the World War One suggested doubts about
current American adventures in Indo-China. The racism and the
anti-urbanism (sometimes thinly-disguised anti-Semitism) of the
old Progressivism could be comfortably abandoned by this new
generation of scholars. They evinced a vigorous will to understand and to act upon America in some fresh way and radicalize it
anew through their own experiences and perceptions.[33]

The young scholars knew the limits of the tradition almost as
well. They felt keenly the absence of any vital school of Marxist
historical interpretation, and the methodological void left by the
inadequacies of Progressivism gave their own work an almost
fanatically empirical character. They abandoned the teleology of
class conflict while struggling to sustain an egalitarian vision
more sophisticated and complete than any non-Socialist view
could possibly accommodate. In political terms, they hardly
knew what to do with their own conclusions: the next generations, resuscitated by direct action, would have to complete the
transition and the simultaneous re-translation of Marxist ideas
into current historical study. These Silent Generation intellectuals offered their writings and their own model as the unfinished
material for the future. In doing so they revolutionized the study
of American history and the self-conception that it gave to future
radicals.

William A. Williams' *The Tragedy of American Diplomacy*
(1959), a careful account of the twentieth-century drive for

foreign markets and the subsequent pattern of US intervention, established a 'revisionist' view of the Cold War and Third World policy that had profound reverberations. By situating the sources of American expansionism in the early republic, and by giving American striving a self-destructive, tragic cast, Williams touched a nerve that Marxists had forgotten existed. Williams also provided the pregnant phrase, 'Corporate Liberalism', and the rough but serviceable definition for the phenomenon. America had, he wrote in *Contours of American History* (1961), answered its need for regulation with a false solution. A modern (and in Williams' own peculiar interpretation, much inferior) version of mercantilism bound together the expansionist, undemocratic corporation with the military-industrial power of the modern state. That state, feckless with regard to the perils it imposed upon humankind, had to be analyzed as a totality, not broken up conceptually into 'liberal' and 'conservative' components; indeed, its historical interpretation depended precisely upon an understanding of how liberal initiatives were integral to the preservation and expansion of the system.[34]

Williams' vision provided the intellectual framework and some of the slogans for the anti-war movement. His careful historical analysis exposed the falsity of Cold War rhetoric and the mistaken interpretations of Third World restiveness. Indeed his work set the tone for later interpretations of US social institutions in general, from schools to prisons to labor unions. Without conceding anything to a CPUSA-style Marxism, it threw the slogans of national security back into the teeth of the Cold Warriors, and posed the question of American democracy anew. Certainly Williams' work had its conceptual limits: it tended toward a mechanical over-interpretation of the state's manipulative capacities and an underestimation of past democratic struggles which created the current liberal institutions. Nevertheless, his critique had an unsurpassed heuristic power in the Veblenesque sense radicalized Americans have always appreciated, tracing the hidden hands of real power within the supposed free market economy.

Mills, with his unremitting hope for the intelligentsia, Marcuse with his roots in middle-European scholarship, and Williams with his faith in a restored historical sensibility—all had this in common: they were, whatever their background and age, New Left (or pre-New Left) because they had abandoned economist Marxism and denied that the state was the main vehicle for Socialist transition. Still, and for all their evident hostility toward the accommodation of their colleagues to permanent Cold War, they remained model-types of what the independent Old Left intellectual had been. They had both feet in the university and the academic traditions even when their minds soared.

They were, in short, ambiguous parents to their ideological children of the wild 1960s. New Left activists, by contrast, saw the university foremost as a convenient base of operations. The differences became steadily more evident as social movements heated up from the early 1960s on. That did not mean the ideas had been discarded; the formulators, to their amazement, found their notions translated into slogans and carried like banners. It did mean the ideas had been cut loose from their specific moorings, for better or worse. That disjuncture signalled the intellectual-political pattern of Marxism among the New Left.

One further step was taken around Williams himself. The thick facticity of Madison intellectualism made it especially appealing to the probing searchers of the nascent academic New Left. The new generation coalesced around the first scholarly journal on the left since the 1930s, *Studies On the Left*, whose initial 1959 issue promised a 'radicalism of the disclosure'. Godchild of Williams, spawned by rebellious veterans of the Communist-linked Labor Youth League, its leading lights consisted largely of New Yorkers *become* radical Americans. They stood somewhere between the Marxism of their youth and the Progressive historians of their graduate training. They sought to draw left conclusions from anti-state premises without falling back into Jeffersonian anti-urban negativity; they tried to imagine a renewed Left which could attack corporate power without retreating to Marxist jargon or losing faith in knowledge, scholarship, and the creation of a responsible citizenry. They attempted, in short, to recuperate the democracy of the small producer into the prospects of a technological society. A most difficult task self-consciously undertaken decades late, it marked a giant conceptual step forward.[35]

Another, less scholarly but more political step was taken, back in New York, by an Old Leftist whose career spanned three radical generations. Abraham J. Muste, had already gone from the ministry to radical labor agitation and education in the early 1920s. In the late 1920s and early 1930s he was the prime mover of the American Workers Party—a unique attempt to naturalize Leninism (and for a moment, Trotskyism) on an American terrain. After the unhappy merger of the AWP into the orthodox Trotskyist movement, Muste returned to the church and to the pacifist Fellowship of Reconciliation that had sprung up during World War Two. In the debacle of the organized left that followed, groups like the FOR and Dorothy Day's Catholic Worker circle spoke to and for the insular dozens and hundreds vocally opposed to atomic diplomacy. Muste and Day also personally opposed 'exclusionism', the ink-blotter test for Communist taints considered obligatory by liberals and favored by many Socialists. Indeed, Muste sought to bring the remnants of the Old Left together in the 1950s for an exchange of views. Not very successful by ordinary standards, his effort was a remarkable sign of moral initiative.

Liberation magazine was Muste's boldest and most successful intellectual coalition. Founded in 1956, as the Cold War had begun to ease, it combined peace activists with civil rights veterans of the Congress for Racial Equality (CORE, which FOR had financially subsidized), independent Socialist and radical thinkers ranging from Dorothy Day to Lewis Mumford, to history professors at Wisconsin. *Liberation* made itself known by its on-the-spot reporting of the burgeoning civil rights struggle in the South, and its dedication to non-violent 'direct action'. But its pages also contained an unprecedented breadth of rethinking basic Socialist values in the atomic age. While its critics correctly pointed to *Liberation*'s religious underpinnings, they tended to miss the subtle populism which renewed the indigenous sense of outraged anti-state morality lost to the surviving Marxist remnants. The *Liberation* group's emphasis on struggle as a community (they, along with the civil rights movement proper, introduced the concept of 'participatory democracy' into American political discourse), their opposition to power politics of any kind, and their unwillingness to place the full blame of the Cold War upon Russians or Americans—all these bedrock convictions of their political life made them impervious to political manipulation. They seemed, whatever their age, to have the moral singlemindedness of youth unconsciously attuned to the coming generation.

In theory, *Liberation* was intended to present non-violence to a wide public; in practice, it achieved a forceful combination of ideas for militant pacifists and disaffiliated radicals. It did not intend, perhaps, to be Marxist at all. Neither did it need to be anti-Marxist. *Liberation* established a perspective within which the old distinctions between historical materialists and idealists became fairly outmoded, as uninteresting as the quarrels of surviving Communist and Trotskyist publications.[36]

For the New Left to manifest itself, other pieces of the historical puzzle remained to be put into place. Most of all, a critique of the surrounding mass culture, a critique both condemning mass manipulation and celebrating the unconscious 'negative moments' of creativity, needed to be developed. Here, too, segments of the Old Left had seen small parts of the future. The young and radical Norman Mailer predicted the drastic revision of conceptual politics to follow the long hiatus. The Old Left had been vanquished, but 'if a revolutionary time should come again, there would be a crucial difference if someone had already delineated a neo-Marxian calculus aimed at comprehending every circuit and process of society . . . until the crises of capitalism in the Twentieth Century would yet be understood . . .'[37]

Understood, that is, not as purely economic phenomenon, but as a complex cultural formation, not for the elite alone, but for the masses. If 'some gigantic synthesis' on a scale equal to *Capital* could be effected to account for whole nature of humanity in its modern situation, wisdom would become possible, which is to say that the legacy of Marxism would not have been wasted after all.

7

The New Left

We New Left Marxists grew up under a mushroom cloud with a silver lining: the nuclear war-threat which, as a byproduct, had erased the all-too-comforting historicism of the various Old Lefts. Compared to that loss, even the failures of Socialism in the East and the West which obsessed our predecessors seemed rather less alarming. They had been so entrapped in the pre-Hiroshima frameworks, the expansion of Socialism or the battle against reverse-Marxist expansion of Stalin's barbarism, that Armageddon became a mere extension of the old logics. Not for us. How could we become enthusiastic about either of the super-powers, armed to the teeth for *our* annihilation? How could we believe in the inevitability of any historical tendency to outrace the doomsday clock? We instinctively thought of ourselves as confronted by two different incarnations of a single menacing system, one world empire under different names.

Then again, the Old Left intellectuals' loss of realistic hope had been at least accompanied, perhaps (they often thought) even caused by the spread of mass culture. They were the last generation to revere, above all things, European high culture and the printed word. We were the first generation of American radicals born into the television era and the all-embracing mass culture. We thought in terms dictated by our surroundings— even in our arcadian idylls, if that is not too much of a contradiction in terms. The media invasion of the mind, worse to Old Left intellectuals than the nuclear arms race, had become part of our assumed reality and one of the rare sources for subversive signals.

Coming of age at the juncture of unprecedented perils and of a consumer-and-technology-inspired utopianism hardly known since the mid-nineteenth century, we believed (and I, for one, still believe) that the possibility of a world transformation lay just then before us. The ubiquitous 'peace and love' sentiment, however commercialized its articulation, portended a great change in the human condition. Personal preparation for the change became part of the popular cultural fabric. Trained in Marxist ideas and graduate studies, we veterans of Civil Rights, student power and sundry other campaigns seriously believed that we might be sometime soon sharing land and sexual partners, indifferent to nationality and language, and that we could bind all the wounds that the human spirit and the planet had suffered. Greater fools us? Perhaps. It was surely a religious idea. But nothing in our lives, before or since, has made so much sense.

The ambiguous space Marxism previously occupied in the lives of American rebels would seem to have been further reduced in this era. But that judgment (which we sometimes pessimistically or optimistically voiced ourselves) proved premature. Marxism helped to explain our soulless enemy, as well as our own descent from Woodstock to the real-life 1970s. Even when, in the first years of New Left mass politics, Marxists outside the sects had no wish to proclaim their intellectual patrimony, Marxist ideas exerted their influence through the informal network of individuals who collectively make possible a new movement. Very soon, when the astonishing turn came to Marxist-sounding slogans, the quality of recuperation became apparent. Without altering the New Left framework much, Marxism had filled in, represented and come to stand for those missing dimensions of political and cultural thought. In the end, Marxism had evolved (as it continues to evolve) into something scarcely recognizable to older generations of American Marxists, something closer to the young Marx or the middle-aged Bruce Springsteen than to the Second or Third Internationals. But the stamp of Marxism, some descendent of Marxism, remained undeniably there.

Behind this curious evolution, a not-so-mysterious absence could be readily discerned. In the period after 1965 there was a renaissance of traditional forms of American radicalism: racial unrest and moral support movements, women's emancipation struggles, a militant 'alternative' press, a utopian experimentation, and so on. Missing—at least in their classical forms—were the two historical conditions ascribed as central to mass radicalization by orthodox Marxism: economic crisis and working-class (especially ethnic) combativeness. The apparent absence of these elements underlined the end of the old Socialist teleology.

In the long run, capitalist expansion would presumably run up against its own self-created barriers; by that time, however, the planet might already have become unliveable. So much for the materialist inevitability of Socialism. Meanwhile the white male blue-collar attachment to Nixon in 1972 and, even more, to Reagan in 1978 symbolized the sociological and political shifts since the 1930s. The big-muscled proletariat of syndicalist lore no longer marches in the front rank of the revolutionary masses. Such changes—not absolute, to be sure, but demarcating a strikingly different era—seemed already in the 1960s to threaten the coherence of Marxism.

Or did they? To speak today of Marxism and Marxists implies a critical self-consciousness impossible twenty, let alone fifty years ago. The more precise identification of the capitalist and state socialist systems as political and cultural constructs with a supra-economic life of their own, centuries (in the case of gender relations, eons) in the making, begins to permit a coming-to-terms with Marxism—itself a product of the same systems—in ways hitherto unimaginable. Location of the historic class struggle (including its national, racial and sexual components) within the general social and cultural conditions of humankind has moved to the foreground of the intellectual agenda. The socialization of production and the built-in crisis of the economic system, keys to the old Marxism, take on a renewed and altered relevance as part of a larger process. Economic crisis mirrors and symptomizes a deeper sickness in the civilization. The socialization is world-wide and extends from production to culture, where a cure may yet be found.

'Marx Against Marx', an Italian extra-Parliamentary slogan, captures a universal desire to transform Marxism's methods into a synthesis equal to the scope of the original. Drawing continual hints of a new universalism from the fragments of natural science, religion and the traditional humanities all suffering from the end of older illusions, spurred on by the crash of empires East and West and by proximity to total annihilation, the search evokes a personal intensity at the outer limits of Enlightenment thought. The New Left, at its best moments, *prepared* Marxist Socialism for such a renovation, in a yet unclaimed future.

Black Experience and the Opening of a New Left

The racial shift in the balance of radical politics had everything to do with the ideological development of the American New Left.

The New Left's predecessors had pioneered, labored toward, and in many cases sacrificed their lives for racial equality. They had inevitably done so in an atmosphere in which Blacks had very largely been the clientele or the intended future allies of a generous-minded and far-sighted Left. The collapse of the Marxist movements and the simultaneous upswing in civil rights in the 1950s reversed the equation; everything now started with the Blacks, and at least until the crest of the anti-war movement on the campuses, would remain so. Behind that strategic reality, a web of political understanding and personal growth entwined the white New Left's self-identity with the non-white world.

Subjectively, the role of Black culture in the teenage lives of the future New Left prepared the way. Only Communist or very racist parents, it is safe to say, perceived the breadth of this influence from sports to music to sexual fantasy. Youngsters grew up with pictures of Black stars on their walls, and lurched into a consumer culture whose comfort seemed almost invisible to those born free of significant material scarcity, but whose positive content came through the teen-oriented culture of records and top-forty radio stations. From the safe haven of the suburbs, the ghetto may have appeared scary but it was also the one place where authentic Americana seemed still to exist. To affirm solidarity with Blacks in any political sense was a minority act; but the sympathy towards Black culture reached further among millions of ordinary teenagers than any previously Left-orchestrated effort could have envisioned. Tell-tale signs of racism in parents, liberal or conservative, provided the proof of a generation gap long before that gap would be interpreted in directly political terms.

The Montgomery Bus Boycott of 1955 re-opened the social agenda closed by the Cold War, if only marginally at first. The charismatic leadership of Martin Luther King, Jr., and the extra-ordinary self-organization of urban Southern Blacks, gave the movement for integration unprecedented public presence and internal resolve. The 'Solid South' cracked. In a second phase, five years later, student-led sit-ins spread through the South and 'freedom rides' dramatized the violence of racist response. Soon, Black children by the tens of thousands would be marching for freedom, a first in American history.

The twin loci of activity, the Black church and the Black campus, suggested the dramatic shift of constituencies for social movements. The Civil Rights movement also thrust the Socialist-connected Congress of Racial Equality into the spotlight, and gave birth to the first of the new radical Black organizations, the

Student Non-Violent Coordinating Committee (SNCC). The un-willingness of the Kennedy administration to order adequate protection for the Freedom Riders, and the effectiveness of direct action in winning specific goals, suggested the limits of government help and the need for greater militancy. The sub-sequent Southern voter registration, conducted in the face of lynch terror and universal intimidation, contested local Demo-cratic powerstructures and forced Northern liberals to put money where their rhetoric was. The gap between front money and federal protection was filled in by the bravery and self-sacrifice of totally committed activists, whose style was existen-tially and instinctively democratic. As pusillanimous liberalism ended at the limits of federal support and guilty fundraising, a central New Left archetype, the SNCC staffer, emerged at a radicalized pole.

The Civil Rights movement arguably resembled the CIO and Knights of Labor more than any other social phenomenon America had seen. Sit-ins were, by this argument, a continuation of sit-down strikes: the activity of young people including chil-dren an extension of the pattern by which larger and larger parts of the community confronted authorities demanding direct rather than demonstrably inadequate representative democracy. The revolutionary nationalist phase which followed in Black America might be compared best to the earlier immigrant mass strikes; it showed a violent rejection of the niggling improve-ments American society offered, and a willingness to die in defiance of ethnocentric legal authorities.

An obscure 1964 pamphlet put the dilemma for liberals and the Old Left correctly: 'the tremendous Negro movement is an American form of radical thought and radical action. The pitiable subordination of American intellectuals to European historical norms and organization is seen nowhere as sharply as in their inability to recognize the specific American radicalism in the Negro movement'.[1]

This is perhaps an overstatement. The rise of a new, distinctive American idealism was greeted by a broad spectrum of intel-lectuals with enthusiasm and vigorous support, open checkbooks as well as open arms. But the overwhelming majority of the 1930s-40s political survivors and their younger counterparts had come to accept the welfare state led by a liberalized Democratic Party as the inevitable starting point of future changes. Rejec-tionism they viewed as a replay of their own youthful folly. Even for those who took a more severe and traditional view, the centrality of the working class to any major social change remained elementary. They could not think any other way, and they could not quite imagine that youth would be so blind as to discard all the lessons of the past. Marxism they understandably connected with their own political conclusions. A different idea of Marxism had as yet no serious cultivators.

We, the New Left Marxists-to-be, had instinctively begun along very different lines. As Fredric Jameson rightly says, late capitalism prospers by absorbing the final 'outside' elements available to it: the Third World and the unconscious. The New Left can readily be seen as a response to this global, systemic process.[2] Our preparatory phases developed through the interpretation of these processes in civil society and in our personal lives.

For those of us born between the war years and the early 1950s, our lives seemed to have led logically to the New Left moment. Save for the children of the Old Left, this generation grew up almost completely ignorant of the struggles that had passed by. We experienced the Red Scare not as a personal threat so much as a climate. Anti-Marxism had become a species of anti-Russianism woven into the national culture. American Marxism, if it ever existed, was circumspectly explained by high-school teachers and college professors as part of the hoary past, a footnote to history marked by such discrepancies as the 1920 'protest' vote for Eugene Debs, or the suspiciously pro-Russian sentiments in some World War Two films shown on late-night television. On the other hand, they could not dismiss so easily current-day American racism, and the presence of movements for racial equality.

But racial equality, except in the mouths of racist demagogues, did not *seem* to have any relation to Marxists or Marxism. Outside the big cities and more advanced campuses (and limited even there to certain neighborhoods), Marxist political activities remained rumor. The older radicals, as a movement, had been atomized. The high tide of McCarthyism left the mark of the heretic, the village atheist, upon the surviving individuals in a New York neighborhood or a Midwest campus town. Organized Communists, Trotskyists and Socialists lived an insular existence, that outsiders neither wished to nor could understand. Some young disciples infiltrated student government, where they advanced the liberal agenda temporarily; or worked inside a civil rights coalition or the Young Democrats, usually without disclosing their secret identity. The self-made radical had to conduct a search for the real thing. En route, he or she was as likely to read about Socialism in the Socialist Labor Party's

Weekly People as the CPUSA's *Worker* (reduced to twice weekly in 1958), to meet an aged pacifist as an avowed Marxist, and to go to a quasi-political Beat poetry reading as attend a Left educational event.

Consequently, for nearly everyone but 'red diaper babies', and also for them in a certain way, the arrival of Marxism trailed behind other forms of personal and political rebellion. This had happened to previous generations of radicals, from the nineteenth century to the 1940s. But now it took on a special poignancy and self-consciousness. Inasmuch as the working class neither appeared within reach of emancipating itself nor demonstrated any interest in Marxist doctrine, the presence of rampant injustice and of desires for drastic change induced a sense of despair (especially when racial efforts lagged) and a thirst for knowledge that might someday be useful. The subject of Socialism remained, for now, either at the plane of useful methodology, or the moral appeal of a disembodied voice from somewhere reaching out into the darkness of middle America. *Monthly Review, Dissent, New Politics,* or smaller and more rare items with their own eccentric political group identity like *News and Letters*, could serve the student equally well. During the 1950s and early sixties the choice of reading tended to be random, depending more on friends and library collection than any preconceived sense of difference. More often than generally has been remembered, some open-minded Old Left veteran who had re-emerged quietly as a professor and aide-de-camp to civil rights groups provided a booklist, and gave Marxist concepts a human face.

The particular varieties of Marxism one stumbled upon did not generally satisfy, at least not completely. Left journal editors had limited contact with younger generations, and the relatively few new books by Marxists mostly had a dated feel. But the paucity of material did lend a psychological advantage: no one would be overwhelmed by it. The feeling of starting over began here for the simple reason that existing organizations and ideas seemed so obviously inadequate to the civil rights revolution or to the problem of nuclear disarmament. Perhaps not since the turn of the century had the sense of virginal beginnings been so absolute.

The hard-working radical student, for instance, could exhaust the entirety of Marxist classics and exegetical works published from Moscow to New York, even flip through the bound library copies of old American Socialist and Communist journals, without any great strain. The experience, for the library-strollers of the time, provided a breadth of knowledge which helped to guard against particular doctrinal fixations. It also bolstered self-confidence. From a social standpoint, some of the older radicals one met qualified as aides, or as mentors for specific occasions. None, except to the blind-eyed young sectarian, could provide leaders. We had no cause to trust anyone over thirty in matters of political guidance; this was not a form of parent-hating but a simple historic reality in most places.

The self-conscious character of the rebellion-in-the-making naturally focused upon explorations of personal life: *Young Werther* or *Catcher in the Rye* updated and politicized. There was, for instance, *Eros and Civilization* (1955), Marcuse's revolutionary reading of Freud. Young women destined to become architects of feminism privately delved into the origins of gender repression; the young romantic understood how art, and sheer play, could offer a glimpse of Socialism within the capitalist era. Sexuality, the eternal quest of youth, received the ultimate theoretical blessing. The instinctive basis for our cultural anti-racism (or, more strongly, admiration of Afro-American culture) had been reaffirmed. No wonder the book became a favored possession and that the dignified old man later found himself, against his will, media-made into a guru of the time, media superstar comparable to the Beatles on one hand and Chairman Mao on the other. Like Mills, Baran, and Williams, Marcuse offered a prototype for *our* Marxism, without seeking to impose any particular political conclusions.

We would discover later that Marcuse had actually supplied the popular gloss for a systematic critique that had lain outside an Old Left unwilling or unable to take its criticism of Western civilization to the very core values. The Frankfurt School exiles, principally Theodor Adorno, Max Horkheimer and Marcuse, scrupulously avoided optimism about the prospects for Socialism or the survival of democratic values. Formally outside politics, especially since the suicide of their more Marxist and surrealist colleague, Walter Benjamin, they lacked any formal need to attach themselves to the West and to place their confidence in Cold War culture. They had long since despaired of the modern fate. But they gave this despair a dialectical edge missing from even the best of avowed Left culture criticism.

Self-confident in the *Kulturgeschichte* that American intellectuals manifestly lacked, these elite German Jews steadily formulated a coherent post-Marxist approach in their little read *Zeitschrift für Sozialforschung*, which emigrated from Frankfurt to Paris and ultimately New York as the editors fled before the victories of Fascism. Writing from intimate experience with Nazism, they turned utopia inside out. They understood better than their American counterparts (who preferred to see Hitler as an alien manifestation) the deep cultural roots of Fascism in modern civilization. The decisive Frankfurt School document, Horkheimer's and Adorno's *Dialectic of the Enlightenment* (1949), made clear that the repression represented in the triumph of Greek classicism over its predecessor mythologies already signalled the constraints that the Enlightenment would codify. A denial of irrationalities that did not fit its expectation, the repression sought to harness the whole of conscious and unconscious thought to programmed work and release (soon, wage-labor and consumption). The effort ultimately evoked the very irrationality it repressed. The supple minds of liberal conformity, Horkheimer and Adorno concluded, ignored the approaching day when nothing would remain of the human sprit but the collective beast feeding upon its own impending self-destruction.

The Frankfurt School anticipated much of the distinctive problematic of the New Left, which would soon disinter its works and reestablish its influence. Yet at the same time the Frankfurters, in their peculiarly European despair, were unable to feel the real pulse of resistance in American popular life. Like Trotsky with his famous aversion to American chewing gum, Adorno found the habits and pleasures of the natives almost beneath civilized contempt. His abysmal misinterpretation of jazz as 'bestial', his overwrought analyses of Donald Duck as the self-punishing 'little man', and of musical absurdist Spike Jones' satires of 'long hair' music as exercises in castration—seemed silly to anyone who had, in fact, grown into rebellion precisely in these environs.[3]

The New Left were by no means the first Marxists to think of culture as political, but previously the constitutive power that culture possessed—ethnic (or racial) traditions on the one hand, *belles lettres*, on the other—had been ghettoized amongst the Left. 'Proletarian Culture' had never been more than a fantasy; middle class 'progressive' culture, including a refurbished 'folk culture', little more than an uncertain constellation of heterogenous elements. The cultural homogenization endemic to postwar consumerism ironically prepared us to reach outside the known frameworks of cultural analysis to new formulations, even when we did not know what exactly we were trying to define. We unconsciously sought out a cultural politics that the

Old Left had never articulated. Race had provided the first big clue, but a new Marxism needed a reformulation of the concept of revolutionary agency.

The most promising of the younger reform Socialists in the late 1950s, former Catholic Worker activist Michael Harrington, unintentionally wrote the script. Harrington dramatized the persistence of poverty in his *The Other America* (1962), but in a special way. Marxist and Progressive writings about the slums had been composed for a century, but Harrington adjusted the effort to the newer reality of the consumer society. Working-class advance had actually contributed to the formation of a bi-polar order, with perhaps a quarter of the population below the basic level of human needs and a disproportionate number of those Black. The New Deal state, which had responded (at least at a consumerist level) to the needs of organized labor and the middle classes, ineffectively treated the problems of the poor, thus creating an unstated gap in economic citizenship.

Harrington himself believed fervently in the possibilities of government intervention, and even more (if possible) in organized labor. But without saying so explicitly, he raised the prospect that failure to respond made a dangerous situation inevitable. Harrington did not himself imagine that spectre to be revolutionary, far from it. But he identified the future constituency of Watts or the other burning inner cities, and hinted that demagogues had plenty of room for action. The lumpen proletarian street-revolutionaries half a dozen years later were offspring of that prediction.[4]

Like Harrington, young idealists in the early and mid-sixties moving from the campus to the slum neighbourhood, were mobilized by the 'rediscovery' of poverty, America's shame. But far more than Harrington, they envisioned the poor reshaping their own fate, if aided by a helping hand from activists. 'We would offer ourselves to the people', Todd Gitlin and Nancy Hollander wrote about the JOIN (Jobs or Income Now) project in the 'hillbilly heaven' of Chicago's New Town; 'offer them a medium for their free expression—a book, an amplification system, a chance to cast their light up from the bottom of this society with the special illumination that comes only from victims. JOIN would emerge, shining or blurry, through the composite prism of the biographies of the people engaged in it, or detached from it, but in any case fixing its substance and its possibilities more exactly and—we hoped—more compellingly than we could with a more orthodox description. Poverty would emerge as more than the sum of separate afflictions and oppressions . . . '⁵

The gift of a book is an interesting detail here, an unconscious link with the older radical movements but offset by the technological-experiential alternative. Veteran Left politicos rightly tended to see the community-organizing mentality as the evidence of a Children's Crusade, or Russian Populism revisited. But they missed a deeper significance. The notion of a sensibility to emerge from the process itself reflected the expectation of self-rule in the Southern campaigns of the early sixties, an expectation so deep that SNCC leader Robert Moses changed his name and disappeared rather than be seen as the Moses of his people. 'Participatory Democracy', – the talismanic slogan of the emerging New Left—was popularized around this time in and through the Southern struggle. As an idea it was both old and new, simultaneously evoking Black insistence on self-emancipation, the general youth revolt against Cold War authoritarianism, and the age-old American radical ideal of direct democracy by the producing classes. Activists viewed it, moreover, as both means and end; as an organizational principle, therapeutic and empowering, it was purposely counterposed to the 'bureaucratic' Old Left ideal of democratic centralism.

By the early 1960s a context again existed for trying to draw together the various threads of mass activity and radical thought. Inspired by the daily heroism of their SNCC colleagues, and satiated with their academic studies, the precocious leadership of Students for a Democratic Society—itself, formally, the youth wing of the social-democratic, Old Left League for Industrial Democracy—met at Port Huron, Michigan in 1962 to assay the prospects for a rebirth of the American Left. *The Port Huron Statement* condensed all the ecletic themes and rhetorics which intoxicated the early New Left: from Fromm and Mills, Williams and Goodman, to echoes of Kennedy and the New Frontier. Not only a radicalized reworking of current idealized liberalism, the *Statement* also blended personal and political moral dimensions in an extraordinary manner.

It spoke for human relationships over the fragmentation blessed by the various existing social systems; it called for more freedom for the young (specifically on campus); it condemned the Cold War restriction of political debate even as it condemned existing Communism; and it urged a democratic, peaceful approach to world problems. By the standards of the Old Left, these did not seem such radical ideas. But by pinpointing the importance of the universities from which a 'new left must start controversy across the land', and by appealing for a level of democracy the various Old Lefts had come to consider unlikely, SDS set a course infinitely adaptable to changing circumstances.[6]

The imitation of Black activism by whites working among their own poor failed miserably. The radicals might mobilize communities on specific issues, but they could not establish bases in the old Socialist or Communist-ethnic fashion because the distance between organizer and organized remained too great. The Black undergraduates in SNCC did better, not only for cultural reasons, but because traditional barriers established by white Southern rule against Black challenges could be breached through specific campaigns like voting rights and desegregation. But even the mass civil rights struggle led to disappointment. The headway made by ordinary Blacks seemed ultimately inconsequential amid deeply entrenched poverty, especially in Northern ghettoes where frustration exploded into the most violent uprisings since the Civil War. The new radicals were forced to recognize, Blacks understandably earlier and more concretely than whites, the need for a more coherent and programmatic alternative.

Was it Socialism, already, that they had in mind? Howard Zinn rightly said that the SNCC activists articulated *some* kind of Socialism, 'but to put it this way freezes what is really a fluid attitude' about means and ends. Its *elan*, its open ended method, 'makes it a threat to *all* Establishments . . . its rejection of authority; its fearlessness in the face of overwhelming power; its indifference to respectability' rendered it powerful but unpredictable.[7]

'We must name the system', SDS President Paul Potter similarly said at the 1965 anti-war demonstration in Washington.[8] Potter evidently did not mean 'capitalism' in the 1930s sense, but the logic of both Cold War camps in their mad arms race and ruthless scramble for power. 'Empire' would have been an accurate term if that had meant not Lenin's Imperialism but the Roman Empire, reconstituted through a myriad of social systems and grown more monstrous with its technological capacity. Enthusiasts of this stage would later decry the invasion of Marxist ideas as an alien force, imported by embittered Black nationalists or by extremist Old Left implants within the student movement. The symptoms existed, and some of the outspoken young Leninists around SDS and the rest of the Movement could be found testing the waters for potential faction-fights and recruits. But the deeper reasons lay within the movement itself, in the problematic of developing a politics and theory equal to the ambition of naming, and overcoming, a system for which the available analyses had fallen short.

Even earlier, the impasse reached by the Civil Rights movement at the time of Martin Luther King, Jr.'s 1963 March on Washington had cast a fateful shadow over mainstream Black alternatives. The enthusiasm of that rally, the vision and moral influence of Dr King, the idealism of young radicals and of liberals seemed to point the way for the nation. Public success, however, disguised inner conflict. The elder Black leaders, original spokesmen for the Civil Rights movement but no strangers to the desire for more power themselves, had never believed in direct democracy with the same sincerity (or naivete) as the SNCC kids. They had no program beyond support for the Democrats, whose entanglement with the arms race, the American empire, and the Dixiecrat alliance precluded serious social transformation. The gap between mass Black enthusiasm and leadership timidity, between sporadic street actions of a peaceful or violent kind and negotiations with the Democrats, widened steadily into a chasm.[9]

This was the historic cue for the return of Black nationalism long considered by liberals and most of the Left as a picturesque legacy or crank fringe. Malcolm X, spellbinding public spokesman of the fast-growing Nation of Islam, emerged into celebrity in the wake of the 1964 riots. For the first time in decades, America had on its hands a portentous figure who proclaimed the need for a revolution. His *Autobiography,* one of the most intensely read books of the 1960s—written by the hand, it may be noted, of Alex Haley, later the author of *Roots*, the single most important political event in the history of American narrative television—vividly demonstrated the logical continuity in Left-Garveyism, from the days of Cyril Briggs and the African Blood Brotherhood down to the contemporary Muslims. Like those earlier phenomena, revolutionary Black Nationalism *had* to lead toward internationalism and heterodox Socialism because it had nowhere else to go for the concepts and mechanisms required to change the society in which it was born and nourished. Brief as Malcolm X's final Socialist period would be, he returned to political dialogue the kind of radical nationalism that would frame New Left thinking about race.

Malcolm's apocalyptic rhetoric ('the enslavement of millions of black people . . . is now bringing White America to her hour of judgment, to her downfall as a respected nation,'[10] a message delivered shortly after Kennedy's assassination) reached out to ghetto Blacks, but also to a fraction of rebellious white youth. As the pre-Civil War reformers had created a constituency with their reform conventions and their moral demands, Malcolm helped call a constituency into existence. Outside the ghettoes, his real following was amongst a vanguard of Black and white student activists. This group would, in a way unimaginable to their mostly liberal parents and to the Communist and anti-Communist survivors of the 1930s-40s Old Left, soon *celebrate* the rage of the urban rioters and regard their actions as entirely just. Malcolm's appeal for a distinct, autonomous Black culture similarly struck many of them as appropriate; not only had the existing culture proven its bankruptcy, but they had come to their own conclusion that cultural change preceded political. Malcolm's assassination under suspicious circumstances in February 1965, removed a powerful demi-Socialist voice of protest. It also suggested the limits on freedom of speech and movement for sworn enemies of the system. The rules would not be what the liberals promised.

Malcolm had come too early for any widescale organizational response on the left to his initiatives. The only Marxist group which responded avidly was the Socialist Workers Party, which eagerly extended its cooperation but which had few resources and little to show for its own theoretical record on Marxism and Black nationalism except old resolutions written by C.L.R. James. But Malcolm had come just in time to precipitate a broader ideological turn toward a new style of Socialism.

In the cycle of protest and frustration, from the Democratic Party convention of 1964 to the streets of Selma, Alabama in 1965, SNCC and other Black radicals were impelled towards a still inchoate version of Marxism. It was not something proclaimed or developed very far, but rather increasingly assumed by the staff as they encountered the limits of liberal support. As the ghettoes burned and the Vietnam War escalated, Martin Luther King himself, widely considered the last hope in American life for moral leadership to a just and peaceful solution, was pulled to the Left. Actually, this move should be seen as a consolidation and personal declaration of his carefully orchestrated position. A self-proclaimed Hegelian sporting a college familiarity with Marxist positions (in his Boston graduate days, reputedly a reader of the *Daily Worker*), King had as his aides for some years several prominent former Communists including Jack O'Dell (by the 1980s, a similarly close advisor to Jesse Jackson). King had known the score all along. Like the protagonist of the Yiddish spiritual-Socialist *Euf Veite Vegn*, he maintained some distance from party Marxists not only for tactical reasons but also because of Marxism's spiritual emptiness. Still, he privately conveyed to C.L.R. James his feelings for a radicalism he could not yet openly avow.[11]

It was something for America that this man, the most beloved insurgent since Eugene Debs and one of the ten most widely admired American figures during his lifetime, should be moving openly toward an internationalist condemnation of American aggression and toward a Christian cooperative view of a future world order. A very elderly W.E.B. DuBois had become a Communist in the 1950s to express his alienation from American society. King shifted to the left as an affirmation of where American society *had* to move if it were not to lose its soul.

Far more than John Kennedy's assassination, King's murder was the central tragedy of the 1960s. In death his failings disappeared, but so did his loving non-violence. Although the American left had a long legacy of repression, from the Haymarket Martyrs, to Sacco and Vanzetti, there was no precedent for the assassinations of Malcolm X and Martin Luther King. The unprovable conspiracy which pointed from every direction to the FBI and the organized ultra-right had succeeded, in its own terms. More than a few Cold War liberals drew a breath of relief—but prematurely. As the rioters moved through the ghetto streets, King's call for a new society and new social relations assumed a chiliastic fervor. Babylon would not finally fall. But by the time the insurgents had finished, its imperial command could never quite be the same again.

Reshaping Marxism

The number and the class backgrounds of participants, their ability to move institutions, had meanwhile given the student anti-war movement great visibility. Its lack of a community-cum-class base tended to flavor their growing Marxist inclinations with delusions that King's Socialistic vision had successfully avoided and that even in Malcolm seemed rhetorical device. The New Left's desires and demands appeared, sometimes even to its participants, out of proportion to its class prerogatives and to realistic prospects of the short run. We envisioned speaking at once for ourselves and for the entire society, or the entire world, just as the vanished radical labor movement and dessicated Marxist parties had attempted to do. We obviously lacked their analytical (or ideological) roots in socialized labor, and in racial and ethnic community life. But in those absences, the New Left created a powerful utopianism based, like the Civil Rights movement, on the American radical tradition. Tinged – but only tinged – by an updated conception of Marxism, a vision of the future was the one thing the New Left could create: our glory and our doom.

Student activism rocketed into national significance with the Berkeley Free Speech Movement of 1964. Berkeley was to New Left practice what Madison had been to theory, and for good historical reasons. Hard-line Marxist ideologues had never been numerous there, or indeed anywhere outside New York. But the Popular Front had peaked during the later 1940s in California, and the prestige of its interracial alliance had never entirely disappeared from the Bay Area. Pockets of progressive and/or bohemian sentiment remained strong on various issues. Demonstrations against HUAC and capital punishment at the very dawn of the sixties already raised expectations.

Berkeley campus politics, heavily influenced by Civil Rights struggles, displayed the essence of the emergent New Left *mentalité*. The indelible image, captured by the world media, of thousands of students surrounding an invading police car while Mario Savio orated from its roof, sent a shockwave of excitement through virtually every campus in the United States. The Berkeley students were not fighting for economic benefits, nor the right to vote, nor even for world peace. They were fighting, in the first place, to break down the barriers between the cold war 'multiversity' and the community, between the California ivory tower and the struggles of sharecroppers in Mississippi (the Free Speech Movement was triggered by the authorities' refusal to allow public campus fundraising for the civil rights movement). Beyond this, the collective eagerness of the students to throw themselves 'against the machine', as Savio urged, to disrupt and destroy the 'bureaucratic manipulation of life', posed essentially non-negotiable demands against late capitalism. The Berkeley students, like their Parisian brothers and sisters a few years later, were demanding nothing less than what the Old Left would have labelled 'Communism': the dismantling of all authority structures in a society of anarchic freedom and abundance. They had abandoned the realm of scarcity (already largely absent from their middle-class upbringings) and were beating upon the door to the realm of freedom.

Politically savvy Red Diaper Babies weaned on the mechanics of radical agitation played crucial roles in building the campus movement. This fact revealed a certain inter-generational Left continuity, but it did not mean that the outbreak was a charade or just a 'front' (nor did the presence of a certain Berkeley librarian who inspired many of the early activist leaders—Hal Draper, last seen as editor of the heterodox Trotskyist *Labor Action*). Whatever the various influences and individual genealogies, the predominant *ethos* was highly original: the melding together of direct-action tactics, vague but emphatic anti-bureaucratic politics and passionate cultural revolt. Moreover the early New Left was bound together by its own generous sense of community—inspired by the stirring example of the southern Civil Rights movements. Otherwise feuding young Marxists, recognizing common problems of mobilization and sometimes overwhelmed by their sudden, unexpected entrance on the stage of national politics, worked together with admirable comraderie. Only later would a new wave of dogmatism, fanned by a distorted affinity to a far away Cultural Revolution, massively reinstate the influences of old-fashion ideologues and 'chemically pure' party lines.[12]

Meanwhile the escalation of American violence against Vietnam, and of the number of American boys in the nightly body count, steadily altered the political equations. Events radicalized the student revolt at a dizzying rate while simultaneously investing it with profound public responsibilities for organizing opposition to the war. Later liberal commentators would simplistically blame the war for perverting American liberalism and for driving young idealists to madness and self-destruction. We don't remember it that way.

In Vietnam, as GIs used to say, you found out who you are. And here the unholy secret to the alliance between domestic liberalism and international support of dictators and murderers was revealed. Challenge to that alliance and to the integrated functions of the welfare-warfare state brought the moral claims of American democracy up short as had no issue since slavery. Once again, the utopians and the oppressed (the latter epitomized in those Black youth destined for the military maw) joined in protest. Once again, the mainstream agonized and divided over the inevitable consequences. The best of that mainstream, our honest professors, articulated those consequences with great lucidity in the spring 1965 national teach-in movement. Here we learned in classrooms lessons that we had never learned before.

Prior to 1965, the leaders of Students for a Democratic Society stubbornly considered anti-war projects as a diversion from the main domestic issues and as an obstacle to realistic political coalitions. We at the base had the morbid expectation of a negotiated but American-dictated 'peace' that would leave the ordinary Vietnamese stranded and the Kennedy wing of the Democratic party in power at home. Older SDSers had retained ambivalent hopes for the poverty programs launched to expand the Democratic Party electorate by drawing inner-city residents into the political process; like thirties radicals working with the Wagner Act, they welcomed the sanction—and the money. Mutual discouragement with the results, and the concurrent radicalization of student unrest, gave these Old New Leftists the cue to exit from leadership and prepared the way for rejuvenation and transformation of Marxist ideas among us, their more radical successors.

The Clear Lake, Iowa SDS convention of 1966 can be seen as a turning point. The organization's senior figures, with the exception of their key parliamentarian (no one younger seemed to understand procedure), stayed on the fringes and could be heard grumbling good-naturedly that the young had inherited the organization and the prerogative to destroy it in their own fashion. Figurehead President Carl Oglesby expressed the Protestant anguish of Norman Thomas gone Kierkegaard, with the best voice on the white left. Greg Calvert and Carl Davidson, brains of the newer forces, preached Student Syndicalism (in part, an adaptation of old IWW and French Syndicalist ideas, in part slapping a name upon a student tendency already in motion). The minority of avowed socialists agonized over the sectarian expression of Marxist ideas, and over the vague and unfocused emerging dialogue. Campus activists had learned much about the problems of student mobilization and administration maneuvering; 'participatory democracy' worked as a perspective, a public ideology, but failed to explain the mechanics of agitation or the strategic problems that could already be seen to lie ahead. 'Student Syndicalism' was a stopgap. Undogmatic Marxists took comfort in the openness of the conventioneers to Socialist ideas better presented, and in the background of those who seemed to give Marxism a New Left flavor.[13]

Increasingly Midwestern and Western, isolationist and Republican in their family traditions, these young radicals offered definitive proof that the social composition of the left had altered. Many of them children of professionals in commercial towns, they could have passed for Debsian Socialists except that they shared a background in Black-influenced popular culture, the desires for self-expression and self-realization, with their East and West Coast comrades. Here the great divide within the history of the American Left seemed to close, and with it, the basis of the old quarrels appeared to vanish. To the children of the Middle Border in particular, the differences which had divided the Old Left for decades could not have seemed less relevant. For nearly all the SDSers, wherever they were based, the key arena had become the campus, the make-or-break issue the war—with its various links to the draft, student freedoms and government racism. To us, the graduate students, fell the lion's share of the intellectual initiative. No one else was on hand and in touch with the constituents.

Intellectuals that we were, we felt instinctively that the weakness of this generation was its lack of firm training in the critical traditions of thought which Europeans seemed to understand so well. (Older American radicals had not been too strong along these lines either.) A small and generally distrusted fraction of campus Marxists ignored current reality to study such questions, keeping to their library carrels in the gathering crisis. For ourselves, we had to learn and teach simultaneously, at a more popular level. Political opportunity beckoned, and a thousand different political projects put the knowledge and skills acquired to work in the immediate situation. Most of us responded with wild enthusiasm and great practicality. It would be the best moment of our lives.

We gave ourselves to the same tasks that any previous radical intelligentsia would have tackled in our place: popularization and communication. The local underground newspaper (produced in dozens of locations by 1968-69), a more significant communications medium than all the national publications put together and the most important grassroots information network since the heyday of the Socialist Party, became at once a means for practical and theoretical expression. Here, the cultural notions of the Frankfurt School (filtered through the Situationists) re-emerged in the layout, as well as in the rhetoric of protest against mainstream culture. Investigative reporting became a self-taught art well before Hunter S. Thompson dramatized the techniques on an expense account we could not have imagined. (Then again, fine marijuana could be had for $15/ounce in 1968 in some parts of the country, and plenty of love could be had, if not for free, at a less dear price than in past or future.) Radical-sounding ads for records ('The Man Can't Jail Our Music') and neighbourhood 'head shops' recalled the old bases of financial support for the Socialist and ethnic press gone by. We could proclaim the revolution and pay the bills simultaneously, if only with financial juggling. The overwhelming campus (and sometimes neighborhood) popularity of the local underground paper demonstrated that the New Left had arrived as a social movement.[14]

Meanwhile, our political education continued. Excoriating the university's links to the military (while publishing analyses of the trustees' personal holdings), laying the groundwork for negotiations of a teaching assistants' association contract, operating the campus radical bookshop—these and a thousand other such chores, quite apart from tumultuous demonstrations and mobilizations with all their related requirements, made us political veterans overnight. Few would regret the loss of scholarly time, partly because we managed to integrate so many assignments with our studies and partly because we possessed a level of energy we would never have again. These very activities put us structurally at odds with our presumed identity as intellectuals bound for assimilation into the multiversity. We sought to save learning from its corruption, but in doing so struggled for the vision of a university unimaginable within capitalism.

Marxism, heretofore an eclectic combination of ideas acquired through self-education and through the bibliographies and lectures supplied by our amiable university mentors, began to gain structure as a kind of Process Theology of the New Left. The *telos* was no longer foreseeable, the god of the Russian Revolution dead and of the Chinese Revolution unconvincing to all but a small minority. But Marxism supplied the method of critique for capitalist institutions. On some campuses, 'countertexts' blossomed, pamphlet-length refutations of existing standard works; in many more places, 'free university' courses offered alternatives, mostly to the social sciences and the humanities. Intense and continuous study classes took up a bewildering multitude of questions, often relating to 'Corporate Liberalism', *i.e.*, the contradiction of university/Democratic Party commitment to domestic social policy and *de facto* support for US military aggression. Compared to similar study groups among previous and later Marxist movements, few New Left circles took up the texts of Marx and Lenin. Occasionally, study groups undertook criticism of the literature in an entire field, such as labor history, and put together extensive bibliographical aids—perhaps because of a Marxist premonition that radicalism would return to the working class and the radical ex-students with it. Younger Marxists outside the universities, giving (or taking) study classes among activist groups from the Black Panthers to GIs, had already come to similar conclusions.

This was the New Left's training school, as much as, if not more than, the scattered 'radical' courses in the official curriculum. But what was the training school for? When the Students for a Democratic Society established their Radical Education Project in 1966, the leadership aimed at educating the rank-and-file undergraduate in much the same way that the old Socialists, Wobblies and Communists sought to give the new recruit some basic feel for doctrine. 'READ, DURN YOU, READ,' a Wobbly paper once headlined, and we didn't measure up any better or worse as internal educators than our Wobbly predecessors had. The experiment had only limited effect because action outran education and the forms of organization.

Undergraduate radicals, the true frontline of full-scale mobilization on the campus, quickly became our teachers as much as our students. They made the most of the suddenly massive anti-war sentiment and the Student Power fever. One could see them working the dormitories in the aftermath of a police or National Guard invasion of campus, peddling papers, setting up study groups, establishing informal cadre for the next action. Like the Black movement, they had the unmistakeable American touch: their organizations were the result rather than the cause of mass mobilization. Like 1930s radical unionists, they also skipped the leftwing meetings to spend their time with their constituents.

What did Marxism mean to them, already the third generation of activists since the days of *Port Huron* six or seven years previous? That would never become altogether clear, any more than it had for the workers who passed through the IWW and 'red' unions of the CIO, or for ordinary Blacks who passed through Civil Rights battles. Their instinctive leaders in a specific dormitory or undergraduate organization might or might not be the budding scholar of radical ideas, our most intimate contacts. They were not, leaders or activist-for-a-day, 'anti-intellectual' in the sense that their detractors, liberals and conservatives defending university complicity and governmental war policy, continually pronounced. Activist undergraduates took to complaining, at the end of the sixties, about the anti-intellectualism of *their* younger sisters and brothers, hanging on them the then-common term, 'high school anarchists'. They were hungry for *useful* ideas, supplied to them by their fellow students, by us, by friendly professors, by the books in the library, and above all by the underground press. They talked about these ideas constantly. We provided a provisional worldview, although more a critique of what existed than a projection of what might come. The 'cultural revolution', as a preparatory experience in the future social relations, was more theirs than ours. No doubt we failed them by providing too little of the complexities in coherent form, in the journals and magazines we set forth. Our work tended to be skewed between popular vulgarization and inaccessible scholarship. We felt sure we had time to overcome these obvious weaknesses. We were wrong.

When Richard Nixon remarked that any further escalation of the Indochina War beyond the Cambodian incursion (and the accompanying Kent State incident) would have brought half a million students to burn down the White House, he described both the power and the limits of the campus movement. It practically accomplished one dimension of its goals: disengagement from the war and an end to the draft. But the universities would obviously not permit a democratic restructuring nor any permanent repudiation of military contracts and research. Students threw rocks, troopers answered with gas, and the campus administrations with an eye on their trustees and their account books, set themselves (to our way of thinking) on the side of Mammon.[15]

In the end, the faith in a great impending transformation faded. Outside forces thrust the campus into a cycle of bitterness and in-fighting when it might have become a model of democratic resilience. Too often, students and their leaders failed to explain their own activities carefully enough. Too many professors, like the vast majority of administrators, had determined to regain their prerogatives regardless of the price. These self-satisfied scholars (some of whom, incredibly, cited their Marxist credentials in support of police clubs) had rarely expressed serious moral qualms about university complicity with the war effort and with manipulation of Third World institutions generally. More sage and humanitarian scholars recalled later that they had, all too quickly, lost the most intellectually vital and challenging, if maddening and disruptive, generation of students in academic history. We, the older heads of the student Left, felt equally helpless to change the course of events, to maintain the verve of protest and of eager learning alike. All our failings were about to double back upon us, more damaging than our darkest fears for the New Left's political future.

Fragmentation

The implosion of the organized student Left seemingly denied the significance of this brief history and the use of Marxist ideas—but no more than had the demise of the old Socialist movement, or the Wobblies' eclipse into sentimental melancholy, or the descent of the Popular Front into sectarian self-negation, or the debauch of Trotskyist intellectualism in a noxious conservatism. The New Left simply plunged the dagger into itself more swiftly and more dramatically. At the 1969 SDS Convention, only two years since Marxist ideas had first been freely batted around on the dais and only a year since black (anarchist) and red (communist with the small 'c') flags had been crossed on the convention stage, the leading two or three factions declared themselves each the *true* Marxist-Leninists. It had the look of madness.[16]

Impatience born of escalating government violence and exaggerated by the political inexperience of leadership and ranks, operated heavily against us. Older radicals of many varieties could easily warn what not to do. But what the New Left was supposed to do in order to confront government escalation of violence on a proportionate scale of militancy and within the confines of its own, mostly campus political environment—that we had to grapple with alone. That the New Left should not romanticize Third World revolutions was obvious to the experienced (*i.e.*, over twenty-year old) activist. But how to present the popular case for Third World guerrillas battling overwhelming firepower? Agitation blurred complexity, as those veterans who honestly recalled their own agitational experiences could appreciate.

When all the old answers had been thrown out, when no universal class showed itself the successor to the industrial proletariat, a personal identification with Czech teenagers in jeans facing Russian tanks, and with Vietnamese guerrillas facing American technological firepower, seemed elementary and perhaps sufficient. On television, it all looked somehow similar. Unlike the old Marxists, young revolutionaries understandably viewed the seeming prospects for transformation, for salvation of the earth from otherwise inevitable devastation, as an opportunity that might not come again. The revolution had to be made soon, even if no one could say for certain how.

Leninism appeared to offer an organizing strategy. As an SDS militant and leader of Columbia University's tennis squad (later a prominent historian of American Communism) put it to me, 'Every team needs a coach'. This was not the Leninism of any organization that had ever been in existence, of course. But it bore a strong resemblance to Popular Front Communism in one essential respect: the form of constituency had become secondary; the command theory had escaped the historical context.

SDSers tried, mostly unconsciously, to fashion an equivalent constituency in student militancy (update of industrial worker) and anti-racism (update of anti-fascism). Living a transitory life among a transitory population on campus, too distant in every sense from the outside communities they sought to reach, they could not make up the deficits. If the talk about Leninism bolstered morale in the short run, it also diverted necessary attention from creating styles of organization appropriate to fall back upon when 'the Revolution' failed.

The desperate combination of white guilt and perverse workerism, the desire to take commands from Black radicals and to whip the white working class into line somehow, possessed a certain logic. Campus activity had not stopped the war, nor brought significant social change at home. There was no end in sight to the Nixons and the Humphreys. The world beyond the campus had to be approached, embraced, perhaps conquered. But this ostensibly reasonable premise had a deep psychological flaw. Leninism crystallized as a form of detachment from the immediate constituency, born of frustration over the New Left's inability to create large, stable organizations among undergraduates. Unable to cope with their impotence as elected or self-appointed leaders for masses of students who did not want or perhaps even need that kind of leadership, an entire SDS stratum of factionalists turned directly to theories that promised them vanguard status. Confounded by the limits of New Left success, they reverted to self-insulation from all the organic traditions of American radicalism. (One prominent SDS and later Maoist sect leader was, reputedly, the son of former Communist Party functionaries at once notoriously hardline and organizationally inept; if not literally possessed of a genetic weakness, the family had helped ruin two generations of Marxism.)

In historical retrospect, the results had touches of comic opera. Hostile groups of SDSers waved copies of Mao's Little Red Book at each other. Would-be political leaders dressed, talked and even spat tobacco in the Mike Gold manner, proclaiming their working-class identities. Acid heads competed with admirers of Stalin for the same girlfriends or boyfriends. A young Leninist art student explained to me that he intended to create a popular newspaper-style comic strip to educate the masses, 'but without the humor'. Friends of many years standing found themselves on opposite sides because, like their counterparts in the 1920s Communist movement, they happened to live in different towns and therefore fell willy-nilly under one hegemony or another.

Beneath the comic opera lay human tragedy. Destructionists and incompetents found their way to the upper ranks and the leadership milieu of the organization. As a veteran staffer complained to me, every administration up until 1969, regardless of political shadings, had published the SDS newspaper, full of letters, miscellaneous articles and unpredictable ideologies. The self-proclaimed masters in the science of leadership could not get it together between ideological wars, drugs, and fits of personal uncertainty. They summoned up a brave front—and they folded. The last persona of the New Left had taken flight more incongruously, crashed more embarrassingly, than all its predecessors combined.

The white New Left at large had in fact turned itself inside out again and again, seeking the revolutionary subject, from radicalized student to sympathizer with Black revolution to witting and unwitting participant in the rise of Feminism. Marxism had in the process gone from playing a simple educational role to providing omniscient guidance on all theoretical and practical questions, and finally (for most activists, anyway) had retreated once more into the shadows as students recommenced their own 'long march' to individual careers and private life. Exhausted by disappointment and all too aware of what dreary alternatives lay ahead, the militants threw in the towel. The vast majority of activists had already quit or had plunged themselves into purely local activities when the national offices closed up shop. The fact that a handful of the outstanding leaders and many locals of considerable reputation had joined the factional foray was yet another proof that the malaise was common currency, the end of an era now unavoidable.

The fate of various Leninisms in this confusion and backtracking showed most clearly the collapse of other, more familiar possibilities. Most of the Old Left groups had kept their distance from SDS in particular, and the telltale sign of Leninism, for some years, was an extraordinarily narrow-minded economism linked to a sincere (and for that time, rare) interest in working-class issues. The garish tabloid of the Maoist Progressive Labor Party looked like a caricature of the *Daily Worker* at its least effective, and the reports of extreme discipline (no drugs, no promiscuity, no traveling long distances without leadership permission) seemed as distant from New Left styles and sensibilities as imaginable. Leninism, as it was then understood, constituted a moral counteroffensive against hedonism and the campus culture.

The National Question lifted Leninist stock upward, as the

Vietnam War expanded and ghetto riots, police repression and white backlash pointed at once to the necessity for community movements and the unlikelihood of spontaneous working-class risings. Progressive Labor, several burgeoning vanguard groups within SDS and lesser Trotskyist entities labored hard to explain imperialism, as their cadre worked in student strikes and pilot factory-community programs. So long as the student movement lasted, these efforts offset (or rather, provided the other side of) the deepening drug culture nihilism—twin signs of growing disenchantment with New Left solutions. Lacking a protective environment, lacking the expectation of semi-imminent revolutionary change, they too turned in upon themselves.[17]

Something similar happened to the Black Left after King's assassination. Black student movements had begun their turn toward versions of Marxism, but a Marxism adequate to the current American crisis proved most difficult to locate and use. Grand political plans, overarching theoretical syntheses were attempted—none met with notable, lasting success. In the short run, and with the political pressure at fever-pitch, the ideas did not satisfy the activists and sympathizers who needed them most. The Black movement, dogged by its own special charisma and gender-identity problems, hounded by COINTELPRO, no more able than the white New Left to take a strategic step backward, soon faded blind-eyed into dogma and thence to oblivion.

SNCC showed the effects of the pressure in its outright Marxist conversion. The organization had early abandoned the litmus test of members and friends for hidden Communist background or sympathies, and in 1965 it had come out forcefully against the War in Vietnam. SNCC eagerly identified itself with the rising tide of 'Black Power' consciousness, as if that identification filled the gap in political strategy. Repression by local, state and federal authorities confirmed their self-defined outlaw status. They might have trouble sorting out their exact ideas about Marxism, but Marxist revolutionaries of some kind they were going to be. One need only consider for a moment how hard Black Communists had worked for respectability among the Harlem elites and the liberal middle classes to see the generational difference separating them from the SNCC leadership.

The change from the early sixties was clearest on the campuses, where the first generation of a large-scale Black intelligentsia struggled to find its identity. SNCC and other early organizations had found their shock troops in the Black Southern schools. Now suddenly, and due largely to political pressures, small numbers gained entrance into major Northern universities.

These students felt torn between the unprecedented attention they enjoyed, and their widespread commitment to more sweeping change. They believed above all in their own Blackness, and in another era might have remained simply nationalists. Amid mounting protests, they demanded more Black admissions and Black studies; amid increasing disillusionment with their position on the campus, they too looked to Marxism for answers—but not the old Marxism. A member of this generation recalls, 'the closest we came to accepting the fundamentals of Marxism was through their applications in Fanon's, Nkrumah's and Toure's works. To many of us, China was a positive yellow blur of 800 million folk . . . [and] the Soviet Union was just another kind of racist European country'.[18]

These were not actually the worst places to start, and besides, everyone has to start somewhere. But such beginnings led to no carefully thought out political objectives between immediate demands and 'the revolution'. Demands for Black Studies programs, sometimes made in a caricature of guerrilla styles, afforded a temporary middle ground with worthy goals but no tenable strategic prospect. Open Admissions, the unrealized democratic aim of an urban universty generation, lacked the government, administration, and faculty support to turn the resentment into something great and positive. Black Left critics later blamed the minority students for their own 'petty-bourgeois' approach; fair as the charge might be, it does not capture the tragedy of the idealistic students, Black and white, who dreamed the university could live up to its claims as teacher and resource for all the people.

In the streets, meanwhile, an extreme version of the nationalist program, the Black Panther Party, briefly skyrocketed to the center of political attention. The Panthers, at some levels, never consisted of more than an image. They first projected themselves in angry confrontations with Oakland police, and soon became a powerful force by virtue of a newspaper which, along with the Muslim *Muhammed Speaks,* constituted almost the entire national Black press. The Panthers captured the grievances and aspirations of an angry ghetto, and the imagination of white radicals, not only with confrontationism but also with their flair for literary brilliance and public relations, and through their problematic but sincere desire to work with white radicals for a Socialist solution.

The Black Panther, with a weekly circulation of up to 100,000, became for several years the ghetto street hawker's hot item, something no Marxist paper including the *Daily Worker* in its days of high repute had ever managed even in Harlem. It raged, it postured, but it delivered a forceful anti-capitalist message that Eldridge Cleaver and Huey Newton, referred to as 'Yankee Doodle Socialism' and 'Intercommunalism', respectively. With all the craziness, this was part of a distinctively native Marxist-utopian fusion. Perhaps it could not have put itself forward so quickly, so dramatically, on any other basis. But the bravado disguised the absence of any feasible future. SNCC and the Panthers, like two failing magazines attempting to combine their shrinking resources, disappeared almost simultaneously.[19]

A more obviously Marxist Black class movement of significance, indeed the most important organized working-class movement of the 1960s, the League of Revolutionary Black Workers based in Detroit, never gained the national spotlight. It was vitally important nonetheless, as the key Black Power connection with the older Marxism and the most successful linking of Black students with a proletarian community.

Its origins lay in the wildcat strikes of the 1950s against both automakers and the UAW, whose leadership had earned for their members substantial economic benefits in return for virtually unchallenged management prerogative over conditions of production. By the later 1960s, the overwhelmingly Black workers in the most intensive jobs faced 'niggermation', the intensification of work, with undirected restlessness. Class and race merged under these conditions. John Watson, civil rights veteran and a careful student of Marxism (via study classes with C.L.R. James' local disciples), launched the well-circulated tabloid, *Inner City Voice,* soon moving on to student editorship of Wayne State University's daily newspaper, *The South End.*

Both papers had a distinctly Black Marxist character, eclectic in content and underground newspaper-like in presentation, but clearly beyond any existing Leninist ideologies or organizations. *The South End,* reflecting the tempo of the factories and neighborhoods where it was widely distributed without charge, arguably became the most successful daily radical newspaper outside New York and the Bay Area in nearly a half century. It articulated above all a challenge to various regional UAW locals on behalf of revolutionary extra-union groups, not so much caucuses in the Old Left power-seeking tradition as propaganda organizations set upon establishing a bridge to social transformation and workers' control.

But the League and its Marxism could never overcome the burdens of the recent and distant past, the non-labor character of the existing Black movement and the deadening institutional power of organized labor officialdom. Veteran Black Marxist James Forman, former SNCC executive secretary, sought to pose the Detroit example as an alternative to the street-tough Black Panther style. The effort was too ambitious, launched (in 1971) as the Movement turned decisively downward, and with a New Left style of consciousness-raising that butted up against the hard realities of a non-revolutionary era. Forman, Watson and others spoke at strikes with mass Black involvement much as had the Wobblies, without hope of organizational base-building. They lacked the Wobblies' calm confidence in an industrial-democratic future. Nor could the League transform itself, in anything short of a revolutionary era, into a replacement of existing unions. All the plans for this auspicious Black Marxism, including a short-lived publishing company, an aborted film company and numerous other schemes, went down the drain. One more experiment had died.[20]

Another Dimension of Light and Sound

By 1971, the New Left had come to a crashing halt. A close observer of the culture could readily perceive that the beloved popular rock music had become repetitive, the early burst of poetry had mostly faded, and the drugs had become both more expensive and lower quality. And yet, certain hopes remained.

For those hopes, the Women's Liberation Movement could very largely take credit. In immediate terms, it had developed out of the guts of the Civil Rights movement and the New Left, organized and led by women who collectively recognized their political disadvantage in male-dominated organizations. Through working papers, convention workshops and articles in the left press, Feminists had put their case forward even in Old Left organizations, but without any decisive effect. They made a collective break in 1968-69, with a variety of new affiliations.

In the closing days of the sixties and first few years of the seventies, Feminist literature appeared in a flood of bright and witty pamphlets and periodicals on subjects ranging from the overrated vaginal orgasm to the unwritten women's history. Challenges, really, more than anything else, they focused attention upon the emancipation of women as a goal in itself, not as an adjunct to any other program. They also reached far beyond the customary audiences of radical intellectuals, as far in their own way as the anti-war movement had a few years earlier.

For good reasons, none of these organizations reached the

national status, membership or relative durability of SNCC or SDS. Even more than the diffuse New Left, they were a combination of local entities which discovered and developed a hitherto submerged women's culture. As consciousness-raising, the form proved vital; as strategy, it was fraught with difficulty precisely because the left and the wider climate of expectation had wound down before serious plans could even be made.[21]

In this light, Marxist ideas seemed at first useful mainly for heroic analogy—the rise of women complementing the rise of workers or Blacks—but soon became more useful for constructing a model for the sociology of oppression. Structural feminist notions, hyphenated into 'Marxism-Feminism', were mobilized to explain the exploited status of women in the labor-market. Their prime constituency, the pink collar worker and younger professional, lacked the institutional mechanisms and the political circumstances to make the most of that analysis. Even carefully adapted, Marxism left unexplained both the genesis and the ultimate undoing of gender oppression: the roots and framework for a Socialist vision. Once male left groups had been properly assailed, the dubiousness of wholesale alternatives such as gender in direct replacement of class became all the more apparent (and, like Black Cultural Nationalism, its advocates were suspected of arrangements with the New Right).

As a spokeswoman for one of the high-level discussion groups wrote in the late 1970s: 'We have not worked out what this means, this hyphen. We think that a revolution which proceeds from the insights of Marxism and feminism is what we want; our own practice as a group leaves everything but the formalistic aspects of such a revolution to be delineated.'[22] But that was precisely the problem. When the social movements around them disappeared leaving Feminism a last remnant of radical times passed, the hyphen became a foremost means of self-identification, a methodological and moral code. But more than that it could not be.

In happier days, a little less than a decade earlier, Feminism sparked the last intellectual burst of the New Left, an outgrowth and a celebration in the face of widespread political collapse. During 1968-70, most of the magazines and journals that would remain the principal intellectual legacy of New Left Marxism began publication, found an initial audience, and set out their editors' precocious visions. Hardly an editor had enough funds before publication for a second issue, hardly a journal had the level of organization for a pre-publication mass mailing.[23]

The ideas flowed. History, sociology, economics, anthropology and a multitude of fields all had their radical critics (a medical students' journal called itself *The Radical Proctologist*), and in the early days most of those critics saw themselves as reaching out beyond academic barriers, offering information to a new and more powerful movement-in-the-making. It was an illusion, but a useful one, as the fury of publication itself swiftly became in part a substitute for the declining possibilities of political activity.

The feminist slogan, 'the personal is the political', might have been festooned upon these publications, and not only because special 'women's issues' usually proved bestsellers. The effort to forge a collective intelligence brought all the difficulties of political personality into close range. Dominant individual figures often gathered others around themselves, but usually yielded after a time of rough testing, with feminism the baseline of criticism. Marxist intellectualism had never seen anything like its acidic dissolution of the male bonding and of the vigorous confidence (but often just pompous posing) of the radical thinker. We New Left males, objects (or, we thought, victims) of the critique, resented it beyond words. Unlike the generations of male activists who never yielded, at heart we knew the critics were right.

Growing Up and Growing Older: The 1970s

We shared one last illusion with our political foes, the vanguardists who had precipitated the breakup of New Left organizations. The working class, redefined in some way, might save the New Left by taking over its best ideas and putting them into action. Since we had become vigorous (or more vigorous) Marxists, with whatever feminist amendments, this was a natural premise soon pursued to an illogical end. Since the energy had left the campus and, for the most part, the ghettoes too, it was also a fallback strategic conclusion. Intellectuals might yet provide the ideas which made a new understanding of working-class action and transformation possible.

Factory and strike-oriented community groups sprouted during 1970-73, and in different, unideological forms another half-dozen years later. New Left Marxism, for these moments, regained an understanding of working-class life as it continued in the face of layoffs and decrepit union leadership. Marxists also gained a renewed appreciation for the difficulties earlier generations of working-class militants, born or made, had endured. It was a profound historic insight, if no one knew very well what to do with it.

This re-emergent workerism also touched upon something novel. The workplace unrest of the mid and late 1960s had gone almost unnoticed amid the campus excitement. Struggles over the pace of work, waged by sons and daughters of the generation that built the CIO, now faced off against the results of the earlier generation's institutional residue. The centralized power of the functionaries, and the constant change in technology that kept informal work-groups off balance, weighed heavily against success. New Left idealists came in mostly at the end of the uprising, soon enough to grasp the spirit but not soon enough to lead the regroupment of rebel forces outside specific localities or specific unions.

But there were unique moments of New Left and working-class *rapprochment* here. Dope-smoking Vietnam vets or angry young women workers touched by women's liberation slogans could share something with the campus activists who put underground-style graphics into shop-oriented newspapers and who hated the conditions of straight work with a similar passion. This would prove an insufficient basis for permanent unity of intellectuals with workers in the old Marxist sense. But it carried the energy of the sixties a little further. Especially where reform-minded union leaders had, for their own reasons, given campus activists entry into labor circles, the results could be startling: a St. Louis group brought Black militants, campus revolutionaries and Klan members into a network that for several years distributed a newspaper with a 10,000 local circulation, much of it paid, and became the authentic voice of rank-and-file discontent. Neither Old Left syndicalist nor New Left, such experiments almost reached a new synthesis as a new generation of industrial workers launched impetuous, typically unsuccessful struggles against the alienation of the assembly-line or typing-pool.[24]

Such efforts also brought the remnants of the New Left squarely in contact with the successors to Marxist traditionalism, bringing unexpected benefits to both. At the dawn of the seventies, the proliferating Leninist groups had eradicated virtually every sign of New Left identity. Preoccupied with the central goal of creating a vanguard organization and increasingly distant from reality in attempting to do so, young would-be American Bolsheviks hitched their energies to outworn ideas. As nearly a decade passed, a Marxist-Leninist account later notes, 'The communist movement has only the vaguest of analyses . . . worse yet, no unity around which theoretical matters we must resolve, and how we can resolve them'. Most effort had gone, and would continue to go, into 'competitive polemics'.[25]

Despite immanent tendencies to move beyond the existing limits of neo-Leninist theory and practice, the general effort petered out. The prospect remained of little bands, now much like the smaller Trotskyist sects, publishing their rhetorical journals to diminishing audiences—with the difference that their writers included former political leaders of note (*Grundrisse* translator Martin Nicolaus for one, and at least one major cultural figure, Amiri Baraka). Not since the forties had so much effort and expectation (albeit limited sharply to participants) ended in so little. But individually, this would not be so important. Ex-Maoist, ex-Trotskyist and ex-SDS intellectuals and community activists often found themselves years later side-by-side, all pushing forty, with the same objectives and much the same reservations about Marxism. For hundreds of dedicated industrial activists, New Left enthusiasm and neo-Leninism had proven opposite paths towards the enduring reality of working-class life.

Not a great deal could be accomplished, in traditional tactical-strategic terms, beyond the election of local union officials and the creation of new health and welfare adjuncts in now declining factory populations. The historic vacuum of the labor movement brought the outsiders inside, where they made themselves part of the moral infrastructure, a reliable presence on the picketline and the state assembly, holding on and awaiting another turn of the cycle. Their Marxism, perhaps the most orthodox and (outside their private circles) the least often expressed, had come down to the flinty reality of class and the dogged necessity of exhausting every means for labor improvement within the system. In their spare hours they listened to Bruce Springsteen, smoked marijuana and sometimes went to church: each affording a mood and a spiritual kinship otherwise unavailable to them. They had become the *alte genossen* of blue-collar Marxism.

For those (most eloquently among the Leninist survivors and the conservative wing of the Democratic Socialists) who seized every opportunity to dispute the sincerity and accomplishments of the New Left, the further lives of its ordinary activists offered impressive counter-evidence. As in previous generations, the vast majority had gone the normal way of families, jobs and personal retrenchment, putting political interests and radical attitudes on the backburner, whether temporarily or permanently no one could tell. Many thousands did not fall victim to the *Big Chill* syndrome of lifelong nostalgia save in one important sense. They taught in colleges—especially in the blue-collar schools—with a dedication they had given to their politics, while continuing to work with local peace and reform groups, marching on Washington when the opportunity arose, and giving to scholarship something like the role they had anticipated for it. But they remained also somewhat out of time; they had not ceased to be in love with a moment of expectation and exhilaration never seen again.

Black activist veterans fell to a somewhat different fate. In a scattering of cities over the next decade or so, yesterday's insurrectionaries came face to face with the survivors of the Old Left advancing on political power. Just behind the victories of Richard Hatcher in Gary, Indiana, Coleman Young in Detroit and later Harold Washington in Chicago could be seen the shadow of the Popular Front. It had nourished these politicians and their advisors during the 1940s-50s, and its old friends in the neighborhoods and union offices worked hard for their election. It was, in a real sense, the last gasp of a vanished age. Power had come too late for the radical dreams.

It was nonetheless, because of the bitterness of white resistance across the class lines, something of a crusade for the basic democratic values nominally vindicated in the Second World War: equality and brotherhood, a new level of cosmopolitan consciousness and caring. Each victory brought a momentary sense of triumph for the nascent Rainbow Coalition. But no campaign seriously promised the impossible, Socialism in one city or even a significant redivision of wealth at the urban level. In power, Black politicians operated somewhat as the Communists' left-wing opponents had always predicted: in coalition with the Black petty bourgeoisie and the white bankers, harnessing Black and reform energy for a better racial atmosphere and a more equitable share of power. Black local officials, like Black congressmen, took important if largely symbolic national and international policy positions. They might one day make the resurgence of a wider radical coalition easier. Yet still poor, still subjected to manipulation on the state and federal level, these cities were far from expectations of the Negro-labor alliance of the 1930s-40s or the Black Renaissance in the heart of the American empire envisioned during the 1960s. They threw into question the Marxist origins (which were mostly unavowed) of the larger strategy.

The attempt to amalgamate these energies in a Left-Nationalist coalition during the 1970s came to naught. The fidelity of the successful Black politicians and now conservative nationalists to the Democratic Party showed the universal dilemma for the Black Left, in all its variants. Marxists from several generations could contribute their energies and their ideas to an uncertain common fund; they had no easy answers to the automated attrition among the Black working class, the timidity and conservatism of mainstream unions, and the paradoxes in local electoral success.[25]

Much the same obtained in other kinds of ghettoes. In Chicago and then New York, the Young Lords, first and second generation Puerto-Ricans, became a force overnight, and overnight disappeared amid repression and faction-fighting. Chicanos in the Southwest, influenced by the United Farm Workers and by charismatic leaders like Cesar Chavez and Reies Tijerina, moved into similar confrontations with local and state police, and the same raised-fist intense expectation of revolutionary-nationalist convergence, and the same malaise afterward. Scattered Asian-American radicals, understandably influenced by Maoism, ran a similar gauntlet. Perhaps only Native Americans, with their severely anti-historical interpretations of their own oppression, survived as a continuous movement, and they, too, lost their leadership to brutal government treatment.[27]

Over the course of time, intellectuals in each of these communities set up new institutions and new publications, with university backing or without it, to see through the difficult times and look beyond to political reorientation. A new sophistication was achieved in journals such as *The Black Scholar* and the Puerto Rican *Libertad*. Marxism found a powerful renewed articulation in these pages, not as an 'open sesame' but as a source for political history and for a logic of the now-rediscovered National Question in all its guises. How effectively these intellectuals had sunk roots into their respective communities remained for now an open question.

Whatever their limitations, such bodies of intellectuals had reestablished the decisive connection with the history of US ethnic radicalism. The differences from the past ethnic lefts threatened, however, to disguise the significance of the connections even from observers conversant with Marxism and some of the relevant languages. An important radical institution like *Centro Cultural Puertoriqueno Pedro Albizu Campos*, the political arm of the radical *Movimento para Liberacion Nacional* (MLN) maintains a high school, a monthly newspaper, a library and a social center on Chicago's South Side. But the organization holds no illusion that the necessary sense of Puerto Rican self-consciousness and political combativeness will emerge primarily through that time-honored medium of the immigrant Left, the printed word.

Nor are these newer activists bedeviled by a faith in the strict rationalism that the Left has traditionally believed itself to embody. The religious cadre of Filipino, Puerto Rican and Central American radicalism finds reflections in the immigrant community, and gains new importance in the absence of a secular intellectual leadership. Seeking as they do to guide their flocks away from the deracinating consumer mentality of American life, radical guides lean naturally toward spiritual claims. And they have good material reasons. While the weakened American Left can supply immigrants little more than emotional solidarity, the Catholic Church allots them funds and property with sometimes considerable autonomous powers. Like the Left leadership of generations past, the Church has its own reasons for doing so. But orders do not reach down always or consistently from the top to the bottom. Yesterday's inner-city Irish parish, the heartland of anti-radicalism since the failure of the Knights of Labor, has here and there become today's Sanctuary Church, yesterday's persecuted Irish nationalist today's internationalist religious Socialist.

A veteran Italian-American radical once said in an interview: 'When I was young, the workers supported me and the priests were against me; now I am old, and the workers oppose me, but the priests support me.' He did not say it with a heavy sense of failure. Life continues, radicalism renews itself, heedless of ideologies and expectations. This is the greatest, and the most hopeful, lesson of all.

The great virtue of the New Left was its having broken with the absolutes of the older Marxism. Seemingly emancipated from the past, the New Left set out to become the political reflection of the Black mass movement for Civil Rights, the student movement against the war, and finally, when all else had been lost, the Women's Liberation movement. It moved faster than anyone could have imagined, because it carried within itself so much of the richness that past Lefts had struggled to create. The New Left began where the Old Left had halted: with the race question, and with popular culture. It reinvented the Woman Question on the very terrain where the Socialist Party had failed. It absorbed the moral and spiritual critique of imperialism that no Leninist movement had been able to formulate. Most of all, it recuperated a Utopianism which had been regarded since before 1920 as pathetic and unworthy of revolutionary consideration, but which remained deep in the American character.

Such freedom to experiment had its down side, which became increasingly obvious as time went on. The New Left had a strong tendency to run away from its deepest problems, and then return to them guiltily, with the wrong conclusions. Ultimately, it failed those mass movements twice over: it could not build solidly upon their accomplishments; and it increasingly misrepresented their meaning as it grew more distant from them in time. The Civil Rights movement had been fought for simple dignity. The student movement had demanded US withdrawal from Vietnam and democratic participation in the classroom. The women's movement stood for equality. Revolutionary ideas every one, but not taken out of a rediscovered Leninist lexicon. In all fairness, the non-dogmatists had no better answers when the political lights went out. No one knew what the next stage would bring.

Conclusion

As we look back at Marxism's development in the US, the twin themes of redemption from the exile of the historical *galut*, and movement forward *through* history to the plenitude of a multi-racial, multi-cultural gender-egalitarian democratic society, can be found in a thousand guises. This is not to deny the materialist interpretation which has proven so helpful in identifying capitalism's specific exploitative character, or to deny the importance of the Marxist organizations where so many radicals and revolutionaries defined their lives' tasks. But the millenialism of the indigenous radical forces and cultural alienation of the immigrants together set the subjective tone for Marxism's early evolution. The eclipse of small property democracy and the simultaneous rise of heroic industrialization with all its accoutrements prompted a decisive but historically limited phase of hegemonic 'proletarian' politics. The emerging centrality of America's economic world empire and the expansion of the consumer society have decisively returned the class question to its broader context where the familiar themes resonate once more.

The interpretation of that context as life-space and as theoretical framework has been, and will no doubt remain, the central task of New Left Marxism and its legacy to future radical movements. But it is a task that can be posed only in abstract form by the intellectual constellations at present. The central social context of contemporary Marxist interpretation, the academy of the 1970s and 1980s, has made a previously unthinkable quantity of research and technical discussion possible in a multitude of fields. The same context has rendered the significance of the ideas all but incomprehensible between specialties. Outside the specialties, outside the university, the advances and retreats remain little known and less understood. On any issue other than foreign policy, perhaps, their importance cannot be tested without the return of a larger social movement.

Outside the academy, Marxist (and post-Marxist) intellectualism remain a sort of underground stream, underground because obscure in an era of apparent political apathy. A distinguished community of political-minded scholars or scholarly-minded political journals staffed by official and ex-officio academics seeks an elusive public to listen and to debate issues. A wider scattering of cultural movements and publications, usually ephemeral, emerge with a certain *éclat* and disappear, exhausted and untenured but having left a mark. Discussion, at least, remains wide open to all comers. *Political Affairs* or *Dissent* have no more (and no less) claim upon the territory than the radical artists' *Cultural Correspondence* or the radical geographers' *Antipode*. If a Yale faculty member, a Marxist labor historian proud of his Communist background, is part of the intellectual dialogue today, then so is a fourteen-year old girl who in the grim year of 1986 publishes a 'zine' dedicated (according to her own description) 'to peace, anarchy, justice and uprising'.[1]

Efforts to leap all these boundaries, to achieve the unity of theory and practice dreamed of in earlier days have proven enlightening failures. Fredy Perlman, post-Marxist extraordinaire, provides a valuable case in point. A Czechoslovakian Jewish immigrant to the USA, student of C. Wright Mills at Columbia during the mid-1950s and printer for the avant-garde Living Theatre, Perlman emerged in 1969 (after various adventures in the Paris May of 1968, where he developed an intellectual attachment to the Situationists) as a major New Left theoretician-pamphleteer-translator. That year he published *The Reproduction of Daily Life*, a colorful treatment of commodity fetishism, the principal theme of most of his publications. With collaborators, he translated Guy Debord's Situationist classic, *The Society of the Spectacle*, another version of the same subject, and founded a Detroit cooperative printshop where he published his own treatises and others', including his collaborative translation of I.M. Rubin's famous *Essays on Marx's Theory of Value*. His own books sometimes appeared in four colors, the most brilliant mixture of radical thought and illustration since the days of his spiritual guide, William Blake.

Perlman began with the Anarcho-Marxist politicial proposition that capital could not demand the contemporary range of technical competence without inspiring the individual will and the collective capacity to revolt. Like C.L.R. James (but without crediting Lenin or Leninism, which Perlman viewed as inherently statist and counter-revolutionary), he had drawn the logical conclusion from the continued socialization of production. Intellectuals might supply necessary insight, but they must (in order to remain revolutionaries) refrain from creating new representations, *i.e.*, vanguard parties to rein in spontaneous experiments at free activity. Praxis itself—as free and fearless, one often thought, as Perlman's own wide-ranging activity—helped to show the way forward in refusing the specializations and false categories assigned by capital. Unlike most New Left Marxists Perlman seemed to know just who he was; unlike the sectarians, he wasn't shamming.

The collapse of the New Left and the retreat of radical labor in Detroit turned Perlman against this historical optimism. Over half-a-dozen years in the 1970s, Perlman came to regard the denouement of Marxism as inevitable in the contortions of state capitalism (he translated two anarchist histories of the Russian Revolution and wrote a huge, epistolary novel of communications between Yugoslavian and American radicals) and the degradation of Socialist ideas generally inherent in the demands of nationalism in all its varieties. Like James, but from a more extreme position, he had come to see past Marxism as an engine for capitalism's further development; he still saw Zion in the distance, but only by looking back in time.

Perlman's career culminated, only a few years before his death at 51, with the critique of civilization. Here, he filled out one of his initial and most basic notions, 'Imperialism is not the "last stage" of Capitalism; it is also the first.' That is, the expropriation of indigenous peoples, the creation of a permanent division of labor with captured slaves as the first proletariat, foreshadowed all future degradation. While younger Perlman anticipated redemption in the uprising of the modern working class, older Perlman developed a theory of authority structures, tribal conflict, and ecological destruction as the overwhelming facts of all 'progress'.[2]

In previous eras, Perlman's intellectual evolution would have been dismissed by left thinkers as a confused return to idealism, premonition perhaps of a Niebuhrian pessimism and acquiescence by default to anti-Communism a la mode. Perlman, as his old comrades observed, had something very different in mind. Leaning heavily upon the lyric anthropo-history *Beyond Geography: The Western Spirit Against the Wilderness* by Frederick W.Turner, Perlman made a striking case for the creative, nurturent qualities of primordial culture and the pathology of the state from its beginnings onward. In this vision, the 'Crisis Cults', uprisings from primitive Christians in the Roman Empire to Cathars to Ghost Dancers, became the true precursors to a modern radical movement. They sought not to replace the state's historical agenda with their own, but to wipe out the agenda.

As the 1980s boiled with the triumph of Reaganism and the debacle of European left alternatives, with unprecedented ecological destruction and with Third World desperation, radical thinkers could not so easily brush aside the attack upon history. Indeed, where Perlman had found Beelzebub in the Leviathan state, others, influenced by Marxism, found god (or at least spirituality) hidden in the revolt *against and through* the historical process. Liberation Theology provided a millenarian anti-imperialist rationale for the rejection of the West's expanded intrusion into syncretic societies still alive with indigenous cultural survivals. Militant scholars of Latin America, whatever their own relationship to religion, argued for the existence of a separate historical trajectory in the Southern half of the hemisphere, a retention of the Counter-Reformation's anti-capitalist religiosity now enlivened by Marxist ideas and pervasive social-economic crisis. The most sophisticated of the Latin American revolutionaries themselves, high officials of the Sandinista government, swore allegiance to Jose Mariátegui, father of *indigenismo*, while also proclaiming their fidelity to 'true Christianity'. Like Mao's Communism, Burmese U Nu's Buddhist Socialism, Arab and African Socialism, an inescapable theme in Latin America has been the separation of communal traditions from imperial intrusion and the attempt to reconcile Western technologies with collective indigenous aims. However these efforts may have failed in the past forty years, the task remains as inevitable as the search for a cooperative order.[3]

US intellectuals as a class remained by and large determinedly secular, fitful and uneasy with if not actually ignorant of such developments. Scarcely seen beneath their collective nose, intellectual currents attuned to versions of religious radicalism began to take shape. A spate of radical religious publications, Catholic, Protestant and even Jewish, reached out toward intellectual constituencies alien to the left. Developments in South Africa and the Phillipines underlined the importance of the information and the political following gathered. A sophisticated and wide-ranging theological discussion commenced in the light of world developments and Marxist theory. Such a development had been unknown since at least the days of the Spiritualists. If not intellectually decisive in itself, it hinted at other changes at large.[4]

Critics on the Right and the social-democratic Left, so far as they could interpret the significance of Liberation Theology at all, saw its development as another form of Third Worldist geopolitical orientation, a mask for Communism. Like current Socialist Workers Party leaders who declare Trotskyism to be a theory of Latin American revolution, American enthusiasts for the Sandinistas appear to the suspicious like consummate adaptationists. A similarity could indeed be drawn, but not the one that the critics thought. Serious, scholarly reportage of Third World conditions and events, one of the most enduring developments of the New Left, had during the 1970s and 1980s slowly, patiently and perhaps unconsciously built up a perspective which escaped the old West-centered interpretations. The venerable NACLA *Report on the Americas,* twenty years old by the middle of the 1980s, could be seen as the flagship of a Marxism which had no longer any need to describe itself in those terms. Struggling for a position outside the familiar Cold War debates, the eclectic supporters of Latin America (or more precisely opponents of US intervention) regardless of their political or religious affiliation began to feel the pull of the Latin American revolutionaries' own subjectivity.[5]

The critics—especially those who all too eagerly recast Latin American revolutions in Cold War terms—unwittingly passed over the deeper conceptual difficulties of Liberation Theology. But so too, with understandable enthusiasm, did most supporters. The most sophisticated of the radical theologians have come to see their movement as the recuperation of the prehistorical sense of totality in human oneness with nature. Along the road of recovery, 'god is revealed in the negation of god', true Christianity in the actions of historic rebels, culminating in the Anarchist, Socialist and Communist movements which offer an antidote to corrupted institutional Christianity. Thereby, Liberation Theology comes to stand in line of historical descent from the struggles and ultimate failure of secular radical movements. Christology, the theory of salvation based in the Biblical story of liberation, offers hope both of return 'to the garden', and an even more impressive example than Leninism of strategic intellectual doctrine readily graspable by a semi-literate Third World population seeking a more prosperous way of life. It is simultaneously escape from history and self-realization through material reality.[6]

But for all its historical-theoretical fructification, Christology is also inherently a theory out of time. It prepares leaders and populations for great measures of collective suffering. It has no way of accommodating the gift that the West brought along with its destructive economies: individuation, the expansion of the individual personality, not through the classic bourgeois framework of 'great books' and 'great music' nor for the elite alone, but through the sources of self-education and entertainment readily available to great numbers. At its highest stages of development, this individuation has promised and continues to promise what Jeremy Shapiro calls the 'universal semiotic of technological experience in which all the oppositions of two-dimensional civilization are irreversibly homogenized and subjected to self-regulating laws of a synchronic system in which the traditional distinctions of form and matter, subject and object, the conscious, the beautiful and the necessary, are overcome.'[7] Certainly the levels of affluence necessary to sustain American-style hedonistic individualism are unlikely elsewhere. But the transistor may be more essential to the surviving tribesman than to the Yuppie jogger.

Myopic misunderstanding of mass desires is not a Christological or Third World problem alone. North American intellectuals who seriously argued—increasingly punching out their analysis on the computer—for the abolition of television were guilty of a related error. They sought the familiar handholds of the Western genteel tradition, guides in an uncertain world. And they fell, like Fredy Perlman, into the irresolvable conundrum at the end of the twentieth century. How *else* could the masses of the world emancipate themselves save by incorporating old myths into new frameworks, drawing the most ancient symbols and modern vehicles for mythology together? What else could the future possibly hold, beyond mere survival, than a universality, translatability and simultaneity of all cultural experience rendered both holy and *fun?*

The unconscious trajectory of New Left Marxism (and post-Marxism) has been, however precariously, in this general direction. The study of empire has tended to merge Leninism's view into a more universal and structural understanding. The interpretation of history, although focused upon the moment of industrial transformation, has sought out the collective subjectivity of the crowd. And the critique of culture, particularly popular culture, pushed hard upon the borders of the unknown.

Can there be another unifying metaphysic to replace the single standard of proletarian class struggle? Resacralization may be a first and overly ambitious approximation. Taken singly, none of the other immediate candidates—the potential universalism of individuation within a semiotic system, the life-or-death chiliasm of Third World struggles, and the no less life-or-death resistance against nuclear war and toxic annihilation—can properly absorb and transcend the Marxist tradition. Between them stands a wide middle ground of workplace alienation (whatever the workplace), of intense but tolerable exploitation and of brief solidarities. Between them stands also the complexity of ethnic-cultural life in the United States, where nationalisms and internationalisms, oral cultures and techno-cultures mix at accelerated speeds. For want of an alternative organizing principle, the market and capital now hold the key. But they hold it with shaking hands. As Ralph Ellison wrote in *The Invisible Man*, remonstrating against Marxist strictures: history is a gambler. No one knows what will happen next. The point of theory, however, is to make guesswork intelligent.

American Marxism Takes a Ph.D., and so What?

A favorite sport of right-wing commentators from the late 1970s has been the attack upon the New Left greybeard, the mutton-chop sideburned college professor who forces his Marxist ideas upon hapless undergraduates. This attack cannot be denied its industrial-sized grain of truth. Radicals in the academy have found themselves trapped inside a massive contradiction, not between theory and reality (as the Right claims) but between theory and practice, between (in the theoretical version) materialism and idealism.

On the one side we have the critique of inequality, the absence of social justice. On the other side, we have the macrotheories of idealism. On the one side, the steady effort of low-profile political presence in any and every arena, on the other side, the tenacious dreams of some splendid vindication. New Left Marxism has given the terms new names as scholarship proceeds. It has not changed the categories in fifteen years.

The complex dynamics of this situation demand new efforts to understand the stasis temporarily reached within the system—identifying the conflicts which lie hidden beneath the apparent triumph as links in a chain of events reaching over centuries and continents. In several areas of concern, the critique of capitalism and social class has edged toward a depth and precision that previous generations of American Marxist scholars would have considered almost unimaginable. Two *caveats* are in order before examining some details of the interpretation. First, the 'New Left' mentors, those who set the methodological pace, were themselves mostly of the older generation. They staked out the ground, frequently with the encouragement of their students and in the glare of the sixties political background which made the subsequent (but perhaps less original) work by their genuinely New Left disciples possible. Second, as Stanley Diamond argued in the first issue of his influential journal, *Dialectical Anthropology* (1975), loyalty to Marx's intention and not to any writ had come to be the premise of Marxist renewal.[8] Did the post-Old Left scholarship and the demi-Marxist interpretation make 'New Left Marxism' a misnomer? That was a question the New Left Marxist was hard-put to answer unequivocally.

Sociologists had been perfectly situated to elaborate the critique of domination. When radicalism entered the university, young sociologists discovered the historical-material reality behind Parsonian systems. As Immanuel Wallerstein remembers, for his generation of college radicals, somewhere between the evocation of the thirties and the expectation of the sixties, Third World imperatives became suddenly and painfully obvious. Wallerstein reasoned back from 'underdevelopment' to the sources of 'development' since the sixteenth century, with capitalism the unifying mode of production and the international division of labor its key tool. All dependence theory comes together here. Within this framework, the development of more states and peripheral states, of imperial centers and outposts of exploitation, becomes the story of modern nationalism in its various stages.[9]

Wallerstein's *The Modern World System* (1974), the central text elaborating these points, has arguably been the most influential single book of the post-New Left era. Critics have shrewdly noted that Parsonian functionalism, disguised in the thicket of Marxist political convictions, has returned suspiciously to the essential interpretation. All sub-systems resemble each other and fit into a single, overarching system; transformation of the system piecemeal ultimately serves as readjustment of integration *grosso modo*. In the extreme form of the argument, all 'underdevelopment' becomes the direct product of capitalist development, and all 'pre-capitalist' economies become capitalist by definition. How this accounts for the subjectivity of the Third World, landlord or *campesino*, urbanite, female, Christian or Rastafarian remains obscure. Where scholarly respect for the sacred and for consciousness fails, recognizable human subjects tend to disappear.[10]

At the popular level of academic practice rather than theory, the critique of domination found its way into the basic college curriculum, with many of the same strengths and limitations. Thus a leading criminology textbook explains the ultimate source of crime as the creation of an industrial reserve army, and the criminal as a primitive rebel acting upon the contradiction between potentiality and actuality under capitalism. In its very existence as a popular teaching tool, regardless of the relative lack of sophistication in its formulations, this work constitutes a breakthrough, on the order of materialism's injection into late-nineteenth-century thought. Other related studies, in the history of education for example, likewise traced evolutionary developments previously described as beneficent (emphatically including purported 'victories' of the common people, such as American public schooling) as fresh means to formalize the control that the system increasingly exercised over the poor. Pedestrian versions of Foucault sported reductionism as if it were a gem. They had *discovered* the truth behind the veil of state generosity, and proclaimed that truth to the world. American radicals, scholars and students thrive on such revelations every bit as much as did A.M. Simons and his study classes. To have the dirty secrets of capitalism elucidated is a triumph, but (as the key authors themselves candidly admit) this only brings the analysis to the first crucial stage of materialist interpretation.[11]

Popular radical economics expresses similar tendencies even more strongly. Dual market and industrial segmentation theory, grafted a Marxist idealism upon marginal economics, inscribing a critique of poverty and super-exploitation across the traditionally cheery view of labor mobility. New Left theorists as early as the 1960s put forward the view that poverty results from the absence of high-wage jobs for the poor. More historically-minded theorists traced this dual market to capitalism's accommodation of organized labor after World War Two: white ethnic unionists would continue to receive upward-tending wages in return for loss of control over production and in return for a separation from the emerging Black labor force destined for the worst factory jobs or no jobs. Feminist theorists of the dual labor market have added their own variables to this equation: the postwar devaluation of female labor, and the simultaneous growth of clerical work, placed an impossible burden upon the prospects of class solidarity—or at least a burden defined as impossible by the existing labor movement.

The direct link between this mode of analysis and classical Marxism was made by Harry Braverman in *Labor and Monopoly Capital* (1974). Braverman, veteran machinist and heretical Trotskyist, remained true to the older Marxism's concentration upon wage-labor, in particular the 'deskilling' of work through the continuous refinement of management prerogatives previously held by skilled labor. Braverman became a true 'New Left Marxist' at an advanced age by virtue of his indifference to traditional Marxist happy endings. The decline of skill, as he viewed it, led not to proletarian revolution but to unparalleled social degradation. Braverman's conclusions echoed that elder moral critique of capitalism, in the tradition of Thorstein Veblen, which (as Paul Attewell observed) regained 'enormous popularity, in the seventies, and for good reasons'. The decisive. shift away from industrial production had become palpable. Younger theorists on the same trail closed the circle with their studies of management strategies. American capital clearly intended to divide the workforce by ethnicity and race, paying disproportionately high wages at the top and low at the bottom, while deskilling across the board. The CIO had momentarily challenged but could not overcome this strategy; seniority itself as a form of job security was also a divisive 'property relation' between workers. Hierarchical Capital indeed created its opposite in the disciplined workforce Austin Lewis described, but successfully overcame the contradictions through technical controls (the repeated breakup of informal workgroups) and through manipulation of distinctions. The synthesis of these perceptions in the work of younger radical economists resembled nothing so much as the 'equilibrium' theories of Bukharin, by which class society re-established its hegemony at each stage after uncertainties and opposition. The *telos* of Marxism, or any other redemption in a dynamic system of analysis, was nowhere to be found.

James O'Connor, chief interpreter of state intervention, struggled hard to give the argument more philosophical depth and political resonance. The State's efforts to achieve Habermasian 'legitimitation', that happy equilibrium, governs its ideological actions, just as the global profit level governs its economic-political interventions. The state must, of its nature, lean towards the monopoly sector in its benefits, as it must emphasize (except perhaps in crisis moments) Keynesian benefits for its chief supporters. Moreover, by the 1970s-80s the state also had to weigh the ideological benefits of the welfare society against the necessity to reduce gaps between social costs and state revenues.[12]

But what if these contradictions could be resolved, or rather at least postponed into the foreseeable future? Or what if crisis simply led to chaos? Had the oppressed given any definitive signal of their capacity to transform society? To this last question, historians of many kinds applied themselves with vigor.

Most radical historians, consciously or unconsciously, adapted a methodology that was strikingly kindred to phenomenology. They could not prove, and did not necessarily themselves believe after a time, that the current working class would transform society. But they could demonstrate the previously undemonstrated in American history: the vital presence of class as an element in the historical process. The working class *existed*, the lower classes existed in a Whitmanian sense, living and dying, enjoying and anguishing, changing with each incoming group and each generation. The keynote, dignity, carried something of the ethical imperative innate to the older Marxism, but diffused or transmogrified into what the historians' ultimate opponents, semioticians, would call 'historicism'.

The social history approach, in particular, became vivid for the young radicals drawn to, or part of, the *Narodnik* blue-collar orientation. As the political breakthrough faded into fantasy, history came increasingly to take the place of the present. History occupied the strategic location that novel-writing had created during the 1910s and literary criticism had taken over in the 1930s-40s: Queen Discipline for American Marxism. The young militants-cum-historians intended not only scholarly history, but more to the point of their own collective past, history understood as interpreted, an historical worldview for activists. Such history, scholarly or didactic, did not lend itself easily to Marxist methodological discussions, possibly a point in its favor. Yet the excitement of historical discovery, whether of the poisonous liberal roots of US foreign policy or of radical ancestors for radicals of all kinds—blue-collar, gay or feminist—was for the early 1970s hardly less palpable than the prospect of permanent degradation in the proletarian present.

Such historical scholarship became markedly less convincing the closer it approached that present. Paul Berman has waggishly characterized the perfect monograph from this school as a detailed study of the pretzel benders of Leonia, New Jersey, during some past obscure moment of glory. Outspoken Marxists with a rather more pessimistic view of lower class initiatives, like historian of slavery Eugene Genovese, twitted the militant scholars for their sentimentalist replacement of decisive action with picturesque behavior. The charges had merit, but neither for the reasons nor with the implications that the critics suggested. Models of American imperial involvement in Latin America, for instance, needed only adjustment from the early twentieth century onward. By contrast, depictions of working-class domestic life, of consciousness and politics, of women's political and social movements and even of the Black family grew steadily more schematic as social history by the time they reached the 1920s. The nineteenth century moment of industrialization became the moment for analysis, because society afterward offered fewer conceptual handholds and more political difficulty. Many careful monographic studies appeared, informed by a vague but undeniable Marxism, from 1975 on. But even methodologically daring researches proceeded via a paradox: a difficult present grew dim, while the presumed golden age of social politics glowed with color, rang with music. Epitomized in Irving Howe's reminiscences of an almost vanished Yiddish culture, these accounts suggested an outcome somehow less certain, less final than the depressingly real events surrounding the real-life scholars.[13]

The very progression of radical scholarship, the filling in of much of the historical narrative and genealogy, exposed the original conceptual limitations, throwing older and younger scholars into a revealing crisis of confidence. How *did* victims of the American past speak for themselves, once the certainty of Socialist triumph had been discretely abandoned? Could fairness, the liberal Democrats' current (and impressively unsuccessful) rallying cry, substitute for the categories they had pursued so long in their efforts to escape the past limits of Marxist interpretations? What recasting of class, race and gender lay beyond the Second International, Third International, and New Left versions? How much, for that matter, could history reveal beyond the dilemmas of the past?

The fundamental dilemma had already been posed by the pioneering *Studies On the Left,* shrewd analytical interpreter of America's Corporate Liberal ideology but unable itself to interpret the sub-political text of the emerging 1960s 'personal politics'. So it would be for my own *Radical America* which survived the New Left with a bundle of vibrant ideas only to be plunged into the long night of the 1970s-1980s. So it would be for countless efforts at clarification, individual or collective, scholarly or popular. To some Marxist scholars, the workplace became the secure haven of class consciousness in history; to others, penetration of community life in history, drawing upon anthropological discourse, yielded fascinating conclusions with no overarching historical dynamic. For still others, an almost aristocratic Marxism embracing a version of Gramsci's concept of hegemony explained the *one* presumably coherent and class-conscious group in America, *viz.* the ruling classes. Radical scholarship threatened to become scholarly art-work, for want of a better purpose.

Black studies and women's studies encouraged fresh lines of approach. Pan-African historians had been striving for decades to make the simple point that had been so clear in Hegel's dialectic of slave and master. The master is the fixed quantity, appearances notwithstanding; it is the slave who moves, who can finally live without the Other and who in the face of all difficulty makes history.

The two new disciplines seemed to concretize the subject, to place it in history and in society. Their genius lay in detail, and in mostly hidden assumptions which returned back beyond Marxism to older American forms of radical inquiry. Such a pathbreaking narrative as Vincent Harding's *There Is a River*, a premier history of the epoch from slavery to emancipation, read like a steady stream bathing the past, supplemental to the rushing current of *Black Reconstruction* with its false eddies and explosive flow. Manning Marable's widely-hailed studies in Afro-American history scanned events with a clear eye trained by DuBois. Current political uncertainty and a nagging despair at white America's moral unresponsiveness haunted the search for ultimate implications. These authors, too, seemed to await another social development not yet in sight.[14]

Joan Kelly's bold theoretical claims that the relationship of man and woman be placed upon a platform as high as that of class relationships marked a parallel, and conceptually more dramatic, advance of women's studies. The careful analyses of dual labor markets, the reinterpretation of suffrage struggles, the new light shed on women's labor and leisure—all demonstrated that the links could be put into place. But where did they go? Not many steps could be taken in the largest conceptual framework, for want of archeological details of gender oppression's origins, or at the other end of history, because the reinterpretation had to await concrete evidence of social movements beyond the limits of women's advance during the 1960s-1970s.[15]

Marxism and Culture

In the wake of widespread political despair, it seemed to many New Left intellectuals that only the subject remained, a subject by no means fully compensated for the loss of personal and methodological certainty by the presence of revolutions somewhere else in the world. The epicenter of methodological discussions—if it could be said to exist at any particular spot anymore—returned to the English departments from which it had fled thirty years earlier and thence to the newer outposts of film, television and semiotic studies.

Fredric Jameson may be said to personify this development at its radical edges. Almost single-handedly (but actually with a large supporting group of teachers, theoreticians and foot-workers in the dissident journals), Jameson injected a critique of form based upon a critical interpretation of European sources, into an American literary criticism still in crisis from the disintegration of the New Criticism. Jameson's distinction lay principally in his vigorous absorption of structuralism's insights and modernism's field of interest to a committed, historic and political reading of the current subject matter. Like his British equivalent, Terry Eagleton, Jameson brought political questions back to the discipline, without either the vulgar claims to 'science' or the glib dismissal of non- and anti-Marxists that had so characterized the old Communist criticism. Jameson's personal example encouraged a variety of sixties veterans and younger scholars, also committed writers, to feel themselves part of serious discussions. He also earned the admirable hatred of ex-left neo-conservatives like Hilton Kramer and William Phillips who recognized a threat to their prestige.

According to the shrewd and persuasive argument of Andreas Huyssen, if poststructuralism is 'primarily a discourse of and about modernism', the prestige French theories presented to American academic audiences can be seen as an *'archeology of modernity'*, modernity at its final phase. There is something very funny about Americans, whose popular culture excited French Surrealists and reputedly inspired Existentialism, formally entering the main theoretical discussion as it loses its connective thread to reality. Postmodernism, if it represents the crisis in modernism itself, marks the historical moment when—in Jameson's words—the avant-garde becomes a necessary accompaniment to the market. But contrary to Jameson's pessimism about the accessibility of understanding in and through history via popular symbols and signs, this process may be the *only possible means* by which the divisions between high and low culture reflecting the ancient division of mental and manual labor can at last be broken. If so, history may become understandable for the *first* time. Modernism, the last of the genteel illusions, had to collapse in a welter of popular culture before this possibility became realizable.[16]

Resacralization, the renewal of the sacred amid the apparently mundane details of life, becomes here a metaphor which encompasses more than the contemporary resurgence of formal religion. The search for a 'lost unity' (Hegel's phrase for religious yearning) in the signs and signals of popular culture, successor to the 'appreciation' of high culture in nineteenth-century European intellectual life, is today a transparently spiritual enterprise. Once again, Europeans have had to remind American intellectuals of what lies before their eyes. Americans have found their gods in Hollywood and the television studios, via the images which displace the traditional apotheosis in the religious service. The tardy growth of culture studies—recently given the pedigree of post-modernist interpretations by prestigeous European theorists fascinated with American culture—seems to have yielded a theology of its own, as impenetrable to the uninitiated as the most exotic religious text and as precious to the initiates. This latter development has not been either democratic or particularly fruitful in any broader theoretical terms. But the intense effort devoted to cultural interpretation demonstrates how desperately a clarification is sought after. In the framework of political renewal it may well mark the long-delayed approach to popular culture, which according to this valorization would become, indeed has evidently become at least in epiphanic moments, home to the wandering consciousness, holy city where pilgrims of every race and sect mingle.

Perhaps, in negation after negation, shedding off every possible illusion, we have come to the stage prophesized by Adorno in *Minima Moralia* 'That there is no longer a folk does not mean . . . as the Romantics have propagated, that the masses are worse. Rather, it is precisely in the new, radically alienated form of society that the untruth of the old is first being revealed.'[17] This aphorism could be read in an optimistic sense: mass culture has educated the masses, in ways not yet fully understood. In *Cultural Correspondence*, a journal which sought to explore the quotidien stretching from Country & Western music to the Sunday funny pages, co-editor Dave Wagner searches for abstractions equal to the prospect, affirming:

'That mass culture—is, taken as a whole, a total response by

Capital to the historical possibilities of the specifically modern mass which it first creates and which now continues to create itself.

'That the culture of the masses in its quotidien is objectively and historically concrete; that is, both in its aspect as the subjectivity of capital objectifying itself for consumption . . . and in its aspect as a response to the demand for objective and historical self-recognition by the masses in its daily life.

'That the mass concretizes its demand for objective self-recognition first in the interstices of daily life, *i.e.*, mass cultural production . . . and later by endorsing its own creations in their mediated or alienated forms as capital appropriates their movement in its interstices with the movement of its own subjectivity (*i.e.*, the market).

'That the objective recognition of their own subjectivity on the part of the masses is covert, disguised and mediated by individuality in the process of which it continually moves in their guise toward the overt form of universal subjectivity.'[18]

Here, the promise of technology's 'universal semiotic', predicted by Shapiro just as the New Left collapsed, may be realized in mass life. Class society is overcome by the force of its own historical momentum, through the details of daily experience—however the final transformation is accomplished. That would be a happy outcome to the seemingly opposite but actually congruent movements, the 1960s social struggles and the deepening of mass culture subjectivity since. It would also vindicate the spirit both of homegrown radicalism, with its genius for direct democracy; and of immigrant radicalism, the socialism of the masses. If we don't run out of time, it will surely happen, not only in the USA but as the ultimate cross-cultural fertilization process reaching around the world. America has committed too many sins to become a beacon of nations. But we may yet make our positive contribution with a trans-racial, trans-lingual, trans-historic example.

Whatever the outcome, one cannot escape a sense of inevitability in the larger drift of events, theory and popular consciousness discussed in this book. Grant, if not the historical pessimism of a Fredy Perlman, that the long-term strength of the system has been to absorb the elements apparently alien to it and to convert new kinds of demands into sources for continued expansion. Some fundamental weakness has inevitably and effectively been turned against the potential forces of liberation. No generation after the disillusionment with Stalin could seriously believe that a proper vanguard would have made the revolution in 1871, 1877,

1886, 1912, 1937, 1947 or 1969. None could believe, either, that class society would exhaust itself, short of annihilation, until sources of a new and universal (*i.e.*, no longer Western) consciousness had come to light. Paradoxically, mass culture which saps and destroys the folkish remnants that bourgeois exploitation has left alive is also a prime source of universal consciousness. We have come to this stage because we could come by no other path.

The apparent impasse in our present era is surely the result of a meta-historical process which has taken place behind the backs of the left (as well as everyone else). If the history of American Marxism continues to have value, it is to teach us that we have all been made fools of in the ruses of history. But we have also been, at our best, God's own fools. The glimmers of wisdom gained at a great price, along with an undying revolutionary faith, have allowed all types and generations of radicals to keep a light in the window. Whatever their human weaknesses and failures, the old Marxists stood for more than they were themselves. And so have we. And so will those who follow us.

Notes

Introduction

1. Richard Hofstadter, *The American Political Tradition and the Men Who Made It* (New York 1948), p.viii.

2. Daniel Bell, 'Marxian Socialism in the United States', in Donald Drew Egbert and Stow Persons, eds., *Socialism and American Life, I* (Princeton 1952), p. 217.

3. See for example Hartmut Keil and John Jentz, eds., *German Workers in Industrial Chicago, 1850-1910: A Comparative Perspective* (DeKalb, 1985); and Rudolph Vecoli's memorable polemic against the scholarship of immigrant conservatism, *'Contadini* in Chicago: A Critique of *The Uprooted'*, in Herbert G. Gutman and Gregory S. Kealey, eds., *Many Pasts: Readings in American Social History, 1865-Present, II* (Englewood Cliffs 1973).

4. Perry Anderson, *In the Tracks of Historical Materialism* (London, 1983), Chapter III.

5. For a partial statement, see Paul Buhle and Thomas H. Fiehrer, 'Liberation Theology in Latin America: Dispensations Old and New', in Mike Davis, Fred Pfeil and Michael Sprinker, eds., *The Year Left, An American Socialist Yearbook, 1985* (London 1985).

6. Karl Marx, *Grundrisse: Foundations of the Critique of Political Economy (Rough Draft)*, translated by Martin Nicolaus (London 1973), p. 884.

Chapter One

1. Karl Marx and Frederick Engels, *The Communist Manifesto* (New York Labor News, 1961 edition), especially pp. 18-19.

2. R. Lawrence Moore, *European Socialists and the American Promised Land*, (New York 1970), Chapters II-III.

3. Alfred F. Young, 'Revolutionary Mechanics,' Franklin Rosemont, 'Workingmen's Parties,' and Eric Foner, 'Workers and Slavery,' in Paul Buhle and Alan Dawley, eds., *Working for Democracy: American Workers from the Revolution to the Present* (Urbana 1985).

4. Cedric Robinson, *Black Marxism: The Making of a Black Radical Tradition* (London 1983), pp. 243-44.

5. Bruce Levine, ' "Beggarly Sans-Coulottes" ' A study of German-American Workers in Two Revolutions, 1848-1860,' and Dirk Hoerder and Hartmut Keil, 'The American Case and German Social Democracy at the Turn of the Twentieth Century, 1878-1907', papers presented at the conference on the impact of socialism in the United States, University of Paris, May 1983.

6. See Paul Buhle, 'German Socialists and the Roots of American Working-Class Radicalism,' in Hartmut Keil and John B. Jentz, eds., *German Workers in Industrial Chicago, 1850-1910: A Comparative Perspective* (DeKalb 1983).

7. Edward Aveling and Eleanor Max Aveling, *The Working Class Movement in America* (London 1889), pp. 198-200.

8. *Ibid*, pp. 208-09.

9. *Arbeiter Stimme* (New York), Oct. 8, 1876.

10. *Ibid*, Nov.26, 1876.

11. See 'Die Jubiläumsnummern der "New Yorker Volkszeitung," 1888, 1903, 1928,' in Dirk Hoerder and Thomas Weber, (eds.) *Glimpses of the German-American Press* (Bremen, 1985). This collection of writings from the jubilee numbers is perhaps the most useful single valuable source available on nineteenth century German-American Socialism.

12. David Montgomery, *Beyond Equality: Labor and the Radical Republicans, 1862-1872* (New York 1967), pp.189-96.

13. Charles Leinenweber, 'Immigration and the Decline of Internationalism in the American Working Class Movement, 1864–1919', unpublished dissertation, University of California, Berkeley 1969, Ch.6.

14. Conveyed best in David Lyons, 'The World of P.J.McGuire: a Study of the American Labor Movement, 1870–90', unpublished dissertation, University of Minnesota, 1972; and in Hermann Schlüter, *Die Internationale in Amerika: Ein Beitrag zur Geschichte der Arbeiter-Bewegung in der Vereinigten Staaten* (Chicago 1918).

15. Saul K. Padover, ed., and trans., *Karl Marx On the First International* (New York 1973), pp.543, 547.

16. Hubert Perrier, ' "Americanizing Socialism": Some Comments on the Quest for a Viable Strategy, 1871–1886', presented at the Paris Conference, 1983.

17. Philip S.Foner and Brewster Chamberlin, eds., Brewster Chamberlin and Angela Chamberlin, trans., *Friedrich A. Sorge's Labor Movement in the United States: A History of the American Working Class from Colonial Times to 1890* (Westport, 1977), p. 155.

18. *Arbeiter Stimme*, Sept.24, 1876.

19. *Vorbote* (Chicago) Feb.14, Dec.5, 12, 14 1874. Renate Kiesewetter, 'Die Institution der deutsch-amerikanischen Arbeiterpresse in Chicago: Zur Geschichte des 'Vorboten' und der 'Chicagoer Arbeiterzeitung', in *Glimpses of the German-American Press* has a wonderful historical perspective on the *Vorbote* and its milieu.

20. Horst Groschopp, 'Kulturarbeit und der Kulturarbeiter in der Geschichte der deutschen Arbeiterbewegung vor 1914,' in *Der sozialistische Kulturarbeiter* (Berlin, 1983), p.7. The value of this scholarship about socialist culture, undertaken in the DDR, cannot be overestimated. Groschopp's scholarship and his leadership of collective labor is yet too little appreciated.

21. See Philip Foner's useful *The Workingman's Party in America* (Minneapolis 1983).

22. Reminiscent accounts in the *Volkszeitung* jubilee numbers, especially James Fuchs, 'Errinerunges eines Radaktionsmitgleides', pp.120–221, and Christ, Ludwig, 'Zum goldenen Jubilem unserer Volkszeitung', p.125, in

Glimpses of the German-American Press. See also Hermann Schluter's *The Brewing Industry and the Brewery Workers' Movement in America* (Cincinnati 1910).

23. *Vorbote*, Dec.7, 1884.

24. Quoted in *Der Sozialist* (New York), June 19, 1886, with a rejoinder from the more orthodox Adolf Douai.

25. Joseph Chada, 'A Survey of Radicalism in the Bohemian-American Community', unpublished paper, Chicago Historical Society, 1954.

26. *Frederick Sorge's The Labor Movement in America*, p. 242.

27. Hermann Schlüter, 'Die Anfänge der Deutschen Arbeiterbewegung in New York und ihre Presse', *New Yorker Volkszeitung*, Feb. 21, 1903, reprinted into *Glimpses of the German-American Radical Press*, pp.44–57.

28. David Montgomery, *Workers' Control in America: Studies in the History of Work, Technology, and Labor Struggles* (Cambridge 1979), Ch.1; and the primary document, George E. McNeill, *The Labor Movement, the Problem of Today* (Boston 1887). So far as I know, the emerging socialist-labor press has never been adequately characterized. See, however, an early and earnest effort by Howard Quint, *The Forging of American Socialism* (Indianapolis 1964 edition), Ch.5.

29. J.S. Hertz, *Di Yiddish Sotsialistishe Bevegung* (New York 1954), Ch. 2–4.

30. Morris Hillquit, *The History of Socialism in the United States* (New York 1903), pp.322–23; Henry Kuhn, 'Reminiscence of Daniel DeLeon', in *Daniel DeLeon: The Man and His Work, a Symposium* (New York 1919), p.4.

31. Leon Kobrin, *Mayne Fuftzig Yohr in Amerika* (New York, 1966), Sect.I, Ch.5–7; Jakob Milch, 'Di Geburt fun der "Tsukunft" un ihr Bedeutung', *Tsukunft*, XVII (1912); A. Liessin, 'Tsum 25 Yoriger Yubeliaum fun, "Tsukunft",' *Tsukunft*, XXII (January 1917).

32. Daniel DeLeon, *Reform or Revolution?* (New York, 1924 ed) , p.24.

33. Daniel DeLeon, *Two Pages from Roman History* (New York 1903).

34. *The People* (New York), July 3, 1892.

35. Robert Rives LaMonte, 'The New Intellectuals', *New Review*, II (January 1914), p.45.

36. Bertram Wolfe's pamphlet, *Marx and America* (New York 1934), put this view forward most concisely; Philip Foner, *From the Founding of the A.F. of L. to the Emergence of American Imperialism History of the Labor Movement in the United States, II:* (New York 1955) puts it forward the most untiringly.

Chapter Two

1. See Paul Buhle, 'American Horror', in Franklin Rosemont, ed., *Surrealism and Its Popular Accomplices* (San Francisco 1981); Harry Levin, *The Power of Blackness* (New York 1958).

2. Joseph Jablonski, 'Millennial Soundings: Chiliasts, Cathari and Mystical Feminism in the American Grain', in Paul Buhle, Jayne Cortez, Philip Lamantia, Nancy Joyce Peters, Franklin Rosemont and Penelope Rosemont, eds., *Free Spirits, I* (San Francisco 1982).

3. The Rev. Samuel May, quoted in Mari Jo Buhle and Paul Buhle, eds., *A Concise History of Woman Suffrage* (Urbana 1978), p.9, from *The Liberator*, June 26, 1857.

4. *The Revolution,* (New York) May 18, 1869; *ibid*, Aug.26, 1869.

5. Karl Marx, *Capital, I,* ed. by Frederick Engels (New York 1939), p.329. Philip S. Foner comments at length on Marx and Engels' erratic treatment of the

subject, in *American Socialism and Black Americans, from the Age of Jackson to World War II* (Westport 1977), Ch.2–3.

6. See David Harris, *Socialist Origins in the U.S., American Forerunners of Marx, 1817–32* (Amsterdam 1966); Alan Dawley, *Class and Community: The Industrial Revolution in Lynn* (Cambridge 1976); Sean Wilentz, *Chants Democratic* (New York 1984).

7. See David S. Reynolds, *George Lippard* (Boston 1982), for the most incisive treatment.

8. C. Osborne Ward, *The Ancient Lowly, II* (Chicago, 1907 ed.), p.686.

9. Quoted in Herbert G. Gutman, *Work, Culture and Society in Industrializing America* (New York, 1976), p.100.

10. Madelaine B. Stern, *The Pantarch: A Biography of Stephen Pearl Andrews* (Austin 1968), pp.109–110.

11. *The Banner of Light* (Boston), Jan.11, 1879; see also Mari Jo Buhle and Florence Howe, 'Afterword', to Elizabeth Stuart Phelps, *The Silent Partner and 'The Tenth of January'* (Old Westbury 1983 edition); and Lizzie M. Doten, *Poems of Progress* (Boston 1873).

12. See for instance 'A Lecture on Constitutional Equality,' reprinted into Madelaine Stern, ed., *The Victoria Woodhull Reader* (Weston, Mass., 1974), volume not consecutively paged.

13. See Mari Jo Buhle, 'Socialism and Feminism in the United States, 1820–1920', unpublished dissertation, University of Wisconsin, 1974, Ch. 2, for a close account of the split not otherwise available.

14. Andrew Jackson Davis, *Arabula, or the Divine Guest* (Boston 1867), p.172.

15. Horace Traubel, Richard M. Bucke and Thomas Harned, *In Re Walt Whitman* (Philadelphia 1893).

16. See Franklin Rosemont, 'Free Play and No Limit: Edward Bellamy's Utopia', in *Surrealism and Its Popular Accomplices;* and Mari Jo Buhle, *Women and American Socialism*, Ch.2. I take sharp exception to Arthur Lipow, *Authoritarian Socialism in America: Edward Bellamy and the Nationalist Movement* (Berkeley 1982), as unfair to Bellamy and his followers, but find the account by Howard Quint, *The Forging of American Socialism* (Indianapolis 1964 ed.), Ch.3, still reliable. See also Quint's discussion of genteel Christian Socialism, Ch.4, which space reasons have prevented me from discussing here.

17. Lawrence Goodwyn, *Democratic Promise: The Populist Movement in America* (New York 1976); Norman Pollack, *The Populist Response to Industrial America: Midwestern Populist Thought* (Cambridge 1962); James R. Green, *Grass-Roots Socialism: Radical Movements in the Southwest, 1895–1943* (Baton Rouge 1978), Ch.1, remains the basic account of the transition.

18. Joseph R. Buchanan, *Diary of a Labor Agitator* (New York. 1903), remains the most satisfactory account of the revolutionary Socialist ideology; see also Paul Avrich, *The Haymarket Tragedy* (Princeton 1984).

19. Particular sinners in this regard are Gerald Grob, *Workers and Utopia A Study of Ideological Conflict in the American Labor Movement, 1865–1900* (Evanston, 1961); and Philip S. Foner, *The History of the Labor Movement in the United States, II* (New York 1955).

20. Report of a speech, *The People* (Providence), Apr.25, 1886.

21. Paul Buhle, 'The Knights of Labor in Rhode Island,' in 'Labor and Community Militance in Rhode Island', a special issue of the *Radical History Review,* 17 (Spring 1978).

22. *The People* (Providence), Dec.12, 1887.

23. Leon Fink, *Workingman's Democracy* (Urbana, 1983), carefully analyzes Knights' economic and political activity in various localities; in my view he places

too positive an interpretation upon the political outcome of their efforts.

24. Nick Salvatore, *Eugene Debs, Citizen and Socialist* (Urbana 1982), Parts I–II.

25. Horace Traubel, 'Debs' *The Conservator,* XIV (May 1903), p.40.

26. Upton Sinclair, *Samuel the Seeker* ([n.p.], 1910).

27. Kalmon Marmor, *Morris Vinchevky, Zayn Lebn, Zayn Shafn, I,* Ch.13 (New York 1927); the most satisfactory secondary account of political and social influence within *Yiddishkayt* remains Charles Madison, *Yiddish Literature: Its Scope and Major Writers* (New York 1968).

28. Morris Winchevsky, 'Karl Marx un Lasal,' and 'Eugene V. Debs,' in *Moris Vinchevsky,* VIII.

29. Daniel DeLeon, *Reform or Revolution* (New York, 1924 ed.), p.19.

Chapter Three

1. Interview with Hugo Gellert, OHAL Archives, Tamiment Library, New York University. Rebecca Zurier has wonderfully captured this spirit in her *Art for the Masses (1911–1917): A Radical Magazine and Its Graphics* (New Haven 1985).

2. Austin Lewis, *The Militant Proletariat* (Chicago 1911), pp.36–37.

3. Horace Traubel, 'Collect: And This is Civilization', *The Conservator,* X (August 1902), p. 83.

4. Mari Jo Buhle, *Women and American Socialism* (Urbana 1981), Chs. 2–4.

5. Walter Thomas Mills, *The Struggle for Existence* (Chicago 1904) and the more extended discussion in Paul Buhle, 'Marxism in the United States, 1900–1940,' unpublished dissertation, University of Wisconsin 1975, Ch.I.

6. Ernest Untermann, *Science and Revolution* (Chicago 1906), 192. The Untermann Papers, Wisconsin State Historical Society, have many illuminating documents on the popular socialist uses of Marxism and on the frustrations of the theoreticians.

7. (A.M. Simons), 'Editorial', *International Socialist Review,* II (Mar., 1902), 697. And see the biography, Kent & Gretchen Kreuter, *An American Dissenter: The Life of Algie Martin Simons, 1870–1950* (Lexington 1969).

8. A.M. Simons, *The American Farmer* (Chicago 1902), p.11.

9. See Paul Buhle, 'Introduction' to Ameringer, *The Life and Deeds of Uncle Sam* (Chicago 1985 edition).

10. Harry Rogoff, *Nine Yiddish Writers (n.p., n.d.)* has a fine chapter on Liessin. See also the extremely informative special issue of *Tsukunft* dedicated to Liessin, his life and his work, Vol. 24 (Apr., 1919), and the rather more critical interpretation by communist leader M. Olgin, 'Liessen un di 'Tsukunft', *Der Homer,* III (Sept., 1928).

11. Karl Kautsky to Boudin, July 4, 1910, Louis B. Boudin Collection, Columbia University; N. Baranoff, 'The Art of Being Omniscient', translated into the *New York Daily Call,* June 25, 1911.

12. Paul M. Sweezy, 'The Influence of Marxian Economics on American Thought and Practice', in D.D. Egbert and Stow Persons, eds., *Socialism and American Life, I* (Princeton, 1952), p. 463; Kerr to Boudin, Nov. 30, 1906 and Dec. 6, 1906, Boudin Collection.

13. Robert Hyfler, *Prophets of the Left: American Socialist Thought in the Twentieth Century* (Westport, 1984), Ch.II.

14. Horace Traubel, 'Craftsmen', *The Conservator,* VII (January 1897), p.168.

15. Austin Lewis, 'Introduction', to *Landmarks of Scientific Socialism*

(Chicago 1907), pp.10, 13–15, 17. This was Lewis' excerpt and translation of *Anti-Dühring*, the only American edition then in circulation. The characterization of the iww as the reflection of truly modern industrial conditions has been developed most recently by the 'extra-parliamentarist' Italian journal *Primo Maggio* in the 1970s and other Italian theorists. See, *e.g.*, S. Bologna, 'Composizione di classe e teoria del partito alle origini del movimento consiliare', in *Operai e stato* (Milan 1972), and M. Tronto, *Operai e capitale* (Turin 1971 edition). Their discussion is also summarized by Bruno Cartosio, 'Italian and West-German Research on the Industrial Workers of the World', European Association for American Studies Biennial Conference, Amsterdam, April 1980.

16. Daniel DeLeon, *Preamble to the I.W.W.*, later republished as *The Socialist Reconstruction of Society* (New York 1935 edition), pp. 53, 49–51, 55, 62.

17. Expressed the most clearly in a series of essays collected as DeLeon, *Industrial Unionism* (New York 1920).

18. Robert Rives LaMonte, 'A Forgotten "Tramp" ', *Industrial Union Bulletin* (Chicago), Apr.13, 1907.

19. Material on the Italian-American revolutionaries remains scandalously inadequate. Edwin Fenton, 'Immigrants and Unions, A Case Study: Italians and American Labor, 1870–1920', dissertation, Harvard University, 1957, is valuable but unsympathetic; see one all-too-brief case study, Paul Buhle, 'Italian-American Radicals and Labor in Rhode Island, 1905–1930', *Radical History Review,* 17 (Spring 1978). Serious scholarship awaits the availability of Rudolph Vecoli's still largely unpublished essays. Until then, the rich sources remain virtually untapped. Compare, *e.g.*, the syndicalist style in 'La degenerazione reformista', *Il Proletario* (New York), Nov.18, 1910 or 'Lo Sciopero dei tesitori di Paterson', March 3, 1913, *Il Proletario*, with the later adaptationist style of the Amalagamated Clothing Workers, 'Unionismo e Socialismo', *Il Lavoro* (New York), Sept.7, 1918, or Giovanitti himself mainstreamed, in 'Il Tramonto Della Forca', *Il Lavoro*, July 27, 1918.

20. Justus Ebert, *The Trial of a New Society* (Cleveland, n.d. [1913?]), and the fuller discussion of other Wobbly intellectuals' delineation of this idea, in Buhle, 'Marxism in the U.S.,' Ch.II. The Intellectual-political side of the iww has been badly neglected by traditional historians such as Melvyn Dubofsky, *We Shall Be All: A History of the Industrial Workers of the World* (New York 1969). The viewpoint of the ordinary Wobbly is captured, as far as it can be at this late date, in Stewart Bird, Dan Georgakas and Deborah Shaffer, *Solidarity Forever: An Oral History of the IWW* (Chicago 1985).

21. Floyd Dell, *Intellectual Vagabondage: An Apology for the Intelligensia* (New York 1926), p. 107.

22. John Reed, 'Broadway Night', *The Masses,* VIII, (May 1916), p. 20.

23. Floyd Dell, 'Books', *Liberator,* I (December 1918), p. 45.

24. Floyd Dell, 'Burlesquerie', *The Masses,* VIII (January, 1916), pp. 14–15.

25. Arturo Giovannitti, 'What I Think of the Masses', *The Masses,* VIII (June 1916) p.5.

26. See 'Some Reasons Why Negroes Should Vote the Socialist Ticket', *The Messenger,* I, (Nov., 1917), p.34.

27. William English Walling, *The Larger Aspects of Socialism* (New York 1913), p.xiv; Walling, *Progressivism – And After* (New York 1914), pp.xxxii, 319. See my discussion of the *New Review*, its origins and its importance, in 'Marxism in the U.S.' Ch.III.

28. Noah Shteinberg, *Yung Amerika* (New York 1920); Itche Goldberg, 'Di Shturmfeugel fun Yidish Kultur-Renasans (Chaim Zhitlovsky)', *Essayen* (New York 1981); Chaim Zhitlovsky, *Fredrikh Nitshe and Zayn Filosofer Antviklung-Gang* (New York 1920); and see my essay on Rivkin, 'Di Filosof fun Yidishkayt,

Barukh Rivkin,' *Problemen* (Jan. and Feb., 1984).

29. Fraina's editorials reprinted in 'The Modern Dance' *Cultural Correspondence*, 6–7 (Spring 1978). Theodore Draper's *Roots of American Communism* (New York 1957), to Draper's lasting credit, recalled Fraina from obscurity. Unfortunately, Draper's lack of knowledge about the immigrant groups at large, and his tendency to read back into history the denoument of the communist movement, badly mars his otherwise sympathetic and insightful account of the Socialist left.

30. Louis C. Fraina, *Revolutionary Socialism* (New York 1918), pp. 3, 65–66, 36, 197. 191, 193, 165.

31. William J. Ghent, 'Letter' to the *New York Call*, Dec.4, 1909.

32. *For the Common Good: Finnish Immigrants and the Radical Response to Industrial America,* ed. Michael Karni and Douglas Ollila (Superior 1977), especially Karni, 'The Founding of the Finnish Socialist Federation and the Minnesota Strike of 1907.'

33. Joseph Stipanovich's study remains the classic treatment of the South Slavs (Slovene, Croats and Serbs), 'Immigrant Workers and Immigrant Intellectuals in Progressive America: A History of the Yugoslav Socialist Federation', unpublished dissertation, University of Minnesota, 1978.

34. Editorial, 'The Tide of Thought', *The World* (Oakland, California), Apr.4, 1918. See my extended discussion of socialist response to mass strikes, 'Marxism in the U.S.', Ch. IV.

35. Frank quoted in Martin J. Sklar, 'On the Proletarian Revolution and the End of Political-Economic Society.' *Radical America,* III (May–June 1969) pp.24–25.

36. Eric Hobsbawm, 'Problems of Communist History', *New Left Review,* 54 (Mar.–Apr.1969).

37. Maria Woroby, 'Russian-American Radicalism', Immigrant Radicalism File at Tamiment Library, New York University.

38. 'What's the Matter with the Socialist Movement Today?', *Appeal to Reason* (Girard, Kansas), Sept. 3, 1921.

Chapter Four

1. *Workers World* (Kansas City), Sept. 19, 1919.

2. 'Y.F.' (Isaac Ferguson), 'Has It Been Worthwhile?' *Communist* (New York), May 15, 1920.

3. *International Press Correspondence,* July 6, 1927; see Mari Jo Buhle, *Women and American Socialism* (Urbana 1981), 'Heritage Lost and Regained', for further discussion.

4. J.B.S. Hardman, 'Communism in America', *New Republic,* XVI (Sept.3, 1930), p.64.

5. See Paul Novick, 'Recollections: On the Founding of the Morning Freiheit', *Morning Freiheit* (New York), Apr.6, 1975. Also Melech Epstein's account of the Jewish transition to Communism, in *Jewish Labor in the U.S.A.* (New York 1953), p.110; and complaints from old time ethnic leftists that the center had swung into the communist movement: *Workers' Challenge* (New York), May 27, 1922.

6. Rudolf Baranik, 'The Lithuanian-American Left', research for immigration and radicalism project, on deposit in Immigrant Radicalism File, Tamiment Library. It may be said that this is the first important point on which Theodore Draper's pioneering study of early Communism, *American Communism and*

Soviet Russia (1960) definitively breaks down. In fairness, little work had been done on the immigrant groups at the time of his writing. But many thousands of ordinary early Party members remained alive then, and Draper evinced little interest in them. See Paul Buhle, 'Marxism in the United States', Chapter 5, for a study of local evidence on the very important question of early polycentrism and avowed resistance to centralizing party authority. I am, finally, grateful for an unrecorded discussion with the late Charles S. Zimmerman on the subject of the TUEL and its aftermath.

7. Dan Georgakas, 'The Greek-American Left', Immigrant Radicalism File; see also Ralph E. Shaffer, 'Communism in California: 'Orders from Moscow' or Independent Western Radicalism?' *Science & Society,* XXXIV (Winter 1970). A valuable if overly rosy recollection of the early Communist turn toward reform unionism is Arne Swabeck, 'American Trade Union Problems, II', *New International,* II (March 1935). My interview with a much-aged Swabeck, OHAL Archives, also includes a reminiscence of Scandinavian-American Socialist and Communist activity. Evidence of Italian-American Communist activity is much present in the short-lived Chicago daily, *Il Lavoratore,* and in the Anthony Capraro Papers, Immigration History Research Center, University of Minnesota; the aftermath of rapid decline and defection is discussed in interview with Joseph Giganti, OHAL Archives; and Vittorio Vidali transcript, OHAL Archives. Lowell Dyson, *Red Harvest: The Communist Party and American Farmers* (Lincoln 1982). James Weinstein, *Decline of American Socialism, 1912–1925* (New York 1967) has a detailed discussion of Communist activity in and around the Farmer-Labor movements. And see Max Shachtman Interview, Columbia University, on early 1920s Communist labor activities.

8. See Ruthenberg's caustic on undisciplined immigrant socialists in *Socialist Party National Proceedings, 1912* (Chicago 1912), p.89; and Theodore Draper, *American Communism and Soviet Russia* (New York 1960), pp. 157–82, the best section of a largely disappointing discussion.

9. My discussions with founding Communists confirms this view: see in particular Meyer Zackheim, Ruth Lipshitz and Philip Caplowitz, OHAL Archives.

10. The best evidence for this hidden internal life is available in the Chicago Foreign Language Press Survey files, Chicago Historical Society, in the reportage of banquet and youth activities reported in left ethnic papers. Not to be ignored is the evidence on Communist activity among ostensibly minor but regionally important ethnic groups. See interviews with Joseph Figueredo and Jose Alvarez, OHAL Archives, and Karl Yoneda, *Ganbatte* (Los Angeles 1984) for reflections on Portuguese, Spanish-Cuban, and Japanese respectively.

11. Bertram Wolfe, 'Problems of Party Training', *Workers Monthly,* V (June 1926) 'Towards Leninism', *ibid.,* V (Jan., 1927), and 'What Is Workers' Education?', *ibid.,* VI (Feb., 1926).

12. Betram Wolfe and Jack Stachel, 'Lenin, the American Workingclass and the Party', *ibid.,* VI (Feb., 1926), pp. 156–58.

13. See, *e.g.*, Bertram Wolfe, 'A Program for the Period of Prosperity', *ibid.,* VLI (July-Aug., 1927); or Jay Lovestone, 'Some Immediate Party Problems', *Communist,* VII (July 1928).

14. William Z. Foster, *The Bankruptcy of the American Labor Movement* (Chicago, n.d., 1927?), pp.2, 37.

15. 'Destroy the LaFollette Illusion', *Daily Worker* (New York), Oct.24, 1924.

16. See William Montgomery Brown, *Communism and Christianism: Analyzed and Contrasted from the Marxian and Darwinian Points of View* (Galion, Ohio, 1925 edition) and Paul Buhle, 'Radical Religious History: Fragments of a Legacy', *The Witness,* CXVII (July 1984). See also, Eugene P. Link,

Labor-Religion Prophet: The Times and Life of Harry F. Ward (Boulder 1984). Also useful is the Willard Uphaus Interview, OHAL Archives.

17. See the forthcoming reprint of *The Crusader*, edited by Robert Hill. I am grateful to Hill for his insights into Briggs. See Draper, *Roots of American Communism*, Ch.15, for some factual data.

18. Mark Solomon, 'Red and Black: Negroes and Communism, 1929–1932', unpublished dissertation, Harvard University, 1972, p.61.

19. Harold Cruse, *The Crisis of the Negro Intellectual* (New York 1967), Section 11; See also Draper, *American Communism and Soviet Russia*, Ch.15.

20. Interview with Luigi Nardella, OHAL Archives; Earl Browder to Daniel Bell, June 15, 1955, Bell Collection; Robert Jay Alperin, 'Organization in the Communist Party, USA, 1931–1938', unpublished dissertation, Northwestern University 1959, has an abundance of material from the TUUL days. See 428–430 on Party conclusions about the limits of success in the early 1930s.

21. See Paul Buhle, 'Jews and American Communism: The Cultural Question', *Radical History Review, 23 (1980)*, and interviews with Nina Goldstein, Itche Goldberg, I.E. Ronch and Sam Davis, OHAL Archive. See also Kenneth Kann, *Joe Rappoport, the Life of a Jewish Radical* (Philadelphia 1981) for a rank-and-file interpretation.

22. This subject has been discussed often, but with much acrimony and mostly unsuccessfully, most especially by anti-communist critics or embittered former functionaries (such as Theodore Draper). Mark Naison's *Communists in Harlem During the Depression* (Urbana 1983) literally marked a new stage in historical understanding, with his sophisticated and sympathetic treatment of the Popular Front mentality.

23. Al Richmond, *A Long View from the Left* (Boston 1973), p. 248.

24. J.R. Johnson [C.L.R. James], 'The Socialist Party', n.d. [1939?], Socialist Party Papers, Duke University.

25. In 1932, The Socialist Party could still boast sixteen non-English language newspapers which considered themselves generally sympathetic, and at least a dozen other English-language papers with some local influence, such as *Racine Labor* and *Kenosha Labor* and the daily *Milwaukee Leader* from Wisconsin, the *Reading Labor Advocate* from Pennsylvania, as well as the nationally circulated *American Guardian* from Oklahoma City and *The New Leader*. See Frank A. Warren, *An Alternative Vision: The Socialist Party in the 1930's* (Bloomington 1974). I regret that I have had to delete, for space reasons, a discussion of Socialist Party activities in the South, especially among sharecroppers. See H.L. Mitchell's autobiography, *Mean Things Happening in This Land* (Montclair, N.J. 1979). Among the more valuable oral materials on the Socialist Party of the 1930s, see Alice Dodge Wolfson on trade unionism, Paul Andreas Rasmussen on work among the unorganized, and Anton Kerzic on fraternal-cooperative activity. OHAL Archives.

26. See Jay Lovestone, 'Marxists and the Unions', *Workers Age* (New York), Mar. 26, 1938; Will Herberg, 'A Review of "I Confess," ' *Modern Quarterly*, XI (Fall 1939), p.68.

27. Burr McClosky, 'I Appeal the Ruling of the Chair,' in Alice and Staughton Lynd, eds., *Rank and File* (Boston 1973), p.161; stenographic report of discussions of Americans with Trotsky in June, 1940, reprinted into Tim Wohlforth, *The Struggle for Marxism in the United States (New York 1968), p. 39. The Auto League Report* from the Socialist Party, in the Daniel Bell File, is valuable reflection on Trotskyist activity as seen by Detroit Socialists.

28. Will Weinstone, 'Report on the XI Plenum,' *Communist*, X (Oct., 1931), p. 785.

29. Robert Jay Alperin, 'Organization,' pp. 305–06, 336–337.

30. See Paul Buhle, 'Marxism in the U.S.,' Ch. 6 for a substantial treatment of this question; and Earl Browder to Daniel Bell, August, 1955, Daniel Bell File; and Alperin, 'Organization', pp.272, 276, 292, 301.

31. George Charney, *A Long Journey* (Chicago 1968), p. 79.

32. Browder to Bell, August, 1955, Bell File; Alperin, 'Organization', pp. 103, 106, 175.

33. See for example, Browder, 'Forward', to *People's Front* (New York 1938), 13; 'Some Remarks on the 20th Anniversary of the CPUSA,' *Communist*, XVIII (Sept., 1939), p.802.

34. Alperin, 'Organization', 27; Max Shachtman, 'The Stalinist Convention', *New International*, IV (July 1938), p.205.

35. See Alperin, 'Organization', p.98, on urging of Bittelman's writings in the *Communist* as the minimum commitment, and p.103, on the insufficiency of this effort.

Chapter Five

1. Haim Kantarovich to V.F.Calverton, June 10, 1924, Calverton Collection, New York Public Library.

2. Halma Gnizi, 'V.F. Calverton, Independent Radical', unpublished dissertation, City University of New York, 1968, is an overly-close intellectual history reading, but contains more insight than the standard treatments on Calverton, as Daniel Aaron, *Writers On the Left* (New York 1961), Ch. 13.

3. Arthur S. Calhoun, 'The Sociology of Literary Expression', *Social Forces*, VI (Sept., 1927), p. 148.

4. Among his flood of books in this early period: *Sex Expression in Literature* (New York 1926); *The Bankruptcy of Marriage* (New York 1928); Calverton and Schmalhausen, eds., *Woman's Coming of Age* (New York 1931).

5. Kazin, *Starting Out in the Thirties* (Boston, 1965 edition), pp. 34–35; a kinder and more appropriate criticism of him can be found in Bernard Smith, *Forces in American Criticism* (New York 1939), p. 372.

6. Calverton, 'Introduction: Modern Anthropology and the Theory of Cultural Compulsives,' in Calverton, ed., *The Making of Man: An Outline of Anthropology* (New York 1931) pp.27–30. Harold Cruse has sought to revive Calverton's theory: see *Crisis of the Negro Intellectual* (New York 1967), pp. 158–62 for an appreciation of Calverton's efforts.

7. See the attacks on Calverton: A.B. Magil, 'The "Marxism" of V.F. Calverton', *Communist*, VIII (May 1929): and A. Landy, 'Cultural Compulsives or Calverton's Latest Caricature of Marxism', *ibid.*, X (Oct., 1931); Calverton, *Where Angels Fear to Tread* (New York 1940), published posthumously.

8. See Paul Buhle, 'Marxism in the U.S.', Ch. VII, and 'Louis C. Fraina-Lewis Corey, 1894–1953', unpublished Master's thesis, University of Connecticut, 1968; no full-length biographical treatment has yet been given to the subject. I am grateful to his daughter, Esther Corey, for a discussion of her father's life: see Esther Corey interview, OHAL Archives, Tamiment Library, New York University.

9. Lewis Corey, *The Decline of American Capitalism* (New York 1934), Ch.II-IV.

10. Alexander Bittelman and V.J.Jerome, *Leninism the Only Marxism Today* (New York 1934); the most acute critic of Corey's venture into marginal economics was Paul Mattick, 'The Literary Caravan', *Modern Monthly*, VIII (Oct., 1934), p.565; on Corey's subsequent fate, see Buhle, 'Louis C. Fraina-Lewis Corey', and Esther Corey, 'Lewis Corey (Louis C. Fraina), 1892–1953: A

Bibliography with Autobiographical Notes', *Labor History*, IV (Spring 1963), pp. 101–131.

11. Cristiano Comporesi, 'The Meaning of Sidney Hook', *TELOS*, 12 (Summer, 1972), remains the best source of discussion; see also Lewis Feuer, 'From Ideology to Philosophy: Sidney Hook's Writings on Marxism', in Paul Kurtz, ed., *Sidney Hook and the Contemporary World* (New York 1968). For the Communist abuse of Hook and his response, see Earl Browder, 'The Revisionism of Sidney Hook', *Communist*, XII (March 1933) and Sidney Hook, 'Manners and Morals of Apache-Radicalism', *Modern Monthly*, IX (June 1935).

12. See, *e.g.*, William F. Warde [George Novack], 'Engels on the Dialectics of Nature', *Fourth International*, I (December, 1940); D.C. Lucas, 'Engels on Dialectics of Nature', *Communist*, XI (Oct., 1940), and Leon Trotsky, *In Defense of Marxism* (New York 1940), pp. 84–85. For the revolt against dialectics at the end of the 1930s, see, *e.g.*, William Phillips, 'The Devil Theory of the Dialectic', *Partisan Review*, VI (Fall, 1938).

13. Bertram Wolfe, 'Books – America's Coming of Age', *Communist* VI, (Nov., 1927), p. 459; and A.L. [Avrom Landy], 'Applied Historical Materialism', *ibid.*, VI (Apr., 1927), p.92, an introduction to documents by Marx and Engels. On Beard and his importance, see James P. O'Brien, 'The Legacy of Beardian History', *Radical America*, IV (November, 1970).

14. Alexander Bittelman, 'Things I Have Learned', unpublished autobiography, Tamiment Library; also Herbert Aptheker, 'American Negro Slave Revolts', *Science & Society*, I (Summer, 1937); James S. Allen, 'The Struggle for Land in the Reconstruction Period', *ibid.*, I (Summer, 1937). The older approach to Black Reconstruction is discussed in Paul Buhle, 'Marxist Historiography in the U.S., 1900–1940', *Radical America*, IV (November, 1970).

15. W.E.B. DuBois, *Black Reconstruction* (Cleveland, 1969 edition) pp. 634–35; see Paul Richards, 'W.E.B. DuBois and American Social History: Evolution of a Marxist', *Radical America*, IV (November, 1970); for the controversy around Black history, see, *e.g.* B.D. Amis, 'Black Peonage', *The Communist*, X (February, 1931), a bitter review of Carter Woodson's *The Rural Negro;* Herbert Biel, 'Class Conflicts in the South', *ibid.*, XVIII (Mar., 1939) and Richard Enmale [Herbert Morais], 'Introduction', to James S. Allen's *Reconstruction: the Battle for Democracy, 1865–1876* (New York 1937), and Allen's Chapter 6 in particular. I wish to mention Paul Richards and Noel Ignatin as having driven home, to me and to others, the importance of DuBois' insights for the entirety of U.S. radical politics.

16. Ralph Ellison, 'The World and the Jug', in *Shadow & Act* (New York 1953).

17. Abner Berry and Hershel Walker interviews, OHAL Archives, make this point most abundantly clear; Harry Haywood, *Black Bolshevik* (Chicago 1978), Ch. 15–18, makes some of the same points, but with a bitterness and a dogmatism that make insight problematic.

18. Foster to Calverton, July 2, 1925, Calverton Papers; the standard discussion of the literary scene in the 1920s, *e.g.*, Daniel Aaron, *Writers On the Left*, fails to consider rich sources such as the *Industrial Pioneer* or the *Hammer*. The work remains to be done.

19. See the sympathetic but not wholly uncritical treatment of Gold's dilemma in Michael Folsom, ed., *Mike Gold: A Literary Anthology* (New York 1972), 'Introduction: The Pariah of American Letters'.

20. 'Send Us a Critic', reprinted in Folsom, ed., *Mike Gold*, pp. 138–39.

21. Sh. Niger, *Lezer, Dikhter, Kritiker, I* (New York 1928), Ch.3.

22. Buhle, 'Marxism in the U.S.', Ch. VII for further discussion; Douglas C. Wixson, 'Introduction', to *The Weed King & Other Stories* (Westport, 1985) has

supplied an excellent antidote to the myth of Communist-leaning writers' supine attitude toward Party leaders.

23. Granville Hicks, *The Great Tradition in American Literature* (New York, 1934 edition), pp.28–29, 41, 57, 88–89, 100, 124, 188–96, 207–15, 227–37, 258–60, 287–330.

24. Kazin, *On Native Grounds: An Interpretation of Modern American Prose Literature* (Garden City, 1956 edition), p.324.

25. John Howard Lawson, ' "Inner Conflict" and Proletarian Art', *New Masses*, XI (Apr.17, 1934), pp.207–08.

26. William Phillips and Philip Rahv, 'Some Aspects of Literary Criticism', *Science & Society*, I (1937), p. 217.

27. See the lucid commentary by James T. Farrell, *A Note on Literary Criticism* (New York 1936). For all the critical discussion since, Farrell's interpretation has never been bested. But see a recent, more positive interpretation of the proletarian literature itself, specifically in women's issues: Joseph R. Urgo, 'Proletarian Literature and Feminism: The Gastonia Novels and Feminist Protest', *Minnesota Review*, NS 24 (Spring, 1985).

28. *New Masses* back cover, XXIX (Sept. 27, 1938). Hardly a single non-sectarian account of the *New Masses* exists and especially of its popular culture component, although David R. Peck's unpublished dissertation, 'The Development of an American Marxist Literary Criticism: The Monthly *New Masses*', Temple University, 1968, is of interest.

29. Larry Ceplair and Steven Englund, *The Inquisition in Hollywood* (Garden City 1980) have made a beginning in unraveling the Communist role in Hollywood, but mainly as backdrop for the later repression. Again, the bulk of scholarship remains to be done. For a unique view, see Warren Susman, 'The Culture of the Thirties', in *Culture as History: The Transformation of American Society in the Twentieth Century.* (New York 1984).

30. *Baseball and Social Conscience: Lester Rodney Interviewed by Paul Buhle and Michael Furmanovsky* (Los Angeles 1984), pp.39–40.

31. Edmund Wilson, *To the Finland Station* (New York 1939).

32. See Irving Howe's extreme sharp critique of Trilling's rightward swing and its implications in Howe, 'The Age of Conformity', William Phillips and William Rahv, eds., *The Partisan Review Anthology* (1962).

Chapter Six

1. Conversation with Joseph Starobin, 1968.

2. Bertram Wolfe and Jack Stachel, 'Lenin, the American Workingclass and the Party', *Workers Monthly*, VI (Apr, 1926), pp.274–76.

3. Joseph Starobin, *American Crisis in Communism, 1943–1957* (Cambridge 1972) pp. 39–41.

4. Mary Inman, *In Woman's Defense* (Los Angeles 1940). In response, Party theoretician Avrom Landy wrote *Marxism and the Woman Question* (New York 1943), and Inman, out of the Party, years later delivered a riposte, *Thirteen Years of CPUSA Misleadership on the Woman Question* (Los Angeles 1948). Women who continued to raise the Woman Question found themselves demoted or excluded. See Hoddee Edwards, OHAL Archives.

5. The interview with Louise Thompson explores the positive side of this relationship, while the interview with 'Queen Mother' Audley Moore points to the internal crisis of the Party on the 'Negro Question'. OHAL Archives. See also Mark Naison, *Communists in Harlem During the Depression* (Urbana 1983), Ch.12.

6. Research by Dan Georgakas, the Greek-American Left, Immigrant Radicalism file, Tamiment Library; Zoltan Deak, ed., *This Noble Flame: An Anthology of a Hungarian Newspaper in America; 1902–1982* (New York 1982), gives a good picture of Hungarian-American enthusiasm for Allied victory. It is important to point out that for some groups such as Ukrainians whose home countries had been invaded by Soviet troops, the Popular Front ended early and the United Front did not greatly succeed in reviving popular support. See Maria Woroby, 'Ukrainian-American Left', Immigrant Radicalism File, Tamiment Library.

7. Itche Goldberg, leading pedagogue of the Jewish People's Fraternal Order, quotes himself in 'Di Yiddishe Kultur un di Yiddishe Shule in Amerike', *In Dienst fun Folk: Almanakh fun Yiddish Folks Orden* (New York 1947), p. 70.

8. B. Rivkin, *Grunt Tendentsin fun Yiddish Literatur* (New York 1949), Ch.1, 3–4. See also Rivkin, *Yiddish Yom-Tevim* (New York 1950), and Rivkin, *H. Layvik* (Buenos Aires 1955), and Mina Rivkin, ed., *B. Rivkin, Lebn un Shafn* (New York 1953). Some of the other outstanding Yiddish literary-critical works to appear from the Yiddishe Kultur Farband milieu of Yiddishists drifting away from the Communist movement included historical studies by Kalmon Marmor, *Yosef Bovshover* (New York 1952) and *Dud Edelshtot* (New York 1950); by Nachman Maysel, ed., *Tsum Hundert Geburtstakh fun Moris Rozenfeld* (New York 1962); and the encyclopedic *Amerike in Yidishn Vort: Antologie* (1955), ed. by Nachman Maysel. The journals *Yiddishe Kultur* and *Zamlungen*, reflecting the drift, had a standard of quality not found in the rest of the quasi-Communist cultural press.

9. Quoted in Starobin, *Crisis in American Communism*, p.64; see also a characteristic non-Communist Progressive approach to this period, Lawrence Lader, *Power on the Left: American Radical Movements Since 1946* (New York 1979), Ch.1–5.

10. *Baseball and Social Conscience: Lester Rodney Interviewed by Paul Buhle and Michael Furmanovsky* (Los Angeles 1984), pp.131–134.

11. Best seen in Steve Nelson, James R. Barrett and Rob Ruck, *Steve Nelson, American Radical* (Pittsburgh 1981), Ch.9.

12. William Z. Foster, *Twilight of World Capitalism* (New York 1949).

13. Best reflected in Gil Green, *Cold War Fugitive* (New York 1984) and Lader, *Power On the Left*, Ch.6, 7, 9. The political demoralization of the Party rank-and-file following the 1956 events is captured best by Clancy Sigal, *Going Away* (Boston 1963).

14. *Monthly Review* Series, OHAL Archives.

15. John Bellamy Foster, *The Theory of Monopoly Capitalism: An Elaboration of Marxian Political Economy* (New York, 1986); and Paul Sweezy, *Modern Capitalism and Other Essays* (New York 1971), which has a representative sampling of his 1950s writing.

16. The best account is in the transcription of a WP veterans' meeting, Paul Buhle, ed., *The Legacy of the Workers Party, 1940–1949: Recollections and Reflections* (New York 1985).

17. James recorded this melancholy result in *The Balance Sheet Completed* (New York 1950). Interviews with Braverman and David Herreshoff, OHAL Archives, discuss the activity of the 'Cochranites' from a more positive standpoint; *The Legacy of the Workers Party* discusses the political disintegration of the Shachtman group into Cold War unionism.

18. The best overall account of this intellectual development is Paul Buhle, 'Marxism in the U.S.A.', in Paul Buhle, ed., *CLR James: His Life and Work* (London 1986). See also the essential primary document, C.L.R. James with Raya Dunayevskaya and Grace Lee, *State Capitalism and World Revolution*

(Chicago, 1986 edition).

19. James, *Notes on Dialectics* (Westport 1980), p.178. Italics in the original removed for quotation.

20. Engels, *Anti-Dühring* (Moscow 1969), pp.328, 331. James along with his collaborators Dunayevskaya and Lee put this interpretation of Engels forward with the greatest force in *The Invading Socialist Society* (Detroit 1972 edition), one of the essential James documents still not widely available. See the Raya Dunayevskaya Papers, Wayne State University, for more documentation and criticisms of James.

21. J.R. Johnson [CLR James], 'The Revolutionary Answer to the Negro Problem in the U.S.', 1947 Resolution, Socialist Workers Party convention, reprinted in James, *The Future in the Present* (Westport 1977).

22. See, *e.g.*, Albert Gates, 'Politics in the Stratosphere', *New International*, IX (Nov., 1943).

23. C.L.R. James, Raya Dunayevskaya and Grace Lee, *State Capitalism and World Revolution* (Detroit, 1969 edition), p.34.

24. Clement Greenberg, 'Avant-Garde and Kitsch', reprinted into Bernard Rosenberg and David Manning White, eds., *Mass Culture: The Popular Arts in America* (New York 1957). Alan Wald's Interpretations of Trotskyist intellectuals have led the way to a closer understanding of the subject. See in particular his forthcoming book on the New York Intellectuals.

25. Irving Howe, *A Margin of Hope* (New York 1982), pp.30–31.

26. Irving Howe, *World of Our Fathers* (New York 1976), Ch.17, is perhaps the most moving account of the moods and mentality; and Howe's autobiographical account, *A Margin of Hope*, Ch. 5–8. See also James Burkhart Gilbert, *Writers and Partisans: A History of Literary Radicalism in America* (New York 1968), Ch.4–6.

27. See Rahv, 'This Quarter', *Modern Occasions*, I (Winter 1971). I have a dim memory of receiving an exchange copy and finding myself at the same loss of how to respond as I felt when receiving the (by-then) Euro-Communist *Morgen Freiheit* English-language pages. Did the editors *really* want *Radical America* in return? Obviously they did. But the limitations on real communication struck me as overwhelming. They, the more theoretically adventurous or generationally sympathetic of the Old Left from all its factions, were reaching out. We had too little to give them in return.

28. Stephen Whitfield, *A Critical American: The Politics of Dwight Mac-Donald* (New Haven 1984), Ch.5–8. See also Robert Cummings and Lewis Cosers' comments, session on *Politics, The Legacy of the Workers Party*, and Robert Cummings, 'Dwight MacDonald in the 1940s', *New Politics*, New Series, I, (Summer, 1986).

29. Irving Howe, *A Margin of Hope*, p.246.

30. For a rather more acerbic treatment of Howe's intellectual and political evolution, see Julius Jacobson, 'Socialism and the Third Camp', *New Politics*, New Series, I (Summer, 1986).

31. T.B. Bottomore, *Social Critics in North America: Radical Thought in North America* (New York 1968), Ch.6; David Horowitz, *C. Wright Mills: an American Utopian* (New York 1983).

32. Frederick C. Stern, *F.O. Matthiessen, Christian Socialist as Critic* (Chapel Hill 1981) is the outstanding study. See Ch.4–6 for *The American Renaissance* and Matthiessen's later studies. See also Giles B. Gunn, *F.O.Matthiessen: The Critical Achievement* (Seattle 1975), for a close literary-critical view.

33. Interviews with William Preston and George Rawick, OHAL Archives. See also an essay which fairly reflects the Madisonian polemic against corrupt Cold War professordom, and the unvanquished desire for a reborn radicalism in

Harvey Goldberg and William Appleman Williams, 'Introduction: Thoughts About American Radicalism', in Harvey Goldberg, ed., *American Radicals, some Problems and Personalities* (New York 1957).

34. David M.Noble, *The End of American History: Democracy, Capitalism, and the Metaphor of Two Worlds in Anglo-American Historical Writing, 1880–1930* (Minneapolis 1985), Ch.6, is the best recent account of Williams' importance.

35. See James Weinstein and David Eakins, 'Introduction,' in Weinstein and Eakins, eds., *For a New America: Essays in History and Politics from Studies On the Left 1959–1967* (New York 1970). A wider intellectual history of *Studies* remains to be written. My forthcoming anthology of interviews and essays on Madison intellectual life, 1950–70, will cast further light on the subject.

36. Jo Ann Ooiman Robinson, *Abraham Went Out: A Biography of A.J.Muste* (Philadelphia, 1981), Ch.8; also see Sidney Lens' insightful memoir of the early *Liberation* milieu and the distinguishing difference between *Dissent* and *Liberation*, in Lens, *Unrepentent Radical* (Boston, 1980), pp.221–24; and some reflections on the political-cultural importance of anarchist pacifism in the 1950s in Lawrence Ferlinghetti interview, OHAL Archives.

37. Norman Mailer, 'The White Negro', reprinted into Gene Feldman and Max Gartenberg, eds., *The Beat Generation and the Angry Young Men* (New York 1958), p.394. Of course, the essay, originally published in *Dissent*, has been reprinted several places. I cite the source I picked up as a 50 cent paperback on a drugstore rack at age 14. I didn't understand all the essays, but it seemed pretty exciting stuff.

Chapter Seven

1. *Negro Americans Take the Lead* (Detroit 1964) p.17: a product of C.L.R. James' group by this time considerably reduced. A good general historical interpretation of the Civil Rights Movement is contained in Manning Marable, *Black American Politics, from the Washington Marches to Jesse Jackson* (London 1985), Ch.1.

2. Fredric Jameson, 'Periodizing the Sixties', in Sohnya Sayers, Anders Stephanson, Stanley Aronowitz, Fredric Jameson, eds., *The Sixties Without Apologies* (Minneapolis 1984), p.207. For a less articulate, earlier version of the same essential theory, see Paul Buhle, 'The Eclipse of the New Left', *Radical America,* VIII (Fall 1973).

3. Max Horkheimer and Theodor W.Adorno, *Dialectic of Enlightenment,* translated by John Cumming (New York 1972). Marcuse struggled to respond in kind to New Left enthusiasm, aggressively praising certain aspects of Black culture, in *Counter-Revolution and Revolt* (Boston 1972).

4. Michael Harrington, *The Other America: Poverty in the United States* (Baltimore, 1969 edition), especially Ch. 4. Harrington himself gives an account of how eagerly the book was received by the Democrats, and how little he anticipated the New Left/Black Power upsweep: Michael Harrington, *Fragments of a Century* (New York 1973), Ch.5–6.

5. Todd Gitlin and Nancy Hollander, *Uptown: Poor Whites in Chicago* (New York 1970), pp.xxiii–xxiv. Wini Breines, *Community & Organization in the New Left, 1962–1968: The Great Refusal* (S.Hadley, Mass., 1982), contains a fine if perhaps overly nostalgic view of the early New Left's democratic spirit.

6. *The Port Huron Statement* (Chicago, 1964 edition), p.62.

7. Howard Zinn, *SNCC: The New Abolitionists* (Boston 1964), p.274.

8. Kirkpatrick Sale, *SDS* (New York 1973), p. 188.

9. Marable, *Black American Politics*, Ch.2.

10. Benjamin Goodman, ed., *The End of White World Supremacy: Four Speeches by Malcolm X* (New York 1971), p.121.

11. C.L.R. James and Martin Glaberman, 'Letters', in Paul Buhle, ed., *CLR James: His Life and Work* (London 1986); see also Stephen B. Oates, *Let the Trumpet Sound: The Life of Martin Luther King, Jr.* (New York 1982); Interview with Abner Berry, OHAL Archives; and John J. Ansbro, *The Education of Martin Luther King* (Maryknoll 1982). A different and more critical view of King is presented in Marable, *Black American Politics*, Ch.2–3.

12. Well conveyed in Paul Jacobs and Saul Landau, *The New Radicals: A Report with Documents* (New York 1966), Ch.6.

13. Kirkpatrick Sales, *SDS*, (New York 1973), Ch.15.

14. For a documentary interpretation of 1960s counter-culture and its radical connections see Paul Buhle, ed., 'Fifteen Years of Radical America: An Anthology', *Radical America*, XVI (May–June, 1982).

15. Sheldon Wolin and John H. Schaar, *The Berkeley Rebellion and Beyond* (New York 1970) remains the most admirable interpretation.

16. See Kirkpatrick Sale, *SDS*, Ch. 23–25.

17. See James P. O'Brien, 'American Leninism in the 1970s', *Radical America*, XI (Nov. 1977–Feb. 1978). A brilliant evocation of the depressed political mood of the early 1970s and the half-crazy response of radicals is Max Crawford, *The Bad Communist* (New York 1979).

18. S.E.Anderson, 'Black Studies: Racial Consciousness and the Class Struggle, 1960–76', *Black Scholar*, XIII (1977), p.40.

19. See Floyd B.Barbour, ed., *The Black Power Revolt* (Boston 1968), Robert L.Allen's incisive *Black Awakening in Capitalist America: An Analytic History* (Garden City 1970); and the harsh treatment of the Black petty bourgeoisie in Marable, *Black American Politics*, Ch.3.

20. Dan Georgakas and Marvin Surkin, *Detroit: I Do Mind Dying, a Study in Urban Revolution* (New York 1975).

21. For the historic background, see Sara Evans, *The Roots of Women's Liberation in the Civil Rights Movement and the New Left* (New York, 1979); a relatively current interpretation of theory if not practice can be found in Natalie J. Sokoloff, *Between Money and Love: The Dialectics of Women's Home and Market Work* (New York, 1980).

22. Rosalin Petchevsky, 'Dissolving the Hyphen: A Report on Marxist-Feminist Groups 1–5,' in Zillah Eisenstein, ed., *Capitalist Patriarchy and the Case for Socialist Feminism* (New York 1979), p.375.

23. To take a personal example: *Radical America*, the unofficial journal of SDS (it had no official journal) which I nurtured. It was published with a run of three thousand copies six times a year, printed on a single-sheet press, collated and stapled by SDS activists or sympathetic hippies, dragged home to pack into mailing bags for SDS chapters and bookstores. All this was accomplished on less than $10,000 per year, with no donations larger than $100, a membership subscription price of $2, and a cover-price that ranged between 50 cents and $1. It was possible because of the manic energy and faith that existed at the time: the real material conditions for the launching of New Left Marxism.

24. I am indebted to an exchange of letters with Stan Weir on this subject; see also George Lipsitz interview, OHAL Archives; and perhaps the most evocative document of the left industrial collectives, the Sojourner Truth Organization's *Workplace Papers* (Chicago 1980), an anthology with documents of ten years' agitation.

25. The Proletarian Unity League, *Two, Three, Many Parties of a New Type? Against the Ultra-Left Line* (New York 1977), p.29.

26. Marable, *Black American Politics,* Ch.3–4.

27. See, *e.g.* Patricia Bell Blawis, *Tijerina and the Land Grants: Mexican Americans in Struggle for Their Heritage* (New York 1971); and 'Solidarity with Puerto Rico: March 1 Bloc Documents,' *Urgent Tasks,* I (May, 1977); for the artistic-political side, see, *e.g.,* Lezlie Salkowitz-Montoya and Malaquias Montoya, 'A Critical Perspective on the State of Chicano Art'. *Metamorfosis,* III (1980) and a response Shifra M. Goldman. 'Response: Another Opinion on the State of Chicano Art', *ibid.,* III (1980–81). Also Eddie DeJesus, 'The Fight for Equality of the Puerto Rican Worker in New York City', a special issue of the National Congress for Puerto Rican Rights publication, *Puerto Rican Worker* (June 1, 1985).

Conclusion

1. Quoted in 'Fan Noose', *Inside Joke,* 95 (1986). This publication, which keeps track of the 'zines', is an admirable source for sub-visable cultural dissent and evidence of the lively radicalism in post-New Left generations.

2. Fredy Perlman, *The Reproduction of Daily Life* (Detroit 1969); Perlman, *The Incoherence of the Intellectual* (Detroit 1970); Perlman, *Against His-story, Against Leviathan* (Detroit 1983); and Perlman, *Anti-Semitism and the Beirut Pogrom* (Seattle 1983), among other works. All remain available from Black & Red, Detroit.

3. The most practical work of American radicals in publishing Latin American works has been done by Orbis Press, of the Maryknoll Fathers. Theoretical work of U.S. supporters of Liberation Theology remains, for the most part, explanation and exposition of Latin American developments. See, *e.g.* Paul Buhle and Thomas Fiehrer, 'Liberation Theology in Latin America: Dispensations Old and New,' in Mike Davis, Fred Pfeil and Michael Sprinker, eds., *The Year Left: An American Socialist Yearbook, 1985* (London 1985); the special *Monthly Review* issue, 'Religion and the Left', Vol.36 (July–August 1984). But Americans have contributed more original work along the lines of interpreting other utopian perspectives. See, for example, the lucid and helpful explanation by Anson Rabinbach, 'Benjamin, Bloch and Modern German Jewish Messianism', *New German Critique, 34 (Winter 1985)* and the special *Telos* issue, 'Religion and Politics', 58 (Winter 1983–84).

4. Some of more important religious-radical publications: *The National Catholic Reporter;* the Episcopalian *Witness*; the evangelical *Sojourner*; and even, arguably, the *Maryknoll Magazine.*

5. Jack Barnes, 'Their Trotsky and Ours: Communist Continuity Today', *New International,* I (Fall 1983).

6. See Frei Betto, 'God Bursts Forth in the Experiment of Life,' in Pablo Richard, *et.al., The Idols of Death and the God of Life: A Theology,* tr. Barbara E. Campbell and Bonnie Shepard (Maryknoll 1983). This book, in my view, is the theologically deepest interpretation from a Liberation Theology perspective now available in English. See also Joel Kovell, *Against the State of Nuclear Terror* (Boston 1983), which like much of Kovell's recent work seeks to bridge the gap between secular left rationalism and the 'numinous', spiritual energy abounding in the vicinity of radical movements.

7. Jeremy J. Shapiro, 'One-Dimensionality: The Universal Semiotic of Technological Experience', in Paul Breines, ed., *Critical Interruptions* (Chicago 1970), pp.137–38. This hope is held out, although in a less optimistic and more focused anti-imperialist way, by several newer intellectual entities such as the journal *Wedge.* See, *e.g.,* 'In the Shadow of the West: An Interview with Edward

Said', and Rosa Club, 'As the World Burns', in 7–8 (Winter/Spring 1985).

8. Stanley Diamond, 'The Marxist Tradition as Dialectical Anthropology', *Dialectical Anthropology*, I (1975) and his assessment after ten years, 'Questions', *ibid.*, IX (June, 1985). The same point comes across in a general sort of way in the useful survey-anthologies edited by Bertell Ollman and Edward Vernoff, *The Left Academy, I–II* (New York, 1982 and 1984).

9. Immanuel Wallerstein, 'Symposium: From the '60s to the '80s', *Cultural Correspondence*, 12 (1981). An early intellectual study, Richard Guarasci, *The Theory and Practice of American Marxism, 1957–1970* (Lanham, Md., 1970), also seeks to make the point that New Left theory was largely pre-determined by the early theorists. By way of evidence, he mentions (178n) that my own *Radical America* was the 'only theoretical journal of the New Left.' This is a bit of an exaggeration. But close enough to be painfully true, if one counts 1970 as the end of the New Left.

10. See Zeev Gorin, 'Socialist Societies and World System Theory: A Critical Survey', *Science & Society*, LVIX (Fall 1985).

11. See Richard Quinney, *Criminology* (Boston 1975). I am most grateful to Quinney for a frank discussion of the Marxist sociological critique and its limits.

12. Paul Attawell, *Radical Political Economy since the Sixties* (New Brunswick 1984), Ch.2–4. This is a lucid but perhaps, given the scope, a necessarily one-sided account of New Left Marxism. It altogether lacks the utopian kernel, as if the current academic status had been written back into the genesis of the intellectual generation.

13. See Paul Berman, 'The World of the Radical Historian', *Village Voice*, Mar. 18, 1981.

14. See Vincent Harding, *There Is a River* (New York 1984), and Harding's dialogue with Ken Lawrence in Paul Buhle, ed., *CLR James: His Life and Work* (London 1986), for reflections on the influence of the elder Black historians upon the younger generations; Marable's *Black American Politics* (1985) is the maturest version thus far of his work. The 'aristocratic Marxism' is best characterized by the work of Eugene D.Genovese. But see *Roll, Jordan, Roll: The World the Slaves Made* (New York 1972) for Genovese's ardent and often successful if not precisely historical effort to look at slavery from the point of view of the slave rather than of the master.

15. Joan Kelly-Gadol, 'The Social Relations of the Sexes: The Methodological Implications of Women's History', *Signs*, I (Summer, 1976).

16. Andreas Huyssens, 'Mapping the Postmodern', *New German Critique, 33 (Fall, 1984)*. Designed as a disciplinary journal, NGC has been, especially in the 1980s, among the most reliable guides to broad intellectual developments. Unlike the erratic *Telos*, it has not been drawn by its Euro-tropism into the debacle of so many erstwhile European left intellectuals, and the neoconservative 'defense of the West' which has been the sorriest result.

17. Theodor Adorno, *Minima Moralia: Reflections from a Damaged Life*, translated by E.F.N. Jephcott (London 1974), p.204.

18. Dave Wagner, 'Philosophical Steps', *Cultural Correspondence*, I (1975), pp. 12–13. For a fuller exposition, see my introduction to the *Cultural Correspondence* anthology, *Popular Culture in America* (Minneapolis 1987), and David Marc's provocative essay in that volume, 'The Critic's Code.'

Index